ANCIENT INDIA

ANCIENT INDIA

S. KRISHNASWAMI AIYANGAR
VINCENT A. SMITH

GYAN

Published by

GYAN

Gyan Publishing House
5, Ansari Road
Daryaganj, New Delhi-110002
Phone: 011-47034999, 9811692060
E-mail: books@gyanbooks.com

Distribution Network
gyanbooks.com
India, USA, Canada, UK, Australia

ISBN: 978-93-7316-489-2 (PB)

First Published, 1911

2nd Impression 2025

Printed at: Gyan Press, Delhi.

ANCIENT INDIA
Author: S. KRISHNASWAMI AIYANGAR, VINCENT A. SMITH

ANCIENT INDIA

ANCIENT INDIA

BY

S. KRISHNASWAMI AIYANGAR, M.A.

Member of the Royal Asiatic Society of Great Britain and Ireland
Fellow of the Royal Historical Society, London.

Member of the Board of Studies, and Examiner in History and Economics, University of Madras

Mysore Education Service

WITH AN INTRODUCTION

BY

VINCENT A. SMITH, M.A., I.C.S. (*retired*)

Author of the 'Early History of India'

LONDON: LUZAC & Co., 46 GREAT RUSSELL STREET

MADRAS: S.P.C.K. DEPOSITORY, VEPERY

1911

INSCRIBED TO THE MEMORY

OF

JOHN WEIR

[INSPECTOR-GENERAL OF EDUCATION IN MYSORE]

(November 1, 1909—July 31, 1911)

PREFACE

THE first chapter deals with the early portion of Indian History, and so the title 'Ancient India' has been given to the book. The other chapters deal with a variety of subjects, and are based on lectures given on different occasions. One was originally prepared as my thesis for the M.A. Degree Examination of the University of Madras.

The favourable reception given to my early work by historical and oriental scholars encouraged me to put my researches into a more permanent form, which a liberal grant from the Madras School Book and Literature Society has enabled me to do.

I have to thank the editors and publishers who have so kindly allowed me to reproduce articles which first appeared in their respective periodicals. Amongst these are Sir Richard Temple, Mr. G. A. Natesan, the Committee of the South Indian Association, Mylapore, and the Mythic Society, Bangalore. I also desire to acknowledge the assistance which has been given me in the publication of the work by the Rev. Canon Sell, and my obligation to Mr. Vincent A. Smith for his valuable Introduction.

CHAMARAJENDRAPET,
BANGALORE CITY,
August 1, 1911.

S. K.

CONTENTS

MAPS

INTRODUCTION

THE request made to me by Mr. S. Krishnaswami Aiyangar that I should prefix to his volume of collected essays on the literary and political history of Southern India, a few words of introduction met with ready acceptance, because nothing gives me greater pleasure than to watch the steady progress made by Indian-born students in the investigation of the ancient history of their country. It would be easy to name many recent Indian authors who have made important and solid contributions to accurate knowledge of the early history of India. Among such writers, Mr. Krishnaswami Aiyangar holds an honourable place and if he had leisure greater than that which official duties permit, he might, perhaps, produce that *Early History of Southern India* which is so much wanted and can be written only by a scholar familiar with the country and one or more of the Dravidian vernaculars. The collection of papers now offered to the public does not profess to be such a history. It is simply a reissue of essays printed on various occasions at different times, and in some cases now subjected to slight revision. A volume of the kind which is rather materials for history than history itself, necessarily suffers from unavoidable overlapping and repetition, and from a lack of unity. But notwithstanding the defects inherent in an assemblage of detached essays

I can cordially recommend this book as being a readable and generally sound introduction to the study in detail of the history of the South.

The first chapter, 'A Historical Survey up to A. D. 700' is a well-written summary. The hypothesis (p. 17) that the Sakas of Seistan were disturbed and set in motion towards India by pressure from the Sassanian dynasty of Persia established in A. D. 226 may yet be verified. The next three chapters give an excellent general review of the salient facts of early South Indian history so far as known. If the author (p. 67) is correct in saying that the Gurjjaras are mentioned in the Tamil epic poem called *Maṇimēkhalai*, the composition of that work cannot be much anterior to A. D. 500, inasmuch as the Gurjjaras do not seem to have entered India before the middle of the fifth century. He holds (p. 75) that the epic is earlier than the time of Varahamihira (A. D. 533), because the poet uses a reckoning of the asterisms which was superseded by the improved system of the Hellenizing astronomer.

Many of the essays now collected, I may observe, make valuable contributions to the history and chronology of Indian, and especially of Tamil literature. The older histories of Indian literature were restricted to the discussion of works written in Sanskrit and Prakrit. The ideal history of the vast literature of India should give almost equal attention to the noble works in the Southern languages, among which Tamil is pre-eminent. The translations published by Mr. Gover, Dr. Pope, and a few other scholars suffice to prove the high ethical and artistic value of the Tamil compositions. So far as I can judge Mr. Krishnaswami Aiyangar is right in dating the best period of Tamil literature in the second and third centuries of the Christian era.

The most important and generally interesting chapter in the book is the sixth (pp. 90–191), which gives an admirable abstract of the political history of the Cholas, with a detailed account of their system of Government and village administration, well deserving of attentive study. The Chola dynasty was singularly prolific in kings of more than ordinary capacity, from the middle of the ninth century to the end of the reign of Kulōttunga in A.D. 1118. It is clear from the details on record that the administration of the kingdom was 'highly systematized' from an early date. For instance, there is abundant evidence that 'the lands under cultivation were carefully surveyed and holdings registered at least a century before the famous Domesday record of William the Conqueror'. The re-survey of 1086 was exactly contemporaneous with the English record.

'The Cholas were great builders; builders not only of cities and temples (sometimes for strategic purposes sometimes in obedience to the dictates of their vanity), but also of useful irrigation works'. It is lamentable to be obliged to record the disgraceful fact that 'when the lower Coleroon anicut (dam) was built, the structure (that is to say, the noble temple of Gangaikoṇḍapuram), was dismantled of a large part of the splendid granite sculptures which adorned it, and the enclosing wall was almost wholly destroyed in order to obtain material for the work.' By the kindness of Mr. Rea,

I have been supplied with photographs of some of the surviving figure sculptures, a few of which will be published in my forthcoming *History of Fine Art in India and Ceylon.* They may, perhaps, be considered the finest known Hindu sculptures, and certainly take rank among the best. A fully illustrated monograph on Gangaikoṇḍapuram and Chola art generally would be of great interest.

The discussion in Chapter VII of 'Sri Rāmānujācharya, his Life and Times', throws much light upon an important epoch in the story of Indian religious development.

The origin and growth of the State of Mysore are treated at length in two chapters. But the identification of the ancient Mahisha Maṇḍala with Mysore must, as Dr. Fleet has shown, be given up. Māhishmatī appears to have been the capital of the Mahishas, and is now represented by Māndhāta on the Narbada.

The later chapters dealing with certain special problems, chiefly concerned with Tamil religious and literary history, are of less general interest.

OXFORD,
February 8, 1911.

VINCENT A. SMITH.

CHAPTER I

A HISTORICAL SURVEY UP TO A.D. 700

In attempting to look back upon our own history, the first essential would appear to be the marking of a few of the more salient features, so that we may group round these a number of minor events and incidents. This will give us perspective; and whatever imperfection there may be in detail it will make the whole presentable. If, at this distance, we take a retrospect, the history of India of the Aryan invasions would appear, like our own Himalayas at a great distance, all smooth but for a few peaks of commanding height. 'Happy is the nation whose annals are a blank,' said Carlyle, and if we can derive comfort from this seeming blankness, we shall perhaps be in a delusion. I shall attempt, therefore, to present in outline the outstanding features with a view to clothing these later on to make them as presentable looking as we may.

We have to begin with the Aryans in their own homes wherever they might have been and move along with them. This will be extra-Indian in character and withal essential to the proper understanding of their doings in India. We shall name this the Pre-Indian age of the Indo-Aryans *circ.* 3000 B.C. During this age the Aryans advance up to the Indian frontier. They are a nomadic-agricultural folk, already differentiated from their Iranian brethren, developing some of the features peculiar to the Indo-Aryans of the Rig-Veda.

The next step in advance takes them across the frontier into India. During this stage of their migration we find them in occupation of the land of the five rivers. It is here for the first time that the Aryans come in contact with the aboriginal inhabitants of India and the struggle for possession of the country begins. The more rudimentary civilization, of course, gives way to the more advanced and vigorous. It is again in the land of the five rivers that the simple civilization and compact tribal organization take form and are pictured to us in the Rig-Veda. The rich soil and flourishing communities catch the eyes and attract the desires of the neighbouring, but still primitive, cousins of these Indian Aryans. To make room for these new arrivals, not without a fight perhaps, the Indo-Aryans move forward across the rivers to the Doab of the Ganges and the Jumna. All this may be ascribed roughly to the half millennium 2000–1500 B.C.

As the Greek cousins of these Indo-Aryans did, so these latter underwent a similar course of development according to their own environment, geographical and political. In the Gangetic Doab, we find the Aryans developing more powerful communities, which, instead of becoming city-states as in Greece, led to strong monarchies ruling great tribes and vast kingdoms, particularly as the country was more open. It was in these regions that the great inter-tribal wars typified in the *Mahābhārata* must have taken place. At least, the incidents referred to in the great epic have their theatre here. Hence this period of history has come to be known that of the *Mahābhārata*. It is here for the first time that the Aryans get into touch, not only with the uncivilized aborigines who are the feature of the Punjab plains, as even the later *Brihat Kathā* makes it clear, but also with the civilized Dravidians of India. It is here, as with the Greeks in Attica and

Boeotia, that the Aryans change their policy of usurpation to that of amalgamation, which alone was possible under the circumstances. To these events is ascribed the period included in the centuries between 1500–1000 B.C.

From here the further expansion eastwards could not be in the wholesale fashion as heretofore, but had to be in driblets. This expansion takes the form of a few powerful kingdoms farther east than the Doab. What the Kurus (or Kauravas) and the Pānchālas were to the Doab, the Kōsalas and Vidēhas were to the further east of those times. It is these regions that the *Rāmāyana* describes. The period taken up in the expansion (or infiltration) into these regions may have been the quarter millennium 1000–750 B.C.

During these periods the Indo-Aryans were rearing those great edifices of learning and religion, which have given this land of ours all its claims to greatness in the various departments of human activity. The pre-Vedic Aryans brought in their traditions, which they could elaborate at leisure in the Punjab. These, in course of time, were put into shape in the hymns of the Veda, which, as time advanced, required to be explained by an elaborate commentary. These commentaries are the Brāhmaṇas. These in their turn led to the further disquisitions called the Āranyakas culminating in the philosophical flights of the Upanishads. This transformation, or rather elaboration, has been going on steadily up to the period we arrived at in the last section. This is not all. Certain scientific inquiries had to be made for the proper understanding of the Vedas and the Vedic ritual. Their need was met by the elaboration of the Vedāngas namely, (1) Kalpa which included geometry so far as it applied to the construction of sacrificial altars, (2) Siksha or phonetics, (3) Chandas or metre, (4) Viyākarana or grammar, (5) Nirukta or study of words, (6) Jyōtisha or astronomy. These Vedāngas find brief treatment in the Brāhmaṇas or Upanishads and acquire the necessary scientific cast in the age we have come to just now.

This development leads us on to the so-called Sūtra period, because this growing mass of literature required to be put in a shape which could easily be mastered. The alphabet, no doubt, had been invented already (or adapted thoroughly to Indian requirements), though perhaps it was not brought quite into common usage. This period overlaps the next and may be taken to occupy the four centuries between 750 B.C. and say 350 B.C. So far then we have to rely entirely upon such evidence as is available in our sacred literature, and scholars have allotted these to very varying periods.

The Aryan home is placed within the Arctic Circle by Mr. Tilak, and he ascribes a very early period (7000 B.C.) indeed for the earliest hymns of the Rig-Veda; while European scholars would bring it to 1500 B.C. Mr. Tilak rests his arguments upon certain solar and other astronomical phenomena referred to in the earlier hymns which upon his hypothesis find clear explanation. The late Mr. Shankar Balakrishna Dikshit refers certain at least of the Brāhmaṇas to 3800 B.C.; there being a reference in the Śatapada Brāhmaṇa to the Pleiades being in the Equinox, which is verifiable astronomically. Dr. Thibaut considers that the verse referred to is a late interpolation. So our position here is not very secure, and therefore our chronology respecting this period cannot lay claim to much accuracy. The ultimate downward limit of our period may be taken to be accurate, as it brings in an unlooked for synchronism. Pythagoras,[1] the Greek philosopher, is believed to have learned in India not only his theory of transmigration, but also his theory of numbers from our Sankya system. Drs. Goldstücker

[1] A. B. Keith disputes this. J.R.A.S., vol. 1909, pp. 569 et seq.

and Bhandarkar refer the grammarian Pāṇini to this period, and if this be correct it brings the history of South India into touch with that of the North.

Taking a fresh starting point, therefore, somewhere in the sixth century B. C., we find ourselves upon somewhat firmer ground as outside light begins to beat in upon us. In the centuries on either side of 750 B. C. the Aryans begin penetrating into the Mahākāntāra round about the Vindhyas, the memory of which is preserved in the tradition regarding Agustia's advent into the south. If the Rāmāyana could be trusted to be correct regarding its geographical details, the great forest extends up to the Pampa Saras, which is on the north bank of the Tungabhadra near modern Hampe, though the Saras (or tank) must have been forgotten under the name, as the author of the Tamil Rāmāyana makes it, Pampānadi. The advent of Agustia introduces reclamation of the jungle into arable land, and he is the reputed author of the first Tamil grammar. Whoever this Agustia was, Rishi or some one else by that name, he does for Tamil what Pāṇini did for Sanskrit. That he criticizes Pāṇini appears to be in evidence in one of the very few quotations that have come down to us. It would thus appear that the Aryan migration into south India has to be referred to this period of the Sūtras.

When the whole of India, north and south, is getting organized, the overgrowth of ritualism, and perhaps of religion becoming too much of a mystery, sets thoughtful people thinking about this very subject. There appear in the sixth century B.C. two great men who have contributed very much to bring about a mighty transformation. It is certainly in the fitness of things that these should have flourished in the spots favoured by nature, where before their time the daring flights of speculation into the mystery of the Unknown reached its grand climacteric under the Indian Pisistratus as he is called, or Rajarishi Janaka. These two great sons of India are Mahā Vīra Vardhamāna, the founder of the religion of the Jīna, and Gautama Sākyamuni, the Buddha. The new teachings of the latter, and the appeal they made to the people have long been recognized as the potent cause of the development of the languages of the people. This influence from the distant north found ready response even in the distant south, with which communication appears to have been maintained by way of the sea, while yet the Daṇḍakāranya had not been penetrated by a great highway, the Dakshiṇāpatha. In another way the advent of the Buddha has also been of advantage to students of history. His religion it was that took India from her blissful isolation, and led her to take her place among the world Powers, but this was not as yet.

With the advent of Buddhism comes into prominence the kingdom of Magadha, perhaps semi-Aryan, as it was in the borderland of Āryāvarta. The capitals of this kingdom appear to have been Rājagriha, Kaikeyi's father's kingdom, and Vaiśāli, also spoken of in the Rāmāyana. Bimbisara of the Śaiśunaga dynasty and his patricide son Ajātaśatru were contemporaries of the Buddha. Before the Buddha attained nirvāna, Buddhism had obtained a great hold upon the people of India, and Buddhist monks and nuns had gone about carrying the Buddhist gospel.

This age when two religious reformers flourished, and in which the foundation of the greatness of the kingdom of Magadha was laid is remarkable in many ways. This is the age in which an Indian contingent fought in the battles of Thermopylae and Plataea in Greece, 'in cotton clothes, cane bows, and iron-tipped arrows'. This was possible because of the twentieth satrapy on the west bank of the Indus, formed by the adventurous skill of the Carian admiral of Darius Hystaspes, by name Skylax. The date of the navigation of the Indus by this admiral and the foundation of the satrapy are placed at about 510 B.C. Not far from this period India, then known to the Aryans, was divided into sixteen kingdoms and a number of autonomous tribes. For besides the accepted line of advance of the Aryans, there appear to have been two other streams of migration—one skirting the lower Himalayas and the other moving down the valley of the Indus. The tribes are found along the mountain borders east of the Ganges, some of them also along the upper reaches of the Punjab rivers. Several of them were governed by their own tribal meetings, held in the hall of the tribe—Santhāgāra.

I mention only one of them, because it was a kingdom previously. I mean the Vidēhas of modern Tirhut whose King Janaka has already been mentioned. These were a section of the great Vajjian clan and were during this period under the government of a republic, whose headman, as in the case of other republics as well, was called a Rajah, answering to the Roman consul or Athenian archon. It is from one of these clans of northern Bihar that the Buddha himself was born.

The kingdoms were, proceeding from the west in geographical order, Kāmbhōja with capital Dvāraka, answering to modern Sindh and Gujarat; Gāndhara, eastern Afghanistan between the Afghan mountains and a little way to the east of the Indus with its capital Taxila (near Shah Deri); Avanti, the modern Mālva with its capital Ujjain; the Assaka (Asmaka or Asvaka) with its capital Pōtali or Pōtana on the banks of the Godavari (modern Paitan); the Sūrasēnas with their capital Madhura, the modern Muttra; the Matsyas west of the Jumna answering to the cis-Sutlej Sikh States or Phulkian States; the two Pānchālas round about Kanouj and Kampilla; the Kurus occupying the country round about Delhi; Vamśa, the country of the Vatsas with its capital Kōśambi; Chēdi, one at least of the tribes having had their local habitat in Bundlekhand, the other being located somewhere in Nepal; the Mallas round about Kuśinãra along the Nepal Tarai; the Vajjians, a confederation of eight clans of which the chief were the Licchavis of Vaisãli and the Vidēhas of Mithila; the Kōsalas whose kingdom during this period included Srãvasti in Nepal on the one side and Benares on the other with Sākēta in the middle; the Kāśis round modern Benares; Maghada round Patna including in it southern Behar up to Bhagalpur on the Ganges; and Anga with its capital Champa not far from Bhagalpur.

It is clear from the above that so far the southern expansion had come up only to the Godavari. This is not inconsistent with the state of things portrayed in the Rāmāyana, which nowhere mentions an Aryan kingdom nor an Aryan settlement of any importance beyond Janasthāna along the upper reaches of the Godavari. The political feature of this period is the struggle for supremacy between the neighbours, the Kōsalas and the Magadhas. The Śaiśunagas particularly under Bimbisāra and his patricide son Ajātaśatru were successful in expanding Magadha to include Vaiśāli and the Licchavi country and keeping Kōsala well within bounds. It was during their rule that Rajagriha was fortified and the capital changed to Vaiśāli. It was a successor of Ajātaśatru, by name Udayana, who enlarged his predecessor's fort of Pāṭalīpura into the great capital of Magadha. The fall of this great dynasty was, however, at hand and was probably brought about by dissensions within and invasion from without. The invasion of Chaṇḍa Pajjota[1] (Pradhyōta) of Ujjain must have weakened

[1] This is the father of Vāsavadattā, Queen of Udayana of Kōśambhi. It was this king who is described in the *Brihat Kathā* as Chanda Mahāsena. That the two refer to the same king is clear from *Priyadarsika*.

the State much and a palace revolution did the rest. The Śaiśunagas were overthrown and the Nandas came to power. The ill-gotten power lasted for two generations only, and the Nandas, in turn, were overthrown by Chandragupta Maurya.

It is while this revolution in politics was gradually working out in the middle kingdoms that the western frontiers were thrown into confusion by the advent of one of the world's conquering heroes. Starting from Macedonia, the young champion of Hellenism, Alexander the Great, marched eastwards combining with the warlike instincts of the general the insatiable curiosity of the explorer. Meeting with feeble resistance on the way across the empire of Persia, he marched along the left banks of the Kophen (Cabul river) and crossed the Indus somewhere above Attock, with the friendly hospitality of Omphes of Taxila, whose jealousy towards his powerful neighbour Porus threw him into the arms of Alexander. It cost Alexander a great effort of skill and daring before he could take the hill fort of Aornos (identified with Mahāban). This done he marched down the Peshawar plain to the banks of the Jhelum. Here at last he met his match. Pōrus was after all worsted; but so far compelled Alexander's admiration, as to get his kingdom restored to him. It was probably extended, under the viceroy Philip. Alexander's further advance upon the Magadha kingdom was prevented by a mutiny among his troops, and he had to turn back, never to return. Having been thus baulked in his attempt to bring about Alexander's intervention, Chandragupta was able to levy troops in the Punjab among the several war-like tribes, and brought about the revolution which, thanks to the exertions of the most astute diplomatist of the times Chāṇakya (or Kauṭilya or Vishṇugupta), gave him the kingdom of Magadha. The accession of this first Maurya is placed in the year 321 B.C. and provides us with the first reliable date in the history of India. During the first decade of his reign, he was able so far to organize his resources that he was master of Hindustan up to the frontiers. Pōrus was assassinated in the meanwhile. It was in 305 B.C. or a few years earlier that one of the most promising among Alexander's generals, who had made himself ruler of Asia after his master's death, attempted the conquest of the east. This time the east outmatched the west. Seleucus Nicator (the victorious) had to agree to a humiliating treaty, giving up to Chandragupta Alexander's eastern viceroyalty under Philip, i.e. the country of Afghanistan.

After this, Chandragupta's empire stretched from the mountains running across Afghanistan to the Bay of Bengal, and from the Himalayas to the Vindhyas. This vast empire was organized on the time-honoured basis of local autonomy, with the condition attached of providing contingents to the imperial army and of acknowledging supremacy. No other closer arrangement could have been made on account of mere distance alone. The empire might have lasted on, if only the members of such a federated empire understood each other better and had acted up to the agreements entered into, or in the absence thereof, had consulted the common interests of all. This perhaps was too much in advance of the times to expect.

Chandragupta's successor Bindusāra followed in the wake of his predecessor and considerably added to the empire. He entrusted the two important frontiers to his two sons, the eldest being viceroy of the northwest at Taxila, while the younger, the more famous Asōka, was the viceroy at Vidīsa (Bhilsa) of the Dakshiṇāpatha.

From Bindusāra we pass on with pleasure to his son Asōka, the Constantine of India. Asōka was viceroy of the then most difficult frontier when his father died. Asōka had to assert his claim as against an elder brother, the viceroy of Taxila, and overthrew him at last. Having thus got the throne, he began his reign in the manner of both of his predecessors. His only acquisition to the empire, however, is explicitly stated to be Kalingam, the Mahānadi Delta, and Orissa. The rest of the Dakshiṇāpatha must have been conquered and brought under, while yet his father was alive. Passing over the Buddhist delineation of the character of Asōka, almost as the evil principle incarnate, we find him accepting Buddhism, after his conquest of Kalingam, out of remorse for the bloodshed, on account of which he is said to have given up Brahmanism in which he was born. The merciful doctrines he taught, the hospitals he built both for man and animal, the interest he took to send the Gospel of the Enlightened far and wide, and the pains he bestowed upon the collecting and consolidating of the teaching of the Great One are matters of common knowledge. In spite of the great changes that had taken place, the administration of the empire went on in the time-honoured method, with little change of principle though the personnel changed. This empire now extended in the south into Mysore, and the southern frontier may be regarded as about 12° N. lat. Along the frontiers of this vast empire and particular places within it, he cut on rocks and pillars his own instructions to his officials and people. Besides this, he erected innumerable stūpas or topes to hold the remains of the great Arhats. These are the material most reliable for his history. His missionary enterprise carried the teachings of the Buddha at least to as far as Syria. From his own edicts we learn that he negotiated with five kingdoms along the southern frontier. They were, Chola, Pandya, Keraḷa, and Satīyaputra in India and Ceylon close to it. At the westernmost extremity of Asia and eastern Europe his influence prevailed. He entered into diplomatic relations with Antiochus of Syria, Ptolemy II of Egypt, Magas of Cyrene, Antigonus Gonatas of Macedonia and Alexander of Epirus. According to Professor Mahaffy, Buddhist monks preached in Palestine and Syria a couple of centuries before Christ. He is said to have sent 84,000 missionaries to different parts of India and dominions beyond. Among them, his brother and sister (or son and daughter) he sent to Ceylon. Having done the best he could to further Buddhism and having ruled his vast empire in the most humane spirit possible, he resigned the responsibilities of this earthly existence to weakling successors.

Asoka was followed by four successors and the dynasty came to an end by the accession to the empire of the Sēnāpathi Pushyamitra, the founder of the so-called Sunga dynasty. He is believed to have assassinated the last Maurya Brihadratha on the occasion of a review of the army. There appears to have been a loyalist in the person of the minister, the Maurya Sachiva[1] of the *Māḷavikāgnimitra*, which after all is better authority for the period, as Kāḷidāsa claims to base his facts upon others' accounts which may have been contemporary, as we have reason to infer. This usurpation was not unchallenged from outside. Pushyamitra could hardly have secured his position when he was threatened by two great enemies from without—Menander (Milinda of Buddhistic tradition) from across the north-western frontier and Kāravēla, the Kalingaraja from the south. Having laid waste the country as far east as even Sākēta (possibly that in Oudh) and besieging Mādhyamika (near Chitor in Rajaputana), Menander retired and no other Euro-

[1] This according to the drama was a brother-in-law of the king of Vidarbha, who demands his release of Agnimitra. The commentary makes Maurya Sachiva almost a proper name.

pean attempted the conquest of India from the land side ever since; nor any at all up to the days of Vasco-de-Gama. It is a part of this army, according to Vincent Smith, that was defeated by Prince Vasumitra on the banks of the Sindhu between Rajaputana and central India and not on the banks of the Indus. This appears a needless limitation of authority for one, who thought of celebrating a Rājasūya and who had his son Agnimitra, viceroy of Mālva.

Pushyamitra got the upper hand of even the other enemy of Kalinga, which appears to have kept at peace with the empire since the conquest of Asoka. Pushyamitra's was the age of the grammarian Patanjali, and from his time there was a revival of Brahmanism. There appears to be no foundation in fact for regarding him as a persecutor. Agnimitra, while yet his father's viceroy, had conquered Vidharba, the modern Central Provinces, and placed it under two kings of the same family subsidiary to himself.

Brilliant as Pushyamitra's achievements were, they did not avail much to keep his dynasty long in power. The Punjab and the north-west frontier were in a state of flux, and those pulsating movements began among the great Mongol tribes on the Chinese frontier, which were soon felt on the banks of the Indus. A domestic revolution subverted the dynasty of the Sungas after three generations, and there was a line of rulers of the Kāṇvāyana family for less than half a century. This in turn was overthrown by the Āndhras, a purely South Indian dynasty of the Dravidians, whose territory occupied the region between Kalingam and the Krishna.

The overthrow of the Brahman Kaṇvas and the accession of the Āndhras in 27 B.C. mark an epoch in Indian history. It opens to our view India south of the Vindhyas which hitherto remained a *terra incognita*. We shall have to treat of Indian history hereafter in three compartments, namely, that of Hindustan up to the Vindhyas, that of the Dekhan between the Vindhyas and the Krishna, and that of India south of the river Krishna.

The age of the Sungas and the Kaṇvas was to Hindustan the age of Sanskrit revival and there appears to be some historical foundation for the tradition which places a Vikramāditya at the latter end of this age. It was at the same time an age of domestic revolution. The ebb in the fortunes of the kingdom of Asia under the descendants of Seleucus was felt in Central Asia, and it was communicated thence to India. After the successful invasion of the east, Antiochus the Great fared badly in the contest he had brought on himself from the Romans. Under his immediate successors, two kingdoms came into existence, the Parthian under Arsakas and Bactria under its own Greek viceroy. This viceroy whose independence had been recognized tried to extend his territory eastwards and was himself overthrown by a usurper. This latter carried arms up to and perhaps even beyond the Indus and was assassinated by his own son. It was his successor Menander who invaded Pushyamitra's dominions and had to draw back because of the movements among the Śakas who themselves moved because of the Yueh-chi beyond ousting them. It is these Śakas that marched into India and founded kingdoms in the Punjab and the lower Indus, perhaps under the Parthian suzerainty of Mithridatis I. These Śakas appear to have been finally beaten back and gave their name to Sakastān (Seistan). In this enterprise a ruler of Mālva distinguished himself. He was the patron of Kāḷidāsa and his name has been handed down to us by a grateful people as that of the saviour of India. There still were Śakas or Kshētrapas on the right bank of the Indus and of these we shall have to speak in the section on the Dekhan.

The Śakas of the Punjab were overthrown by a branch of Yueh-chi about A.D. 50, and with the first rulers of the dynasty this part of India came into touch with Rome on the one side and China on the other.

Third in succession in this dynasty of Gāndhāra is Kanishka, famous in Buddhist history and one of the most powerful of Indian emperors. Scholars disagree regarding the actual date of the accession of Kanishka and his successors, but all agree as to his greatness. He was more successful in an invasion of the neighbouring parts of Chinese territory, where his predecessor failed and was able to hold his own against the Parthians. His fame rests, however, upon his acceptance of Buddhism and his successful attempts to make the 'middle country' of China accept it. After a successful reign, when his frontiers extended to Pāṭalīpura on the one side and touched the Parthian and Chinese Empires in the west and north and the sea in the south, Kanishka died or was assassinated by a discontented army about the middle of the second century A.D. Two or three of his successors continued from Peshawar to rule this empire which, up to the very last, appears to have included the country from Muttra on the east to Cabul in the west. When the last of them, Vasudeva, passed away the empire broke up about the first quarter of the third century.

To turn now to the Dekhan. Among the powers mentioned as under the empire of Asōka we find the Āndhras, who appear to have been then along the east coast. They develop gradually, expanding westwards so as to occupy all the Dekhan from sea to sea. In the decadence that followed the death of Asōka, the Āndhras seem to have had their own share, and they may possibly have helped Kāravēla of Kalinga, when he invaded Magadha in the middle of the second century B.C. When the Kaṇvas were overthrown the Āndhras extend their power northwards and occupy

Magadha, having had their flank protected by the hills and rivers from the Yavana invasions of Menander. During all the transactions described in the last section, the Āndhra power in the interior was unaffected; and these had to be active only on the west where the Kshētrapas or the Śaka Satraps of the Parthians were pushing their arms southwards. The Āndhras had to counteract this and do so by making Paitan an alternative capital to Dhanakaṭaka in the east.

The later rulers among them showed themselves quite successful against these Śakas, particularly Vilivāyakūra II [1] (the Baleokuros of the Greeks). He was able to beat off the Kshētrapas from the south, where their power went as far down as the Malaya country along the coast. His son followed in the wake of the father, and after two more generations the dynasty came to an end, about the same time the Kushāṇa rule died out in the north.

On the south-eastern side of the Āndhras we see a new power rising, namely, that of the Pallavas, regarded the same as Pahlava or Parthiva (Parthian). The earliest records of these come from places far north of Kanchi which, later on, became the capital of the Pallavas. The Pallavas have not yet come to be a political factor.

South of this region we find a number of petty States, and farther south still the three kingdoms of Chola, Pandya and Kēraḷa and beyond these Ceylon. These Powers appear to have actively helped the Āndhras, as each of these States (at least certain rulers among them), claim to have defeated 'the Aryan forces'. A somewhat later Tamilian ruler of Kēraḷa, with his capital at modern Kranganore, claims to have beaten some princes 'on the banks of the Ganges.' These three States had their own local rivalries, and as history opens upon

1 Called Gōtamīputra Śātakarni by some historians.

this part of the country, the Cholas are in the ascendant. This ascendancy passes to the Chera or Kērala ruler when we reach the end of this period, that is about the end of second century A.D. This period all known circumstances point to as the era of great Tamil literary activity and the development of the local prākrits—among the latter Paiśāchi. It is in this language and under the Āndhras that Gunāḍya composed his Brihat Kathā.

It is an unfortunate coincidence that in Indian history the century following is enveloped in mist as regards all the three regions into which we have divided the country. When again the mist lifts, the Pallavas are found dominant in the south; the Chāḷukyas occupy the Dekhan and the Guptas are prominent in the north. Thus there appears to have been a great interregnum in India, which may be accounted for somewhat as follows. The great Arsakian dynasty of Parthia was making way before the Sassanian Persians. The rise of this new power in Persia put pressure upon the Śakas of Seistān, who perhaps moved eastwards to join their cousins along the lower Indus and Guzerat. This must have thrown the whole western frontier in confusion. From this salient angle the Śakas, among whom there might have been some Parthians, pushed themselves eastward into Mālva and southward into the Dekhan. This puts an end to the Dekhan power. A similar incursion into the Punjab would overthrow the Kushāṇa dynasty there. When we come upon the Guptas, we find them just at the place where, under the circumstances, we ought to expect resistance to the advance of this aggressive power. The next Dekhan power is the Chāḷukya, in the south of the Bombay Presidency, about Bijāpur. It is also perhaps out of this confusion there arises the 'foreign Pallava' State in the Nellore District. This aggression provokes resistance and the organizer of the general resistance

2

rises up out of the struggle. With respect to South India, the Chera ascendancy is questioned by the united Chola and Pandya, and these wear out each other. This leads to the break-up of one empire into a number of petty principalities, which fall an easy prey to the rising Pallavas.

When the light of day breaks in upon the theatre of our history at the beginning of the fourth century A. D., there is a wedge of the Śakas driven in between the Dekhan and Hindustan. These Śakas, known in this region the Kshētrapas, had already overthrown the Āndhras of the Dekhan and were in secure occupation of the land of Vikramāditya—Mālva with its capital Ujjain. These had been continually here from the beginning of the Christian era and, getting eventually the better of the Āndhras, they had become a great Power under the greatest of their rulers Rudradāman. One of the records bearing upon the history of this ruler's reign throws a curious light upon the times. Armies passed and repassed and dynasties rose and fell, but the peaceful pursuits of the agriculturist and the artisan went on undisturbed. The grant has reference to the repairing of a tank, by name Sudarśana, constructed in the reign of Asoka, but damaged owing to a breach. This was repaired under Rudradāman and adequate provision was made for its up-keep in the manner usual in the country, foreigner as he was in that region. But for this sensible continuity of administrative policy, the evil consequences of the rapid succession of invasions would have been immensely more detrimental to the country.

It was in the region set over against Mālva that the next great Indian Power comes into being. A certain officer, possibly of the Āndhras, by name or title, Gupta, had a petty province in and about Kośambi south-west of Allahabad. His son passed away unnoticed also. It was the grandson Chandragupta, who became the founder of a dynasty. His period of rule was certainly a golden age in Indian history. Chandragupta married a Licchavi princess of Vaiśāli, which gave him such influence and, what is more, such powerful aid that he was able easily to make himself the ruler of what was ancient Magadha. He not only beat back the advancing tide of Kshētrapa aggression in central India, but also uprooted the power of these Śaka rulers. Having made himself so far successful, he founded an era in A.D. 319, known as the Gupta era. Chandragupta's reign was devoted to securing what under the Mauryas was Magadha. Having been happily so successful in this, he had also the discernment to join with him in this work of empire building his eldest son Samudragupta, the Napoleon of India.

Samudragupta well deserves the comparison. He was not only a great conqueror but also a capable administrator; and both the father and son were skilled in the fine arts. Samudragupta is described as a 'rūpakrit' which scholars interpret as a dramatist. The word ordinarily means a sculptor. He seems to have early conceived the idea of uniting the whole of India into one empire, and this idea he began to put into practice with all the uncompromising zeal begotten of confidence in his capacity. Leaving in the extreme east, Kāmarūpa (Assam), Davaka (middle) and Samatata (the Delta) independent allies upon his eastern frontier, he conquered the whole of Hindustan excepting the Punjab. (His father Chandragupta carried his conquests up to the Arabian sea). This done he started on a career of conquest to the south. Starting from Patna, he passed rapidly through the Mahānadi valley down the east coast, coming up to Kanchi in the south where the Pallavas had already made themselves secure. Taking a turn to the north-west, he passed through the Mahārāshṭra country and Khandesh and entered his territory again. From the eleven kingdoms he passed through, he exacted allegiance but otherwise left them autonomous. He then entered into satisfactory political engagements with the autonomous tribes of the Punjab, Rajputana and Mālva; and with Nepal and the tribes along its borders. Not content with this, he not only entered into diplomatic relations with the Kushāṇa rulers of the Ghāndhāra and Kabul, but also with the chief Kushāṇa ruler on the Oxus. In the south he received a mission from Mēghavarṇa of Ceylon, who requested permission to build a Buddhistic monastery at Gaya. Having achieved so much, he got his exploits set in the best Sanskrit verse and inscribed it upon an Asoka pillar now at Allahabad. What was mere vanity in Samudragupta is comfort to the historian. He was succeeded by his son Chandragupta Vikramāditya who, through an equally long reign with his father and grandfather, preserved the grand fabric of empire handed down to him, and made his reign so glorious that scholars now find it the most suitable to ascribe to the traditional Vikramāditya. With the Guptas, Brahmanism and Sanskrit literature take a fresh start, though Buddhism was not persecuted as such.

If the ambassadors of the Ceylonese king are to be trusted, Buddhism seems to have already decayed considerably. Somewhat later, however, the Chinese pilgrim Fa Hian visited the country, and passed across the whole of Hindustan from Taxila to the mouths of the Ganges. His observations are all the more valuable, as they were those of a man who notes them only by the way. If Fa Hian is to be believed Buddhism was not in such a bad way. The whole administration was very creditable and criminal law was mild, capital punishments having been few. There appears to have been nothing harassing in the Government. People enjoyed a large measure of freedom and considerable wealth. Private benefactions were large and the whole country wore a look of great prosperity. The roads were well looked after and kept clear of marauders; and through all his long journey Fa Hian was not subjected to any molestation whatever, Buddhist though he was. The Guptas were Vaishṇavas, but like Indian monarchs their benefactions were distributed alike among all religions in the country. Tolerance may be a virtue or a weakness; but the most powerful Hindu dynasty was tolerant in the highest degree. Fa Hian spent a number of years in learning Sanskrit and was rewarded by gaining valuable Buddhist works in that language.

In the reign of Chandragupta Vikramāditya, that great scourge of the world, the Huns, broke in upon the Gupta Empire as they did upon the Roman Empire. Skandagupta his grandson not only repaired the mischief done to the empire in the reign of his father Kumāragupta I, but also beat back the Huns. But a later invasion of these made him fall back, and the Huns under Toramāna established themselves in Mālva, and the country in the north-west, having overthrown the Śaka rulers of Gāndhāra by the way. It was as a result of this mishap to the empire that Guzerat separated under Sēnāpati Bhaṭṭāraka, who founded the Vallabhi dynasty which lasted on till they were overthrown by the Muḥammadan invasions about A. D. 770. Although the empire was divided the ruler of Mālva Yaśodharman and the Emperor Bālāditya, now confined to Magadha, both defeated Mihiraguḷa, the fiendish son of Toramāna. Mihiraguḷa was taken prisoner, but was restored by the magnanimity of Bālāditya. He lived to hand down his name to posterity, as an infamous tyrant of Kashmir, a despoiler of temples and monasteries; as one who cultivated cruelty almost as a fine art. With the continued incursions of these Huns the Gupta Empire comes to an end. Before taking leave of this empire it is but doing justice to a great dynasty of emperors, who not only built an empire, but took great pains to administer it upon the most enlightened principles, despotic as their authority was, to quote a small passage from Fa Hian regarding free hospitals, which were due perhaps to the influence of that humane predecessor of the Guptas, Asoka. These hospitals were endowed by benevolent and educated citizens. 'Hither come all poor or helpless patients suffering from all kinds of infirmities. They are well taken care of and a doctor attends them, food and medicine being supplied according to their wants. Thus they are made quite comfortable, and when they are well they may go away.' Comment would be superfluous. The overthrow of the Guptas brings Indian history to almost the end of the sixth century A. D.

Turning to the Dekhan, during the period the disintegration that came upon it in consequence of the successful wars of the Mālva Kshētrapas continued, and the whole region was broken up into a number of petty principalities. When Samudragupta undertook his great invasion of this region, it was composed of eleven kingdoms, possibly more. Even then the western half remained a little more compact having been divided between Daivarāshṭra and Erāṇḍapalla, corresponding respectively to the modern Mahārāshṭra and Kāndesh. It is from the former that the first powerful dynasty works its way up. During the period of the later Guptas, when they were engaged in that death grapple with the Huns, the Chāḷukyas gradually occupied the territory of their northern neighbour and pushed down the Krishna to occupy the country since known as Vengi. Here they come into touch with the Pallavas, with whom they had to maintain perpetual war along the borders.

The farther south was also getting consolidated under the new rulers, the Pallavas of Kanchi. When Samudragupta came to the south, Vishṇugopa was the ruler of Kanchi. His successors at Kanchi gradually annexed other Pallava States in the neighbourhood, and expanded southwards, adding the smaller States between the dominions under Kanchi and the Chola and Keraḷa kingdoms. Along the banks of the Krishna then these rising Pallavas had to keep vigilant, as against the Chāḷukyas. The accession of the Pallavas marks the rise of Brahmanism in the south, and these Pallavas were great temple-builders and patrons of Tamil literature, for some of the earliest of the rock-cut temples dedicated to Śiva and Vishṇu belong to this period.

When we emerge out of this formative period, States re-form in India, and the whole country falls into three well-marked divisions, namely, the empire of Hindustan under the supremacy of Thanēsvara, the Dekhan under the Chāḷukyas, and the farther south under the Pallavas. These shall be taken in this order, as it was during this period that there were a few Chinese pilgrims, chief among whom was Hieun Thsang. Not only this; we have also more of indigenous historical material to hand; to mention only a few—Bana's Harshacharita, inscriptions of all the three, Nandikkalambakam, the Prabandhas of the Vaishṇavas, the works of the Śaiva Aḍiyārs, etc.

It will preserve chronological continuity to begin with South India first. The Pallava power from the northern frontier of this region proved a bulwark against the advancing Chāḷukya power. About A. D. 500, while the Gupta emperors were engaged in fighting the Huns, the Pallavas had become the chief southern power; while the Dekhan also had been united under Kīrtivarman and his brother Mangaḷīsa. When Mahēndra Pallava's death leaves the Pallava dominions to his son Narasimhavarman, one of the greatest among the dynasty, the Chāḷukya Power simultaneously passes to the greatest among them Pulikēsin II. The accession of these princes to power took place about the same time that a certain combination of circumstances brought about the accession of Harshavardhana Śīlāditya of Thanēsvar, later on of Kanouj. We must now turn to this ruler.

Out of the confusion caused by the incursions of Mihiragula, the Hun king of Sagala (the capital of ancient Madra Dēsa), there arose, in the line of march of the enemy and in the far-famed region of battles where more than once the fate of India was to be decided, a chieftain by name Prabhākaravardhana, who was connected by marriage with the imperial Guptas. Prabhākara beat back the Huns through his two valiant sons, the elder Rājyavardhana and the younger, a lad of fifteen, Harshavardhana. The latter commanding the rear, while his brother marched ahead, was still in the region below the mountains on his way, when he heard his father was taken ill and returned. The elder soon followed, having crushed the enemy and placed the frontier in a condition of safety. Prabhākara died and was succeeded by his eldest son, who heard of a misfortune that befell his only sister Rājyasrī married to Grahavarman of Magadha. The latter had been killed by the ruler of Mālva and Rājyasrī had been thrown into prison. Rājyavardhana marched upon Mālva, and having defeated the king of that country, was on the march homeward when he was entrapped by Śaśanka of Bengal. Rājyavardhana was assassinated by Śaśanka and Rājyasrī had to escape to the Vindhyan forests to save herself. Harshavardhana appears to have been unwilling to accept the responsibility of rule, but he had to do so all the same.

His first task was to go in search of his sister, and find where she was, which he soon did and just saved her from death. He then turned to Śaśanka and reduced him to subjection. This done, he set to himself the task of rebuilding the empire, as it was under the Guptas. Throughout a comparatively long reign he was constantly engaged in war for about thirty years, and brought the whole of Hindustan under his sway, his authority having been acknowledged by the Brahminical ruler of Kāmarūpa (Assam) and the Śaiva ruler of Bengal on the one side to the far off Vallabhi and Kashmir at the other extremity. In one direction a limit was set to his arms, and so his achievement fell far short of his ambition, which was probably that of Samudragupta. Harsha undertook an invasion of the Dekhan, but the Vindhyan passes were so well guarded by Pulikēsin of the Dekhan that Harsha was actually defeated. Like many another great man he recognized the limitation to his own capacity and acquiesced in this defeat, as he never again made any other attempt on this side. Thus, having reconstructed an Empire of Hindustan, he turned his attention to maintaining this empire.

It was during the later part of his reign that Hiuen Thsang, the great master of the Law from China, travelled in India. He found the administration of the empire as satisfactory as his predecessor of a couple of centuries ago had done, except that the land and water ways were not so secure as in the age of the Guptas. The emperor was constantly on the move and his camp was almost a moving city. Criminal justice appears to have been prompt, but somewhat severer than in the previous age. There was a regular system of official records, although none of these have come down to us. Harsha, a great scholar and poet himself, gave a stimulus to learning, and, according to the Chinese scholar, education appears to have been widespread. In his court, and under his direct patronage, poets flourished in such numbers that his name ranks among typical patrons of letters. By nature or by education, he appears to have been extremely tolerant.[1] His eclecticism was much like that of Akbar; but latterly, and through the influence of Hiuen Thsang, he leant more and more to the Mahāyāna school of Buddhism. The great Buddhist festival he celebrated at Kanouj and the toleration feast he held at Allahabad show that he entertained very broad and enlightened views upon religion. Although he had to carry on wars incessantly for thirty years, he seems to have been led into war out of sheer necessity, rather than of a taste for it. The stories regarding his acts of persecution have to be considerably discounted. When he passed away in A. D. 648 he does not appear to have left a proper successor. A minister of his Arjuna usurped the empire. The usurpation proved a failure, through the intercession of a Chinese ambassador. Harsha sent a Brahman as ambassador to China. When this ambassador returned, China sent a return embassy under Wang-Hiuen-t'se. When this latter arrived the usurpation had taken place. The usurper illtreated the ambassador who fled to Tibet for protection. Returning with Tibetan help, he overthrew the usurper, and thus came to an end the last Hindu empire, of Hindustan. During the centuries following A. D. 700 up to the Muḥammadan conquest, there never was built up another empire of any duration and the want of a central power accounts for the conquest, with comparative ease, of India by the Muḥammadans.

At about the same time also came to an end the great Pallava Power in South India. Since administering the check to Harsha, Pulikēsin had to grapple with the Pallava Narasimhavarman, the builder of the cave-temples at Māmallāpuram, the seven pagodas. One of the Pallava generals, marched up to the capital

[1] This is the age and Benares the place where Sankaracharya is believed to have written his *Bhāshyam*.

of the Chāḷukyas at Bādami and destroyed it so completely that there was an interregnum of thirteen years after Pulikēsin. His successors, however, often carried the war into the Pallava territory, the northern frontier having been undisturbed. It was to maintain peace on this Pallava frontier that Pulikēsin organized a separate viceroyalty at Vengi under his brother, who in his turn became the founder of a dynasty.

A sad calamity overtook the Chāḷukyas about the latter half of the seventh century A.D. This was the overthrow of their dynasty and the usurpation of the Chāḷukya Empire by the Rāshṭrakūṭas, with their capital farther, and therefore safer, from the Pallavas. This gave the Pallavas a little respite; but after the temporary occupation of Kanchi by the Rāshṭrakūṭa Vairamēgha, the Pallava Empire breaks up into smaller States, from out of which the great Chola Empire is eventually to rise.

Amidst all this ceaseless flux of the political units that constituted India through all these ages, there stands out one fact, namely, that whenever great empires were in existence, such as the Maurya or Gupta or even that of Harsha, India enjoyed not only internal tranquillity and the blessings of a good administration, but also security on the frontiers. Whenever this imperial unity was wanting, it follows as unmistakably that the anarchical elements inside asserted themselves. This state of division invited an invader, and he was readily forthcoming, so that if there is one feature which can be said to be the dominant feature of the history of India during the millenium ending A.D. 700, that feature is the attempt to build a permanent empire. In spite of all these disturbances there still was a good measure of peace and plenty in the country, and what follows, as a necessary consequence thereof, considerable success in making life not only tolerable but comfortable. The literary and artistic achievements of the period are things we may well be proud of; and this has been due entirely to a broad outlook into the future by our ancestors. It is only to be regretted that they did not discover a method of reconciling the opposing principle of local autonomy with imperial unity. This accounts for all the ills that followed.

The history of Hindu India has a unity of its own, if only the material available be used constructively. This unity would become the clearer, if we could but bring together all the available information. It is every day becoming more and more possible, thanks to the exertions of orientalists, to write such a history.

CHAPTER II

HISTORY OF SOUTH INDIA

A GOOD map of India, will show very clearly that India, south of the Himalayas, falls naturally into three divisions, namely, the river plains of Hindustan in the north, the plateau of Mālva Dekhan in the middle, and the plains below the Ghauts bounding the Dekhan plateau. Historically each of these natural divisions may be treated separately. Hindustan has a history of its own, coming into touch with that of the Dekhan only at particular epochs. The Dekhan has its periods of history quite distinct from that of Hindustan; while the history of South India and that of the Dekhan come into contact much oftener, and the general movements of both regions show a great deal more of connexion and interaction. The reason for this state of things is not hard to understand. In the early dawn of history in India, between the first two divisions there was an impenetrable forest called Mahākāntāra (or the great forest) flanking the Vindhyas, and proving with them a great barrier to the freedom of movements of the population. With respect to the Dekhan and the south there has never been any such barrier either of mountain or forest. Hence it is we are justified in treating of the history of this part of India—India south of the Vindhyas—as one whole, though it is possible and often necessary to treat it in compartments.

The history of peninsular India begins, then, somewhat later than that of Hindustan; for the Dravidian civilization of the south, though much more ancient than its history, owes its history to Aryan immigration, as much as does north India. This immigration of the Aryans took place certainly much later than Vedic times. Of the period that intervened between this immigration and the beginning of historical times in south India, we have but few traces of evidence, and these are more often indirect than direct.

The first definite mention of kingdoms in the south, which can be accepted as historical, undoubtedly is that in the thirteenth edict of Asōka. This we have to regard as the historical starting point, until the chronology of the Puranas and the Epics are settled beyond doubt. Even as such we have to come down to the Christian era for any detailed knowledge of South India.

For this knowledge we are more dependent upon the so-called auxiliaries to history than any history we have, even of the chronicle kind. The evidence is to be found in the monuments of human industry and art, and the inscriptions that have come down to us on coins, metallic plates, or upon stones. The inscriptions do not take us very far, and the information contained in them, though reliable and often clear, is not quite so full as one would wish they were. The monuments have begun to be studied only recently, and, so far, the results they have yielded, though quite satisfactory, are not full enough. There is much to be done here before results can be achieved. The traditionary evidence is of a different character. It is far fuller, though very careful sifting is required before any reliance can be placed upon it. These traditions may be grouped into ethnography and folklore, and literature. The customs, habits, and the various and varying practices of the people tell their own tale, not only in regard to the movements of the people and their change of habitat, but also give us the clue to their history.

The literary tradition is often more fixed and perhaps more reliable, though again considerable care has to be bestowed in the collection, classification and evaluation of the evidence. On a general consideration of these various items of information so far available, the history of South India would fall into six periods:—

(1) Early period—to the fifth century A. D.

(2) Pallava period—fifth to ninth century A. D.

(3) The Chola ascendancy—ninth to fourteenth century A. D.

(4) The ascendancy of Vijayanagar—fourteenth to sixteenth century A. D.

(5) The Musalmān-Maharatta period—sixteenth to eighteenth century A. D.

(6) The British period—eighteenth and nineteenth century A. D.

Corresponding to this there are for the Dekhan:—

(1) Āndhra period—to fifth century A.D.

(2) Early Chāḷukya period—fifth to seventh, and Rāshṭrakūṭa—seventh to tenth century A. D.

(3) The later Chāḷukya period—tenth to fourteenth century A. D.

(4) Vijayanagar.

(5) Musalmān-Maharatta.

(6) The British period.

The earliest period of South Indian history, in contradistinction to that of the Dekhan, depends entirely upon literary evidence. In fact for the first period there is nothing else except for a few Asōka and Sātavāhana records. Even Sātavāhana history depends in great part upon the accounts given in the Puranas—chiefly the Matsya, Vishṇu and the Vāyu. So far, therefore, as the movement of political power is concerned, South India and the Dekhan were marked off respectively as the spheres of the Sātavāhanas and 'the three kings' and several (seven according to Tamil literature) chieftains. The kings are respectively Chera,

Chola, and Pandya; and the chieftains have their strongholds on hillocks, like the doorgs of the Pāḷayagars of a later generation. The region specially remarkable for these chieftaincies was the hilly strip of country running through South Arcot, Salem, and Coimbatore districts, at the foot of the ghauts where they move out to meet each other. Kanchi was the head-quarters of one, Tirukoilūr of another, Anji, Kāri, and Ōri belong to the Salem district; Pēhan, Evvi and a few others to Madura and Tinnevelly; while Āmur (Ambur) and Vellore belonged to yet another chieftain of Māvilangai.

There was some commercial activity during this time, although the period must have been full of wars as well. Happy confusion prevailed in matters religious, a single street often containing shrines sacred to the bright beneficent Vedic deities and the blood-thirsty and vengeful devil worship. Alongside both of these are the quiet abodes of the holy ones of the Jains and the Buddhists as well. There appear to have been the rudiments of good government, mostly in some sort of self government, and justice was administered with even-handed impartiality. The authorities present to us, no doubt, idealized picture of the state of society; but behind the work of art it is easy to discover the bed-rock of fact. There seems to have been more unity in society, and the hard hidebound exclusiveness (which is only too apparent now), does not find much vogue. Buddhist and Jain influences are at work; but the worship of Śiva and Vishṇu seem to carry the largest clientele.

This old order changeth yielding place to new, and we find instead a struggling body of warring political atoms. From out of this struggle arises the great Pallava power, and we pass into the second period. It often appears that the history of India, before the British supremacy was established, can be considered only as a perpetual struggle to found an empire. Regarded in this manner, the establishment of that European power would be the natural result of the political evolution of the country as a whole. This view seems to be clearly right with respect to South India in particular, and thus can be seen a parallelism in Indian history to that of Greece in pre-Macedonian times.

At the commencement of the first of these periods the Cholas are in the ascendancy. They give place to the Cheras, who in turn make room for the Pandya. The Pandya supremacy passes away and the Pallavas rise into importance. The latest scientific estimate of the age of all these vicissitudes is the fifth century; but there is a volume of evidence in favour of pushing this period back a few centuries. Here the investigation will have to go hand in hand both in Sanskrit and Tamil. This is not the place nor the occasion for an elaborate exmination of the connexion between the two languages, but it must be remarked in passing that one of the earliest Tamil Kāvyas is based on the *Brihat Kathā* of Guṇāḍya, who flourished in the court of a Sātavāhana at Paitan. This gives us the ultimate lower limit; while the fifth century would be the ultimate upper limit for this period of efflorescence of Tamil.

There is one great landmark between the first period and the second, and that is the invasion of the south by the great Samudragupta. He came south down to Kanchi and then turned north-west from it. The contemporary of this Gupta was Vishṇugōpa of Kanchi, which name figures among the early rulers of Kanchi in the Pallava records. With them we come upon firmer historical ground. Simultaneously with these rise into importance the early Chāḷukyas, in the region that had, in the earlier period, been in the possession of the Sātavāhanas. These latter had to maintain their possessions as against the Kshētrapas, first from Guzerat and then against them from Mālva. In this struggle they were finally overthrown, and it is from among the feudatories of these Sātavāhanas that the

Chāḷukyas rise. The Āndhra or Sātavāhana rule is characterized by almost the same social features as the farther south; but in point of religion they seem to have been great patrons of the Jains and Buddhists. Trade guilds and commercial corporations seem to have been in existence; and a brisk commercial intercourse appears to have been maintained both with the interior by way of land, and with the outer world by way of water. The Prakrit dialects seem to have been cultivated with care, and the Paiśāchi *Brihat Kathā* is evidence of this culture. Prathishṭāna (Paitan), Patri, Vallabhipaṭan, are said to have been great marts and ports of exit for commerce on the west coast; while equally important in the east and south were places like Tamralipti, Kaṭaka, Tonḍi, Puhār, Korkai, etc., on the Coromandel; Cranganore, Tonḍi, Vaikkarai on the Arabian Sea Coast. Other places referred to are Kaṭāha, Sambahava and some islands, and regions about the Persian Gulf.

Through the centuries of its sway, the Sātavāhana dynasty had its power extending from sea to sea, and we are not quite sure how it actually passed out of existence. The usual break-up probably followed, a great external impact, and when again we gain a glimpse we see the Chāḷukyas well on their way to hegemony in the Dekhan. From A. D. 500 to 750 we find the Chāḷukyas and the Pallavas constantly at war. The Pallavas gain the upper hand and destroy the capital of the Chāḷukyas at Badami about A. D. 640. In consequence there is an interregnum for thirteen years. During the next two generations the Pallavas suffer similar disasters from the Chāḷukyas. Kanchi has often to stand siege and even suffer occupation by an enemy. The constant wars on the Pallava frontier wear them out, and an internal revolution does the rest. The Chāḷukyas fall and the Rāshṭrakūṭas rise in their place. The Pallavas attempt to assert their independence; but the attempt is frustrated by the energetic action of the Rāshṭrakūṭa Dantidurga Vairamēgha. With this passes away Pallava greatness, and their territory becomes broken up into a number of chieftaincies, the first of these being overthrown by the Chola Āditya before A.D. 900. This same ruler of the Chola dynasty also overthrew the Kongu country, and thus began the Chola empire in the Dekhan.

The period of Pallava ascendancy is remarkable in many ways. It was the period of great religious activity, when Buddhism had to give way before the rising tide of Paurānic Hinduism, both Śaiva and Vaishṇava. According to Mr. Venkayya the earliest Pallavas of the Prakrit records were Buddhists; the next ones were Vaishṇava and the last ones Śaiva. This was also the period when cave-temples, and other temples, as well, came to be constructed in large numbers. There was also considerable activity in literature. Many of the Tamil classics that we have at present have to be ascribed to this period. In the Dekhan also there was similar activity, the Kailāsanātha temple at Ellora having been built during the period.

When the Pallava power broke about the end of the eighth century A.D., and the Cholas were beginning to rise, South India was divided in political allegiance, the border line passing through the fringe of the plateau. Just in the region where we are, there was the dynasty of the Gangas ruling over the plain districts of Mysore, with their capitals at Kolar and Talakad at different times. The Pallavas and Pandyas seem to have been at war, which ended in the complete overthrow of the former. The Pandya activity in the north received a check from the Ganga feudatories of the Rāshṭrakūṭas in a battle fought so far out as Tirupparambiyam near Kumbhakonam. The Pandya Varaguṇa had to withdraw, and this was the time propitious to the rise of a new dynasty of enterprising rulers, such as the Cholas were. They rise into prominence no doubt by the acquisition of the Pallava and the Kongu kingdoms. This latter acquisition brings the Cholas into touch with the Rāshṭrakūṭas through their southern feudatories the Gangas. The Rāshṭrakūṭas and the rising Cholas go to war. Krishna III of the former dynasty is so far successful that he is in occupation of Kanchi. Later on Rajāditya, the son of Parāntaka I, falls in a battle fought in A.D. 949–50 with a Ganga feudatory, Būtuga; and this for a time checks the rising tide of Chola aggression. About a quarter of a century thence the Rāshṭrakūṭas fall a victim to a domestic revolution, and a scion of the western Chāḷukyas rises into importance. This revolution gives the Cholas the requisite leisure to organize their resources, and when they reappear under Rājarāja they are already a great power. The Chāḷukyas similarly have a succession of able and energetic rulers. The plateau becomes the debatable frontier between the two powers, and this struggle continues for six or seven generations, with varying success, until at last the Cholas and the Chāḷukyas mark off their spheres of influence as it were. The Cholas remain below the Ghats, and the territory in the plateau remains nominally under the Chāḷukyas. The end of this struggle—a battle royal between two equally matched powers—well organized and with great resources—brings into prominence a number of feudatory states, chief among which have to be mentioned the Yādavas of Devagiri, the Kākatīyas of Warangal, and the Hoysalas of Dvārasamudra. In the south the chiefs of minor principalities rise into importance; but the leading part is taken by a succession war for the Pandya throne, in which the Ceylonese on the one hand, and the Cholas and their feudatories on the other take part. This civil dissension contributes to weaken all parties, the Cholas fall, and the Pandyas and the Hoysalas fight for the quarry, as the Hoysalas and the Yādavas did before on the break up of the Chāḷukya Empire. At the time that Marco Polo was sailing along the Indian coast, Narasimha Hoysala and Sundara Pandya were ruling in the south; the Yādavas were under Ramadeva, and the Kākatīyas under Pratapa Rudra II. It was into this world of South India thus politically divided that Alā'u'd-dín Khilji broke in. When next his general, Mālik Kāfur, undertook a more systematic raid into the south, the kingdoms were in a high state of decay. They were all crushed and the Musalmān stood arbiter for a time.

This is the period of high watermark of Hindu progress all round. Modern Hinduism assumes the shape in which we find it to-day. The indigenous literature as well as the classical Sanskrit receive considerable patronage and blossom into full maturity to pass into artificiality. Religion has been readjusted to the requirements of the masses, and administration had come to be highly organized upon surprisingly modern lines. Revivalism in religion and re-invigoration was the order of the day. It is upon a world so situated that the flood wave of Muslim incursion broke in, overturning everything. As in nature so in politics action provokes re-action against it. This incursion, and the consequent confusion and apprehension, provoked local re-action, wherever there were local ruling families. The Muslim outposts are beaten in and the empire is in no position to assert its authority. The local efforts are gathered up in the foundation of a large and united Hindu Empire known to history as that of Vijianagar. This empire lasts from the middle of the fourteenth century to the end of the sixteenth, when in its turn it falls before a coalition of the Musalmān kingdoms of the Dekhan. The two chief Musalmān States of Golkonda and Bijāpur divide the south between themselves, the Karnatic Bālaghāt going to the one, and the pā'īn ghāt to the other. In the former, arises the kingdom of Mysore, and in the latter the Nawābship of Arcot. Happily the first one remains to-day under its native ruler, though under the ægis of the British Empire; while the other is represented by a titular scion of the family thus founded. It is this other that gave the occasion for the European merchant companies to drop their quills and try the sword. It is this pleasant diversion of some of the Company's clerks, be it by accident or by design, that was the small beginning of that great political phenomenon—the British empire in India as we see it to-day. It is these attempts, which have never ceased to be made from the beginning of history, that have culminated in the empire that for the first time holds sway from the 'Roof of the World' to Cape Comorin and from the Mekran coast to the Mekong valley.

No attempt has been made in this chapter to trace the history of South India on any large scale—a task of the greatest magnitude and difficulty. I have only attempted to indicate the many issues, both principal and subsidiary, that would require careful study and investigation. There is room for much good work on all these periods, the earlier more than the later generally. The first is a virgin field for any explorer, while much yet remains to be done in the second. The periods intervening the brighter epochs are so far a mere blank The history of these intervals of darkness could be worked out by a study of the places where local chieftains flourished; while the Pallava period has to be worked up by a study of the Ganga and other dynasties coeval with the Pallava. There is much useful work to be done along the lines indicated, and work, too, that would be all the better for the co-operation and co-ordination of individual effort.

The Mythic Society of Bangalore has been ushered into being and will provide the requisite common platform, and under its auspices I have every hope that individual workers will not be long in coming forward to lend their assistance.

CHAPTER III

STRUGGLE FOR EMPIRE IN SOUTH INDIA

FROM the dawn of history, empire has been a problem of such importance that a talented historian, Maspero, has named his history of the Tigres and Euphrates valley, during the second and third millenniums B.C., *The Passing Away of Empires.* This has been the case with empires ever since Pericles played his noble rôle of empire-building on the stage of Athenian politics down to our own times, characterized by imperialism as represented by Chamberlain and Cecil Rhodes. So far as India is concerned this has been the problem from the days of Chandragupta—nay even from the days of the *Mahābhārata*—to the comparatively late times of Mahadaji Scindia. It is a common complaint of historians that in Indian history there is no central argument round which to marshal facts so as to present a connected and consistent whole. This, no doubt, is true to a certain extent and the Hindu period of Indian history has, in consequence, been given the distinguishing epithet 'formative', that is, the period when States were in process of formation. I would rather give this distinction to the earlier part of the Hindu period; and characterize the later one 'the struggle for Empire'. It was in this struggle that the States that had been formed were brought into a larger union with the inevitable tendency to break up. Empire is after all a compromise between the opposing principles of local autonomy and imperial unity. While for a time one of the two rival principles may be in the ascendant, the other is always in existence to take advantage of any weakening in it. This, in essence, has been the case with Indian empires, with the distinction that personality played a far more prominent part than the principle underlying it. This latter peculiarity it is that makes the struggle assume in India the appearance of a rise and fall of dynasties, without much affecting the even tenor of life of the people, or their civilization.

India has through historical times been divided into three distinguishable geographical parts despite much historical unity. These are Hindustan, the Dekhan and the farther south. Before the establishment of the British empire these parts had each a distinct history of its own and were never, more than temporarily, united into a consistent whole. There occasionally arose great rulers like Asoka or Samudragupta, who made an attempt at welding them into one, but the attempt was practically successful only for their lifetime. Asoka's boundary in the south was a line drawn from Pondicherry to Cannanore and the parts outside it lay beyond his authority. With regard to Samudragupta it was even less—his claim to authority over the Dekhan States having been one of sufferance rather than of actual rule. He claims to have conquered the States of the Dekhan and to have restored them to the defeated rulers. So it is possible to consider the history of any one of these three geographical parts by itself, and without reference to the other two. Thus I can now give a summary of the struggle for empire in the south between the rulers of the Dekhan and of South India.

The earliest known historical reference to these is in the inscriptions of Asoka where he refers to the Chola, Pandya, Kērala, Satīyaputra and the ruler of Ceylon. But of the actual state of the country or of its rulers we know but little; but from literature

(Tamil) of an ancient character we may gain a glimpse of the political condition of South India in the early centuries of the Christian Era. It is then that we see, as I have pointed out in the chapter on the *The Augustan Age of Tamil Literature*, that States were formed by the amalgamation, mainly by conquest, of the smaller communities into the larger kingdoms, so that at the beginning of the Christian Era we find three well-defined and compact kingdoms of the Chera, Chola, and Pandya. These lay claim to having overcome the Aryan forces, and thus perhaps indicate their having played a not unimportant part in the wars of the Dekhan rulers against the northern invaders, the Kshētrapas of Guzerat and Mālva. The Dekhan contemporaries of the three crowned kings of the south (Chera, Chola, Pandya) and the seven chiefs were the Āndhrabbrityas. Of this dynasty the most distinguished rulers were Gōtamīputra Sātakarni and his successor Pulimāyi or Pulōmavit. These beat back the Kshētrapa Nahapana from the south and kept his successors confined to Guzerat and thus saved the south. The territories under their rule included the present Nizām's Dominions and the Mahārāshṭra, with their capitals at Guntoor (Dharanikōt or Dhanakaṭaka) and at Paitan on the Godavari. The constant references in Tamil literature to Karikāla Chola's erecting his tiger-emblem on the Himalayas, and the father of Śenguṭṭuvan's having had for his northern boundary the Himalayas, would warrant the inference that they carried their arms successfully towards the north. The more so as Karīkāla is said in the *Śilappadhikāram*, to have received presents (tributes as they are called) from the rulers of Mālva (Avanti), Bundalkhand (Vajranāḍu) and Magadha. It would thus appear that the struggle for empire had already begun, and this probably continued for a couple of centuries, when we see the Āndhrabbritya power going out of existence.

So also in the south we lose the thread, and we have barely any mention of a great ruler. There is thus a hiatus in the available records which would indicate an anarchy consequent on the fall of the greater Powers that held sway. This anarchy was taken advantage of by the rising power of the Guptas, who, under Samudragupta and probably under his father, conquered the Dekhan States, and restored them to their former rulers, perhaps, as a matter of policy. This state of vassalage could not have lasted long, and from out of this anarchy there arose two great Powers, the Pallavas in the south and the Chāḷukyas in Mahārāshṭra. These two dynasties, with their capitals respectively at Kanchi and at Badami (near Bijāpur), continued the same struggle for empire and were seen fighting constantly on the Tungabhadra-Krishna frontier. As a consequence of this perpetual antagonism, we see the Chāḷukyas, following the example of the Āndhrabbrityas, create a frontier province with head-quarters at Rājamahēndri. This was done by the great Chāḷukya Emperor Pulikēsin II, who made his younger brother the viceroy. That this was a wise measure and was called for by the necessity of the case is amply borne out by his great enemy Narasimhavarman Pallavamalla's attacking Badami and burning it down, so as to cause an interregnum of thirteen years. These two great rulers were the imperial contemporaries of the Chinese traveller, Yuwan Chwang (Hieun Thsang), and of his host Harshavardhana Śīlāditya of Kanouj. This was about the middle of the seventh century after Christ. A little after the end of that century, both these powerful dynasties wore out each other so thoroughly that they went out of existence and gave way to others to take their place in the Dekhan and in the south after the inevitable anarchy. We see about this time the political centre of gravity shifting. The rising Rāshṭrakūṭa power is on its trial and not merely has to make good its claim; but it also has to contend against factions within the camp. Now it was the rōle of the Gangas of Mysore to extend their territory northward and southward. In this latter direction they received a check from the Pandyas under Varaguṇa, who turned back the Gangas after inflicting a defeat on them at Tirupparambian near Kumbakonam. The Pandya was too far off to defend the Mysore frontier against the Gangas and not long after this we find the Rāshṭrakūṭas tightening their grip upon the Mysore country, and putting their southern frontier in a state of defence, at a time when a new power comes into being immediately to the south of Mysore.

This was no other than the great Chola dynasty, whose inscriptions in large numbers give us an insight into their greatness and the political condition of the times. Taking their origin somewhere in the Tanjore district (near Pudukotta) they mastered possession of the Chola country; and when the third in succession, but the first great ruler, Parāntaka came to the throne about A. D. 900, their authority extended over Chola, Toṇḍa and Kongumanḍalam. It was he that fought against and beat back aggression on the Pandya, Kēraḷa and Ganga frontiers. When he passed away in the middle of the century, he left to his sons the wars all along the northern frontier. It is now that the Chola fortunes fell so low that the Rāshṭrakūṭa ruler, Krishna III, was in occupation of Kanchi for a while, and that Rājāditya, the Chola ruler, for the time being, was slain in a battle at Takkōlam about A. D. 950, chiefly through the exertions of Perumānaḍi Būtuga, the Ganga feudatory of the Dekhan rulers. About a twenty years after this, the Rāshṭrakūṭas were overthrown by a scion of the Chāḷukyas, and the confusion in the Dekhan was the opportunity for the Cholas of the south. While yet the Chāḷukyas were struggling to make good their newly acquired position, the Cholas began to recover so well that, when the great Chola, Rājarāja the Great, ascended the throne in A.D. 985, he found himself in possession of the Chola, Toṇḍa and Kongumaṇḍalams, and he had to fight the Kēraḷas on the west coast and the Gangas in their own country. This latter power was overthrown about the year A.D. 1000, thanks to the exertions of this great Chola, ably seconded by those of his greater son Rājēndra, the Gangaikoṇḍa Chola, so that the debatable frontier hereafter was Yeḍatorēnāḍ, 2000. While the son was thus fighting to establish peace on this frontier, the father had vastly added to his empire by a stroke of policy in the north by the addition of the whole of the eastern Chāḷukya kingdom of Vengaimaṇḍalam.

This kingdom beginning as a viceroyalty under Kubja Vishnuvardhana, the younger brother of Pulikēsin II, the Chāḷukya, continued to acknowledge allegiance to the Chāḷukyas, probably till these latter were overthrown. Then the eastern kingdom continued in comparative peace till the Cholas made their frontier contiguous to the eastern Chāḷukya frontier. Rājarāja now gave his daughter in marriage to Vimalāditya, and restored the conquered kingdom to his son-in-law, who was only too glad to have the powerful Chola to help him in case of attack either from the west or from the north. The eastern Chāḷukya territory, it must be said to the credit of the far-seeing policy of Rājarāja, remained ever after faithful to the Cholas and continued an integral part of the empire.

When Rājarāja died in A.D. 1013, he left behind him to his son, the Gangaikoṇḍa Chola, practically the whole of the Madras presidency except Madura and Tinnevelly. Only the Chāḷukya frontier was in dispute. The son had to fight on this frontier and if his inscriptions can be taken as unpimeachable evidence he secured it. He sighed for new worlds to conquer in his own small way, and carried his arms successfully across Kalingam (Ganjam), etc. He fought battles on the Ganges and in Burma, earning thus the high-sounding surname of the Gangaikoṇḍa Chola, the magnificent ruins of whose capital at Gangaikoṇḍa-Sōḷapuram (in the Woḍiyarpālayam taluka) attest his greatness to this day. When in his turn the Gangaikoṇḍa Chola (the hero of the Kanarese Rājasēkhara Vilāsam), had to leave his earthly empire to his son Rajādhirāja in A.D. 1042, the frontiers were all aflame in revolt, and this condition of the Chola empire was made the worse by the Chāḷukya ruler of the time having been a great warrior.

Three generations of rulers had lived and passed away in the seven and a half lakh country[1] of the Chāḷukyas and their exertions left the empire quiet in all other directions except that of the Chola frontier. On this frontier there was constant war even in the days of Rājarāja and his son, so that, when Sōmēsvara Āhavamalla ascended the throne of his fathers A.D. 1044, he had to continue the work of his father and grandfather. Meanwhile Rajādhirāja had had time to introduce order into his own empire, and to bring the revolted frontiers back to their allegiance. When the warrior-king Sōmēsvara broke in upon him Rajādhirāja was ready to meet him. The wars were long and wearying and the results were often doubtful. They made at last a resolute attempt to decide once for all this debate of arms, and the result was the great battle fought in the year A.D. 1052 at Koppam on the Tungabhadra. Rajādhirāja fell in it and, for the time, victory was with the Chāḷukyas; but Rājēndra, the younger brother of the Chola, brought up reinforcements and retrieved the fortunes of the Cholas and thus earned

[1] This refers either to the revenue, or to the number of villages.

his title to be crowned on the field of battle. Now began the battle royal between the contending rulers which was not to end for a couple of generations, and, when it did, it had worn out both parties so much that the empires were ripe for breaking up. Rājēndra Chola II was able during his reign to invade the Chāḷukya dominions themselves, and lays claim to having erected a pillar of victory at Kollāpuram (Kolhapur). One unlooked for consequence of these long and wearisome wars was the advent into prominence of a number of great chieftains, who beginning as pillars of empire eventually proved, in their successors, its destruction. Having had to fight over the wars of his elder brother again, and having to maintain the Chola arms and prestige strenuously during his time, as against the Chāḷukyas, Rājēndra died in A.D. 1060 or 1061. His younger brother Vīrarājēndra assumed the imperial purple and along with it the responsibilities. He was already a handy man for the heavy work. One of the Mysore Inscriptions thus speaks of him and his rule—'a new ruler! A kingdom fit for a hero! Now is the occasion for us'.

The Chāḷukyas were busy on the frontier. Between Vīrarājēndra and Sōmēswara several battles were fought in the Ceded districts. The Chāḷukyas regarded Koḷlippākkai somewhere in the Chitaldroog district as the door of the south and appointed the most trusted official to guard this region. At the accession of Vīrarājēndra the whole of the Mysore country—the three divisions composing it, namely, Gangavāḍi, Nolambavāḍi and Banavase, all but the last only nominally, was under the second but the most capable of Sōmēsvara's sons. Another son was not far off and had a viceroyalty in the Ceded districts with head-quarters at Kampli, and bearing the title Vengaimanḍalēsvara without the territory to give him the title. It would appear from the inscriptions that the Chāḷukyas advanced up to the Pālār, from which river Vīrarājēndra had to chase them back. After this the normal condition of affairs was restored, and the five Chola invasions had for their objective the territory at the angle between the Tungabhadra and the Krishna. Vīrarāja once occupied Kampli and planted a 'Pillar of Victory there'.

The Chola claims to have won three times in battles at Kūḍal Sangaman at the junction of the rivers. In most of these Vikramāditya, the second son of Sōmēsvara, played a distinguished part. On the last occasion when the Chola was there, having accepted the challenge of Sōmēsvara I, he had to wait long and neither Sōmēsvara nor his army appeared. While the Chola was about to break up camp and move on, Vikramāditya appeared at the head of his army and showed a readier inclination to treat than to fight. This parleying ended in a treaty between the Chola ruler and the Chāḷukya prince who set the seal by taking the Chola princess as his wife.

This change of front on the part of Vikramāditya has to be explained. While the Chola was waiting, Sōmēsvara Āhavamalla died by drowning himself in the Tungabhadra as a result of an attack of a malignant fever. There was a change of rulers at Rājamahēndri. Rājarāja Chāḷukya, the nephew and son-in-law of the Gangaikonḍa chola, had died leaving a son and a daughter. This son does not appear in the transactions immediately following Rājarāja's death. The western Chāḷukyas moved east, but Vīrarājēndra was too quick for them. He won a victory at Bezwada (Vijayavāḍi) and appointed a brother of the late King as Viceroy at Rājamahēndri. Vīrarājēndra thus secured himself on this side of his empire and returned, sending out an expedition across Kalingam to Central India. In this political condition of his frontiers Sōmēsvara Āhavamalla died, and his eldest son Sōmēsvara Bhūvanaikamalla succeeded. Vikramāditya did not wish to play the rôle of a lieutenant to his less distinguished, though elder, brother, but could not strike single-handed. Hence the inclination to enter into an alliance with the powerful Chola on the frontier.

This done, Vikramāditya moved through the southern part of his brother's dominions to feel the temper of the greater viceroys of the empire. Some time in the course of this progress, Vīrarājēndra died at Gangaikoṇḍa Śōḷapuram the capital. This unsettled the plans of Vikramāditya who hurried there, set his brother-in-law on the throne and returned to his more direct sphere of activity. Soon after the new Chola ruler fell a victim to a revolution, and another young ambitious man was upon the Chola throne. Vikramāditya had to bide his time, and waited six more years before he thought he could venture upon his dangerous career towards empire. The young man who ascended the Chola throne in A.D. 1070 was no other than Kulōttunga, the son of the Chāḷukya Rājarāja and grandson, through his mother, of the Gangaikoṇḍa Chola. He appears to have been brought up in his grandfather's house and seems to have distinguished himself, while yet a prince, in distant expeditions in central India. As Yuvaraja, he is said, in his inscriptions, to have captured a herd of elephants at Vairāgaram and to have taken Chakragōṭṭam. This latter is in the territory of Dhāra where the great Bhōja had recently ruled, and it might have been that Kulōttunga had to play a leading part in the expedition sent out by Vīrarājēndra. Vīrarājēndra is said also to have sent an expedition to the Talaing country. As Yuvaraja of the Chāḷukya Rājarāja, Kulōttunga could not have gone there. This is further borne out by 'Kulōttunga's having uplifted the lotus goddess in the direction of the rising sun.' This could, perhaps, be made to mean the Telugu country, which is not quite to the east of the Chola country.

It would thus be clear, bearing in mind that the name of Kulōttunga does not figure in the transactions after the battle of Bezwada, that Kulōttunga spent his youth in the immediate entourage of the great Cholas. He appears to have been quite content to accept a lieutenancy from his uncles, but not from any of his cousins. Further there is nothing to connect Kulōttunga with the revolution after Vīrarājēndra's death. This may have been the natural consequence of the Chāḷukya intervention, and Kulōttunga merely reaped the benefit arising therefrom, having had reason to believe, as some of his inscriptions and the *Kalingattupparani* show, that he was adopted by the Gangaikonḍa Chola, though this latter had three sons to succeed him and another older than these who preferred quiet life to sovereignty. It was this Kulōttunga who upset the calculation of Vikramāditya, and, under the circumstances of his accession, fought against Vikramāditya in his schemes of self-aggrandizement.

Kulōttunga had his own frontiers to quiet before he could think of Vikramāditya, and this respite on this frontier was taken advantage of by Vikramāditya to gain greater hold upon the Mysore country. In this he was successful in the main. When he, therefore, thought his time had come to put his plans into operation, Kulōttunga was ready. Sōmēsvara Bhuvanaikamalla had reasons to suspect Vikramāditya, and this latter deemed it unsafe to reside at court. Vikramāditya made up his mind, and with his brother Jayasimha got things ready in the south against his elder brother and sovereign. Sōmēsvara asked for help and Kulōttunga gladly agreed; but before Kulōttunga could arrive Vikramāditya had won, and Sōmēsvara was thrown into prison. This was in A. D. 1076. After an invasion or two of the Mysore country to wrest the southern half of it from the Cholas, and another into the Telugu country, Vikramāditya allowed matters to settle themselves in the frontier between the Cholas and the Chāḷukyas. Each of these sovereigns ruled over his respective empire for half a century, generally in peace. Vikramāditya sent out two expeditions across the Narbudda, Central India, (Dhāra and Dāhala), having been distracted by wars, civil and external, in the earlier part of his reign. He dispatched contingents to help rulers at such a great distance as Kāmarūpa (Assam). Kulōttunga conquered and even colonized the south and west up to Kōṭṭāru near Cape Comorin, and subjugated the Kalingams (Orissa) through his general Karuṇākara Toṇḍamān.

Affairs on the Mysore frontier were developing fast for a final issue, and chiefly through the strenuous exertions of a Mysore chief, Vishṇuvardhana Hoyśala, and the warlike instincts of his general Gangarāja. Gangavāḍi and Noḷambavāḍi were lost to the Chola in A. D. 1116 and only nominally added to the Chāḷukyan empire. This marks the beginning of the disruption. The southern viceroys who stood firm by the side of Vikramāditya in his wars against the Chola, and even in his usurpation, naturally expected the reward of their services in nominal allegiance, if not actual independence. This had to be acquiesced in and the ambition of some of these redoubtable champions of the prince, the aspirant to the throne, proved the bane of the emperor and his empire. Vikramāditya was, however, saved the humiliation of a break-up of the empire by the exertions of the loyal Sinda chieftain, Achugi II of Gulburga (in the Nizam's Dominions). He defeated in a night attack at Kannēgala the Hoyśala forces and chased them back to Bēlūr, their head-quarters. Their allies in the revolt, the Kaḍambas of Hangal and Goa had also to find shelter in their strongholds. So when Vikramāditya died in A. D. 1126, the empire was left intact no doubt, but without chances of continuing much longer, unless it found a succession of very capable rulers, which the empire was fated not to have.

Kulōttunga was more fortunate. Doubtless he had to acquiesce in the loss of southern Mysore, but he acquired a hold upon Kalingam. What was more he had capable sons, distinguished in war and trained in administration to succeed him, when he died A. D. 1118. There were three successors who maintained the empire intact and when the Chola Empire fell, it fell from the impact of simultaneous Pandya, Kērala and Kākatīya invasions from the south, west and north. Both these emperors were great administrators, each in his way. They had perfected the Government, as it had been handed down to them, and were otherwise patrons of letters. They adopted a policy of enlightened liberalism in religion. After a couple of generations of weak rulers, the Chāḷukya empire was subjected to the double misfortune of disorganization and dissensions within, and the onset of a powerful invader without. This double calamity was averted by a man of genius Bijjala, who usurped the empire and infused some fresh life into it for a quarter of a century. The new power of the Kākatīyas of Wārangal was emerging into a great career, and the process of disintegration was going on, though, in the meanwhile, unobserved only by those whom it concerned the most. The Hoyśalas pressed from the south, Yādavas from the north-west and the Kākatīyas from the east. The empire was dead and these shared the quarry. Like the Chola empire somewhat later, this empire was parcelled out among numbers of petty chieftains, who claimed independence, and had to maintain it by perpetual readiness to fight. At the commencement of the thirteenth century there stood out the Yādavas of Deogiri, the Kākatīyas of Wārangal or Telingana, the Hoyśalas of Dvārasamudra, and a number of small chiefs in lieu of the great Chola empire and the Pandyas and Kērala. At the end of the first decade there broke in into this world south of the Vindhyas the great Muslim wave of invasion under Mālik Kāfur. Overthrowing in succession the great feudatory principalities of Deogiri, Wārangal and Dvārasamudra, Kāfur Mālik advanced south as far as Ramēswaram. Leaving small garrisons behind, he went back to mature his own plans of king-making and becoming king. The general movement against this occupation of the country by the Muḥammadans culminated in the great Hindu empire of Vijayanaggar. The garrisons were driven out and the threads of these isolated risings were gathered together by the genius of one man, who placed the headquarters of the rising empire in the frontier outpost of the south to guard at least this last citadel against the Muslim conquest. This story, however, belongs to another period.

CHAPTER IV

INDIA AT THE DAWN OF THE CHRISTIAN ERA

INDIA the wonderland of the east, as it is even now called, was made known to the west, when the world-conqueror, Alexander the Great, forced open her gates on the north-west. Our knowledge of India at all of a definite character may be said to extend no farther than this period, as, according to the most recent authority, his connexion with India was not much more than a great raid. It is matter of common knowledge that he had to give up his idea of carrying his conquests right up to the eastern limits of the land, (according to his own notion of the configuration of the earth), owing to a mutiny among his soldiers headed by his cavalry commander Koinos. Before leaving India, however, he divided his conquests on this side of the Indian Caucasus into three vice-royalties as follows:

I. Paropanisadae, the country west of the Indus, with Oxyartes, the father of Roxana, for its viceroy.

II. The Punjab including in it the kingdom of Taxila, and that of Porus, that of the Sophytes together with the territories of the Oxydrachoi and the Malloi, under the viceroy Philip, son of Machetas; leaving the civil administration in the hands of the native princes.

III. Sindh including the kingdom of Mousikanos, Oxykanos, Sambus and Maeris of Patalene under Peithon, the son of Agenor, for its viceroy.

Philip was murdered in a mutiny, before the death of Alexander, and his place was taken by Eudamos who remained in India till called away in 317 B.C. to help Eumenes against Antigonus of Asia, the most powerful among the Diadochi. When the Macedonian Empire was partitioned a second time in 321 B.C. (consequent on the death of Perdiccas, the regent of the first partition), the Indian province, east of the Indus, was left out of account, as Peithon had to withdraw to the western bank of the great river. About 305 B.C. Seleucus Nikator made an attempt to revive the empire of Alexander in this region, but had to relinquish his hold upon the whole of Afghanistan, and enter into a humiliating treaty with Chandragupta, the Maurya emperor of India. This personage is believed to have been in the camp of Alexander in the Punjab, and, thrown upon his own resources as the great Macedonian turned away from the banks of the Ravi, he took advantage of the confusion resulting from the departure of Alexander to overthrow the ruling Nanda in Magadha, and set himself up as the first emperor of India known to history. In the course of fifteen years he was able to make himself so strong as to fight Seleucus, not only on equal terms but also to extort from him such a valuable cession of territory as Afghanistan up to the Hindu-Kush. For three generations this dynasty held its power undiminished. His grandson Asoka, the great Buddhist Emperor of India, was able to hold his own with the successors of Seleucus, and maintained with them the diplomatic relations thus begun by his grandfather. It seems to be well attested that both Seleucus Nikator and Ptolemy Philadelphus had sent ambassadors to the courts of Chandragupta and Bindusara, although scholars are not wanting yet who consider the particular edict of Asoka a mere boast. With the death of Asoka about 230 B.C. the Mauryan empire loses its hold upon the more powerful and distant of its vassals, and the days of the dynasty are numbered.

From this event to the year A. D. 319 the date of the rise to power of the Imperial Guptas, the history of India is yet quite uncertain, although we are able to gain a few glimpses as to the general features of the history of that period. The Asiatic empire of the Seleucidae was attacked simultaneously by the Romans and the Gauls from the west and north-west, and the Parthians from the east. About the beginning of the second century B. C., Parthia made good her independence under Arsakes Mithridates I and Baktria under Eukratides.[1] This was but the reflex action of the movements of the nomad tribes in the far-off plains of Mongolia. The great tribe of the Hiung-nu fell, with all the fervour of neighbourly love, upon the Yuet-chi, and dislodged them from their then habitat in the plains of Zungaria. These in their turn fell upon the Wu-sung, killed the Wu-sung chieftain in battle, and marched further upon the region then in the occupation of the Se, Sŏk or Śakas. These last had to make room for them along the right bank of the Oxus and occupy the country protected by the Indian Caucasus. The Yuet-chi were themselves defeated by the son of the late Wu-sung chieftain. When his father fell in battle he found a secure asylum with the Hiung-nu, who now helped him to regain his lost patrimony. It was in the course of these movements that the Śakas and possibly some of the Hiung-nu moved down the Kabul valley into India, and occupied the country on the right bank of the Indus, right down even to Gujarat. It is one of their out-settlements on the Jumna that the coins and other antiquities of Muttra would seem to warrant.

[1] V. A. Smith, *Early History of India*, p. 210 ff.

While all this was taking place across the borders of India, in India itself there was going forward a revolution of no less consequence. The Mauryan empire was overthrown by Pushyamitra Sunga, the Maurya general, in spite of the loyalist minister, a brother-in-law of Yegñasēna Sātakarni of the Dekhan. The usurper's strength was tried by a triple war:—(1) against Menander, ruler of Kabul; (2) against Kāravela, the Kalinga ruler of Orissa; (3) against the loyalist Yegñasēna and in behalf of a counter-claimant to the throne of the kingdom of Vidharba. Though for the time successful against all these, the empire had suffered vital injuries. The Dekhan kingdom or viceroyalty becomes so powerful that the Āndhras establish an imperial position themselves, and render their quota of service by holding out against the Śaka invaders from the north-west and west. It must have been in the course of these wars that the occasion should have arisen for the founding of the era which now goes by the name of Vikramāditya, and that under the name of Śaka. As to both these eras and the circumstances of their origin, there is very considerable difference of opinion among scholars. In the course of the political shiftings described above, a clan of the Yuehchi, by name Kushāna, was able to push its way into India and establish a kingdom in the Punjab including Kāsmir. The greatest ruler among them, whose empire came into touch with the Chinese Empire on the one side and the Parthian on the other, is Kanishka, the Constantine of the Buddhism of the greater vehicle (Mahāyānism). Learned scholars associate him with both the eras above referred to, while there are yet others, who would dissociate him from either and refer him to a period later than both. None of them, however, take him beyond the period I have marked at the beginning. At the very beginning of the Christian era then the Punjab and the frontier province, including Kāsmir, were under the Kushānas or their immediate predecessors or their successors. Gujarat and Mālva, including northern Konkan, were under the Śakas.

During the period marked out above, we have been passing from the supremacy of Buddhism (if such an expression can be regarded as appropriate at all), through a reassertion of the Brahman ascendancy, on to a final compromise, ending on the one side in Mahāyānist Buddhism, and on the other in the Hinduism of the Gita. For as Professor Kern maintains, on the authority of the Tibetan historian Tāranath and the Saddharma-puṇḍarīka, the founder of the Mādhyamika school of Buddhism, Nāgārjuna was a disciple of the Brahman Rāhuḷabhadra who was much indebted to Sage Krishna. Paraphrased, this means no less than that these teachers drew a part of their inspiration from the Gita.[1] This is borne out by the importance that attaches to Bhakti (devotion) in Mahāyānist Buddhism and later Hinduism.

During all this period of active mutations both in religion and politics, South India would appear to have been out of this great vortex. This is a delusion due more to lack of information than to a lack of history. The edicts of Asoka mention the Chola, Pandya, Kerala, Satīyaputra, and Ceylon, among those with whom he entered into diplomatic relations. He thought it worth his while to send his son and daughter to Ceylon as missionaries. These facts put it beyond a doubt that there was some communication between Magadha and Ceylon, generally by way of the sea. It cannot be that the neighbouring coast was not also brought into touch with the north. The edicts of Asoka, found in the Chitaldroog district, make it certain that there was some connexion, and in all

[1] *Manual of Indian Buddhism*, p. 122.

likelihood by way of land, and by the east coast. The Ceylonese tradition, as embodied in the *Mahāvamśa*, is quite in support of this conclusion. Between the Mahārāshṭra and Mālva there was a great trunk road notwithstanding the great forest region between them. This road it is that has given us the name Dakshiṇāpatha (Dekhan). Most likely this road wound its way over the hills by way of Burhanpur into western Mālva. The middle region was the forest, which it continued to be even up to the days of Harsha.

During this period, and for a long time after, Hindustan (the country north of the Vindhyas), kept touch with the outer world by way of land mainly; the south kept itself in contact with the rest of the world chiefly by way of the sea. That the Hindus did not always wait for others to come to them for goods is in evidence in a variety of ways. There is, first, the statement of Cornelius Nepos, who says that Q. Metellus Celer received from the king of the Suevi some Indians, who had been driven by storm into Germany in the course of a voyage of commerce.[1] This is quite a precise fact, and is borne out by a number of tales of voyages with the horrors attending navigation depicted in the liveliest colours in certain classes of writings both in Sanskrit and Tamil. Among the places mentioned in the latter classes of sources are those in the East Indian Archipelago, such as Java (Śāvaham), Sambhava (Karpūrasambhavam), Kaṭāha (Sumatra), and Kāḷaham (Burma) not to mention China. It would thus appear that there was some very considerable activity in maritime commerce. They used to have lighthouses to warn ships and one such is described at the great port at the mouth of the Kavery, a big palmyra trunk carrying on the top of it a huge oil lamp.

[1] Macrindle, *Ancient India*, p. 110.

On either coast were towns of great commercial importance. Beginning with the coast of the Arabian Sea and passing over the ports beyond the region of South India, the first town of importance is what thel classical geographers call Tyndis (Toṇḍi) where Quilandy now stands. Opposite to it lies what was called Liuke (White Island) now going under the name Sacrifice Rock or 'Veḷḷiyan Kallu' among the people. The Ophir of these geographers is located by some at the site of modern Beypore. South from this was the great mart of Muziris (Muyirikkōḍu, Koḍungalur or Cranganur) the port of Vanji or Karur, the capital of the Cheras, with the river-mouth Pseudostomos (Aḷi-mukham or false mouth). This is the port to which navigators turned their course when, through the enterprise of Harpalos, the south-west monsoon was discovered. Passing this port we come next to Bakare (Vaikkarai) the port of Nyeacinda in the territory of the Pandion of Madura (Nīrkkunṛam in the kingdom of the Pandyans at Madura). After this the classical geographers mention only Cape Comorin (Kumāri). Passing Kumāri they lead us into the Argalic (Argali in Tamil, Mahodadi in Sanskrit) gulf, and thence into the port of Kolkoi (Korkai). It is here that the island of Taprabane naturally finds mention. The origin of this name for Ceylon has been the cause of very ingenious speculation. It is regarded by some as the equivalent of Tamraparni (the Tambapanni of the Buddhists). There is another derivation more fanciful than this, namely, tap Rāvaṇa as a corruption of dīpa Rāvaṇa. The more likely and much less ingenious origin would be dīp Ruan, Ruan being one of the kingdoms in the Island of Ceylon, about the beginning of the Christiau era, according to the *Mahāvaṃśa*; and that the kingdom to which sailors should inevitably go from the Argalic gulf. Proceeding still further through the gulf these sailors came to the eastern emporium of Tondi, the great mart for Chinese wares, and commodities from the Eastern Archipelago. Further north of this was Puhār at the mouth of the Kavery; the next port of importance on this side was Maisolos as Pliny calls it (Masulipatam).[1]

To take up the political geography of south India as a whole then, the country south of the Krishna was divided among 'the three crowned kings' and seven chieftains, with an eighth coming somewhat later. It is the coast region and the more open country that belonged to the kings, while the middle regions of hills and forests belonged to the chieftains, and perhaps even a few tribes (Nagas and others). The east coast from near the mouth of the Krishna to the south of Tondi, in the Zamindari of Ramnad, belonged to the Chola, although midway between the kingdom proper and its northern viceroyalty of Kanchi lay the hill-country round Tirukoilur, in the possession of a class of chieftains named Malayamān, very often loyal supporters of their suzerain, occasionally truculent and rebellious. South of the Chola kingdom lay that of the Pandya, which extended from coast to coast, and embraced within its borders the modern districts of Madura and Tinnevelli, and the State of Travancore, taking in also a part of Coimbatore and Cochin. This included in it the chieftaincies of Āay (the Aioi of Ptolemy) round the Podyil hill in the western ghats, and of Evvi round about the port of Korkai in Tinnevelli. There was besides the domains of Pēhan round the Palnis, which comes under their sphere of influence as well. North of this and along the western ghats on the sea-side lay the territory of the Chera: a territory stretching right across the Palghat gap through Salem and Coimba-

[1] Kanakasabhai's *Tamils*, 1800 years ago, ch. iii and Macrindle's *Ancient India* and Ptolemy.

tore. South Mysore was parcelled out among a number of chieftains corresponding to the modern Pāḷayagars, whose allegiance was at the disposal of either, but the more powerful, of their neighbour kings. Such were the Irungō of Arayam, Pāri of Parambunāḍ, Adiyamān of Tagaḍūr (Dharmapuri) and Ōri of the Kollimalais. The first of these was within Mysore territory proper, and to the east of his domain lay the Gangas, and Kongu to the south.

These chieftaincies were the bone of contention between the Cholas and the Cheras. When the period under treatment begins, the Cholas are supreme under Karikāl, who ascended the throne, probably after defeating the Chera and Pandya in a battle at Veṇṇil (Koilveṇṇi as it is now called) in the Tanjore district. He was a remarkable sovereign who, in many ways, contributed to the permanent welfare of his subjects, and has consequently been handed down to posterity as a beneficent and wise monarch. He constructed the embankments for the Kavery, and his chief port Puhār was the great emporium of the east coast. His reign was long and, taken along with those of his two predecessors and the successor next following him, constitutes the period of the first Chola ascendancy in the south. In the reign of his successor a great catastrophe befell Puhār, and the city and port were both destroyed. This was a hard blow to the ascendancy of the Cholas. But Karikāl had, after defeating his contemporary Chera, given one of his daughters in marriage to the son of his vanquished rival. This alliance stood the Cholas in good stead. Karikāl's successor began his reign with a victory, which his heir-apparent won for him, against the Chera and Pandya combined, at Kāriyār, probably in the Salem district. When Puhār was destroyed there was a civil war, owing perhaps to the untimely death of the young Chola prince; and the Chera ruler for the time being, advanced through the central region. He intervened in favour of his cousins with effect, as against the rival claimants of royal blood, and restored the Chola dynasty to some power; but the ascendancy surely enough passed from them to the Chera. The Chera ascendancy under the Red-Chera (Śenguṭṭuvan) lasted only one generation; in the reign of his successor the Pandyas rose to greater importance and the Chera suffered defeat and imprisonment at his hands. This Pandya ascendancy probably lasted on somewhat longer till about the rise of the Pallavas in Kanchi. This course of the political centre of gravity of power in southern India is borne out in very important particulars by the Ceylon chronicle, called the *Mahāvaṃśa*. According to this work, the Cholas were naturally the greatest enemies of the Singalese rulers. There were usurpers from the Chola country in Ceylon in the first century B.C.; and there were invasions and counter-invasions as well. On one occasion the Chola invaders carried away 12,000 inhabitants of Ceylon and set them to work at 'the Kavery' as the Chronicle has it.[1] This looks very much like an exploit of Karikāla, seeing that it was he who built the city of Puhār. King Gajabāhu of Ceylon was present at the invitation of the Red-Chera, to witness the celebration of a sacrifice and the consecration of the temple to the 'Chaste Lady' (Pattiny Devi) at Vanji, on the west coast.

The ascendancy of the Chera, however, passed away, as already mentioned, to the Pandyas in the course of one single generation. The Red-Chera was succeeded by his son, 'the Chera of the elephant look', who was his father's viceroy at Toṇḍi, and figured prominently in the wars of his predecessor in the middle region. He was defeated and taken prisoner in a battle, which

[1] Upham's *Mahāvaṃśa*, vol. i, p. 228.

he had to fight with the contemporary Pandyan, designated the victor, at Talaiālangānam. With this mishap to the ruler the Chera ascendancy passes away. The Pandyans of Madura take their turn now, and continued to hold the position of hegemony up to the time that the Pallavas rise into importance. This, in brief and in very general terms, was the political history of South India at the beginning and during the early centuries of the Christian Era.

Passing on from the political to the industrial condition of India, we have already described the principal sea-ports, both on the western and eastern seaboard. If, as has been pointed out, there were so many thriving ports and, if foreign merchants sought these for trade at considerable risk of pirates and, if there was so much enterprise in sea-going among the inhabitants of the country, the conclusion is irresistible that the country had a prosperous industry, and so, on examination, it appears certainly to have been. Apart from the complaints of Petronius that fashionable Roman ladies exposed their charms much too immodestly by clothing themselves in the 'webs of woven wind', as he called the muslins imported from India, Pliny says that India drained the Roman Empire annually to the extent of 55,000,000 sesterces, equal to £486,979[1] sending in return goods which sold at a hundred times their value in India.[2] He also remarks in another place, 'this is the price we pay for our luxuries and our women.'

That the industrial arts had received attention and cultivation in early times in India is in evidence to the satisfaction of the most sceptical mind. The early Tamils divided arts into six groups: ploughing (mean-

[1] Mommen gives the total £11,000,000, £6,000,000 for Arabia, £5,000,000 for India.

[2] *Malabar Manual*, vol. i, pp. 250-1.

ing thereby agriculture), handicrafts, painting, commerce and trade, the learned arts, and lastly the fine arts. Of these agriculture and commerce were regarded as of the first importance. Flourishing trade presupposes a volume of industry, the principal of which was weaving then, as it also has been until recently. Cotton, silk and wool seem to have been the materials that were wrought into cloths. Among the woollens we find mention of manufactures from the wool of rats, which was regarded as particularly warm. There are thirty varieties of silks mentioned, each with a distinctive appellation of its own, as distinguished from the imported silks of China which had a separate name. The character of the cotton stuffs that were manufactured is indicated by the comparisons instituted between them and, 'sloughs of serpents' or 'vapour from milk'; and the general description of these as 'those fine textures the thread of which could not be followed even by the eye.'

The chief exports from the country, as the author of the *Periplus* says, were these: 'The produce of the soil like pepper, great quantities of best pearl are likewise purchased here, ivory, silk in the web, spikenard from the Ganges, betel from the countries further to the east, transparent stones of all sorts, diamonds, rubies and tortoise shell from the golden Chersonese or from the islands off the coast of Limurike.' This is all from the port of Muziris on the west coast. He goes on to say: 'There is a great resort of shipping to this port for pepper and betel; the merchants bring out a large quantity of spice, and their other imports are topazes, stibium, coral, flint, glass, brass, and lead, a small quantity of wine as profitable as at Barugaza, cinnabar, fine cloth, arsenic and wheat, not for sale but for the use of the crew'. That Pliny's complaint about the drain was neither imaginary nor hypersensitive is in evidence in a passage descriptive of Muziris in one of the ancient classics of Tamil literature[1]: 'Muśiri to which come the well-rigged ships of the Yavanas, bringing gold and taking away spices in exchange.'

Regarding the trade of the east coast, here follows a description of Puhār as a port; 'Horses were brought from distant lands beyond the seas, pepper was brought in ships; gold and precious stones came from the northern mountains; sandal and aghil came from the mountains towards the west; pearl from the southern seas and coral from the eastern seas. The produce of the region watered by the Ganges; all that is grown on the banks of the Kavery; articles of food from Ilam (Ceylon) and the manufactures of Kāḷaham (Burma)'[2] were brought there for sale. The products of particular importance received in the port of Toṇḍi are aghil (a kind of black aromatic wood), fine silk stuff (from China), candy, sandal, scents, and camphor. All of these articles and salt were carried into the interior by means of wagons drawn by teams of oxen, slowly trudging along through town and village, effecting exchanges with commodities for export. Tolls were paid on the way, and the journey from the coast up the plateau and back again occupied many months. A brisk and thriving commerce with the corresponding volume of internal trade argues peace, and the period to which the above description will apply must have been a period of general peace in the Peninsula. They did not forget in those days to maintain a regular customs establishment, the officials of which piled up the grain and stored up the things that could not immediately be measured and appraised, leaving them in the dockyards carefully sealed with the tiger signet of the king.[3]

1 *Ahanānūru*, 149.

2 *Paṭṭinappālai*, 127 ff. and *The Tamils* 1300 *years ago*, p. 27.

3 *Paṭṭinappālai*, 134–6.

The Tamils built their own ships; and in the other crafts of the skilled artisan they seem to have attained some proficiency, though they availed themselves of experts from distant places. In the building of the royal palace at Puhār, skilled artisans from Magadha, mechanics from Marāḍam (Maharatta), smiths from Avanti (Mālva), carpenters from Yavana, worked[1] together with the artisans of the Tamil land. There is mention of a temple of the most beautiful workmanship, in the same city, built by the Gurjjaras.[2] In the building of forts and in the providing of them with weapons and missiles, both for offence and defence, the Tamils had attained to something like perfection. Twenty-four such weapons are mentioned among the defences of Madura.

Passing on from the industrial to the literary, social and religious condition of the south, which we have so far been considering, we have again to do with the three kingdoms, each with a capital city and a premier port. The Cholas had their capital at Uraiyūr, with Puhār for an alternative capital and chief port; the Pandyas had their capital at Madura, with the port and premier viceroyalty at Korkai; the Cheras had their capital at Vanji, with the principal port and viceroyalty at Toṇḍi. The Cholas had their premier viceroy, who was generally the heir apparent, or at least a prince of the blood, at Kanchi. These towns and ports, therefore, bulk very largely in the literature and literary traditions of the period. The road from Kanchi to Trichinopalli appears to have passed through Tirukkoilūr. From Trichinopoly (i. e. Uraiyūr) to Madura it lay along the more arid parts of the Tanjore district to Koḍumbai in the state of Pudukkōṭṭa, and thence to Neḍunguḷam; from which place the road broke into three, and led up to Madura

1 *Maṇimēkhalai*, Canto xix, ll. 107 and ff.

2 Ibid xviii. l. 145.

in three branches. From this last town a road kept close to the banks of the river Vaigai up to the Palnis; and from there it went up the hills and down again along the banks of the Periyār to the town of Vanji, situated near its mouth. There were also other roads besides; one, at least, from Vanji to the modern Karoor, and thence on to Tirukkoilūr. These roads were not safe in all parts alike, there being certain portions of them that passed through desert regions, inhabited by wild tribes, who were a cause of terror to the wayfarers, particularly those who had something to lose, notwithstanding the fact that robbery was punished with nothing short of impalement. Journeys were none the less frequent for purposes of pilgrimage, or in search of patronage for learning, or for the profits of commerce.

The rulers in those days held before them high ideals of government. Their absolute authority was limited by the 'five great assemblies', as they were called, of ministers, priests, generals, heralds (spies), and ambassadors. There appears to have been a general permit for a learned Brahmin to speak his mind in any durbar; and these often gave out their opinions most fearlessly. This privilege was similarly accorded also to men of learning. I give a few instances in illustration: a Brahmin pilgrim from the Chola country happened to be present at the Chera court, when the Chera king gave orders to his ministers to set his army in motion to avenge an insult that some northern princes, he was told, had given him. The minister's remonstrance and the reluctance of the general were overruled. This Brahmin got up and pointed out, in a speech, that he had warred for the fifty years of his rule in order to safeguard his earthly interests, but had done very little to provide for himself in the life to come. Of course the expedition was countermanded, and the king began to make provision for the future. A young Pandya king of the next generation showed himself too enthusiastic for war, and it fell to the lot of one of the poets at court to wean him of this war craze. In a poem of 850 lines he conveyed the hint to the king; if language can be conceived to be the art of concealing thought, here is an instance *par excellence.* The next instance takes us to the court of the Malayamān of Tirukkoilūr, who neglected his wife. A number of poets of the first rank interceded and restored him to her. The next case that I will mention here is that of a poet, who enjoyed the patronage of successive Chola rulers. He found that at the end of a civil war the victorious Chola was about to put to death his vanquished cousin. The poet pointed out that the victory tarnished the good name of the Cholas, quite as much as a defeat; and that he did not know whether to rejoice for the victorious Chola or weep for the vanquished one. The intercession was certainly effective. These illustrations show in addition the respect that learning commanded. I shall permit myself one more illustration to show this respect. The warlike Pandya referred to already, came to the throne young. He had immediately to go to war against a combination of his two neighbours, and his court was naturally anxious as to the result. The young prince in a poem, full of poetical grace, assured them that he would return victorious, and that, if he should fail, the poets of his court, including Māngudi Marudan, might cease to attend.

The ideal of justice set before them in those days was something unattainable. They strove their utmost to attain to the sublimity of their ideal; and a king was judged good or bad upon the degree of success he achieved in this particular branch of his duties. 'Oh the king! he is to blame if the rains fail; he is to blame if women go astray. What is there in a king's estate, except perpetual anxiety, that people should envy the position of a king for!' Learning went in search of patronage. There must have been a very considerable output of literature. It was doubtless to check the growth of the weed of learning that a body of censors called the Śangam was instituted. It is a number of works, which received the imprimatur of this learned body, that has been the source of all this information regarding this period. This is not the place to enter into the question of the origin of Tamil literature; or of its independence or otherwise; or of its connexion with the literature of Sanskrit. But I may remark, in passing, that Tamil literature (as distinct from language,) cannot lay claim to that independence that its votaries demand for it with more zeal than argument. Learning was somewhat widespread and much sought after. Women had their share of learning, as the number of women poets indicates. Nor was this learning confined to the Brahmin; although he was the sole custodian of the 'northern lore'.

In matters religious there was a happy confusion. Jains, Buddhists, Brahmins, Śaivas, Vaishṇavas, and people of other persuasions, both major and minor, all lived together and at peace with one another. 'There were splendid temples in the city dedicated to the worship of the celestial tree Kalpaka, the celestial elephant Airāvata, Vajrāyudha (the thunderbolt of Indra), Baladeva, Sūrya, Chandra, Śiva, Subrahmaniya, Sātavāhana, of Nigrantha, Kāma (god of love), and Yama (god of death). There were seven viharas reputed to have been built by Indra, the king of the gods in which dwelt no less than 300 monks (Buddhistic). The temple of Yama was outside the walls of the town, in the burial ground in the city of Puhār, the capital of the Cholas.'[1] The three rival systems of the Brahmins, and those of the Jains and the Buddhists flourished together, each with its own clientele unhampered by

[1] *Pattinappālai*, etc.

the others in the prosecution of its own holy rights. The Brahmin was regarded as an inconvenience, by some, but the general feeling was that he was indispensable to the prosperity of the State. A devout Buddhist and an ascetic Jain prince both speak of him with great respect. He was the custodian of the hidden lore; he was the guardian of the sacred fire, the source of material prosperity to the State; he was the person who performed the sacrifices according to the difficult orthodox rites, and who brought timely rain. These are the terms in which these heterodox writers refer to him. He had a function in society and he discharged it faithfully. The whole attitude both of the orthodox and also of the heterodox in matters of religion was pity for the ignorance of the other; but nothing more bitter, as Max Müller has very well pointed out.

Animism seems to have played an important part in the religious system of those days. There was a temple consecrated to the 'Chaste Lady', as she was called, who died in consequence of the murder of her husband. Her images are preserved in temples up to the present times, for, according to Dr. A. K. Kumarasami,[1] some of the images depicted in illustration of the ancient art of Ceylon are of this deified woman. Sati was in vogue; but under well recognized limitations. This was permitted only to women, who had neither natural guardians to fall back upon, nor children to bring up. That it was not uncommon for young women to return to their parents widowed, is vouched for by a comparison that a poet institutes between the approach of darkness and the return of the widowed young woman, whose husband had lately fallen in war. Annual festivals were celebrated with great éclat, and one of the grandest was that to Indra celebrated at Puhār.

[1] J. R. A. S., 1909, p. 292.

I have gathered my facts from a vast body of Tamil literature only recently made available to the student. I now proceed to consider the sources of this information, which are the classical writers; Indian literature, Tamil and Sanskrit; and the Ceylonese chronicle. Of the first group, Strabo wrote in the reigns of Augustus and Tiberius, Pliny published his geography in A. D. 77; the *Periplus of the Erythraean Sea* was written in the first century A.D.; Ptolemy wrote his geography about A.D. 150; the *Peutingerian Tables* were composed in A.D. 222. There were other writers who wrote later, but we are not concerned with them directly. I would draw attention to three points, taken from the works of classical writers.

Pliny remarks: 'At the present day voyages are made to India every year, and companies of archers are carried on board, because the Indian seas are infested by pirates'. Later on he says: 'It (Muziris) is not a desirable place of call, pirates being in the neighbourhood, who occupy a place called Nitrias; and besides, it is not well supplied with wares for traffic'. This was before A. D. 77. Ptolemy regarded this port Muziris as an emporium, and places the country of Aioi south of Bakarai. The *Peutingerian Tables* state clearly that two Roman cohorts were maintained in the same town for the protection of Roman commerce.

Mr. Sewell, who has made an elaborate study of the Roman coins found in India, considers that the coin finds lead to the following conclusions[1]:

1. There was hardly any commerce between Rome and India during the Consulate.

2. With Augustus began an intercourse which, enabling the Romans to obtain oriental luxuries during the early days of the empire, culminated about the time of Nero, who died A. D. 68.

[1] J.R.A.S., 1904, p. 591.

3. From this time forward the trade declined till the date of Caracalla, A. D. 217.

4. From the date of Caracalla it almost entirely ceased.

5. It revived again, though slightly, under the Byzantine emperors.

He also infers that the trade under the early emperors was in luxuries; under the later ones in industrial products, and under the Byzantines the commerce was with the south-west coast only, and not with the interior. He differs from those who find an explanation of this fluctuation in the political and social condition of India itself, and the facilities or their absence for navigating the seas; and considers that the cause is to be sought for in the political and social condition of Rome.

From an examination of the second class of my sources of information alone, we find that there was a period when South India was under great rulers, who gave the country peace and thus provided the indispensable security for commerce. This period can be shown to correspond to that of the Roman empire from Augustus to Caracalla. After this period, we find the country in a condition of political flux. These being so we may still find one, at least, of the most potent causes of this commercial decline in the internal condition of India itself. Pliny and Ptolemy do not mention the Roman cohorts at Muziris which the *Peutingerian Tables* do. The first exploit of the Red Chera is the destruction of the Kaḍambu tree on the sea coast. Another compliment that the poets never miss an opportunity of bestowing upon this patron is that the Chera fleet sailed on the waters of that littoral with a sense of dominion and security. The Kaḍambu mentioned above is explained as a tree of extraordinary power which could not be cut down by ordinary man. I rather think from the context that it has reference to a piratical rendezvous. If this view be correct, the advent of the said Chera brought along with it security. This would be in conformity with Ptolemy's reference to Āay, who was one of the seven chieftains known to literature as 'the last seven patrons'. From the body of works known to Tamil scholars as Śangam works their contemporaneity could easily be established. I have examined this question elsewhere in the chapter on *The Augustan Age of Tamil Literature* and find the name Āay a distinctive name of an individual, and not that of a family. Then Āay must have been the contemporary of, or a little older than, Ptolemy, and the age of Ptolemy would practically be the age of the Red Chera, and the Chera ascendancy. This conclusion only confirms what has been arrived at independently of this class of evidence. Gajabāhu of Ceylon, who visited the Red Chera almost at the end of his reign, ruled according to the Ceylonese chronicle from A.D. 113 to 135. Allowing for the difference between the Ceylonese date of the Nirvāna of the Buddha and that arrived at by modern scholars, as Dr. Fleet, namely, sixty years, the date for Gajabāhu would be A.D. 173 to 193. The Chera ascendancy then would cover the latter two-thirds of the second century A.D. Here has to be brought in the Paiśāchi work *Brihat Kathā*. Among the temples mentioned as having been found at Puhār was one dedicated to Śātavāhana. This personage was the ruler in whose court flourished the minister Gunāḍya, who was the author of this stupendous work which stands at the root of all romantic literature in India, whether in Sanskrit or any vernacular. It was a translation of this work that set the fashion in Tamil for the composition of the romantic epics. The age of the original is still matter under investigation. The latest authority on the question is the Dutch scholar Speyer, who would place it in the third century

A. D. at the earliest—a date clearly impossible according to our line of inquiry. I shall not say more about it here now; but only remark that one of the works, clearly based upon this, has to be referred to a period anterior to the astronomer, Varahamihira A. D. 533. This work, *Maṇimēkhala* refers to the asterism under which the Buddha was born as the fourteenth; which, according to the modern computation, following Varāhamihira, ought to be the seventeenth. The *Ceylon Chronicle* also deserves to be investigated more carefully. So far investigations from different points of view only appear to confirm its chronology, except for the correction made above.

The date of the death of Caracalla corresponds closely to the disappearance of the Śātavāhanas of the Dekhan. According to the latest opinion the power of the Kushānas also vanished about the same period. In South India likewise the Pandya ascendancy passes into darkness. The century following is one of the dark spots in Indian history, until the rise of the Guptas in the north, of the Chāḷukyas in the Dekhan, and of the Pallavas in the south. More research into Tamil literature and the Ceylon Mahāvamśa would yield results worth the trouble, failing coins and other auxiliaries. There may be also something to be gained by a careful study of the traditions that grew up later on.

CHAPTER V

THE MYSORE STATE—A RETROSPECT

THE State of Mysore over which His Highness Sri Krishna Raj Waḍeyar Bahadur, G.C.S.I., presides, lies between 11° 38′ and 15° 2′ north latitude and between 74° 42′ and 78° 36′ east longitude. It occupies just the apex of the triangle which is known as the plateau of the Dekhan. Mysore itself is a somewhat irregular quadrilateral resting upon the shoulders of the eastern and the western ghats, where they make their junction in the cluster of hills round about the Nilgiris. Raised from two to three thousand feet above the sea it has a salubrious climate, and falls into two divisions, each with distinctive physical features. The one is the Malnad (hill country) extending between the western ghats and a line drawn from Shikarpur to Periyapatna and onward even to Biligirirangan hills; then the maidan (plain) all east of it up to the Madras frontier. The quadrilateral measures 290 miles east to west and 230 miles north to south, occupying an area of 29,445 square miles, of which an area of thirteen square miles has been assigned to form the Civil and Military Station of Bangalore, which is directly under the British administration. The population of the State, excluding that of the Civil and Military Station, was returned in the last census (1901) as 5,449,800 (2,751,902 males and 2,697,898 females), averaging 185 to the square mile. More than five millions or 92·63 per cent of the total are Hindus; Musalmāns number 268,131 or 4·92 per cent; and Christians 32,933 or

0·6 per cent. As many as 86,629 are returned as 'animistic' and the Jains number 13,682. Of the total population only five per cent are literate. Of the males only nine per cent are literate.

The State, as it is at present, has been in existence as a single political entity only from A. D. 1800 onwards; but the territory comprised therein has had a history of its own long anterior to this period. There are traditions local and general, connecting this area with the great epics of the *Rāmāyana* and the *Mahābhārata*. As we come down the stream of time, Jain traditions record that the great Mauryan emperor, Chandragupta, retired from the world and spent the evening of life in contemplation at Sravana Beḷgoḷa. His more famous grandson, Asoka, if the *Mahāvaṃśa* is to be believed, sent missionaries to Mahishamanḍala. This name for the territory has not been found either in the inscriptions of Asoka or that of Samudragupta. There is no doubt that both Asoka, and after him the Sātavāhanas and finally Samudragupta, had all of them some historical connexion with the country, but it is not referred to by the name Mahishamanḍala.[1] Be this as it may, we have certain references in Tamil literature to chiefs who have to be located in Mysore and it has to be assumed that, so far as can be known at present, the history of the Mysore country begins with the Christian era at least.

At this period the Gangas occupy the southern portion of Mysore with their capitals, first at Kolar and later on at Talakāḍ. Among those who met the Chera king, Śenguṭṭuvan, in his northern expedition were the Gangas, and they visited him when he was in camp at the foot of the Nilgiris. From this time onwards the province is divided into three distinct parts,

[1] I am glad to find myself supported by Dr. Fleet in this position *vide* p. 425 *et seq.*, I. R. A. S., p. 1910.

each with a history of its own, roughly corresponding to the three British divisions of Ashṭagram, Nandidroog and Nagar. These ancient divisions were Gangavāḍi 96,000, Noḷambavāḍi 32,000 and Banavase 12,000.[1] Of these three, the first was under the Gangas up to the end of the first millennium after Christ; the second was at first divided among the Bāṇas or Mahāvalis, the Vaidumbas, and part perhaps among the Cholas and the Pallavas, till at last the Pallavas conquered them and made the whole an annexe to their dominions. The territory of Banavase maintained itself from the beginning of the Christian era, possibly earlier, to its absorption by the early Chāḷukyas, about the time that Noḷambavāḍi was conquered by the Pallavas.

Up to A.D. 600, then, the three parts of the Mysore province each had an independent history and was struggling to maintain its independence. Then two of them lost it, while the third was more fortunate than either of its neighbours. It is in the history of the third that we have to look for the early history of Mysore, though it was not known by that name. About A.D. 600, when the Chāḷukyas, north of the Krishna, who were in occupation practically of the whole of the Dekhan, and the Pallava masters of the south were fighting for ascendency in India south of the Vindhyas, the province of Mysore, situated at a convenient angle between the two great powers, was allowed to develop on her own lines for a short time.

The Pallavas and Chāḷukyas had to maintain an incessant struggle along the Tungabhadra-Krishna

1 The figures attached to each name seem to indicate either the revenue paid or the value of the produce, as is customary even now in certain localities. Mr. Rice considers it to be the former. Dr. Fleet takes them to stand for the number of townships in the division, in spite of apparent exaggeration. This does not find support in existing practice, which clearly indicates that it is either revenue, or income, sometimes the quantity of seed required.

frontier. In this struggle Banavase loses its individual existence and the Chāḷukyan frontier is advanced into the province of Mysore in the west and the Circars in the east. In the latter region a new viceroyalty is created with a brother of the king for its viceroy, and this latter becomes the founder of a separate dynasty, that of the eastern Chāḷukyas. The two great Powers, however, wear out each other in the struggle, and what follows, as a natural consequence, is the subversion of both. The Chāḷukyas are overthrown by the Rāshṭrakūṭas and the Pallava empire breaks up into a number of petty principalities, owing perhaps to the temporary occupation of Kanchi by the Rāshṭrakūṭa Dantidurga Vairamēgha. All these transactions take place about A.D. 754; and during this time eastern Mysore is closely associated with the fortunes of the Pallavas and southern Mysore or Gangavāḍi is left for a while to herself. The next century is a period of steady advance of the Gangas. It is at the end of this period that the Gangas advance in the southern direction and fight a battle against Varaguṇa Pandya at Tirupparambiyam, near Kumbakonam. Meantime the Rāshṭrakūṭas in the north have had time to consolidate their newly-won empire, shifting their capital to an interior place from Bādāmi once destroyed by the Pallavas. The Rāshṭrakūṭa capital was at Mānyakēta, which is identified with Malkhed in the Nizam's dominions. Having set matters right at head-quarters, these Rāshṭrakūṭas were in a position to advance their arms southward and south-eastward, and the absence of a powerful State facilitated this movement. The Gangas became the feudatories of the Rāshṭrakūṭas, who even occupy Kanchi for a time, stopping for a while the growth of the Chola power just rising above the horizon of South Indian politics. With the beginning of the tenth century after Christ the aspect of affairs in South India was somewhat as follows: the

Rāshṭrakūṭa, Krishna III, having been in temporary occupation of Kanchi, completely shattered the remnant of the Pallavas, while before his time the Gangas had been reduced to subjection by his predecessors. South of the Mysore frontier there arose a new Power which had been for some time forming a State of its own out of the disintegrating Pallava dominions. The great Chola Parāntaka overthrew the Ganga–Pallavas, then the Pandyas and the Kēraḷas, and made for himself, in touch with all three alike, the Chola kingdom which was destined to a far greater future. The net result of all this activity was that the Rāshṭrakūṭa frontier was pushed back past the plateau of Mysore. It was time then for the rising Cholas to measure their strength with that of the Rāshṭrakūṭas, when these latter were overthrown by the Chāḷukyas in A. D. 972. This event facilitated matters considerably for the Cholas, as their previous attempts in this direction had been foiled by the successful resistance of the Ganga feudatories of the Rāshṭrakūṭas. Rājāditya, the heir-apparent to the Chola empire, fell at Takkōlam about the middle of the century, and the Chola advance had been put back by this event for half a century.

The overthrow of the Rāshṭrakūṭas in A. D. 972 was followed by a cessation of activity on their southern frontier, and the Gangas were left to develop themselves as best they might. This was the opportunity for the Cholas, who by now had occupied the Kongu country beyond. Before the Chāḷukyas could consider themselves secure in the north of Mysore, the Cholas pushed their arms northward over the passes and overthrew the Gangas, occupying Talakāḍ in the west and Kolar in the east. Then began, between the two Powers, the Chola from the south and Chāḷukya from the north, one of the most persistent and well-matched struggles for the possession of what is now the State of Mysore. During the first quarter of the tenth century, the southern Power under the great Rājarāja and his son Rājēndra had occupied the country corresponding to the maidan part almost, and the Chāḷukyas were left in possession only of what was Banavase 12,000 and the extreme northern part of Noḷambavāḍi 32,000. Along a frontier stretching from Yeḍatore in the west to Henjēru and Chitaldroog in the east, the two Powers contended for mastery and the contest had become very earnest, when Āhavamalla Sōmēsvara ascended the throne of the Karnāṭaka. Āhavamalla's reign and that of his son Vikramāditya occupied the rest of the century and the first quarter of the next. During this period the Chola empire enjoyed a succession of great rulers ending with Kulōttunga Chola, 'who abolished tolls'. It was in the course of this struggle that this part of the table-land had the chance of being brought under one rule, and the first independent dynasty of Mysore came then into being.

This was the dynasty of Hoysalas, sometimes wrongly designated Beḷḷāḷas, which having been chieftains of a petty district in Hassan, advanced to become one of the great South Indian Powers. The first rulers of this dynasty distinguished themselves against the Cholas on behalf of the Chāḷukyas, and obtained for this service a greatly extended viceroyalty which, while yet Vishṇuvardhana was ruling, embraced the whole of the present province of Mysore. Before he died, he left the Hoysala kingdom with its frontier advanced in the north up to the Krishna. His son and grandson were engaged in consolidating this kingdom and putting it upon a footing of peace and prosperity. The next rulers were in a position to lead up their forces to bear their share in the break-up of the great Chola empire in the south. The Chāḷukya empire had gone past reclamation and the Kalachūrya usurpers had had a bad time of it in maintaining themselves against the Yādavas of Dēvagiri, the Kākatīyas of Wārangal, and the Hoysalas themselves. When this great empire had been divided among the three, the turn for the Cholas came. The Kākatīyas occupied Kanchi for a while, the Pandyas marched upon Trichinopoly and were in occupation of Srīrangam. In this condition, the Cholas found the Hoysalas ready enough friends. The Hoysala Narasimha and his son Sōmēsvara drove out the Pandyas indeed, but took their place and not only occupied Srīrangam but divided themselves also into two branches, one ruling the empire above the Ghats and the other that below.

It is now that the Hoysala empire reached the high water-mark of its prosperity. Then came the great invasion of the Dekhan under Mālik Kāfūr, followed within a quarter of a century by a more systematic conquest by Muḥammad bin Toghlák. First the Yādavas, then the Kākatīyas, and last of all the Hoysalas were overthrown by the former, who advanced farther south and occupied Madura and places round about. With the return of Mālik Kāfūr, the Hindu powers had some respite which they made use of for reconstruction, perhaps not entirely successful, which a fresh advance of the Muḥammadans under Muḥammad bin Toghlák for a time kept back. It required a man of genius to gather together the separate and isolated efforts of petty chieftains, and then arose the great Vijianagar empire, thanks to the guidance of Vidyāraṇya.

The Hoysalas who had, since the burning down of their capital at Haḷebiḍ by Mālik Kāfūr, been at Tonḍanūr, easily succumbed to the rising Power and the State of Mysore was among the earliest acquisitions of Vijayanagar. The varying fortunes of this empire, it will be out of place to trace here. During all the waxing and waning of this great Hindu State on the Tungabhadra, Mysore enjoyed the geographical advantages of her situation and had been divided into three chief viceroyalties—that of Channapatna and Srīrangapatna in the south, and Beḍnūr in the north. In the intrigues at the court of Vijayanaggar, some of the Mysore Naiks played their inglorious parts, till the great catastrophe that overwhelmed the great empire threw them all into confusion for a while. When matters quieted down after the battle of Tālikōṭa, the whole empire was nominally under the ruler at Penukoṇḍa, but the viceroys at Madura and Srīrangapatna regarded themselves as practically independent. Jagadēvarvarāyulu or Rānapeddajagadēvarāyulu had been disgraced, and his possessions were falling into the hands of the viceroy at Srīrangapatna.

In this state of affairs in South India generally, there arose among the number of chieftains, who were the actual rulers of the territory under the Seringapatam viceroy, a Woḍeyar of remarkable ability. This was Raja Woḍeyar of Mysore belonging, as he claimed, to the Yādava family of Guzerat. His first ancestor came into Mysore from the 'banks of the Godavari' two centuries before A.D. 1600, and the family had since been in the enjoyment of a comparatively small bit of territory in and around the taluk of Mysore. It was given to Raja Woḍeyar to enlarge his petty principality into a compact kingdom, and this could be done only by occupying the viceroyalty of Tirumalarāya of Seringapatam.

Raja Woḍeyar took advantage of the differences between Venkaṭapati Rāya at head-quarters at Penukoṇḍa and his nephew Tirumalarāya of Seringapatam, and enlarged his territory by first attacking that of the Chennapatna viceroy and then of his suzerain, the viceroy at Seringapatam. When matters were ripe and he found himself strong enough, he brought on a quarrel with the viceroy, which eventually was taken to be cause enough to go to war. He who had taken measures carefully for the forthcoming eventuality proved the stronger of the combatants. Tirumalarāya had to flee for life, and was eventually killed and Seringapatam fell to Raja Woḍeyar. He, however, deemed it prudent to get his possession ratified by an imperial grant in A.D. 1612. Thus came into being the State of Mysore properly so-called.

Under Raja Woḍeyar and his immediate successors, the State occupied only the districts of the same name, and it was not till the throne passed into a collateral branch under a nephew, Kanṭīravanarasarāja Woḍeyar, that anything like a systematic conquest of the Chennapatna viceroyalty was attempted; and when he laid down the responsibility of royalty he had extended the boundaries of the State very considerably. Next followed Doḍḍa Dēva Raja Woḍeyar, who pursued the policy of his predecessors and extended his territory through the Tumkur and Chitaldroog districts so that when his nephew, Chikkadēva Raja Woḍeyar, came to the throne in the middle of the seventeenth century, about the same time as the Emperor Aurangzeb ruled, he had only to purchase Bangalore from Ekojee in order to complete the state of Mysore, and to occupy the maidan part, leaving the Malnad still under the most able among the Naiks of Ikkēri (near Beḍnūr). The making of Mysore was now complete, and Chikkadēva had to organize the territories. In this great work, he was ably supported, first by his Jain tutor, Vishalakshana Pundit of Yelandūr, and then by Tirumala Iyangar, a friend and fellow pupil. When he died in A.D. 1704, a few years before his imperial contemporary, he left to his deaf-mute son a well-ordered State, including not only the maidan parts of Mysore, but also the bordering districts below the ghats, with a full treasury, and a capable and faithful minister-regent in the person of his life-long friend Tirumala Iyangar.

This state of affairs gave an opportunity for the disorderly elements to assert themselves, which under the strong rule of Kanṭīrava Narasa, and before him of Rāja Woḍeyar, had been kept well in hand. Through the great ability and management of the Brahmin minister, the so-called 'Mooka Arasu' (the dumb-king) passed away after a peaceful reign leaving behind him a son. Under this son, the State was exposed to two great dangers from outside. The Ikkēri Naiks had been weakened, and eventually reduced to nullity, through the double attack from the Bijapur Sultans on the one side and the Mysore Woḍeyars on the other. The removal of this barrier exposed the rising state of Mysore to the invasions of the Musalmāns of the Dekhan and the Mahrattas. When Doḍḍa Krishna Raja was ruling Mysore, the Dalavāys came into notice as a distinct factor in politics. They rendered service to the State by first taking Dēvanahalli and Chikkaballapur and then Sāvandroog, near Bangalore, and by successfully withstanding the Mahrattas. When Krishna I passed away he left behind him no proper heir, and the usual struggles at king-making began. The first nominee did not prove a very apt tool, and the king-makers discovered that they had mistaken their man. He was sent away to Kabbaldroog to perish there, and in his stead a baby, Krishna Raja, was placed upon the throne. The real power in the State actually passed out of the hands of the Maharaja into the hands of the three great functionaries of State—the Dalavāy, the Pradhān and the Sarvādhikāri. Two brothers of the famous Dalavāy family and a cousin divided the three places among themselves, and the administration was carried on smoothly for sometime, when the Maharaja began to chafe under the yoke thus gradually made heavier as he felt. In this state of affairs in Mysore, there was coming into notice a young Musalmān in the Mysore army, who had attracted his General's attention in the siege of Dēvanhalli by the Mysore forces under Nanjaraja, against the Nawab of Sīra. The young man was soon advanced to the position of a squadron commander, and found scope for rendering more useful service to his master in the operations round Trichinopoly during the Karnatic wars of the eighteenth century. Dalavāy Dēvaraja having grown too old, an exchange of offices took place between the brothers, and Nanjaraj assumed command at Trichinopoly, where for distinguished service Ḥaidar had been rewarded with the Foujdāri of Dindigul. When Nanjaraj returned to Mysore, matters were growing ripe for a revolution. Dēvaraj having retired from public life, the Maharaja was getting tired of the yoke of Nanjaraja who was becoming very high-handed, and an attempt was made by the palace party to get rid of the troublesome minister. Ḥaidar's aid was called in and for the while Nanjaraja was compelled to retire on pension. All that he was doing, and more, was entrusted to Ḥaidar, who got rid of Kaṇḍē Rao, whom he had made use of as an apt tool in all his previous transactions. The power over the army and the financial control given to him to stop the inroads of troublesome foes like the Nawab of Sīra and the Mahrattas, made him the arbiter of the situation, and he then became the ruler of the State, though he still preserved the monarchy of the Woḍeyars by nominating one from among the young cousins of the Royal family, when Krishna Raja II passed away. The circumstances of the selection are thus described by Wilks: 'He ordered all the children to be collected from the different branches of the house, who, according to ancient precedent, were entitled to furnish a successor to the throne. The ceremonial observed on this occasion, however childish, was in perfect accordance with the feelings which he intended to delude, and sufficiently adapted to the superstition of the fatalist. The hall of audience was strewed round with fruits, sweetmeats and flowers, playthings of various descriptions, arms, books, male and female ornaments, bags of money, and every varied object of puerile or manly pursuit; the children were introduced together and were all invited to help themselves to whatever they liked best; the greater number were quickly engaged in a scramble for the fruits, sweetmeats and toys; but one child was attracted by a brilliant little dagger, which he took up in his right hand, and soon afterwards a lime in his left. "That is the Rajah", exclaimed Ḥaidar. "His first care is military protection, his second to realize the produce of his dominion, bring him hither, and let me embrace him." The assembly was in a universal murmur of applause, and he ordered the child to be conducted to the Hindu palace and prepared for installation.'

It was the rôle of Ḥaidar to enlarge the boundaries of the Mysore kingdom beyond its former boundaries, so as to include within its dominions the countries right up to the Krishna in the north and as far as Dindigul in the south. He had to contend against the Nizām and the more powerful Mahrattas in the north and the English Company in the east and south. In spite of reverses he maintained the territories of Mysore intact and left them all to his son, who for the first time did away with the fiction of a Mahāraja. Tīpū Sultan followed in the wake of his father and cherished ambitions, which constantly led him to trample upon his neighbour's rights. This eventually led to a combination among them and Tīpū had to accept the inevitable. He never gave up organizing himself for a final struggle, which led to the fall of Seringapatam, and the restoration of the Hindu dynasty of the Woḍeyars under Krishna Raja Woḍeyar. All this brings us to the nineteenth century which begins with the Mysore State as it is at present. The young Maharaja's administration was to be conducted by the Regent Pūrniah. Sir Barry Close was then British Resident, with Sir Arthur Wellesley as Commander of the forces. Pūrniah carried on the administration till A. D. 1812, when the Maharaja assumed the responsibilities of his high office. Pūrniah then retired to Seringapatam, to bring a busy life to a close there, so long the scene of his activity.

The young Maharaja, thus freed from the influence of the only man who was likely, during those troublous times, to steer into a safe harbour the ship of State, was, but with difficulty, able to hold his own against the disorderly elements then abounding in the country. His generosity was proverbial and is remembered even to this day. Disorders broke out simultaneously in several parts of the State and in the neighbouring British districts. It was thought that the Maharaja was too ready to listen to advisers who were by no means competent to give him wise counsel. His princely generosity was used as a handle to depose him. Some debts, which the Maharaja had contracted, were paid off by the British Government, and the Maharaja was told that, as this state of things could not proceed any further, he would have to lead a retired life with a pension suited to his rank and dignity. Needless to say the Maharaja protested. The Governor-General was, however, determined to act upon the fourth and fifth articles of the subsidiary treaty, and accordingly formal notice was given to the Rajah. Thus commenced in A. D. 1831 the fifty years of British administration of Mysore.

FAMILY TREES

[N.B.—*Dotted lines indicate succession not in regular line.*]

Yadu (1399 to 1423).

Hiri Beṭad Chamaraj I (1423 to 1458). Chamaraja.

Timmaraja Woḍeyar (1458 to 1478).

Hiri Chamarajarasa II (1478 to 1513).

Beṭad Chamaraj III (1513 to 1552).

Timmaraj (1552 to 1571). Krishnaraj. Bōḷe Chamaraja IV (1571 to 1576).

Beṭad Wodeyar (1576 to 1578). Rajādhi Rāja. Betad Chamaraja V. (1578 to 1617). Muppin Dēvaraj.

Narasa Raja. Beṭad Wodeyar. Nanjraj. Chamaraj. Immaḍi Raja (1637–8).

Chamaraja Wodeyar VI (1617 to 1673).

Rāja Wodeyar (died young). Kanṭīrava Narasa (1638 to 1659).

Dod Dēvaraj. Chikka Dēvarajēndra. Kempa Dēvayya (1659 to 1672). Mari Deva

Chikka Dēvaraj (1672 to 1704). Kantīrava Narasa.

Kanṭīrava Narasa (1704 to 1713).

Dod Krishna Raj (1713 to 1731).

Chamaraja VII (1731 to 1734). Chikka Krishnaraja (1734 to 1766).

Nanjaraja (1767 to 1770). Chamaraja VIII (1770 to 1775).

Chamaraja IX (1775 to 1796).

Krishna Raja III (1800 to 1868).

Chamarājēndra X (1868 to 1894).

H. H. Sri Krishna Raja Wodeyar (1894—
(The Present Ruler).

Prince, Kanṭīrava Narasa Raja Wodeyar
(The Yuvaraj).

CHAPTER VI

THE CHOLA EMPIRE IN SOUTH INDIA

PART I—HISTORY

1. The Ancient Cholas: The name Chola is given to a people, as well as to a dynasty of rulers, not only in ordinary parlance but also in literature, and reaches to the highest antiquity that literature or usage can take us. Who the people were, and where they came from, it seems well-nigh impossible to determine at present. That they were in the country that they occupied in historical times very much earlier than the beginning of history for South India, does not admit of any doubt whatsoever. The Cholas, as rulers, find mention in the *Mahābhārata* and the Epic and Puranic literature generally. The chronology of these, however, is yet matter for investigation. The first undoubted historical mention[1] of these Cholas is in the second and thirteenth rock edicts of the great Mauryan emperor Asoka, who refers to these friendly Powers along with the great Potentates that made themselves heir to the empire of Alexander the Great. Passing down the stream of time, from the days of the great Maurya, whose fame spread through the whole of Asia, and even eastern Europe and Africa, the Cholas are spoken of as a source of trouble to the Ceylonese rulers set over against them in the neighbouring island. In the century immediately preceding

[1] V. A. Smith's *Asoka* (2nd ed.), pp. 156 and 174.

Christ there were six Tamil usurpers from the country of 'Soli',[1] according to the *Mahāvamśa*. In the centuries immediately following the advent of Christ, however, we seem to be at the gray dawn of South Indian history. The period between this and the rise of the Pallavas is the period of the high water-mark of Tamil literature; and our information, though not up to the requirements of modern historical criticism, is certainly more in volume and not altogether valueless. It is most convincingly clear from this body of literature that there was a powerful dynasty of Chola rulers in the early centuries of the Christian Era.

Before dealing with this dynasty of rulers there are a few names that find mention in this body of literature which have to be considered. These are most of them Puranic names[2] that have been adopted into this body of literature by the genealogist. Genealogy making was regarded as a particular pastime of the eleventh century bards; but these genealogists seem to have had a much anterior vogue. Among the names mentioned in this manner are those of 'Sibi, who gave his life to save a dove; Kavēra the father of the river Kavery; Muśugundan who helped Indra; Manu who ran his car over his son in justice to a cow. Passing these over, there still is left a reference of a different character, when we come to a Chola called Perunjōṟruchchōḻan. The first part of the word means 'the great food supplier'; and this is explained by reference to the Chola's having fed the armies of both the Pāndava and Kaurava combatants on the occasion of the Great War. This, however, is a feature claimed alike by all the three—Chera, Chola and Pandya. One fact stands out clear from all this—

1 Upham, *Mahāvamśa*, vol. i, p. 218.

2 *Śilappadhikāram*, Canto xxiii, ll. 58-9 and pp. 488-9; *Maṇimēkhalai*, Canto 1, l. 5, note Pandit Swaminatha Iyer's edition. Also *Vikkiramaśōḻan ulā*.

that when these rulers began to think of their pedigree they found that they could easily graft themselves on the heroes of the *Mahābhārata* either directly or indirectly. Taking leave of these heroes as being beyond the pale of history, there come into view two or three personages who must be regarded as quite historical. The first great Chola among them who demands our attention is the Chola Karikāla. There are a number of his predecessors mentioned in the Sangam works; but in our present state of knowledge of these it would be hazardous to attempt arranging them on any scheme, either genealogical or successional. Karikāla's grandfather would appear to be Vērpahaṛaḍakkai Perunaṟkiḷḷi.[1] He was a contemporary of Kuḍakkō Neḍumśēralādan, the Chera king, and they both fought and fell in battle on the same field. Poets who celebrated this sad catastrophe were contemporaries of Karikāla as well. Karikāla's father is spoken of in these works as Uruvappaharēr Iḷayōn or Iḷanjētchenni. The latter part of this long name means a prince. It would appear therefrom that he never succeeded to the throne. The father died a prince and the grandfather fell in battle, and so the grandson was left, when quite a young boy, heir to the throne of a kingdom not in the enjoyment of peace. Nor were causes wanting for civil dissensions. Young Karikāla found himself a fugitive at Karūr after the disastrous battle in which his grandfather fell along with his Chera enemy. It was from here that he was fetched to ascend the throne by the State elephant from Kaḻumalam (Shiyali). He met with a serious fire accident from which he escaped with difficulty, though he was maimed for the rest of his life. It is from this early accident that he got the rather peculiar name of

[1] *Puṟanānūṟu*. Reference in pp. 8 and 9. Pandit Swaminatha Iyer's edition.

'blackleg'. As a young man he had to sit as judge in a cause, the parties to which feared that the young man might misjudge. He appeared as an old man to them, and the award he gave was as sound as that of a judge of the most mature experience. He had for his uncle a chief by name Piḍarthalaiyan. He had married among the Nāngūr Veḷ family. He had to fight a great battle at Veṇṇil (probably Koilveṇṇi in the Tanjore district),[1] both the Chera and the Pandya having combined against him. His Pandya enemy is not specifically mentioned by name, though the Chera was almost certainly the ''Sēramān Perumśēralādhan'. This Chera felt the defeat so keenly that, like the Italian Charles Albert, he exiled himself and ended his days by starvation. Notwithstanding the sad fate of this great Chera, the war seems to have ended in a treaty which was sealed by a marriage. The heir presumptive, or heir apparent, to the Chera throne married, either then or later, the Chola princess who is called Naṛchchōṇai.[2] Peace had been secured on that side and along with it on the side of the Pandyas as well. He appears to have been among those that were a source of trouble to the Ceylonese; for it was he that built the city of Kaverippaṭṭinam, to which he transferred the head-quarters that had hitherto been at Uraiyūr near Trichinopoly. The construction of this city and the transference of the capital to it, perhaps after the definitive treaty with his immediate neighbours, would argue security on the one side and want of safety on the other. This is exactly what is reflected in the *Mahāvaṃśa*. Gajabāhu I of Ceylon heard from an old woman who was bewailing the loss of her only son, that twelve thousand Ceylonese were carried

[1] *Pōrunarāṛṛuppaḍai*, ll. 143–8 and other references under Karikāla. q. v. above, note (4).

[2] *Silappadikāram*, p. 10 and Canto xxix.

away by the Tamilians, in one of their recent invasions, to work in the 'town of Kavery[1].' Having secured his frontier on the west and south, he transferred his capital to the coast, both for purposes of the flourishing commerce of those days and for the defence of the sea frontier. He is given credit by the poets of the period with having carried his arms victoriously as far north as the Himalayas, on which he is said to have erected the tiger emblem of his family. His northern expedition is specifically mentioned in the *Śilappadhikāram*;[2] and, what is even more, he is said by the same authority to have been on diplomatic terms with the rulers of Magadha, Vajra (Bundalkhand) and Avanti, the second of these being a subdued enemy and the third a positive friend. These specific assertions of a poet, only one generation removed from him, cannot be regarded as mere figments of the imagination. Kaverippaṭṭinam in the days of Karikāla seems to have been a great emporium of trade both inland and over sea. The poem *Paṭṭinappālai* is a mere description of this city in the days of Karikāla. He is besides uniformly credited with having made the embankments for the Kavery.[3] The Chola kingdom reached the height of its glory under him in the days anterior to Rājarāja the Great. He was none the less as a patron of letters. *Paṭṭinappālai* already referred to was composed in his honour for which the author received the reward of a lakh and sixty thousand gold pieces. This lucky author lived on to celebrate another patron, Toṇḍamān Iḷandiṛayan[4] of Kanchi of a later generation.

Other poets there were who flourished in his time and enjoyed his patronage as well. Among these must

[1] Upham's *Mahāvaṃśa*, vol. i, pp. 228–9, ch. 35.

[2] Page 139.

[3] *Epigraphist's report*, 1906, sec. 14. Large Leyden grant Arch. Survey of S. I., vol. iv, etc.

[4] *Perumbaṇāṟṟappaḍai*. Pandit Swaminatha Iyer's *Pattupāṭṭu*.

be mentioned Paranar, Kaḷāthalaiyār, Veṇṇikkuyathiyār, etc., all of Śangam fame. His reign must have been a long one, and when he passed away the succession fell to the lot of a son, or a grandson, by name Neḍumuḍikkiḷḷi, also known with many another attribute. His reign also must have been a comparatively long one. He began with a victory over the Cheras and Pandyas at Kāriyāru.[1] If this is to be connected with a river of the name in the Salem district, the allies must have advanced with a view to taking advantage of the new succession. The Chola was able to make his position good, with the aid of a valiant brother, who was probably the viceroy at Kanchi at the northern end of the Chola dominions. Kiḷḷi's capital was also Kavērippaṭṭinam at the commencement of his reign. It was in his reign that Kavērippaṭṭinam was destroyed by the sea. He was the father of Tonḍamān Iḷandirayan, the ruler of Kanchi celebrated by Rudirāngaṇṇanār in his *Perumbāṇārruppaḍai*. This Tonḍamān was the offspring of a liaison between the Kiḷḷi and a Naga princess who sent him to his father when the boy had grown old enough to leave the mother. A mishap to the ship brought about the neglect, on the part of the anxious father, to celebrate the annual festival to the patron goddess of the city.[2] Hence the destruction of the city. This great calamity struck a deadly blow at the prosperity of the city and its rulers; and this misfortune may have been the occasion of a civil war among the several branches of the Chola family. It was in the course of this war that the Chera ruler Śenguṭṭuvan found occasion to intervene in behalf of his cousin, and defeating his enemies at Nērivāyil,[3] not far from Uraiyūr, restored somewhat the shattered

[1] *Maṇimēkhalai* xix 126—*Puranānūru* 47.

[2] *Maṇimēkhali* xiv, ll. 55-70; xxv, ll. 170-205.

[3] *Śilappadhikāram* xxvii, ll. 115-125 and *Padirruppattu*, sec. 5.

fortunes of the family. During the period of the Chera ascendency thus ushered in, the Cholas were able to maintain an independent existence, though with reduced territory and shorn of much of their glory. The rise of the Pandyas, almost simultaneously with the Pallavas, destroyed what was still left of their greatness and the Cholas of this period pass into darkness. During the period of decadence and decay of the Chola power and the advance of the Chera, the viceroyalty of Kanchi was cut off from the Chola kingdom by the wedge of a Chera viceroyalty in the Salem district.[1] What had happened to the Toṇḍamān of Kanchi, whether he founded a separate family of his own and whether that family had any connexion whatsoever with the Pallavas of history, are problems on which more light has to be thrown by further research before any answer can be ventured. During the three centuries of Pallava ascendency the Cholas are heard of only in a general way, and no particular details are forthcoming. But there is one Chola who may have to be referred to the early part of this, if not to a period somewhat anterior even. This Chola is known by the name Kōchchengaṇ. He is credited with having defeated the Chera Kaṇaik-kālirumporai,[2] whom he threw into prison. He is besides said to have won a bloody battle at Kaḻumalam (Shiyali), though his enemies are not specifically mentioned. The Śaivas claimed him among the Aḍiyārs, while the Vaishṇavas claim him equally among their benefactors. He was a great temple builder, and among these temples are mentioned both Śiva and Vishnu shrines. He is definitely said to have built and dedicated seventy temples to Śiva in a Vaishṇava work.

Passing on into the Age of the Pallavas, the Cholas find mention among those defeated both by

[1] *Padiṟṟuppattu*, sec. 5. *Śilappadhikāram*, Canto xxiv, last lines.
[2] *Puranānūru* 74, *Kalavaḻi* 40, *Periatirumoḻi* 6.

the Pallavas themselves and their hereditary enemies the Chāḷukyas. The wife of the Pandya king whom Tirugnānasambandar converted was a Chola princess. Beyond these few references Chola history during this period is an absolute blank.

2. The Earlier Cholas: The making of the empire now begins. All the time the Pallavas were in the ascendent the Cholas had not passed out of existence, as has been pointed out already. They were a Power maintaining a precarious independence, hemmed in by the Pallavas on the one side and the Pandyas on the other. There appears to have been a branch of them ruling in the Ceded districts,[1] in the days when the Chinese traveller Yuwan Chwang was in India. When the Pallavas began to decline in power in the south, the political condition of peninsular India was somewhat as follows. The Dekhan portion was divided into two parts, the western under the Rāshṭrakūṭas with their capital at Mānyakēta; the eastern under the Chāḷukyas with their capital at Rajamandri. The southern frontier of these was the Pennar, or perhaps a line somewhat farther south. The Pallava territory proper was divided among three connected branches of the Pallava family. The westernmost part of it was under the Gangas, who now begin to play a decisive part in the history of South India. Next last of them was the territory of the Bāṇas called Ganga-Bāṇas, and further east near the coast was the dominion of the Pallavas themselves. It was the founder of the Rāshṭrakūṭas[2] that gave the *coup de grâce* to the tottering Pallava Power; but the new dynasty had presently to turn its attention to the north, where the Gūrjaras were rising fast to an

[1] *Epigraphist's Report*, 1906, sec. 5.

[2] *Bombay Gazetteer*, vol. i, pt. ii, pp. 389-90.
Periyatirumoli III, viii. 10.

imperial position. The Pallavas were, therefore, left unmolested for a time by them. It was under Govinda IV[1] and his son Krishna III[2] that the Rāshṭrakūṭas were able to turn their attention to the south. The former was, however, kept fully engaged as a result of his intervention in a disputed succession to the Eastern Chāḷukya throne. The accession of his son to power was coeval with the rise of a usurper Perumānaḍi Būtuga in the Ganga kingdom. The Rāshtrakūṭas seem to have had a hand in this usurpation[3] as in the disputed succession in Vengi. Govinda's diplomatic efforts bore fruit in his son Krishna's reign. Krishna was able to advance southwards and was for some time in occupation of Kanchi and Tanjore. Simultaneously with this southward move of the Rāshtrakūṭas was the march northwards of the Pandyas. A generation earlier than Krishna the Pandya Varaguṇa[4] advanced north to extend his power into Pallava territory, and was beaten back by a supreme effort on the part of the three connected dynasties, of the Ganga, Pallava, and Bāṇa. The battle at Tirupparambium near Kumbhakonam sealed the doom of the Pandya against achieving an ascendency, and the occasion was taken advantage of by the Cholas. The latter then begin to carve out for themselves from their own patrimony as it were, a small kingdom which grew into a mighty empire in the hands of their more powerful and enterprising successors. The Cholas beginning with Vijayālaya up to Rājarāja the Great, can therefore be called the makers of the Chola empire.

Vijayālaya: The Pandya Varaguṇa already referred to in the previous paragraph came to the throne in

1 *Bombay Gazetteer* I, pt. ii, p. 417.
2 *Epigraphia Indica* vol. iii, 284-285.
3 *Epigraphia Indica* vol. iv. 281.
4 *Epigraphist's Report* for 1906, secs. 8–10.

A.D. 862-3. He invaded the Chola country and directed his attack upon Iḍavai in the same country. It was in the same campaign that he stormed the fortress of Vēmbil.[1] He then marched as far north as Araiśūr on the Pennar in the southern Toṇḍanāḍu from which he issued a grant. Against this aggressive Pandyan there was a combination brought about between the Gangas and the Ganga-Pallavas, before which he thought it prudent to retire. The allies were victorious at Tirupparambium near Kumbhakonam. In the battle the victorious Ganga Prithvīpati I fell, while the Ganga-Pallava Aparājita the overlord was rid of so troublesome an enemy. He seems, however, not to have been able to recover much of the lost ground, perhaps owing to other movements in the north of his territory. The opportunity had now arrived for the Chola. Vijayālaya was ready to take advantage of the situation that was fast developing. He began extending his humble patrimony without awakening suspicion, and in the course of his long reign of thirty-four years at least, he was able to capture Tanjore and make it not only his capital, but also to leave records of his reign in such distant places as Ukkal, Conjeevaram, Tirukkōvilur and Suchīndram[2] near Cape Comorin. Calculating back from the known and verified date of Parāntaka's initial year, Vijayālaya began his reign in about A.D. 846.

Āditya:[3] The successor of Parakēsarivarman Vijayālaya, to whom are referable some at least of the records of a Parakēsarivarman without any other distinctive appellation, was succeeded by his son Āditya I, Rājakēsarivarman. Āditya I continued in

1 *Epigraphist's Report* for 1906, sec. 25.

2 *Epigraphist's Report* for 1909, sec. 35.

3 Ibid. 35 and references under Kielhorn's Southern List *Epi. Ind.*, vol. vii, nos. 676-80.

the forward policy of his father and conquered finally the Pallava Aparājita victor over the Pandya Varaguṇa, and brought himself into touch with the Rāshṭrakūṭas on his northern frontier. If the *Kongudēśarājākkaḷ* is worthy of any credit, he was also the conqueror of Kongu. The history of his successors seems only to confirm this so far. His was also a long reign of twenty-seven years and brings us to the reign of his son Parāntaka I.

Parāntakā I, Parakēsarivarman, Vīranārāyana, etc., A. D. (907–947). Parāntaka succeeded to a kingdom of considerable extent, and his frontiers touched the Pandya country in the south and south-west, Kēraḷa in the west, the Bāṇa and Vaiḍumba country in the north-west, and the eastern Chāḷukya and Rāshṭrakūṭa countries in the north. He first attacked and overthrew the Pandya Rājasimha in battle before A. D. 910 having, perhaps previously, entered into a marriage alliance with the Kēraḷas on his western flank. This secured him safety on the southern side. His next move appears to have been the subjugation of the Bāṇas. He was enabled to follow in this policy unmolested, as the Rāshṭrakūṭas[1] were fully occupied with their own aggressions on their neighbours. Govinda IV of this dynasty was engaged on a fruitless, nay, suicidal intervention in a disputed succession to the eastern Chāḷukya throne. When Parāntaka had repeatedly overthrown two Bāṇas in succession he conferred their patrimony upon his ally the Ganga-Bāṇa Prithvīpati Hastimalla.[2] His next conquest was that of the Vaiḍumbas, and the acquisition of their territory of the Vaḍugavaḷi (the road to the Āndhra or Telugu country). He ensured peace to his vast conquests in such a way that his reign

[1] *Bombay Gazetteer*, vol. i, pt. ii, pp. 416-7.
[2] *South Ind. Ins.*, vol. ii, no. 76.

marks the beginning of the religious activities of the period. The Kaḷāmukha[1] and Pāśupata Śaivas begin to find favour, and the earliest Vaishṇava Āchāryas[2] commence their apostolic work. Parāntaka himself appears to have been a Śaiva[3] and did his pious duty to the great shrine at Chidambaram by renewing the gold plating of the great hall there. In his thirty-seventh[4] year or somewhat earlier he felt himself strong enough to venture on a successful invasion of Ceylon. After a long reign of at least forty years during which he extended and consolidated his patrimony, and secured his frontiers from hostile attack both by conquest and diplomacy, Parāntaka passed away. He left behind him five sons, among whom three appear to have ruled. His eldest son Rājākesarivarman Rājāditya succeeded Parāntaka. The approach of the Cholas towards their southern frontier put the Rāshṭrakūṭas on the alert, and their hand is clearly discernible in the usurpation of the Ganga kingdom by Perumānaḍi Būtuga,[5] a son-in-law of Amōghavarsha and a brother-in-law of Krishna III. This threw that frontier into confusion and insecurity, and Rājāditya promptly marched forth to set matters right. A bloody battle at Takkōlam was the result. Rājāditya was killed on the field of battle by Būtuga, who managed to mount the elephant of the Chola and kill him. This event took place in A.D. 949-50.[6] Krishna III took advantage of his victory to the full, marched into the Chola country and was in occupation of Kanchi for a while; and, what was even more of a calamity to the Cholas,

1 *Epigraphist's Report* for 1909, sec. 37.

2 *Vide* the Chapters on Rāmānuja and Tirumangai Āḷvār.

3 Leyden grant and *Kalingattupparani.*

4 Reference under note 2 above.

5 *Bombay Gazetteer*, vol. i, pt. ii, pp. 304 and 418.

6 J.R.A.S. for 1909, pp. 443-5.

he laid siege to Tanjore.[1] Gaṇḍarādittan, the second son of Parāntaka, succeeded his elder brother and did his best to beat back the enemy and prevent his getting a permanent hold upon the Chola kingdom, not altogether without success. The Rāshṭrakūṭa power had hardly twenty more years to run, and there were already the premonitory symptoms of the coming storm. Anyhow the Cholas had some little respite given them to recover lost ground. Gaṇḍarādittan has left behind him memorials of his rule in the town that bears his name, and the fifth '*Tiruviśaippa*' in which he calls himself ruler of Tanjore. His devoted and pious widow built a temple at Konērirājapuram,[2] and erected a statue of her late husband which is to be seen in the temple even now. He left behind him a son, probably a baby, and was succeeded by his brother Ārinjaya, or as he is sometimes called, Arjuna. The other two sons of Parāntaka were prince Uttamaśīli and one Arikulakēsarin, who held high command both under his father Parāntaka I and under his elder brother Rajakēsarivarman Arinjaya.[3] This last may have been the person referred to by the name Madiraikoṇḍa Rājakēsarivarman. The attribute Madiraikoṇḍa may be due to either a particular achievement of his own or borrowed from his father's. Arinjaya was succeeded by his son Parāntaka II, Sundarachola. In this reign there appears to have been trouble on the Pandya side, and this ended unfavourably for the rebels through the exertions of the Chola, ably supported by the efforts of his general Śiriyavēḷān. The Pandya king had to find 'shelter in the desert'.[4] This seems to be the achievement

[1] *South Ind. Ins.*, vol. iii, 7.
[2] *Epigraphist's Report*, 1909, sec. 41.
[3] *Epigraphist's Report*, secs. 38-9.
[4] Ibid. sec. 40.

that is reflected in the statement that Āditya II 'while a boy played sportively in battle with the head of Vīra Pandya'. The yet unidentified battle of Chevur may also refer to the same achievement against the Pandya. Parāntaka II was succeeded by his son Āditya II, Karikāla, of whom but little is known beyond the achievement against the Pandya, as a boy. He was followed on the throne by his first cousin Parakēsarivarman Uttama Chola. His accession took place in A. D. 969–70. His succession does not appear to have been altogether beyond question. If the recently discovered Tiruvālangāḍu plates[1] are to be believed Rājarāja was probably the favourite. He, however, would seem to have declined to be the cause of a civil war. If Rājarāja really did this he ought in the circumstances, to be counted a genuine patriot. The accession of Uttama Chola was coeval with the invasion of the Rāshṭrakūṭa dominions by the Paramāras of Mālva under Harsha and his successor Munja, who carried their arms up to the capital Mānyakēta itself. This catastrophe was taken advantage of by their enemy within, the Chaḷukyas, who under Taila II overthrew the Rāshtrakūṭas and restored their fallen dynasty to power. The latter's relative Mārasimha, the son of the Ganga Būtuga, was able to do nothing more than recognize one of his nephews as the paramount ruler.[2] This naturally brought on a struggle between the Gangas and the Chaḷukyas, and gave the much-longed for occasion to the Cholas. At this critical moment in South Indian History appeared Rājarāja, the Great.

3. The Great Cholas: Rājarāja was nominated successor when Madhurāntaka Uttama Chola ascended the throne in A. D. 969-70; and became Sovereign in his

1 *Epigraphist's Report* for 1906, secs. 11 and ff.

2 *Bombay Gazetteer*, vol. i, pt. ii, pp. 422-4.

own right in A.D. 985. Except for the Pandyas in the southern corner and the Keralas beyond the ghats, he was master of the Tamil country south of the Pennar. The Pandyas were likely to give trouble; the Keralas might stir; but the greatest vigilance was required on the north-west where the Chāḷukyas were fast setting their newly acquired territory in order to bring the loyal Ganga kingdom into allegiance to themselves. In the eastern Chāḷukya dominions matters were not more satisfactory either. There was about this time an interregnum, which may have been the result of a civil war. These two regions were ripe for intervention by a powerful ruler inclined to make his influence felt. No prudent ruler of any ideas of lasting ambition could think of advancing so far out without setting his flank and rear in safety. For the first ten years Rājarāja I seems to have devoted himself to this work entirely. It is to his twelfth year that we must refer for his first conquest and that is a victory over the Chera fleet in the 'Roads of Kāndaḷūr'. In the course of two years he had conquered Gangappāḍi, Nuḷambappāḍi, Taḍigai-vaḻi, and Vengaināḍu. Of these the first two constituted the bulk of Mysore which, for the next century and more, was the bone of contention between the Cholas and the Chāḷukyas. The last was the territory of the Eastern Chāḷukyas and the interregnum was taken advantage of by the Chola to impose his dominion on them. This seems to have been successfully done by Rājarāja, who gave the second ruler after the interregnum by name Vimalāditya his daughter Kundavvai in marriage. The Eastern Chāḷukyas for the rest of the period of the Chola ascendency were loyal to the supremacy of the Cholas. Taḍigai-vaḻi was between the two former. He had also put down the rebel Pandyas by the fourteenth year. By the sixteenth year Rājarāja had added to his conquests Kollam (Quilon in Travancore) and Kalingam (Orissa). By the twentieth year he had asserted his authority over Īlam (or Ceylon). The conquest of the Ganga and Noḷamba territories were not acquiesced in by the Chāḷukyas as was already pointed out; and now began that duel which lasted on to the year A.D. 1117. It was between the years twenty and twenty-four of Rājarāja that he is said to have invaded Raṭṭappāḍi seven and a half lac country; and he claims having defeated the Chāḷukya Satyaśraya. This twenty-sixth year is the year in which Rājarāja got the bulk of his inscriptions incised in the Tanjore Temple, a record of gifts and offerings made by himself, his queens, his sister the Pallava lady Kundavvaiyar, and others. His list of conquests comes to an end with the mention of his acquisition of 'the twelve thousand ancient islands of the sea' in his twenty-ninth year. This year appears to have been his last and would take us on to the year A. D. 1012. Rājarāja's conquests came to a close practically in A. D. 1005. He had settled the boundary of the Chola empire on the northern and north-western side. A somewhat irregular line drawn from Yeḍatore Nāḍ 2,000 to the Tungabhadra along the line of separation between the Malnad and Maidan districts of Mysore, and then continued along the river to where it meets the Krishna, and then on to the sea, this line would mark off the Chola country proper. Along the coast, however, the Chola power extended through the districts of the Madras Presidency to Vizagapatam, although Kalingam farther north is also among the conquests of Rājarāja. His son Rajēndra was evidently crowned while yet the father was alive in A. D. 1011-2. Rājarāja was known as Arumoḻi Deva when heirapparent under Madhurāntaka. He assumed in the third year of his reign the title Mummuḍichola and towards the close of his reign, the title Jayaimgoṇḍa

He is also known as Rājāśraya. He was, all things considered, the greatest of these great Cholas, not only because of his great conquests, but also in the more humane field of constructive administration.

Rajēndra, the Gangaigoṇḍachola, otherwise Muḍigoṇḍa, Nigarili and Uttamachola, was quite a worthy son of a great father. As a prince he seconded with energy the efforts of his father, and that this was so is borne out by his early records, which state that he 'conquered with his great and warlike army Iḍaitturainādu, Vanavāsi whose warriors (were protected by) walls of continuous forests, Koḷḷippākkai, whose walls were surrounded by śuḷḷi (trees), Maṇṇaikkaḍagam (a town in the Nelamangala Taluk, of the Bangalore District, perhaps represented by Būdihāḷu), of unapproachable strength'. All these are places along the frontier between the Cholas and the Chāḷukyas and are situate along the boundary marked out above His next exploit was the conquest of Īḷam. He took from the king of this island 'the crown of the king, the exceedingly beautiful crown of the queen, the crown of Sundara and the pearl necklace of Indra, which the king of the south (the Pandya) had previously given up to that (king of Īḷam); the whole of Īḷamaṇḍalam'. This, together with the crown, 'the garland of the sun', and the family treasures of the king of Kerala entitled him to the surname Muḍigoṇḍachola which he assumed before the sixth year of his reign. These records lay claim to the conquest of many ancient islands. This is probably a mere echo of his father's achievements. By his ninth year he added the 'impregnable Śāndimattīvu where Paraśurama had lodged a gold crown worthy of Lakshmi the goddess; defeated the Chāḷukya Jayasimha at Muyangi and conquered Raṭṭappāḍi seven and a half lac country; and the principal great mountains (which contained) the nine treasures (of Kubera).' Records of his twelfth year claim for him the following additions to his list of conquests: 'Śakkarakōṭṭam (Chakrakōṭa) belonging to Vikramavīra; Madura-mandalam with the fort of Mudiri-pada; Nāmanaikkōṇam; Panchappaḷḷi of Venjilaivīra; Māśuṇi-desam; the family and other treasures of Dhīraratha of the race of the Moon, after defeating him in the hall of Ādinagar; Oḍḍavishaya whose waters are hard to approach; Kōsalai-nāḍu where Brahmins assemble; Danḍabutti (Danḍabhukti) after having destroyed Dharmapāla in hot battle; Dakkana Lāṭam after having forcibly attacked Ranasūra; Vangāḷadēsam from which Govindachandra fled, having lost his fortune; elephants of rare strength after a hot battle with Mahīpala of Śangukkōṭṭam which touches the sea; and Ganga whose waters sprinkle *tīrthas* on the burning sand.' Many of the details in this long list have to be left unexplained in our present state of historical knowledge; but it would be rash to dismiss these as mere figments of a diseased imagination in the face of the recently discovered Tiruvalangāḍu plates which apparently confirm several of these details. These plates were composed in the sixteenth year of Rajēndra, and contain what looks like a quite unvarnished tale of the contemporary political condition of India, although Rajēndra may not be given credit for all that the record may claim as his conquest. According to this record Rajēndra first conquered the Pandya country and appointed his son Chola-Pandya as viceroy; he then turned upon Kerala and added it on to his son's charge. He then started upon his more distant expeditions overcoming the Chāḷukya Jayasimha. After this he sent his general to the banks of the Ganges. Indraratha of the lunar race was overcome, the wealth of Ranaśūra was seized, and the country of Dharamapāla was subdued. The Chola general got the vanquished kings—among whom was Mahīpāla (of Bengal)—to carry the water of the Ganges for his master. This is plainly an imitation of the supposed achievement of Śenguṭṭuvan Śēra of the Śilappadhikāram; but none the less does it seem to be true that he brought the Ganges water to purify the great tank which he constructed at Gangaikonḍaśōḻapuram, and which he named with pardonable egotism 'the pillar of Victory'. This again is an imitation of the deed ascribed to an ancient Chola who let the water of the Ganges into that of the Kavery. The Chola general then captured the king of Orissa with his younger brother, before Rajēndra returned to his capital. On a subsequent occasion he crossed the sea and captured Kaḍāram, having taken on the way the Nicobars and other places. This oversea achievement of Rajēndra is found graphically described in inscriptions of his nineteenth year, and is believed to be the source of the Kanarese drama Rajasēkheravilāsa. This nineteenth year is probably the last of his conquering years. Allowing the fullest for the possible exaggeration of the panegyrist, there is still enough left to regard Rajēndra as one of the greatest of Indian conquerors. The remaining twelve years of his reign he must have devoted to improving the efficiency of the administration, which had been laid out and handed on by a line of rulers, who take high rank among the world's rulers. Devotee of the war-god as he seems to have been, he could not have neglected the arts of peace, if he applied the great accumulation of wealth, not only to outdo his father's magnificence in the building of a capital and temple at Gangaikonḍaśōḻapuram; but also in the building of a magnificent tank, the bund on one side of which ran sixteen miles in length, and which was intended to irrigate a half from each of two districts. It was an act of modern and civilized vandalism that pulled down the bund and temple walls to build the lower anicut on the Koleroon. Perhaps it was already falling, or had fallen into disrepair very badly; all the same there is not much left, it is said, of this magnificent piece of work, as Pharaoh's *Gazetteer* of the early nineteenth century calls it. Rajēndra's last known year is the thirty-first and this would take us to the year A. D. 1042-3. He had, according to the custom of the family, associated with himself one of his sons from the year A. D. 1018. This son was Rajādhirāja though he was not the eldest, for among those honoured with titles by him on his accession were an uncle (paternal) and an elder brother by name Āḷavandān.

Rajādhirāja, Jayaṃgoṇḍachola: Rajādhirāja ruled from 1042, the thirty-first year of Rajēndra I to the year A. D. 1052, the year of the battle of Koppam where he fell. He and his brother Rajēndra are regarded as brothers of Rajēndra I by Mr. Rice, who does not assign, however, any reason in support of the view. From the statement made as to the break of succession by the death of Rajendra (by mistake for Rajādhirāja) in the battle of Koppam, it would appear that these two brothers were the sons of their predecessor, for otherwise the succession need not be considered as having ceased in the regular line. The two brothers succeeded Rajēndra I one after the other. Rajādhirāja had an uncle (a younger brother of his father), and an elder brother as has been already stated. The fact that he was crowned by Rajēndra I in 1018, while yet the latter was alive, would confirm the view that he was the son of his predecessor. Of this ruler a western Chāḷukya inscription of A. D. 1071, at Annigere[1] in the Darwar district states that 'the wicked Chola who had abandoned the religious observances of his family, penetrated into the Beḷuvola country

[1] *Bombay Gazetteer*, vol. i, pt. ii, p. 441.

and burnt the Jain temples which Ganga Perumānaḍi, the lord of Gangamanḍala, while governing Beḷuvola, had built in Annigerenāḍ;' and that 'the Chola eventually yielded his head to Sōmēsvara in battle, and thus losing his life broke the succession of his family.' This quotation shows that the Chola conquest of Gangavāḍi was no mere idle boast; that the Gangas who had become the feudatories of the western Chālukyas did not acquiesce in the conquest; and that at one time, at least, the Cholas carried fire and sword through the southern part of the Raṭṭa country. Rajādhirāja wherever he was engaged before, had to concentrate all his energies in keeping the frontiers quiet as soon as he became independent ruler after A. D. 1042. There seems to have been a tendency to throw off the yoke on the part of all the subordinate allies of the Chola. He began by conferring upon his uncle, elder brother and four of his younger brothers the dignities of rulers over the Cheras, the Chāḷukyas, the Pallavas, the Gangas, the Pandyas and the people of Lankha. These were so many provinces which carried along with them the responsibilities of Lords or Wardens of the Marches. As to the 'Lord of Kanouj' it is only a title, probably taken from the victory over a king of Ceylon who was reputed to have come from Kanouj. This done, he marched upon his enemies in succession taking the easiest first and meting out exemplary punishment to the traitors. He attacked the three allied Pandyas. The first of them, Mānābharana, was decapitated; the second, Vīra-Kerala, was trampled by an elephant; and the third, Sundara Pandya, was expelled to Mullaiyūr. He destroyed one of the kings of Vēṇaḍ (Travancore), and wearing the garland of *vanji* (symbolical of going to war with a play upon the word, the name of the old capital) put to flight a Chera king and won a naval victory in the 'Roads of Kāndalūr.'

He next turned his attention to the Chāḷukya frontier and this time acted through his general Kēvuḍan. The Chālukyas had to retreat under the princes Vikramāditya, Vijayāditya and Jayasimha, leaving two generals Gaṇḍappaiyan and Gangādharan dead. The victorious Cholas took advantage of this success, pressed on the retreating force and set fire to Koḷḷippākkai one of the Chālukya capitals. Having disposed of his other enemies, he could now turn to Ceylon where four successive rulers suffered disgrace and death at his hands. They were Vikramabāhu, Vikrama Pāndu, Vīrasālamēghan and Srīvallabha Madanarājan. Since the *Mahāvamśa* concedes these victories over the Ceylon kings, Rajādhirāja may be given credit for these achievements of his. On his return from Ceylon, he defeated in an expedition northward Gaṇḍardinakaran, Nāraṇan, Gaṇapati and Madhusūdhanan, before entering the Chāḷukya dominions and destroying their gardens and palaces at Kampili. Collecting the tributes from one and all of these Powers without remission, and collecting 'his sixth share' of the produce he could well assume the title Jayaṃgoṇḍachola and enjoy a brief respite before he lost his life in the battle of Koppam on the Tungabhadra, which would better suit the circumstances of the case than Koppam on the Pālār. This tale of conquests of Rajādhirāja shows that but for his energetic action the empire built by his two predecessors would have gone to pieces. He brought all the revolted provinces back to their allegiance, and handed the empire down to his successors intact; but it was even now that we find among the feudatories of the Chālukya Sōmēsvara the name of the Hoysala Vinayāditya, in whose line was to be born Narasimha and his son Vīra Sōmēsvara, who were to play the role of protectors of the Cholas when their empire was fast crumbling through internecine dissensions and the onsets of the Pandyas. This is yet far ahead.

Rajādhirāja was succeeded by his younger brother Rajēndra, who was present at, and played a prominent part in, the battle of Koppam where his brother fell. The earliest of his inscriptions, that of his third year, mentions his achievement at the battle where he was 'crowned', and so his reign could not have begun much earlier. This does not debar his having been associated with his brother in his career of conquest. An inscription at Heggaḍedēvanakōte in the Mysore district couples Saka 984 with his twelfth year, and this would give Saka 972 or A. D. 1050 for the commencement of his reign, although the battle of Koppam has been calculated to have taken place on May 23, A. D. 1053. Rajēndra then ruled from 1050 to at least A. D. 1062. His chief achievement is the restoration of the fortunes of the Cholas in the battle of Koppam which proves to be the turn in the tide of the Chola conquest. Perhaps already trouble was brewing at home and there might have been others who would have contested the succession. His other achievements are a reconquest of Ceylon, but certain discrepancies of the names of the conquered Ceylon rulers would lead one to suppose that the achievements of Rajēndra might have been only what he had done on behalf of his brother. That he was in Ceylon is borne out by inscriptions of his reign being found there. Rajēndra is credited with having erected a pillar of victory at Kollāpuram (Kolhapur). His daughter, Madhurāntaki, was married to the eastern Chālukya Prince Rajēndra, the son already of the daughter of the Gangaikonḍa Chola, by name Ammangadevi. This prince was to become later on the Chola emperor Kulōttunga Rajēndra was succeeded by his son Rajamāhēndra of whom nothing more is known than that he dispensed justice even better than Manu, the ancient Chola who rode his car over his own son, in justice to a cow which lost its calf through the negligence of the prince. He is said to have made some benefactions to the temple at Srīrangam. There is available an inscription of the second year of his reign. It was in succession to this ruler that we have another great Chola, whose connexion with his predecessors is not so clear and whose accession at the time seems to be regarded an act of usurpation. To understand the nature of the complications thus introduced, we have to go back upon a generation or two of South Indian history. Āhavamalla and his immediate predecessors have had one single object before them constantly; namely, the keeping back of the advancing tide of Chola aggression. In this Āhavamalla was in the main successful. The title Āhavamalla, the great in war, was well-deserved by him and he carried on successfully the wars with the Cholas bequeathed to him by his predecessors.[1] It was also he who either founded (or enlarged) the Chāḷukya capital Kalyāṇi in the Nizam's dominions, and he shifted to it the head-quarters of the empire from Yatagiri also in the Nizam's dominions (thirty miles, south of Malkhed).[2] In this attempt at holding the southern frontier against the Cholas, he was ably seconded by his sons, Sōmēsvara and Vikramāditya, the viceroys respectively of Banavāse and Gangavaḍi. When Āhavamalla died in A. D. 1068.[3] (March 29), he, was succeeded naturally enough by his eldest son, Sōmēsvara Bhuvanaikamalla; but unfortunately for the empire, his younger brother Vikramāditya was certainly the more capable of bearing the burdens of

[1] Satayāśrya and Jayasimha were respectively, rivals of Rājarāja and his son Rajēndra. *Bombay Gazeteer*, vol. i, part ii, 433.

[2] Fleet 450. *Ibid. Epi. Car.* VII. Sh. 20 a. Jayasimha Devar Nija Vijaya Kaṭaka Samanvitam Līla Vilāsadind Etagirila Nelevīḍinoḷ, etc.'

[3] *Epi. Car.* vol. vii, Sk. 136, Shimoga, pt. i.

empire. The other sons of Āhavamalla, Jayasimha and Vishṇuvardhana Vijayāditya, were more inclined to support Vikramāditya rather than Sōmēsvara. During Āhavamalla's lifetime these young princes were already given important viceroyalties and were made to regard themselves 'Pillars of Empire' as their respective titles would show. Sōmēsvara, Vikramāditya and Jayasimha appear to have been sons of the same mother, the Ganga princess[1] as the Vikramānkadēva Charitam appears to warrant and as inscriptions[2] of Sōmēsvara II himself would lead us to believe; while Vijayāditya was possibly their half-brother. While investing Lakshmaṇa as governor of Banavase, in return for valuable services rendered to the empire, Sōmēsvara says: 'junior to me is Vikrama, to him is Singhi junior; to me, Vikrama, and to Singhi you are junior and all the rest are junior to you'.

But from the titles of each of these princes Mr. Rice would infer that Vikramāditya was the son of a Ganga princess, Jayasimha of a Pallava-Nolamba princess and Vijayāditya of an eastern Chāḷukya princess. This is not a necessary inference, the titles of these princes being explained by the mere facts of their conferment upon the princes by the ruling emperor. Such investitures have been the fashion among the Chola emperors, their contemporaries. Rajādhirāja, Rajēndra Vīrārājēndra in succession made it a point to hold investitures of the sort and a number of titles importing authority over foreign states has been bestowed on Chola princes of the blood.[3]

Āhavamalla Sōmēsvara left behind him four sons, the eldest succeeding him, while the second had cherished imperial ambition for sometime at least.

[1] Dr. Fleet thinks she was a Pallava Princess, K. D. 440, note 3.

[2] Vol. vii, Sk. 136, *Epi. Car.*

[3] *Vide* the inscriptions of these in vol. iii, pt. i, *South Ind. Ins.*

To understand the situation among the Cholas, we have similarly to go back upon the rise of their power. The Chola Power rose from the ashes of the Pallavas the earliest conquests of the Cholas having been the Tonḍamanḍalam, re-named Jayaṃgonḍa Cholamandalam and Kongu. One of the mightiest and the most statesman-like exploits of the great Rājarāja (A.D. 985-1016) was the conquest and the subsequent conciliation of the eastern Chāḷukya dominions of Vengi, i. e. the Telugu country. To attach this to him permanently he married one of his daughters Kundavvaiyar to the Chāḷukya Vimalāditya. This was followed in the next reign by a more important marriage—more fruitful of consequences to the Empire. Rajēndra, the Gangaikonḍa Chola, had a daughter Ammanga Devi, who had been given in marriage to the eastern Chaḷukya Rājarāja, probably her own cousin. The offspring of this happy union was a Rajēndra Chola who was to become famous as Kulōttunga, 'the upraiser of the fame of the two families . This grandson of Gangaikonḍa Chola had married the daughter of Rajēndra, the victor over Āhavamalla at Koppam, and when this Rajēndra died, the son-in-law aspired to the Chola empire, although there was a brother and at least a number of sons of Rajādhirāja. This ambition, unwarranted though it appears, seems to have had some support among the royal family. This in fact was the discordant element in the Chola Empire. About A. D. 1070, therefore, Sōmēsvara Bhuvanaikamalla was the emperor of the Chāḷukya dominions, while his younger brother Vikramāditya was an aspirant to the imperial position. In the Chola empire Rajēndra was succeeded by his younger brother Vīrarājēndra, while Rajēndra Chola of the eastern Chāḷukya dynasty was equally an aspirant to the empire, which brought him within an ace of losing his own patrimony of the Chāḷukya kingdom. These transactions, we shall now take up in some detail.

The Chola emperor Vīrarājēndra had the following among his titles, which he probably assumed as a result of his achievements against the western Chālukyas, namely, Sakalabhuvanāśraya, Srīmēdhinīvallabha, and Mahārajādhirāja. He assumed also another Rajāśraya, which before him had been borne by Rājarāja, the Great. Two others, by the former of which alone he was spoken of by the western Chāḷukyas,[1] were Vīra Chola and Karikāla. In one of Rajēndra's inscriptions we find a brother of his, by name Vīra Chola, on whom he conferred the title Karikāla, and if these two persons, Vīrarājēndra the emperor and Vīra Chola the prince, could be identified as the Mysore inscription would justify, Vīrarājēndra was a brother of the two brothers Rajādhirāja and Rajēndra the heroes of Koppam. This along with 'the twenty-third year of (my) father (ஐயர்), who was pleased to conquer the eastern country, the Ganga and Kaḍāram' of the Gangaikoṇḍaśōḷapuram inscription of the fifth year of Vīrarājēndra, would solve another puzzle of Chola genealogy. This quotation refers to the great conqueror Gangaikoṇḍa Chola, Rajēndra the son and successor of Rājarāja the Great. His conquests of territories on the banks of the Ganges and the Irawaddy have now happily been placed beyond a doubt, thanks to the researches of Messrs. Venkyya and Kanakasabhai Pillai,[2] by the identification of Naccāvaram with the Nicobars and Pāppālam which according to the *Mahāvamśa* of Ceylon is a port of Ramañña, i. e. the Talaing country portion of Burma. Thus then the known facts so far clearly point to Vīrarājēndra as the younger brother succeeding the elder, although according to the Kalingattuparani and

1 *Epi. Car.* vol. vii. Sk. 136.

2 Article in the *Madras Review*, November, 1903.

a few inscriptions[1] we have to accommodate a Rājamāhēndra between the victor at Koppam and his successor brother Vīrarājēndra. Either it is that Rājamāhēndra died a *Yuvaraja* without independently reigning or he was set aside; but the latter conclusion does not appear to be warranted, as this Vīrarājēndra had an elder brother in the person of Ālavandan *alias* Rājarāja, and, as will appear, Vīrarājēndra himself was associated with his brother Rajēndra in his expeditions into the Chāḷukya territory. Rājamāhēndra, the son of Rajēndra, then died soon after his father and Vīrarājēndra ascended the throne.

For three generations the Cholas and the Chāḷukyas were contending for mastery in Peninsular India. The Rāshṭrakūṭa Krishna III ably seconded by his feudatories the Gangas had brought the rising Chola power low indeed. As these Rāshṭrakūṭas themselves were subverted, the opportunity for the Cholas arrived and the father and son, Rājarāja and Rājēndra, took the tide at the flood. While the father conquered and organized the younger, the son went on advancing the Chola arms into the Mysore country, took possession of eastern and southern Mysore and advanced the Chola frontier to Yeḍatoreṇāḍ 2,000 in the west and Koḷḷippākkai on the Banavase frontier in the north-west. Laṭṭalūr, Koḷḷippakkai and Henjēru (Penjēru) were the gates of the Chāḷukya empire from the south. This was regarded as of so much importance that the warden of this frontier was a marked official, often a relative of the Chāḷukya emperors. In A. D. 1060 a Raṭṭa, named Singaṇa Deva, was ruler of this part of the country. He has been described as 'a dweller at his lotus feet (of Trailōkyamalla), entitled to the five big drums, Mahāmanḍalesvara, (lord of)

[1] *Ālangudi Ins. of Rājarāja II*, page 191; *South. Ind. Ins.*, vol. iii, pt. ii.

Laṭṭalūr, ornament of the Yaduvamsa, chief of Koḷḷippākkai, determined champion over the chief of Penjēru (Henjēru,) an elephant to the lotus-garden of the Chola and Laḷa feudatories, the door of the southern region,[1] the Kālakūṭa poison to hostile kings, his father-in-law's lion, the Meru of the Raṭṭas—with these and all titles the Mahāmanḍalesvara Singaṇa Deva, was ruling the kingdom (composed of) the Uchchangi thirty, the Sūḷeṇgal seventy, the Manḍali thousand, the four Chola villages, with the stones and treasures, the thousand force and others, putting down the evil and upholding all.'

Having done this great work Rajēndra laid down this earthly authority and position, and then the troubles rose up all over again, as a succession is the occasion for enemies. The rulers who followed next had to fight the wars over again; but then these were only in the farthest frontiers. Ceylon, Madura and Malabar were easily brought back to a sense of allegiance, but not so this Tungabhadra frontier, where it was not a question of allegiance but of mastery. The wars were, therefore, prolonged and continued almost from year to year. Invasions and counter invasions were the order of the day. The Cholas had taken occasion once to plant a pillar of Victory at Kollāpuram (Kolhapur).

The great battle at Koppam in 1053 did not settle the matter finally. Each party claimed the victory though the advantage certainly lay with the Cholas. The Chāḷukyas continued to appoint governors of Gangavāḍi (with head-quarters first at Baḷgāmve and then at Halebīḍu), although the Cholas had the territory certainly under them. When, therefore, Vīrarājēndra came to the throne about A. D. 1062-3 he had to be

[1] (See Shikarpur 323, *Epi. Car.* VII Koḷḷippākke, the door of the south.)

very active on this side. From his inscriptions it appears that he five times fought the Chāḷukyas in the region of the Tungabhadra. In three of these he fought against Sōmēsvara Āhavamalla (A.D. 1044–68). Rajēndra was crowned on the battle-field of Koppam in A.D. 1053, and an inscription of the twelfth year of his reign is known, although this ought to be, according to Prof. Kielhorn's calculation, the eleventh year. This would take us on to A.D. 1062, but this need not be the case, as with respect to the Cholas there was always an overlapping of reigns owing to the practice of Yuvaraja's being associated in the administration by the reigning monarch.[1] The first achievement of Vīrarājēndra was the beating back of prince Vikramāditya from Gangavāḍi. '(He) drove from the battle-field in Gangap-pāḍi into the Tungabhadra the Mahāsāmantas, whose strong hands wielded cruel bows, along with Vikkaḷan who fought under a banner that inspired strength.' In A.D. 1056 Vikramāditya was ruler of Gangavāḍi 96,000, Banavase 12,000 with Harikēsarin of the family of the Kaḍambas of Hāngal, as his deputy in charge of the latter district.[2] In A.D. 1058 Kadambaḷige thousand is placed under Chāḷukya Ganga Perumānaḍi. Two years later, Trailōkymalla, Chāḷukya, Ganga Perumānaḍi Vikramāditya Dēva was ruling the Gangavāḍi 96,000. These inscriptions at Davanigere[3] are borne out by the Shikarpur inscriptions.[4] According to these latter he was viceroy, with head quarters at Baḷḷigave (Baḷgāme), of Gangavāḍi, with Banavāse, Sāntalige and Noḷambavaḍi. During the fifties of the eleventh century A.D. Āhava-

[1] In this case, however, the Yuvaraja was Rājamahēndra and not Vīrarājēndra.

[2] Fleet: *Bombay Gazetteer*, vol. i, pt. ii, p. 440, note 4; also *Ind. Antiquary* (IV. 103).

[3] Nos. 153 and 140, *Epi. Car.* vol. xi.

[4] Nos. 83 and 152, *Epi. Car.* vol. vii.

malla had one of his sons Sōmēsvara Bhuvanaika-malla, governing in the Bellary District and another governing practically the whole of the Mysore Province, with, of course, deputies to help him. Later on Vishṇuvardhana Vijāyaditya was governor of Nolambavāḍi 32,000 (eastern Mysore) with the title Vengimaṇḍalēsvara[1] and head-quarters at Kampili (Kampli) and Jayasimha, ruler of Banavāse alone. Thus it is clear that in a war with the Chola all these princes would figure, and so it is stated in the Chola inscription. Since the first achievement of Vīrarājēndra is against prince Vikrama, it is clear that after the battle of Koppam the Chālukyas were slowly working their way up to Gangavāḍi. Vīrarājēndra naturally had to push back Vikramāditya during the years A.D. 1055–1060. This achievement would fall within the period of the reign of Rajēndra, as, according to Prof. Kielhorn's astronomical calculations, Vīrarājēndra ascended the throne in A.D. 1062–3. This, together with Rājamāhēndra's[2] (son of Rajēndra) having fought against the Chālukya Āhavamalla, would indicate that Vīrarājēndra did not come to the throne by any act of usurpation on his part.

Vīrarājēndra apparently had two objects in view now: (1) the keeping back of this Chāḷukya aggression which was always possible, and which was quite a real danger at the time; and, (2) his active interference, with a view to achieve this, in the affairs of the Vengi kingdom of his brother-in-law, who died about this time. The Telugu country safe on his side, the Chāḷukya advance in the south would be impossible. These objects of the Chola naturally led to great activity on

[1] Not because he was son of an eastern Chāḷukya Princess but he had charge of the Vengi frontier; and wars with Vengi were his province.

[2] *South Ind. Ins.*, vol. iii, pt., ii, p. 191, *Epi. Indica.*, vol. vi, pp. 20-4.

these very frontiers. Hence the appointment of a frontier warden, a royal prince, with his head-quarters at Kampli at the salient angle between the Chola and the Vengi country. The second exploit of Vīrarājēndra, therefore, is a successful invasion of the Circars to prevent Vikramāditya gaining a hold upon the country. How Vikramāditya's intervention was brought about is not detailed in any of the inscriptions which state that: 'He (the Chola Emperor) attacked and destroyed the irresistible, great and powerful army which he (Vikkaḷan) had again dispatched into Vengaināḍu'. 'This must have been brought about somewhat in this wise. The eastern Chāḷukya Rajarāja, the son-in-law of the Gangaikonḍa Chola, died and had at least a son Rajēndra better known as Kulōttunga and a daughter Kundavvai; but we see that, the Vengi country passes into the possession of Vijayāditya, an uncle of Kulōttunga, through the good offices of Vīrarajēndra. This disputed succession ought to have brought Vikramāditya upon the scene. But Vīrarājēndra was nevertheless victorious at last, and placed his nominee Vijayāditya of the eastern Chāḷukya family, (not of the western Chāḷukya family as was hitherto supposed), upon the throne, after a battle at Vijayavāḍi (Bezwada).

The next great achievement was his great victory at Kūḍal Sangamam over the entire body of the Chāḷukya forces. This place is at the junction of the Krishna and the Tungabhadra, just the region wherefrom the Chāḷukyas would hope to bar the northward and north-eastward progress of the Chola. 'The enemy full of hatred, met and fought against (him) a third time, hoping that his (former) defeats would be revenged. (The King) defeated countless Sāmantas, together with these (two) sons of Āhavamalla, who were called Vikkaḷan and Singaṇan at Kūḍal Sangamam on the turbid river. Having sent the brave vanguard in advance, and having himself remained close behind with the kings allied to him, (he) agitated by means of a single *must* elephant that army (of the enemy), which was arrayed (for battle), (and which) resembled the northern ocean. In front of the banner-top he cut to pieces Singaṇan, the King of warlike Kosalai, along with the furious elephants of (his) vanguard. While Kāśavadaṇḍa-nāyaka, Kētarasan, Mārāyan of great strength, the strong Pōttarayan (and) Irāchchayan were fighting (he) started, saying: "Follow Mūvendi, (who wears) a garland of gold!" and cut to pieces many Sāmantas, who were deprived of weapons of war. Then Maduvaṇan who was in command fled; Vikkaḷan fled with dishevelled hair; Singaṇan fled, his pride and courage forsaking (him). Annaḷan and all others descended from the male elephants on which they were fighting in battle, and fled; Āhavamalla too, to whom they were allied, fled before them. The king stopped his fast furious elephant, put on the garland of victory, seized his wives, his family treasures, conches, parasols, trumpets, drums, canopies, white chamaras, the boar banner, the ornamental arch, the female elephant (called Pushpaka and a herd of war-elephants, along with a troop of prancing horses, and amidst (general) applause put on the crown of victory, (set with) jewels of red splendour.'[1] This was the battle of Kūḍal Sangamam and I have quoted the inscription in full to give an idea of how battles were fought in those times. While the Chāḷukya records mention in general the prowess of the Chāḷukyas, they do not give us circumstantial details of any particular battle against Vīrarājēndra in person. Bilhana's Vikramānkadeva Charitam no doubt depicts prince Vikramāditya as conducting expeditions towards the south and credits him with the occupation both of Kanchi and of Gangaikoṇḍaśoḷapuram. This is not during the reign of Vīrarājēndra

[1] No. 20, *Scuth Ind. Ins.*, vol. iii, pt. i.

but after his death, as we shall have to relate. That he invaded Vengi is no doubt likely, but even here the result is entirely different from what the panegyrist would have us believe. Before the close of his fourth year, i.e. prior to the death Somēsvara I, Vīrarājēndra had conquered other chiefs.[1]

But inscriptions of his fifth year, the year of the death of Sōmēsvara Āhavamalla, state that the Chola emperor, having defeated the Keralas at Ulagai and defeated and imprisoned the Pandyas (Kaṉṉiyas) and Chāḷukyas, the king overthrew several chiefs among whom figure the Ganga and Noḷamba chiefs. When he retired to Gangaikoṇḍaśoḷapuram he received an autograph letter from the Chāḷukya Sōmēsvara challenging the Chola king to meet him once more at Kūḍal Sangamam. Vīrarājēndra accepted this and marched to the appointed place Kandai. Not finding the Chāḷukya Sōmēsvara there, he waited a month and then putting to flight such of the Chāḷukya army, as had been there to watch him and, having erected a pillar of victory on the Tungabhadra, inscribed upon it an account of his conquest of Raṭṭappāḍi seven and a half lac country.

Then he 'appointed the liar, who came on a subsequent day, as Vallabha (Chāḷukya king), and tied (round his neck) a beautiful necklace.' These transactions have to be accounted for in this wise: the fifth year of Vīrarājēndra was the year of the death of Sōmēsvara Āhavamalla, who passed away by drowning himself in the Tungabhadra, owing to an attack of malignant fever. This would account for his absence from Kūḍal Sangamam. His death brought matters to an issue between the two brothers Sōmēsvara II and

[1] The chiefs of Poṭṭappi (Kalahasti); Vāran of Kerala, the younger brother of Jananātha of Dhara and the Pandya Prince probably one Vīrakēsarin son of Srīvallabha.

his younger brother Vikramāditya, of whom the latter was the more distinguished in the recent transactions. It was then that he appeared somewhat belated at the Chola camp, and negotiated successfully for Chola help in the event of his attempt to gain the throne as against Sōmēsvara. The treaty was sealed, of course, by the marriage of the Chaḷukya prince with the daughter of the reigning Chola. Though some of the Chola inscriptions give a ludicrous character to this particular transaction, that this was the real import is amply clear from these inscriptions themselves, while the *Vikramānkadēva Charitam* gives naturally enough a glossed version of it in favour of the hero prince Vikrama. This done Vīrarājēndra marched into the Vengi country. Having moved (his camp) he declared: '(We) shall not return without regaining the country of Vengai, which (we had formerly, subdued. You (who are) strong, come and defend (it) if (you) are able!' That army which was chosen for this expedition, drove into the jungle that big army, which resisted its enemy on the great river close to Viśayavāḍi (Bezwada), and which had for its chiefs, Jananāthan, the Danḍanāyaka Rājamayyan, whose *must* elephants trumpeted in herds and Mūpparaśan. 'His elephants drank the water of the Godaveri. He crossed over Kalingan and beyond it dispatched for battle his invincible army as far as the further end of Śakkaragōṭṭom (Chakra-kōṭṭa). He re-conquered the good country of Vengai and bestowed it on Vijayādittyan, whose broad hand held weapons of war and who had taken refuge at his lotus-feet.'

This last affair, as has been explained already, is the outcome of a disputed succession in the Vengai country. After the death of the eastern Chāḷukya Rājarāja (A.D. 1060-1), Kulōttunga (Rajēndra) ought to have succeeded, but this succession appears to have been disputed. The *Kalingattupparani* records that the wife of Gangaikoṇḍa Chola took up the dear child when it was born, and from the signs upon its feet predicted his uplifting both the families in fame. This was nothing more, probably, than the pious grandmotherly wish for the advancement of her grandson. It is very probable that the child was brought up in the grandfather's house, with all the paraphernalia of empire surrounding the young prince. Thus it was made possible for his uncle Vijayāditya to make a successful attempt to place himself on the throne of Vengai, as we find inscriptions of Kulōttunga's early years only in the southern end of his paternal dominions, i. e. the territory round about Madras. In his difficulty Vijayāditya probably sought the strong arm of Vīrarājēndra, to whom a friendly Vengi was of paramount importance. This would, *inter se*, be detrimental to the interests of the Chāḷukyas of Kalyāni. Hence all the warlike transactions between the rival powers, in regard to Vengi in which neither was directly interested. Returning from this victorious expedition to Gangaikoṇḍaśoḷapuram, Vīrarājēndra assumed the paramount title of Rājadhirāja or, as other inscriptions say, Rajādhirajan Rājarāja, 'as was the custom of the family.'

Inscriptions of the sixth year of Vīrarajēndra and also those of his seventh year, add another engagement between the contending powers at Kūḍalsungamam, for the third time, when Vīrarajēndra 'burnt Kampili before Sōmēsvara could untie the necklace which he had put on, and set up a pillar of victory at Karaḍikkal.' This Sōmesvara is correctly identified by Dr. Hultzsch with Sōmēsvara Bhuvanaikamalla, the son of Āhavamalla and the elder brother of Vikramāditya and Jayasimha, who was, according to Dr. Fleet, sometime governor of the Beḷuvoḷa, Purigere, etc.

country earlier; but on a third occasion, he burnt the city of Kampili, before 'Sōmesvara could untie the necklace which he had put on and set up a pillar of victory at Karadikkal.'[1] The untying of the necklace refers to the untying of the necklace of Yuvaraja to assume the higher one of the reigning sovereign, rather than, as Dr. Hultzsch considers, to the incident having taken place in the lifetime of Sōmēsvara I. In an inscription at Shikarpur,[2] Sōmēsvara II assumed the royal insignia on the fourteenth day after the death of his father, as is the Hindu custom even now; and the inscription 83 of vol. III of *South Indian Inscriptions* implies that Vīrarājēndra acted promptly after the death of Āhavamalla, for the Shikarpur inscription says that the Chola king thought of taking advantage of the change of rulers and exclaiming! 'A new reign; a kingdom fit only for a hero; now is the time to invade it; I will surround Guṭṭi and besiege it' The inscription states further down that Vīra Chola turned his back after a cavalry skirmish between the vanguards. If this interpretation is correct these events must have taken place in A. D. 1068. Before the next year, Vīrarājēndra added to his laurels by the over-sea conquest of Kadaram in the Talaing country of Burmah.

All this time of active warfare, we have evidence of Vīrarājēndra's transacting business of a civil character. Whenever he was at Gangaikondaśolapuram, his capital, his secretaries were busy bringing papers and dispatches which he disposed of promptly. It is a pity that there are no inscriptions to give us a hint as to how he arranged for this civil business while he was engaged in war. From the few inscriptions of his time, which we have, he shows himself to have been

[1] This refers to the promptness with which the victory was gained.
[2] Sk. 136, *Epi. Car.*, vol. vii.

an active monarch, who acted up to his responsibilities, and when he passed away about the year A. D. 1070, he left behind him a compact kingdom to his son Adhirājarāja, but the opportunity for Kulōttunga now arrived after having waited for over eight years.

One more point deserves mention here before we close the accouut of Vīrarājēndra. There is a Tamil grammar, by name *Vīrasōḻiyam*, written by Buddhamitra, with a commentary by the author's disciple Perundēvanār. It is called *Vīrasōḻiyam* from the patron of the author who was born at Ponpaṟṟi in Malaikūṟṟam. This Mr. Venkayya would identify with Ponpeṭṭi in the Paṭṭukoṭṭai Taluka, as this would bring him near Toṇḍi, of which Buddhamitra is said by his pupil, the commentator, to have been lord. That the patron, whose name has been associated with the grammar, is none other than Vīrarājēndra is borne out by references to and quotations of inscriptions of Rājēndra Chola I and those referring to the battles of Koppam and Kūḍal Sangamam. No inscription of a later time is mentioned, and the name of Vīrarājēndra as the author's patron is found in the text of the grammar itself. This makes another landmark in Tamil literary history and gives the clue to many a knotty point in the literary chronology of Tamil.

The death of Vīrarājēndra in A. D. 1070, marks another stage in the struggle between the Chola and Chāḷukya Powers. It has already been pointed out that prince Vikramāditya had entered into an agreement with Vīrarājēndra on the Tungabhadra; but the death of his powerful ally and father-in-law made him halt in his course towards achieving the usurpation that he must now have planned already. We have noticed before that the disputed succession at Vengi brought both the Chāḷukya and the Chola upon the scene, but the Chola had the best of it in the fight and Vengi was yet faithful to the Cholas under Vijayāditya. Kulōttunga all this period had been governing, either in his own name or as it appears more likely, as a viceroy of the emperor, the territory in the middle, including in it the region embracing Tiruvoṟṟiyūr, Tiruvālangāḍu in the Kārveṭinagar Zemindari and Kolar.[1] Vikramāditya took a measure of the situation at a glance, and set about putting his neighbourhood in good attitude for his crowning act. Prince Rajēndra Chola was likely to strike in for the Chola empire, and it was of immense importance to secure the Chola succession to his brother-in-law, who had already been associated with his father Vīrarājēndra. This he did, and we have the ruler Adhirājarājēndra in succession to his father. We have inscriptions of his third year, while Vīrarājēndra's dates run into the year, A.D. 1070. So Adhirājarāja would have ruled independently for only part of a year. According to the *Vikramānka Deva Charitam*, Vikramāditya installed his brother-in-law, and the *Kalingattupparani* and *Vikkirama Soḷanulā* mention a king between Vīrarājēndra and Kulōttunga. This apart, an inscription of the third year of Vīrarājēndra mentions that the magistrate Rājarājamūvendavēḷān and the Sēnapathi Rājarāja Paranriparākshasan *alias* Vīrasōḷa Iḷangō, met at Kanchipuram and held an inquiry into the administration of a grant made in the eighth year of Vīrarājēndrdēāva. This same Sēnapathi Rājarāja Paranriparākshasan *alias* Vīrasōḷa Iḷangō figures in the same capacity under Kulōttunga in an inscription of his second year (i. e. 1072) at Tiruvoṟṟiyūr. Thus then it is clear that Adhirājarāja succeeded his father but had only a short reign, for in the same year Rajēndra Chola *alias* Kulōttunga also

[1] This I infer from the fact that the earliest inscriptions of Kulōttunga are found in this region; but this may not have been the case.

ascended the throne of the Chola empire. This unsettled the arrangements of Vikramāditya, who had to bide his time, and it is probable, as the *Vikramānkadeva Charitam* states, that he was on the best of terms, in the meanwhile, with his brother Sōmēsvara.

Leaving Vikramāditya aside, we have to consider the position of the other young prince whose name bulks out so largely in the South Indian politics of the time, namely, Rājakēsarivarman Rajēndra Chola *alias* Kulōttunga Chola. It has already been pointed out that he was the grandson of the Gangaikonḍa Chola, and that it was probable that he was brought up in his grandfather's house, whether he was actually adopted by him or not. There was, in fact, no reason for the adoption as the grandfather appears to have had a number of sons, who were (at least one of them was) associated as lieutenants of the great conquering Chola. One would naturally expect this Rajēndra to succeed his father, when he died in 1061–2 or the next year. In all the transactions about the appointment of Vijayāditya VII as viceroy of Vengi, we do not hear of the name of Kulōttunga, and this would suggest that this young ambitious prince did not regard it as a matter of much moment to him whether he was viceroy of Vengi or not. His ambition was imperial and not viceregal, in this resembling his great contemporary Vikramāditya, who for many years had practically the whole of the southern half of his father's and brother's empire under his control. There is yet another reason for this indifference, but this seems to be the main reason, though it appears to have escaped the notice of the expert editors of these inscriptions, Dr. Hultzsch and Mr. Venkayya. The earlier inscriptions of Kulōttunga state that, as Yuvaraja, he accomplished two great feats: (1) the capture of elephants at Vairāgaram and (2) the capture of the fortress of Chakrākōṭṭam. His inscriptions take us on to his forty-ninth year as emperor, and so he must have ascended the throne, a comparatively young man. Then he may have been Yuvaraja to his father, the eastern Chālukya Rājarāja I, or his grandfather and uncles. If he had been at Vengi all the while, Vijayāditya's succession could not have been possible, altogether setting aside his nephew; but granting that he was at Vengi, where was this Vairāgaram and what is the achievement of catching elephants? If again he was even ousted by Vijayāditya his uncle, the fact of his accession to the eastern Chāḷukya dominions, specifically stated by the Piṭāpuram pillar inscriptions and the copper-plate grants, is not borne out by any of his inscriptions, all of which are dated as from A.D. 1070, the year of his accession to the Chola throne. There appears to be only one explanation for all this. Vairāgaram is Wairagarh in the Central Provinces,[1] north-east of Ajanta, and it is here that as the Chola Yuvaraja, on the occasion of the invasion of Vīrarājēndra, or his grandfather, Rajēndra I, he distinguished himself. His early inscriptions affirm that '(He) gently raised without wearying (her) in the least the lotus-like goddess of the earth residing in the region of the rising sun.' (அருக்கனுதையத் தாசையிலிருக்கும் கமலமனைய நிலமகள் தன்னை முன்னீர்க்குளித்தவன்றுள், திருமாலாதிக்கேழலாகி எடுத்தன்ன யாதும் சலியாவகையினி தெடுத்து தன் குடைநிழல் இன்புற இருத்தி).[2] This land of the rising sun cannot well be the country of Vengi, and if the conquest of part of Burmah by Rajēndra I is accepted, as it must now

[1] I am glad to find Pundit Hira Lal support me in this suggestion to which I was led by Mr. Venkayya's objection to my previous identification of Vairāgaram with a place of similar name in Burmah *vide Epigraphia Indica* x. 26–7.

[2] Note also: காய்கடற்றிசைத்தரத்துப் பூபாலர் திறைவிடுதக்க வெஞ்சொலிகைநிற முறைநிற்ப. *South Ind. Ins.*, No. 76, vol. iii, pt. 2, p. 169, 1–4.

be, this would only mean that Rajēndra Kulōttunga distinguished himself as a prince in the eastern exploits of his grandfather, either during, Rajēndra Chola's, or under Vīrarājēndra when he reconquered Kaḍāram. This would also satisfactorily account for the idea of the Panḍitha Chola (Rājēndra, the Gangaikonda Chola) having been his father according to the *Kalingattupparani* (XIII. 62).

There is still the mention of his rule over Vengi to be explained. This is easily done by the mere fact that he was the legitimate heir whoever else had been viceroy (and Vijayāditya claimed to be nothing else), and when Kulōttunga became emperor he did not wish to assert his claims to, or make a boast of what was certainly a much inferior position.

If this view of Kulōttunga's earlier position be correct, then his achievement against Chakrakōṭṭam, against the ruler of Dhāra might have been accomplished, when Vīrarājēndra dispatched an army into Kalingam and across into Dhāra after his last expedition into Vengi. The Kalinga ruler at the time was Rājarāja whose wife Rājyasundari, daughter of the Dramila (Dravida) King Rajēndra Chola, was the mother of the Kalinga ruler Anantavarman Choda Ganga.[1] This Rajēndra Chola, Dr. Hultzsch suspects, is identical with Vīrarājēndra. Be this as it may, it is probably in this invasion that Kulōṭṭunga found occasion to distinguish himelf against Chakrakōṭṭam.

This view of the early life of Kulōttunga differs from that of Dr. Hultzsch and Mr. Venkayya, who infer it was only a question of usurpation on the part of Vijayāditya, assisted by Vīrarājēndra. This would accord very ill with Kulōttunga's position in the

[1] It is quite possible that this Rajēndra Chola was the Gangaikonda Chola, or Rājēndra Kulōttunga as Mr. Venkayya infers in his Report for 1905.

interim. If he had remained anywhere in the Chola empire, Vīrarājēndra would have taken steps to keep him out of ever-aspiring to the throne. Nor does he figure among the western Chāḷukya relations with Vīrarājēndra. It appears, therefore, that he was biding his time as did Vikramāditya for nine years to work his way up to the empire.

Inscriptions of the second year of Kulōttunga lend support to this view, as No. 64, vol. iii of the *South Indian Inscriptions* implies 'that he felt himself already at that time as a member of the Chola family to which his mother and grandmother belonged, and not as an eastern Chāḷukya, because it mentions as his crest the tiger and not the boar.' In inscriptions of his first four years he styles himself Rājakēsarivarman Rajēndra Chola Deva, while that in his fifth year ascribes to him the title Kulōttunga. In addition to the achievements already referred to while yet a prince only, the inscriptions of his fifth year add that he vanquished the king of Kuntala, that he crowned himself as king of the country on the banks of the Kavery, and that he decapitated an unnamed Pandya king. 'Having made the wheel of his (authority) to go as far as the Golden Circle (i.e. Mount Meru), on the earth, which was surrounded by the moat of the sea, that was (again) surrounded by (his) fame, (the king) newly wedded, in the time when (he was still) heir-apparent (iḷangō), the brilliant goddess of victory at Śakkarakkōṭṭam by deeds of valour, and seized a herd of elephants at Vayirāgaram. (He) unsheathed (his) sword, showed the strength of (his) arm and spurred (his) war-steed, so that the King of Kondala (Kuntala), whose spear had a sharp point, lost his wealth. Having established his fame, having put on (a garland of victory over) the northern region, and having stopped the prostitution of the goddess with the sweet and excellent lotus-flower (i.e. Lakshmi), of the southern region, and the loneliness of the goddess of the good country whose garment is the Ponni (Kavery). (he) put on by right (of inheritance) the pure royal crown of jewels, while the kings of the old earth[1] bore his two feet (on their heads) as a large crown.' This would be the year A.D. 1075 and the Kuntalas here referred to must be the generals of Sōmēsvara II, particularly his brothers, Vikramāditya and Jayasimha, the latter having been at the time viceroy of Banavase. This merely refers to an attempt at intervention on the part of Vikramāditya, as a result of the misfortune to his brother-in-law and the consequent change of rule. But before the eleventh year of Kulōttunga's reign, he had to intervene with greater vigour in the affairs of the Mysore country. But how this was called for has to be explained before proceeding further.

Sōmēsvara Bhuvanaikamalla ruled over the Chāḷukya empire from A.D. 1068 to A.D. 1076 when his reign came to an end. The only epigraphical information available is that Sōmēsvara, having got intoxicated with pride after a few years of rule, neglected the government badly, and his virtuous brother Vikramāditya overthrew him in the interest of good government and established himself instead. Turning to the *Vikramankadeva Charitam* again for details, we have the following which I extract from Dr. Fleet.[2]

'Bilhana tells us, that, for a time, the two brothers lived in friendly fashion at Kalyāna; the younger duly honouring the elder as the chief of his house and his king. Sōmēsvara, however, fell into evil courses, and even tried to do harm to his brother. Thereupon Vikramāditya left Kalyāna taking with him all his followers and also his younger brother, Jayasimha III,

1 *South Ind. Ins.*, p. 142, vol. iii, pt. ii.

2 *Bombay Gazetteer*, pt. ii, vol. i, pp. 444-5.

who, he considered, could not be safely left with the king. Sōmēsvara sent forces in pursuit, to bring the brothers back. But he was unsuccessful and at last desisted from the attempt. Vikramāditya went on to the Tungabhadra on the bank of which river he rested his army for sometime, with the intention of fighting the Chola king. It appears, however, that, for some unexplained reason, he deferred this project in favour of making a triumphal progress through the southern and western parts of the kingdom; for, the narrative goes on to say, that having spent sometime in the Banavase province, he marched through the Malaya country, that Jayakesin the lord of Konkan, i.e. the first Jayakesin in the family of the Kaḍambas of Goa, came to him and brought presents, and that the lord of Āḷupa made submission and received favours in return. It also implies that he visited Kerala, and inflicted some reverses on the king of that country. He then seems to have taken some definite action against the Cholas. But it was stopped by the Chola king, Rajakēsarivarman otherwise called Vīrarājēndra Deva I, making overtures of friendship, and offering him a daughter in marriage, on the condition that he retired to the Tungabhadra. Vikramāditya accepted the proposals and the marriage was duly celebrated. Shortly afterwards, however, the news reached him that his father-in-law was dead, and that the Chola kingdom was in a state of anarchy. He then proceeded at once to Kanchi the Chola capital; put down the rebellion there, and going to Gangakunḍa, secured the throne for his brother-in-law, probably Parakēsarivarman otherwise called Adhirājarājēndra. He then marched back to the Tungabhadra. But he heard, almost immediately, that his brother-in-law had lost his life in a fresh rebellion, and that Rajiga the lord of Vengi,—i.e. the eastern Chālukya king Kulōttunga Chola Deva I, whose original appellation was Rājēndra

Chola—had seized the throne of Kanchi. He at once prepared to march against Rajiga. The latter induced Sōmēsvara II to enter into an alliance against their mutual enemy. When Vikramāditya at length reached Rajiga's forces, Somēsvara's army was encamped, with hostile intentions, not far off in his rear. And in the battle which ensued, and in which Vikramāditya was victorious, Rajiga fled and Somēsvara was taken prisoner. The narrative says that Vikramāditya at first intended to restore his brother to liberty and to the throne. But eventually he decided otherwise. He had himself proclaimed king, and then appointing Jayasimha III, viceroy at Banavase, proceeded to Kalyāṇa and established himself there.'

The above is the account of Vikramāditya's Vidyāpati (poet-laureate); and, apart from a little glozing in favour of his patron and a certain want of chronological sequence, the narration of events is in the main true. A part of this story has already been dealt with before—Vikramāditya's actual motive and how he entered into treaty with Vīrarājēndra, what he did to his brother-in-law and how the affair ended. What has to be specially noted here is the last transaction of the narration: how Sōmēsvara was actually overthrown. It is very likely this achievement of Kulōttunga, that is detailed in inscriptions of his fifth and sixth years, i. e. A. D. 1075-6. It is very probable that Vikrama's elder brother was an incapable ruler or even worse. There is no doubt that Vikramāditya had distinguished himself even during his father's lifetime. Nevertheless, he had carefully prepared his scheme and put it into effect at the psychological moment, and thus showed clearly to the world that in diplomacy, he was not behind any body at the time. It was, however, not a cold-blooded deed of unscrupulous usurpation, for it is quite possible that Sōmēsvara's regime might have brought the empire to the verge of ruin, seeing they had to reckon with a neighbour like Kulōttunga. In this enterprise, Vikramāditya had the support of the viceroys of first rank among his brother's officers, and this could not have been obtained if there had been no counterbalancing virtues in him. Sēuṇa Chandra II of the Yadava family, the premier viceroy of the north-west, Jayakēsin Kaḍamba of Goa; Achugi II of the Sinda family of Yelburga; Eṛeyanga Hoyśala of Gangavāḍi, the son of Vinayāditya the right trusty lieutenant of Sōmēsvara Āhavamalla; and Irukkapāla, the brother of the governor of Noḷambavāḍi; all these heartily helped Vikramāditya and were the main pillars of his empire for the following half century and more. Thus then Vikramāditya allowed Kulōttunga to boast of a victory while he had to be busy at head-quarters to complete his usurpation. This done, there began the battle royal between the contending nations or rather rulers.

The next war, undertaken against the Chola, also appears to have gone against the Chāḷukyas. Inscriptions of the fourteenth and fifteenth years of Kulōttunga lay claim to having turned back an invasion of Vikramāditya from Nangali (about six miles east of Mulbagal) via Manalur (other inscriptions have it Alaṭṭi) to the Tungabhadra; and to having captured Gangamanḍalam and Singaṇam. Having secured his frontier in the north he turned his attention to the south against the Pandyas, and subdued the south-western portion of the Peninsula including in his conquests the Gulf of Mannar, the Podiyil mountain (in the Tinnevelly district), Cape Comorin Kōṭṭāru, the Sahya (the western ghats) and Kuḍamalaināḍu (i. e. Malabar). About this time he appears to have effected conquests in the Malabar country, Viḷiñam and Śālai having been occupied according to the *Kalingattuparani* and the *Vikkiramaśolanula*. That this is not a mere high-falutin assertion of a triumph without success is amply borne out by the utter absence of purely Chāḷukya inscriptions beyond the Shimoga and the Chitaldroog districts, the capitals of the so-called viceroys of Gangavāḍi having been beyond the Gangavāḍi itself (namely, Beḷagāmve first and Bēlūr next); and the appointment of particular governors to hold the southern frontier against the Chola in northern Mysore.

'Lakshmana becoming lord of the Great Banavasenāḍ, Vikramanoḷamba becoming the lord of Noḷamba-Sindavāḍi, Gangamanḍalika (probably Udayāditya) becoming lord of the territory from Âlampara, Bhuvanaikamalla, in view of their being as a long bar to the south, gave them these countries'.[1] Although this arrangement was actually made in the reign of Sōmēsvara II, there was no material alteration of frontier till about the early decades of the following century. These achievements of Kulōttunga must have taken place about A. D. 1085.

If Vikramāditya moved south, about A. D. 1080, then the opportunity would have been taken advantage of by the Pandyas of the south, and Kulōttunga had not only taken steps 'to fix the limits of the southern country,' but also had settled some of his officers on the roads through Kōṭṭāru to hold the country in check, 'while all the heroes in the western hill country (Kuḍamalaināḍu) ascended voluntarily to heaven, (he) was pleased to bestow on the chiefs of his army, who were mounted on horses, *settlements on every road*, including (that which passed) through Kōṭṭāru, in order that the enemies might be scattered, and took his seat on the throne acquired in warfare.'[2]

This war must have taken place soon after Vikramāditya ascended the throne in A. D. 1076 and both the

[1] *Epi. Car.*, vol. vii, p. 202 of the translation.

[2] *Vide* No. 73, *South Ind. Ins.*, vol. iii, pt. II; the officer in charge of Kōṭṭāru was a man of the Chola country.

emperors had learnt by A. D. 1080 (or thereabouts) that it was impossible to decide once for all on this frontier, and matters were left to settle themselves by efflux of time. During the rest of his reign the Chāḷukya emperor devoted himself to peace. His reign had a span of half a century and, during this long period, Bilhaṇa notices an invasion and even occupation of Kanchi and two invasions across the Narbudha. The occupation of Kanchi was nothing more than the attempted invasion of the Chola empire which ended in failure. The other two invasions were active interventions in the affairs of Mālva and Chēdi or Dhāra and Ḍāhala, as, after the death of Bhōja of Dhāra and Karṇa of Ḍāhala, there was constant war. His invasion of Bengal and Kāmarūpa (or Assam) are not likely with the Cholas constantly on the alert, unless these happen to be mere contingents of armies sent to help a friendly Power.

Jayasimha, who had acted with him and had been rewarded with the viceroyalty of Banavase, a position which Vikrama himself occupied under his father, revolted and evidently the revolt had been put down; but nothing further was heard either of Jayasimha or of his other brother Vishṇuvardhana Vijayāditya. With this change Vikramāditya effected an important modification of domestic policy, which produced consequences that could hardly have been foreseen by him. He gave important viceroyalties to chieftains with great local influence[1], sometimes scions of old families, and these became founders of the great feudatory dynasties that played such important parts later on. We see this change taking place during the peaceful regime of the great Chāḷukya Vikramāditya. His empire extended from the Narbudda southwards to the Tungabhadra;

[1] His sons were given only viceroyalties, etc., near headquarters, e.g. Jayakarṇa, *Bombay Gazetteer*, p. 455, vol. i, pt. ii.

and from the junction of the latter with the Krishna, if a line be drawn northwards more or less in a straight line to where the Wardha meets the Godavari and continued up this affluent, we shall have marked the eastern boundary of the Chāḷukya Empire. All the east of this from the southern portion of Ganjam was the Chola empire under his great contemporary Kulōttunga, whose southern limit was Cape Comorin itself except for a small part—the Madura district—which was under the Pandya. The country beyond the western ghats to the sea was under the Chera or Kerala ruler in the same subordinate position as that of the Pandya, though unwilling.

This extensive empire of the Chāḷukyas was divided into Rāshṭra, Vishaya and Grāma, answering exactly to the Manḍalam (province) Nāḍu (division) and Ūr (township). Hitherto viceroys were appointed over the larger divisions, sometimes over more divisions than one; but hereafter it is generally the rule that there is a viceroy over each of these larger divisions. Over the Vishaya, or the district, there was a governor who happened to be a local chief. We hear of Ganga chiefs with head-quarters at Yeḍēhalli and at Āsandi in Kadur district. Each village or township constituted the unit of administration, and had its own assembly or governor according to its history. Besides the viceroys of provinces there were great generals, ministers for peace and war, commissioners of finance, and great noblemen in Mahāsēnāpatis or Danḍanāyakas, Sandhivigrahins (often there is a higher officer the Hēri Karnāṭa-Lāṭa-Sandhivigrahin, great minister for peace and war of the Karnāṭaka and the Lāṭa territories), controllers of the pannāya, pērjjunka and other taxes and lastly the Mahasāmantādhipatis—these last being kept at court, perhaps because they were dangerous elsewhere. The emperor had his capital at Kalyāṇa; but he had also half a dozen other places in important positions, often referred to as Rājadhānis, or alternative capitals which, to judge from their location, would be for administrative convenience, more than to satisfy the vanity of the ruler for the time being. These cities were Kalyāṇa, the capital; Banavase and Baḷagāmve, the head-quarters of the southern viceroyalty; Naḍaviyappaiyanabīḍu, in the north-east of Bijāpur on the frontier of the Nizam's Dominions; Ētagiri, the modern Yetagiri, thirty miles south of Mālkhed; Vijayāpura, the modern Bijāpur; Maṇṇeyakere, also in the Nizam's Dominions, and Vikramāpura or Araśiabīdu. Most of these were head-quarters of viceroyalties, while Ētagiri was the old capital of the dynasty. Even Tiruvikramāpura (named after either the emperor or Vishṇu Kamalāvilāsin) was a capital under Sōmēsvara, with the name Araśiabīdu (the palace of the queen), because one of a number of the lady viceroys[1], during the rule of the Chāḷukyas, had her head-quarters there.

Among the viceroys of Vikramāditya we find the names of a number of chiefs, who became later on the founders of the great feudatory families, though for the while their charges often changed. This has been stated already. Without following the details of the change of viceroys, the provinces were: (1) the Yādava territory of Dēvagiri or, as it was known before this, Sēuna Dēśa with capitals at Sinnar and then at Dēvagiri, including in it all the territory in the north-west of the empire; (2) the Silāharas of northern and southern Konkan, the country along the coast below

[1] Akkadevi the aunt of Sōmēsvara I, was governing Kiśukāḍ seventy in A.D., 1022.

The queens of Sōmēsvara I, and some of his successors had small territories to administer, sometimes directly, often by Deputy.

Vikramāditya had six queens. Of whom we have records of four at least, in government of small districts or administration of revenues. One of them was governing the capital Kalyāṇa and another had a district allotted to her for pin-money. (Angabōgha).

Fleet, *Bombay Gazetteer*, vol. i, pt. ii.

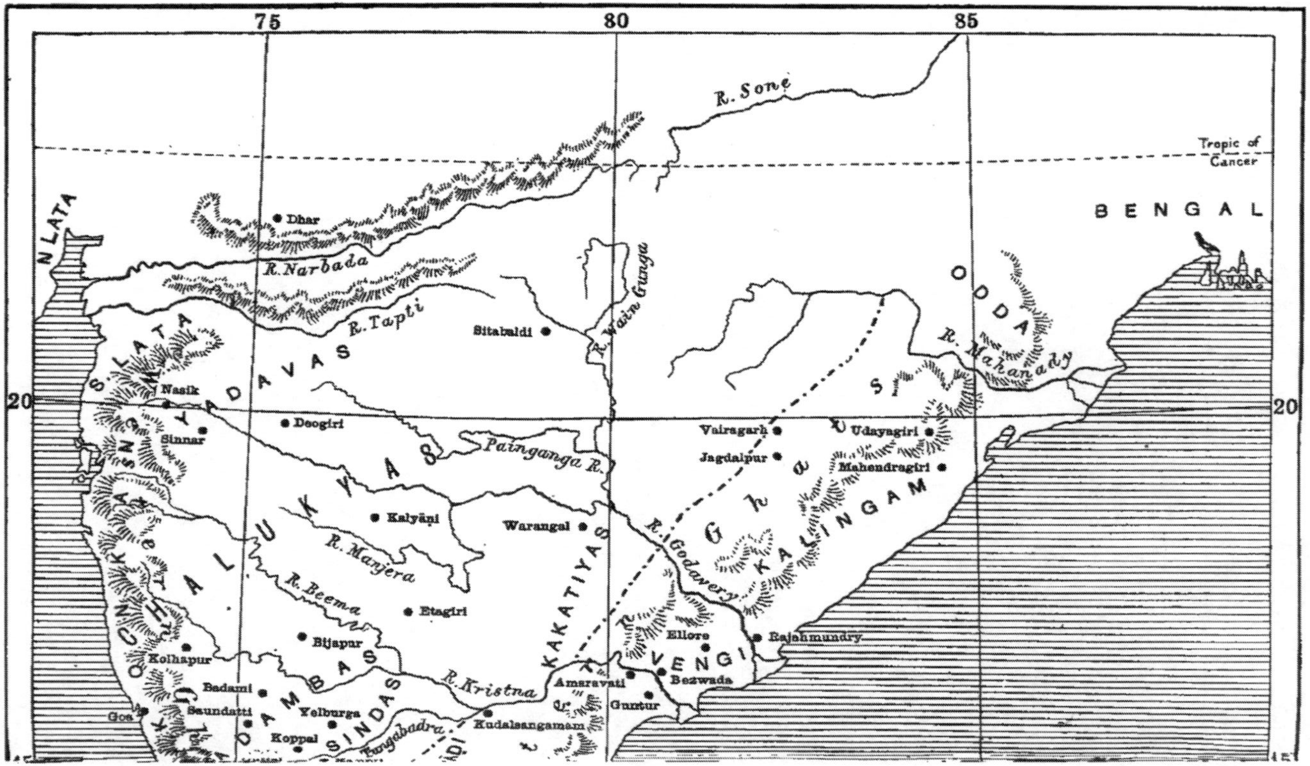
75
80
85
20
20
Tropic of Cancer
BENGAL
R. Sone
R. Narbada
R. Tapti
R. Wain Gunga
R. Mahanady
R. Painganga R.
R. Manjera
R. Beema
R. Godavery
R. Kristna
Tungabadra
ODDA
KALINGAM
VENGI
KAKATIYAS
YADAVAS
CHALUKYAS
KADAMBAS
SINDAS
Dhar
Sitabaldi
Nasik
Sinnar
Deogiri
Kalyāṇi
Warangal
Etagiri
Bijapur
Kolhapur
Badami
Saundatti
Goa
Yelburga
Koppal
Kudalsangamam
Amaravati
Guntur
Bezwada
Ellore
Rajahmundry
Vairagarh
Jagdalpur
Udayagiri
Mahendragiri

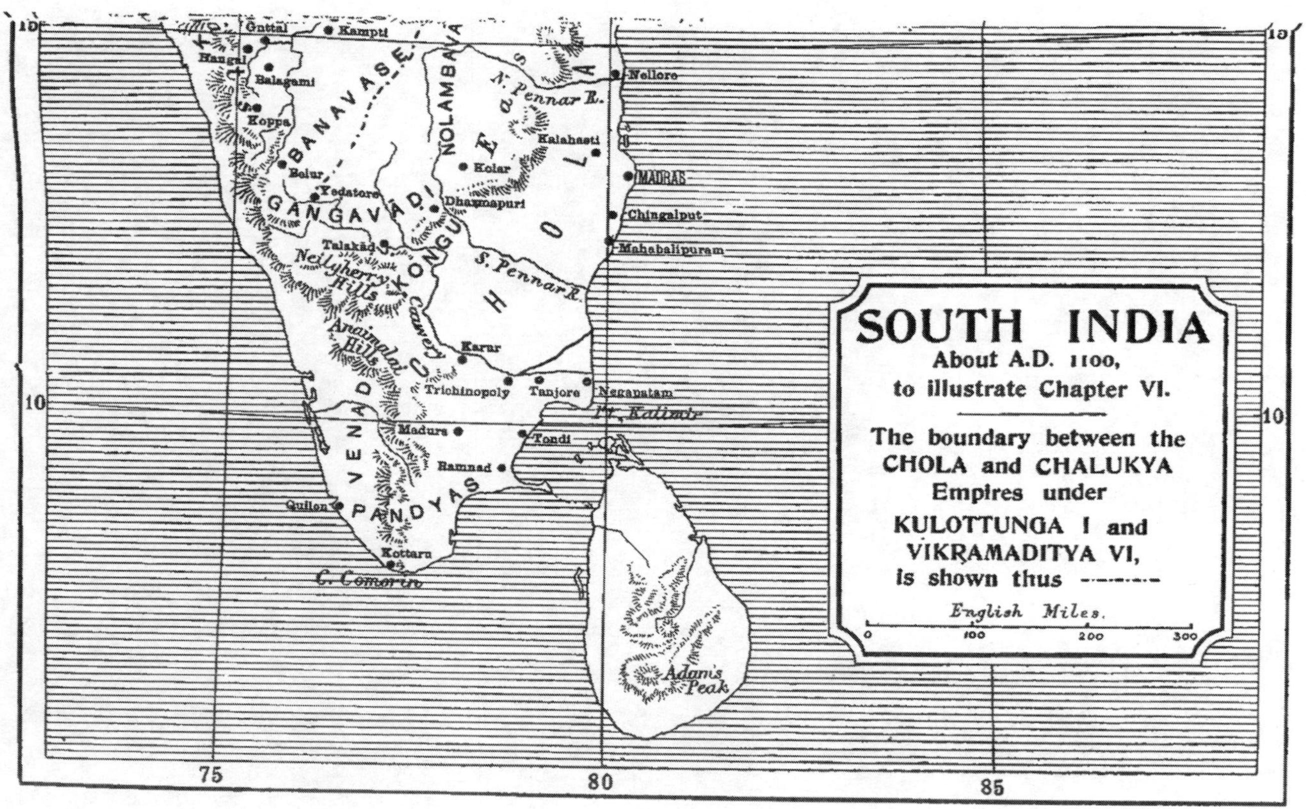
SOUTH INDIA
About A.D. 1100,
to illustrate Chapter VI.
The boundary between the CHOLA and CHALUKYA Empires under KULOTTUNGA I and VIKRAMADITYA VI, is shown thus
English Miles.
0
100
200
300
Guttal
Kampti
Hangal
Balagami
Koppa
Belur
Yedatore
Talakād
BANAVASE
GANGAVĀDI
NOLAMBAVA
KONGU
Neilgherry Hills
Anaimalai Hills
Cauvery
Kolar
Dharmapuri
Kalahasti
Nellore
N. Pennar R.
S. Pennar R.
MADRAS
Chingalput
Mahabalipuram
Karur
Trichinopoly
Tanjore
Negapatam
Madura
Tondi
Ramnad
Quilon
Kottaru
C. Comorin
VENAD
PANDYAS
Adam's Peak
75
80
85
10
15

Bombay; (3) the Silāharas of Kolhapur; (4) next come the Kaḍambas of Goa; (5) to the east of these their cousins the Kaḍambas of Hāngal in Dharwar; (6) east of these come the Sindas of Yelburga; (7) then the Guṭṭas of Guṭṭal in Dharwar; (8) next the Raṭṭas of Saundatti; (9) Banavase, often under the Kaḍambas of Hangal, after Jayasimha's rebellion; (10) Nolambavāḍi, under the Pandya chiefs of Uchchangidurg; (11) Gangavāḍi under the Hoysala Erē-yanga and his sons Beḷḷāla and Vishṇuvardhana; (12) Tārdawāḍi round Bijāpur. Besides these, there were the viceroyalties in the head-quarters territory, namely, round Gobbur, Kammaravāḍi and Sitabaldi in the Nizam's Dominions and the neighbouring parts of the Central Provinces; these three having been under Rāshṭrakūṭa (the first two) and the Haihaya chiefs, respectively.

Except for the rebellion of prince Jayasimha, viceroy of Banavase and the two invasions across the Narbadha before the years A.D. 1088-9, and between that year and A.D. 1098, there was peace throughout the empire. But the monotony of it was broken by an invasion, probably of the eastern Chāḷukya dominions. There are inscriptions referring themselves to Vikramāditya's reign at Drākshārama and at other places beyond his dominions, although Bilhaṇa says that he was for sometime in occupation of Kanchi. But towards the end of his reign, the danger to the empire already showed itself in the advancing power of a Mysore chief. It has more than once been noticed before that the southern provinces of the empire constituted the premier viceroyalty, and it is here that the greatest generalship was called forth. The Hoysalas were making themselves masters in reality of the Gangavāḍi 96,000, of which they had been nominal viceroys for two generations. Vinayāditya first, then Erēyanga his son, and then the latter's son Vishṇuvardhana, through the loyal exertions of Ganga Raja, a dispossessed scion apparently of the Ganga family, now turned out the Cholas and took Talakāḍ, the head-quarters of the Chola viceroyalty on or before A.D. 1117. This enhanced the reputation, and not less the resources of the Hoyśala, who was advancing his power northwards by attacking Noḷambavāḍi and Banavase. This movement appears to have been synchronous with that of the Kaḍambas of Goa and the Silāharas of Konkan. The empire was saved this dismemberment by the watchful activity and energy of the Sinda chieftain, Achugi II, who defeated the Hoysala forces under Ganga Raja, (which had marched up to the Krishnavēṇi (the Krishna river), in a night attack at Kannegāla and chased them to Belūr. He then turned in the other direction and chased the others across the western ghats and took Goa.

Notwithstanding this, Vikramāditya continued to rule till the year A.D. 1126, or possibly A.D. 1127. He appears to have been a liberal patron of letters and religion. In his court flourished the Kasmirian poet Bilhaṇa, who evidently wandered through the country in search of a patron, as did Vijñānēsvara the author of the *Mitākshara* system of Hindu Law. In religion he displayed the usual liberalism of Indian monarchs. From inscription 124 of Shikarpur, we find that as viceroy he got a Jīnālaya constructed at Baḷḷigāve. His father, be it remembered, died a Śaiva. From the founding of Tiruvikramāpura and the construction of palaces, temples, etc., near the temple of Vishṇu Kamalāvilasin, as Bilhaṇa records, he probably was a Vaishṇava. Nevertheless a Dombal inscription of A.D. 1095, records grants made to the Vihāras of Buddha and Āryā Tārādēvi at that town. That Buddhism had its following is borne out by inscription 170 of Shikarpur,[2] that the great minister, the

[2] *Epi. Car*, vol. vii.

Daṇḍanāyaka Rūpabhaṭṭayya, who was in charge of the (Vaḍḍarāvuḷa) principal taxes and the eighteen Agrahāras, established the Jayanti Bauddha Vihāra in Baḷḷigave and made grants to it and for the worship of Tārā Bhagavatī, and of the gods Kēsava, Lōkesvara and Bauddha with all their attendant gods, etc., in A.D. 1068. Vikramāditya had at least six wives, all of whom probably were not alive at once; but of his children we know of only three; Jayakarṇa, viceroy of some territory in the Bijāpur division which he ruled by deputy; Somēsvara III Bhūlōkamalla, who succeeded him; and a daughter Mailāḷa Devi, who married the Kaḍamba Jayakēsin II of Goa. He started an era from A. D. 1076 known as the Chāḷukya Vikrama, which did not get into such general vogue as to supersede the Śaka era. It went out of use in the course of a century. Usurping the empire, Vikramāditya perhaps rendered a service to it by preserving it from dismemberment for another half a century, and we might say that he added to it southern and eastern Mysore. It was this same addition that carried with it unmistakable germs of dismemberment, and, as will be seen later on, the Hoysala benefactors of the empire were the chief instruments, which caused it to break up.

Turning now from the Chāḷukya to the Chola empire, Kulōttunga had by his fifteenth year introduced order into the revolted provinces, in the most persistent of which he even went the length of planting military colonies not in the Roman fashion, but by allotting territory to his officers, who would occupy the settlement at the head of the forces at their command.[1] The next year A. D. 1086, a year

[1] This is borne out by his inscriptions being found at Māramangalam and Akkaśālai on the site of the ancient Korkai, thus supporting Kulōttunga's claim to have shut in the Pandya on the side of the Gulf of Mannar. *Epigraphist's Report* for 1904, p. 12.

before the domesday survey, he seems to have undertaken a re-survey of some parts, at least, of his dominions. This fact is referred to in two inscriptions in the Tanjore district, and the unit of measure was the Srīpāda (the royal foot) of Kulōttunga. But that such surveys used to be, and had been, accurately carried out much earlier is attested by the references to the book (புத்தகம்) in the Tamil and Kaḍitha in the Kanarese countries.[1]

One achievement of Kulōttunga which deserved a whole work to celebrate it in the estimation of his contemporaries, and perhaps himself, is the conquest of Kalingam for him by his general Karuṇākara Toṇḍamān of Vanḍai, or Vanḍalūr. The work referred to is the Tamil poem known as the *Kalingattupparani* of Jayaṃkoṇḍān, who was the Kavichakravarti at the court of Kulōttunga as Bilhaṇa was the Vidyāpati at Kalyāṇa. This conquest of Kalingam is also among the achievements of Vikrama Chola. So far as Kulōttunga is concerned there are clearly two invasions of Kalingam referred to. The Tiruviḍamarudūr inscription of his twenty-sixth year refers to an invasion of Kalingam, but strangely enough his later inscriptions, which narrate accurately his other achievements, omit it. This would warrant the inference that it was not the achievement which invited the classic of Jayaṃkoṇḍān. The next reference to a conquest of Kalingam is in the inscriptions of his forty-second and forty-fifth years. This great conquest therefore ought to have taken place in or before A. D. 1112, while the first one was before A. D. 1095-6. Kalingam figures among places conquered by Rājarāja the Great and his son Rajēndra. After the death in A. D. 1078 of Rājarāja of Trikalinga, his son Anantavarman Choḍa Ganga was on the throne till A. D. 1146.

[1] See Govt. *Epigraphist's Report* for 1900, sec. 25, p. 11.

According to the Tēki plates[1] of Rājarāja Choḍa Ganga, vcieroy of Vengi and the eldest son of Kulōttunga, issued in A. D. 1084, the boundary of the Vengi was Mannēru in the Nellore district in the south and Mahēndragiri in Ganjam in the north. This would show that south Kalingam was already under the Cholas. While therefore the first invasion might possibly have been to drive out some intruder into this remote frontier which was easy of accomplishment, the next one must have been of a formidable character. This probably was the occasion when Vikramāditya penetrated into Vengi (which would account for inscriptions of his reign at Drākshārāma), according to Bilhaṇa, after long years of peace. He must have been compelled to retire. We have seen already that Vīrarājēndra marched into Kalingam, and if Mr. Venkyya's identification of the Rājēndra Chola the father of Rājyasundari, wife of the Kalinga Rājarāja and mother of Anantavarman Choḍa Ganga, with Rājēndra Chola II be correct, then it is possible that Kulōttunga undertook the grand invasion of northern Kalingam or Sapta Kalingam, the king of which according to the *Kalingattupparani* failed to appear with his tribute. This appears to receive support from the fact that the Kalinga Choḍa Ganga's increase of power took place during the years A. D. 1087 to A. D. 1118-19. In the Vizagapatam plates of the latter year he assumes titles and a magnificent genealogy, which are not found in the plates of the earlier year. He further boasts in the latter of having restored 'the fallen lord of Utkala (Orissa) in the eastern region,' and the 'waning lord of Vengi' in the western.[2]

[1] *Epigraphia Indica*, vol. vi, p. 334, et seq.

[2] *Vide* Gov. *Epigraphist's Report for* 1905, p. 53. It may be noticed here that there was some direct relation of a friendly character between the Cholas and the rulers at Kanouj at the time, Madanapāla and his son Gōvindachandra. *Vide Epigraphist's Report for* 1908,

10

If this be the correct view of the event, then the composition of the *Kalingattupparaṇi* will have to be brought down to somewhere near A. D. 1112, rather than to a period of about fifteen years earlier, a date hitherto fixed for it. The credit of this expedition, according to this work, is entirely due to Karuṇākara Toṇḍamān of Vaṇḍai (Vaṇḍalūr), but the inscriptions of Vikrama Chola lay claim to some very creditable performance on the part of the prince. It is very probable that the prince did bear his share in the glorious achievement of the conquest of northern Kalingam.

Before bringing the reign of Kulōttunga to a close, there is one more event of importance to be discussed which took place during the last year of his reign. It is the conquest of Gangappāḍi, for the Chālukyas ostensibly, by the Hoysala chief, Biṭṭa Dēva, helped by his general Ganga Raja. This is recorded in detail only in inscriptions of A. D. 1116 and A. D. 1117, and the conquest could not have taken place very much earlier. Ganga Raja claims to have driven the Chola army across the Kaveri, and having ousted Adiyamān and Narasimha Brahma. The general then occupied Talakāḍ, the Chola capital on the Kaveri. This was the crowning achievement of a series of enterprises by the Mysore chiefs to shake off the yoke of the Cholas imposed upon them over a century since, by another Rājēndra Chola. Thenceforward, the Chāḷukya boundary nominally at least extended to Kongu, Nangali and Kōyatūr in the south. So far as we know at present, Kulōttunga's forty-ninth year is the latest, and this would bring his reign to an end in A. D. 1118, just six years before that of his rival contemporary which took place in A. D. 1126.

sec. 58, Ins. at Gangaikoṇḍa Sōḷapuram, containing the Gāhadwal-genealogy.

This half century was a period of consolidation for the Chola empire, as it also was for the Chāḷukya. The administration was carried on on the lines laid down, as in fact must have been the case even before, to a great extent, by Rājarāja the Great. It is the idea of permanent peace that led to Kulōttunga's military outsettlements in the Pandya, and Kēraḷa frontier, for we find a Tanjore general endowing a temple, with the emperor's sanction, at Śōḷapuram near Kōṭṭāṛu which was not far off Cape Comorin, which is now in the Travancore country. Except the loss of southern and eastern Mysore the empire remained intact. When he died, it was at peace, surrounded by friendly powers all round, except on the Mysore frontier, where further aggression was very carefully checked. The danger when it befell the empire came from all quarters, but in the meanwhile, that the empire held together was due to the far-seeing arrangements of the great Chola monarchs of whom, we may say, this was the last. Kulōttunga had three queens, namely, Dina Chintāmaṇi (probably Madurāntaki, daughter of Rajēndra), Ēḷiśaivallabhi and Tyāgavalli. This last was the queen entitled, according to the *Kalingattupparaṇi*, to issue orders along with Senni (Kulōttunga I). She became chief queen only in A. D. 1095. Hence the latter work must have been composed between A.D. 1095 and A. D. 1118.

I shall show a little later on what the rural government was, and describe in some detail the actual machinery of the Chola administration. That these were not the invention even of the great Rājarāja is borne out by the inscriptions at Tiruppāṛkaḍal, near Kaverīppāk (then known Kavidippākkam), of dates between Parāntaka I and Rājarāja. We find mention here of a number of village committees in addition to those detailed in the following part:—

The tank committee, the garden-supervision committee and the general committee of management. The new ones are :—(1) the great men for the supervision of wards (Kuḍumbu), (2) the great men for the supervision of the fields; (3) the great men numbering two hundred; (4) the great men for the supervision of the village; (5) the great men for supervising Udāsīnas (ascetics). These committees, together with the learned Brahmans (Bhaṭṭar) and other distinguished men of the village, constituted the village assembly. We sometimes come across the Grāma Kōn (chief of the village). There appear to have been individuals in charge of particular wards of the village. The following is an extract from an inscription at Perumbūr near Madurāntakam of A. D. 1081. 'The above (grant) was ordered by Śaṭṭai Govindbhaṭṭar of Irāyūr (in charge of) Srīmadhurāntakacheri, Kuṉṟakuḻi Sōmayājiār of Uṟuppaṭṭūr (in charge of Srī Parāntakachchēri; Kāṭṭugai Nārāyana-kramavittar of Nambūr (in charge of) Srī Iṟumuḍiśoḻachchēri; Srī Krishnabhaṭṭar of Araṇīpuram (in charge of) Srī Simhḷāntakachchēri; Nārāyanabhaṭṭar-Sarvakratuvājapēyayajiar of Pippirai (in charge of) Srīvīrasōḻachchēri, etc.

With reference to the re-survey undertaken in A.D. 1086, I have had to differ from the late Mr. Srinivasa Raghava Aiyangar as to the interpretation of 'calculated' and 'settled produce' (காணிக்கடன் and இறை கட்டினது [1] That these meant the tax as assessed and that as settled after experience, if not experiment, and that such revisions and reductions of land revenue were known in those days are in evidence in the following extract. 'To (the god) Mahādēva of (the temple of) Rajēndra Śōḻīsvara, which Araiyan Madhurāntakan *alias* Kulōttunga-Śoḻa-Kēraḷarajan, the lord

[1] These were interpreted as gross produce and the government demand by the accomplished author of *The Forty years' Progress*, but he was so good as to admit in a kind letter that it was possible 'he was all wrong', as he took the information from Dr. Burnell's *Palæography* and did not consult the inscriptions first hand.

of Mulanjūr in Mannināḍu, a district of Solamandalam had caused to be built at Koṭṭāru *alias* Mummuḍi Solanallūr, in Nānjināḍu (a sub-division) of Uttama Śolavalanāḍu, a district of Rājarāja Pāndinādu, shall be paid, for the expenses required by this god, from the thirtieth year (of my reign) forty-five and a half, three-twentieths, and one-fortieth, Māḍai, by the village of Āndāykkuḍi in the same Nāḍu. According to (the settlement of) payments (that had taken place in the seventh year after the accession of Rājēndra Śōla Dēva), (this) tax was paid instead of the (original) land tax of seventy-nine Kāśu and three-hundred and twenty-four kalam of paddy. The previous name of this village having been cancelled and the name of Rājendra Śolanallūr (having been substituted), let it be entered in the revenue register (vari) as a tax free Devadāna from the thirtieth year (of my reign) including rents, internal revenue, and small rights such as Ūrk-kalanju, Kumārakachāṇam, the fishing rent, the tax on looms, the rent on the goldsmiths, Māḍaikūli, Daśa-vandam, and Kālalavukūli).'[1] The government shewed itself otherwise interested in rural prosperity by the establishment of an agricultural settlement of twenty-four families at Tiruvālangāḍu.[2] The Tiruvānaikkāval inscription of the year A.D. 1117 states that 'as these four and three-quarters (vēli) of land had been lying full of holes and sand as uncultivated dry land, until the forty-seventh year of this king, we (the assembly) agreed to sell the land to Muṇayan Arumoḷidēvaṇ *alias* Villavaraiyan for purchase money of 4, $\frac{1}{20}$, $\frac{1}{80}$ good kāśu current at the time.' About this time land was selling in the Uḍaiyārpāliam Taluka, not very far off, at twenty kāśu per vēli[3] 'Having dug and reclaimed the four and three quarter (vēli) of land, he has to supply for these four

[1] *South Ind. Ins.*, vol. iii, pt. ii, p. 162.
[2] No. 65, vol. iii, pt. ii, *South Ind. Ins.*
[3] *South Ind: Ins.*, vol. iii, pt. ii, p. 152.

and three-quarters (vēli) of land to the temple treasury twenty-three kalam, two tūni and one kuruṇi of paddy by the marakkal called after Rājakēsari ; viz. five kalam for each vēli at the rate of dry land, etc.'[1] . . . Such are the few glimpses we get into the revenue arrangements of those days. The standard coin now appears to be the māḍai, sometimes called madhurāntakan māḍai. This was equal to two kāsu and to five and a half kalams of paddy, the price of which varied sharply according to locality and to time. The tax māḍaikkūli, as a minor tax, perhaps refers to the seigniorage upon coining. The standard dry measure was the marakkāl, either rājakēsari as above or arumoḷidēvan, both of the days of Rājarāja ; and the Ēkanāth measure for ghee or arumoḷidevanuḷakku. There is mention also of canals and roads, as in other Chola inscriptions, and of the use of the rod of sixteen spans for measuring land. More than all, this Kulōttunga's fame stood high as the 'Sungandavirta Chola' (the Chola who abolished tolls). That he was regarded with so much gratitude for this act shews that the tax was oppressive, and that the ruler wise and statesman-like. This one act gave him a place in the popular esteem along with the 'good Cholas of yore'.

Kulōttunga's age was also one of great religious and literary revival. In his reign flourished the Vaishṇava reformer Rāmānuja, who had to betake himself to Mysore to avoid the displeasure of Kulōttunga. Jayaṃkonḍān was his Kavichakravarti and possibly the commentator of the *Śilappadhikāram*, Aḍiyārkkunallār did not live much later, as he quotes twice from Jayaṃkonḍān, once acknowledging the authority by name and another time by the simple mention Kavichakravarti. This would have been far from clear, if made much after Jayaṃkonḍān's time as

[1] *South Ind. Ins.*, vol. iii, pt. ii, p. 171.

there were other Kavichakravartis in the interim. The Śaiva writer Śekkiḻār, author of the *Periyapurāṇam*, also flourished in his court. While dealing with the literary activity of Kulottunga's reign, we might mention that an inscription of his eighteenth year (A. D. 1088), at Srīrangam settles a point or two much animadverted upon recently, consequent on the idea of Caldwell, who thought that before the twelfth or the thirteenth century A. D. there was not much Tamil literature worth the name, and that the Vaishṇava Āḻvārs lived about the same time. This inscription refers to the text '*Tēṭṭar-undiraḷ*' of Kulāsekarāḻvār, one of the latest Āḻvārs. If his text began to be chanted in presence of god Ranganātha on a festival day, he must have lived sometime before at least; but prince Soḻa Keraḷa a little earlier than Kulōttunga made provision for the recital of this and another set of Tirumangaiāḻvār's verses also. All this was before Rāmānuja had made himself the chief of the Vaishṇavas at Srīrangam. In spite of this, Mr. Gopinatha Rao[1] would have us believe that these were contemporaries of Āḻavandār, the great grandfather of Rāmānuja, who died when Rāmānuja had grown up to be a promising young man. It would appear too much of an idiosyncrasy on the part of the Srīvaishṇavas to regard Āḻavandār only as an Āchārya and his Tamilian contemporaries Āḻvārs.

The second point raised by this inscription is about Nammāḻvār, the author of the Tiruvōymoḻi. Three Srīvaishṇava Brahmans are named, Shaṭagopadāsar, Tiruvaḷudināḍudāsar and Kurugaikkāvalan, all names and surnames of Nammāḻvār. An inscription at Ukkal of the time of Rājarāja I names the god himself Tirvōymoḻideva. These lead us to believe, with Dr. Hultzsch, that Nammāḻvār lived much anterior to the eleventh century A. D.

[1] *Vide* articles in the *Madras Review*, for 1905, February and May.

We now come to the decline of the Chola Power. With the death of Kulōttunga the period of the great Cholas comes practically to a close. As already stated, he himself had to acquiesce in the loss of the Gangavāḍi country His successors, even the most capable of them, could barely maintan their position intact for just a century and no more. All the time the Chāḷukya empire was as much on the decline; and it is only when the new powers, that rose out of the ashes of this empire, began their aggressions that the position of the Cholas became seriously endangered.

Vikramachola, Akaḷanka, Tyāgasamudra: Kulōttunga was succeeded by his fourth son Vikrama, who was viceroy at Vengi on behalf of his father. He seems to have been a warlike prince, and engaged early in the wars of this father. He distinguished himself first against 'Telunga Bhīma' of Kolanu (Bhīma Nāyaka of Ellore). He is also said to have burnt the country of Kalinga and this must have reference to some achievement of his during his father's invasions of Kalingam.[1] He was then appointed viceroy of Vengi in succession to his two elder brothers who preceded him in the viceroyalty. It was from this high position that he proceeded to the empire almost at the end of his father's reign, in A. D. 1118. The latest known date of his reign so far is his seventeenth year. His reign seems to have been otherwise uneventful. He continued the policy of his father and maintained court on the same enlightened lines. He is credited with having accepted the dedication of the *Kalingattupparaṇi*[2] by the author Jayṃgonḍān, who in the work celebrated the exploits of Karuṇākara Tonḍamān on the one side, and the greatness of his master on the other. He is believed to have

[1] *Epigraphist's Report* for 1906, sec. 18.
[2] *Kulōttunga Cholanulā.*

been a Vaishṇava, and it seems to be this monarch who is mentioned by Kamban as 'Tyagamāvinōdan.'[1] It was perhaps in his reign that Rāmānuja, the Vaishṇava apostle, returned to his native country, after having gone into a long period of exile.

Kulōttunga II Rājakēsarivarman, Tribhavanachakravartin: Vikrama's son Kulōttunga II succeeded his father. His initial date has not yet been ascertained with certainty, though his latest regnal year is the fourteenth year. He is the Kumāra Kulōttunga of literature. He has been celebrated by his tutor and court poet, Oṭṭakkūttan, in more than one poem of his. It is in this author's *Kulōttungachōḷan Ulā* and *Takkayāgapparaṇi* that the fact is mentioned, with some little elation, that the Vishṇu shrine at Chidambaram was removed and the image thrown into the sea. It was this image that was taken over by Rāmānuja and established at Tirupati. After a reign of fourteen years he was succeeded by his son Rājarāja II. The latest known regnal year of his is fifteen. He was succeeded by Rājādhiraja II. Year thirteen is his latest known year. The period between A. D. 1118 and 1178 is occupied by the reigns of these four rulers. Their period was one of considerable literary activity. Sēkkiḻār, Kamban, Oṭṭakkūttan, Pugaḻēndi and possibly Aḍiyārkkunallār are names that any age might well be proud of. It was in the reign of the last of these that a civil war began in the Pandya dominions and involved in it the Cholas and the Ceylonese. There were two rivals for the crown of the Pandyas at Madura. Parākramabāhu the Great, king of Ceylon, espoused the cause of Parākrama Pandya; while his rival Kulasēkhara had the sympathy of the Chola for the time being. Some, at least, of the Chola feudatories regarded the presence of the Ceylonese as a

[1] *Kamba Rāmāyanam, Yuddhakhāndam, Maruthuppadalam*, 58.

menace to be got rid of at any cost, and one of them, Pallavaraiyar son of Edirili Śoḷa Śambhuvarāyar, distinguished himself in this affair. Lankhāpura Daṇḍanātha, the Ceylonese general, captured and plundered Ramēsvaram, and took Toṇḍi and Pāśa and marched upon Madura. Meanwhile their protege Parākrama Pandya was murdered by his rival, who drove his son a fugitive for shelter. The approach of the Ceylonese was opposed by Kulasēkhara, who was defeated and driven into the Chola country for protection. The Ceylon general having fetched Vīra Pandya, the son of their ally, placed him on the throne, and advanced upon the Chola country itself. It was then that the Chola general, by a supreme effort, managed to compel the Ceylon army to retreat. This war was continued later on in the reign in behalf of Vikrama Pandya, the son of the former Chola ally Kulasēkhara. The Chola army advanced this time right up to Madura, put Vīra Pandya and his children to death, and took possession of Madura. Having erected a pillar of victory there, they gave the kingdom over to their ally and returned. It is this achievement that was the cause of the assumption of the title 'the conqueror of Madura and Īḷam' by Rājādhirāja II and his son Kulōttunga III later on.[1]

Kulōttungachola III, Parakēsari, Tribhuvanachola Vīrarajēndra, and Kōnērinmaikoṇḍān, A. D. 1178 to 1216: Kulōttunga III already distinguished himself in the war of the Pandya succession in the reign of his father; but he had again to intervene in the affairs of the Pandya kingdom. Before the nineteenth year of his reign he had to overthrow the son of Vīra Pandya who was able to restore himself by ousting the Chola protege Vikrama Pandya. This time the Chola not only defeated him at Neṭṭūr, but also put to death

[1] *Epigraphist's Report* for 1899, secs. 23-39.

the former's son and placed Vikrama Pandya on the throne. He then pardoned Vīra Pandya and his ally Vīra Kēraḷa. He had, about the same time to march upon Kanchi and beat off an enemy, who may have been a Telugu Chola chief of the family that came to prominence in the next reign. Kulōttunga III was a great builder and renovator of temples, particularly those of Śiva. He appears to have been the original of the stories regarding some of the great Śiva shrines in the Tanjore district[1].

It was in this reign that some of those feudatory families began to appear, who contributed eventually their share to the general break up of the Chola empire. We have already referred to the family of the Śambuvarāyan near Kanchi. Another family that of the Adigaimāns, descendants of Eḻini (Yavanika) appear at and about Tagaḍūr (Dharmapuri). A third family of importance was that of the Telugu Cholas of Nellore (Trivikramāpura). These were beginning to grow in influence and importance, perhaps owing to the fluctuating wars of the Pandya succession in which many of these had each its share. Kulōttunga, however, enjoyed peace during his reign, except for the disturbances in the southern frontier and in the north, already adverted to, which lasted for thirty-seven years. During this long period great changes had taken place in the politics of the Dekhan. The great Hoysala chieftains, who were such stout pillars of the empire under the Chāḷukya Vikramāditya, began their movements towards independence even while that emperor was alive. Their northern neighbours, the Yadavas, had similarly laid their plans to detach the north-western parts of the empire. The Kākatīya chiefs in the eastern parts had their own ambitions as well. It is these three that stand out among

1 *Epigraphist's Report* for 1908, secs. 63-8.

a host of the feudatories of all degrees of Vikramāditya. What was wanted for the actual dismemberment of the empire was a civil war, or internal dissentions ending in a usurpation. This was just the course that events took in this part of India at the time. Muḥammad of Ghazni had come and gone, and the Rajputs were giving the fullest play to their petty jealousies. Similar feelings actuated the principal Sirdars of the empire in the Dekhan, except for a family or two of loyalists. The weakness and ineptitude of the successors of Vikramāditya led to the Kalachūrya usurpation, and the contest later on between this dynasty and the loyalist general Bamma (Brahma). These changes relieved the Yadavas and Hoysalas of their feelings of loyalty, and they began to settle their frontiers by war. As the Hoysalas, under one of their great rulers, were thus fully occupied in carving out for themselves an empire of their own, the Chola frontier on its most vulnerable side was safe from aggressive movements till late in the reign of Kulōttunga III. The death of Vīra Beḷḷaḷa II took place just a few years earlier than that of his Chola contemporary. His successor Narasimha II felt his Krishna frontier so safe that he could turn his attention to the south where matters were developing fast for his intervention. It was in the reign of Kulōttunga III that the Tamil Grammar *Nannūl* was written by its Jain author Bhava Nandin.[1]

Tribhuvanachchakravartin Rājarāja III, Rajakēsarivarman, succeeded to the throne of the Cholas in the year A.D. 1216. His latest known year is the twenty-eighth year and in all probability his reign came to an end in A.D. 1243-4. At the outset of his reign there seems to have been a contest, although there is nothing known as to its particular character. The fact,

[1] *Epigraphia Indica*, vol. vi, p. 281. *South Ind. Ins.*, vol. iii, No. 62.

however, that Narasimha Hoysala felt it necessary to advance as far as Trichinopoly, and even further, and that he felt justified in assuming the title of benefactor of the Chola would warrant the inference that there was a civil disturbance of some sort. It would seem as though the Pandyas were moving into the Chola kingdom in revenge for the humiliation to which they had been subjected so lately by Kulōttunga III. Narasimha II promptly marched forth in support of his ally, the more readily as the Pandyas, at least the section hostile to the Cholas, found ready support among the Kongus. He reached the heart of the Chola empire, compelled the Pandyas to retreat and even cowed the recalcitrant barons of the empire into submission, and then returned to his dominions. These transactions have to be ascribed to a period before A. D. 1223-4. The next time he intervened was about the year A. D. 1232. This time he came having heard that Rājarāja was a prisoner in the hands of the Kāḍava chief Kōpperunjingadeva, as he styled himself later on. This Pallava chief came into prominence during the Pandya invasion and as was only too probable, as a consequence thereof. His head-quarters were at Sēndamangalam in the South Arcot district.[1] Narasimha moved down as quickly as before and restored the Chola to his own. Two of his generals were ordered to continue operations till the disturbances in the country should be put an end to, and as was to be expected they carried out his orders so well that the restored Chola continued to rule undisturbed till about the year A D. 1242-3. But the storm was gathering all the same. The Telugu Chola Ṭikka, otherwise Gaṇḍagopala, was inclined to move down from his capital at Nellore. Māravarman Sundara Pandya was advancing from the south, and

[1] *Epigraphā Indica*, vol ii, p. 163.

Kōpperunjinga was ready to take advantage of it all in the interior. The confusion was worse confounded by a rival in the person of Rājēndra Choladeva III. Kōpperunjinga assumes royal titles, Sundara Pandya crowns himslf at Muḍikonḍaśoḷapuram, and Vīrā Somēsvara of Mysore prides himself upon having restored the Chola. The last of these, for sometime had a capital at Kaṇṇanūr near Srīrangam, and the Pandyas and the Hoysalas fight in this vicinity. The feudatory Kōpperunjinga beats back the northern invader, and establishes himself independently in the northern parts of the Chola empire. 'It were long to tell, and sad to trace each step from ruin to disgrace.' The empire that the great Cholas built at so great an expense of labour and skill thus passed ingloriously out of existence through the ineptitude of a ruler or perhaps two, who while occupying the position could not command the resources, either of ability in themselves or the sagacity to find and use it in others. This is quite the way with earthly empires and the Chola empire could not be an exception; but this must be said to the credit of its founders and maintainers that they did their work well and wisely so far as they could—nay so far as man could.

PART II—THE CHOLA ADMINISTRATION

(A. D. 900 to 1300)

HAVING attempted, in the previous part to give a connected account of the Chola empire, let me now proceed to bring together what little is known of their system of administration.

To follow in the wake of Sir William Lee-Warner, I shall begin with the unit of administration of the Cholas, which was the village-community, composed either of a single village, or oftener of a group of villages. This union was called in Tamil 'kūṟṟam'

PEDIGREE OF THE CHOLAS

- 1. Vijayālaya. (Parakēsarivarman, thirty-four years.)
  - 2. Āditya I.
    - 3. Parāntaka. (A. D. 907 to *circa* 947.)
      - 4. Rajāditya d. A.D. 949-50.
      - 5. Gandāradittan 956-7.
        - 9. Madurāntaka Parakēsari ; Uttāmachola 969-70 and 16 years.
      - 6. Arinjaya. Madhuraikonda and Rājakēsari.
        - 7. Parāntaka II Parakēsari, Sundara Chola and destroyer of Vīra Pandya.
          - 8. Āditya II (Karikāla) Rajakēsari.
          - Kundavvaiyar, m. Pallavaraiyar Vandyadēvar.
          - 10. Rājarāja I (A.D. 985 to *circa* A.D. 1013).
            - 11. Rajēndra, the Gangaikonda Chola (1011-2 to *circa* A.D. 1042-3).
              - 12. Rājādhirāja, Jayamgonḍa Chola (A. D. 1018 to 1052).
              - 13. Rajēndra (1050 to 1062-3).
                - 14. Rajamāhēndra.
                - Madhurantaki, m. 17. Rajēndra Chola, otherwise Kulōttunga (A. D. 1070 to 1118).
              - 15. Vīrarājēndra (1062-3 or 1063-4, to A. D. *circa* 1070).
                - 16. Adhirājarājēndra.
                - A daughter, m. Vikramāditya VI.
              - Ammāngadēvi, m. Rājarāja I 1022 to 1061-2 or one year later.
                - 17. Rajēndra Chola, otherwise Kulōttunga (A. D. 1070 to 1118), m. Madhurantaki.
                  - Chodaganga, viceroy of Vengi, A.D. 1084.
                  - Mummaḍi Chola, viceroy of Vengi, A. D. 1077.
                  - Vīra Choḍa, viceroy of Vengi, 1078 to 1088-9.
                  - 18. Vikrama Chola (A.D. 1118 to *circa* 1135).
                    - 19. Kulōttunga Chola II (1123 *circa* to 1146).
                      - 20. Rājarāja II (1146 *circa* to 1178).
                        - 21. Rājādhirāja II (A.D. 1171 to 1186).
                          - 22. Kulōttunga Chola II (A.D. 1178 to 1216).
                            - 23. Rājarāja III (1216 *circa* to 1248).
                              - 24. Rajēndra Chola III (A.D. 1245 to 1267).
                                - 25. Tribhuvana Vīra Dēva (A. D. 1331-2).
                  - Three other sons.
            - Kundavvaiyyar, m. East Chāḷukya Vimalāditya (A. D. 1011 to 1022).
              - Ammāngadēvi, m. Rājarāja I (see above).
              - Vijayāditya VII, viceroy of Vengi (1062-3 to 1076).
      - Prince Uttamaśīli.
      - Prince Arikulakēsari.

Note.—The dates of commencement of each ruler are those of the astronomically verified ones of Prof. Kielhorn ; while the terminal dates are based upon the last regnal years as yet available from epigraphical sources. The names of the monarchs that ruled are numbered.

(or sub-division). Each one of these sub-divisions had an assembly of its own called the mahāsabha. This assembly, though subject to supervision by the divisional officers or intendants (Adhikārins), exercised an almost sovereign authority in all the departments of rural administration. To illustrate this rural administration, I shall take as a specimen the village of Ukkal near Māmaṇḍūr on the road between Conjeeveram and Wandiwash. The fourteen published inscriptions from this place give us a better insight into the rural administration than any other equal number I could choose. I extract therefore, from the records the following account of the powers and duties of the assembly :—

Ukkal[1] was in Pāgūr nāḍu sub-division of the Kaliyūr kōṭṭam in the Toṇḍa—or the Jayaṃgoṇḍa Chola—maṇḍalam. According to other records Ukkal belonged to its own sub-division of the same kōṭṭam (Sans-kōshṭaka).

No. 1. The assembly received 200 kaḻanju of gold from Tiruvikrama Bhaṭṭa *alias* Brahmādhirājar, one among the commissioners of Uttaramēruchaturvēdimangalam (Uttaramallur) for feeding twelve Brahmans before the god of Puvanimāṇikkavinnagar received his noon-day offerings.'

No. 2. States that the assembly received 550 kuḻi of land measured by 'the graduated rod', made over to them by Nārāyana Rājasimha, a native of the Chola country, to supply the god with four nāḻi of rice daily. 'Having received the revenue of this land and having exempted it from taxes for as long as the moon and sun exist, we, the assembly, engraved this on stone.'

No. 3. Records that a certain Peṟṟān Ādittan of the Chola country purchased two pieces of land, the first from a private person and the second from the

[1] *South Ind. Ins.*, vol. iii, pt. i.

village assembly, and made over both pieces to the villagers for maintaining a flower-garden. 'The same person had purchased from us, the assembly, for a flower-garden 501 kuḻi of land measured by the graduated rod to the west of the irrigation channel, etc.' 'Having received in full the purchase-money and the revenue of the land . . . and having exempted the flower-garden and (the land assigned) for the maintenance of the garden from taxes for as long as the moon and the sun exist, we, the assembly, engraved this on stone.' 'Having been present in the assembly and having heard this order, I, the arbitrator, Āyirattunūṟṟuvan *alias* Brahmaguṇākhara Vidhyāsthāna Mangaḷāditya Samanjasapriyan, the son of Nālāyiravan wrote this.'

No. 4. Kaṇṇan Ārūrān of the Chola country and a servant of Rājarāja, who got a well sunk and a cistern constructed by the roadside in the name of his royal master, made assignments of paddy for the upkeep of this charity. In order to supply this paddy, we, the assembly, of this village having received from him the revenue and the purchase-money, and having exempted the land from taxes, etc. . . .

No. 5. We have received, 1,000 kādi of paddy from Saḍayan. We, the assembly, shall close (the sluice of) the tank (to collect water for irrigation) and shall cause 500 kādi of paddy to be supplied every year as interest on those 1,000 kādi of paddy. The great men elected for the year (the Perumākkal) shall cause the paddy to be supplied.

No. 6. We, the great assembly of Sivachūḷāmaṇichaturvēdimangalam, including the great men elected for (the management of) charities during this year . . . in our village and the commissioners (in charge of the temple) of Śāttan in our village.' They make a grant to the temple of Mahāśāsta. 'The commissioners of the temple of Śāttan shall protect this charity.' 'The great men elected for the supervision of the tanks shall be entitled to levy a fine of one Kaḷanju of gold in favour of the tank-fund, from those betel-leaf sellers in this village, who sell (betel-leaf) elsewhere but at the temple of Piḍāri.'

No. 7. The inhabitants of our village . . . the lands, everything else that is not the object of deeds of gift, in the environs of the village, the common property (madhyama) of the assembly. We shall sell this land which has thus become common property (of the assembly) to those inhabitants who promise to pay taxes on each kuḷi. No person shall be allowed to produce deeds of gift or deeds of sale (âvaṇam) in order to show that the land thus sold belongs to himself. We, the assembly, shall levy a fine. 'Those inhabitants who do not submit to this, shall be liable to pay into Court (Dharmāsanā) a fine of 108 kānam . . . per day. If through indifference though . . . was thus given to those who pay the fine, and they themselves have fined them, they are not able to remove the obstacles to the possession, the great men elected for the year shall be liable to pay an additional fine of twenty-four kānam.'

No. 8. The assembly received 400 kādi of paddy from Saḍayan to feed two Brahmans from its interest of 100 kādi.

No. 9. The lord Sri Rājarājadēva, being graciously seated in the college (kallūri), on the south or the painted hall (chitrakūṭa at the great hippodrome gate in Tanjore was pleased to order as follows:—

'(The land of) those landholders in villages of Brahmans, in villages of Vaikānasas (a section of Vaishṇavas), in villages of Śramaṇas (Jains), in Śōṇāḍu, in Toṇḍanāḍu, and in Pandināḍu *alias* Rājarājavaḷanāḍu, who have not paid on the land owned by them, the taxes due from villages, along with the other inhabitants of those villages, for three years of which two are completed between the sixteenth and the twenty-third year of my reign, shall become the property of the villages and shall be liable to be sold by the inhabitants of those villages to the exclusion of the (defaulting) landholders. Also (the land of) those who have not paid the taxes due from villages for three years (of which), two are completed, from the twenty-fourth year of my reign shall be liable to be sold by the inhabitants of those villages to the exclusion of the (defaulting) landholders.' 'Accordingly, having been written by the royal secretary, Rajakēsarinallūr Kiḻavan, and having been approved of by the chief secretary Mummuḍichōla Brahmamārāyan, and Mummuḍichola Pōsan (Bhoja), this order was engrossed from dictation on the 143rd day of the twenty-fourth (year of my reign).'

No. 10. We have sold and executed a deed of sale for (i) 3,000 kuḷi measured by the rod of sixteen spans beginning (to measure from the west of the land which was the common property of the assembly . . (ii) five levers to the east of this land, etc. Having received in full the purchase-money and the revenue of the land, we, the great assembly, sold it free of taxes and executed a deed of sale. Having been present in the assembly and having heard the order, I, the accountant and arbitrator of this village, Pōṟṟikuḻi Kalidēvan *alias* Iranḍāyirattunūṟṟuvan wrote this.'

No. 11. We, the great assembly, including the men elected for the year, and the great men elected for the supervision of the tanks, assigned at the request of Chakrapāṇi Nambi. . . . 'Half a measure of land in the fresh clearing (Puduttiruttam on the west of the village of Sōḍiambākkam.'

No. 12. We, the assembly of Sivachūḷāmaṇichaturvēdimangalam, (ordered as follows) :—'To the god of Puvanimāṇikkavishṇugriham in our village shall belong as a divine gift (dēvabhōga), the village called

Sōḍiambākkam, etc. We shall not be entitled to levy any kind of tax from this village. We, (the great men) elected for the year, we, (the great men) elected for the supervision of the tanks, and we, (the great men) elected for the supervision of the gardens, shall not be entitled to claim at the order of the assembly, forced labour (veṭṭi), vedili, vālakkāṇam, from the inhabitants of this village. If a crime or sin becomes public, the god (temple authorities) alone shall punish this village.'

No. 13. A cultivator named Sēnai granted one paṭṭi (Sans. nivartana 40,000 Sq. hastas or hands) from the proceeds of which water and fire-pans had to be supplied to a manṭapa frequented by Brahmans. The great men who manage the affairs of this village in each year shall supervise this charity.

This series of extracts, from inscriptions ranging in time through three centuries, say from A. D. 800 to 1100, shows clearly how rural tracts were governed during those centuries. The village assembly were the sole government of the village (or village-unions) in all its departments. They were the absolute proprietors of the village lands. When fresh clearings were made the assembly became proprietor of the newly acquired lands. When lands were thrown out of cultivation, the Sabha took over the lands to give them to others, who would pay the stipulated taxes per kuḷi. It was the business of the assembly to see that the actual cultivator was not molested in the possession of his holding. Failing in their duty, 'the great men of the year' laid themselves open to be fined by the general assembly. The assembly received deposits of money and grants of land for charitable purposes, and administered the trusts by a board of commissioners, specially appointed for the purpose from year to year. They often sold common village lands for these purposes, and received in return the purchase-money and an additional sum, from the interest of which the assembly had to pay the state dues upon the alienated lands, made tax-free by themselves. They received all the taxes, and made independent grants of villages tax-free for purposes of charity, and could waive all customary claims on landholders. They could take over the lands of villagers for default of payment of taxes, the collection of which, however, appears to have been made with great elasticity. This is not all; they could even transfer jurisdiction over villages to other corporations, such as temple-authorities. Where they did not feel themselves competent to interfere they sought instruction from head-quarters, as in No. 9 quoted above, where the lands concerned were those made over to other proprietors. This record is a copy of a circular order issued by Rājarāja the Great. It was drafted by the royal secretary on the verbal instructions of the emperor himself, and approved of by the chief secretary (Ōlaināyakam), Srīkishnarāma *alias* Mummuḍichōla Brahmamārāyan, and Perundaram Īrāyiravan Pallavaiyan *alias* Mummuḍicōhla Pōśan (Bhōja), and then despatched to the mahāsabhas. These sabhas had treasuries of their own, as would appear from the inscriptions of Rājarāja at Tanjore which refer to up-country treasuries.

The great assembly of the village, or kūṟṟam was divided into several committees. There were certainly three—the great men elected for the year (a committee of the assembly for general management), the great men elected for the supervision of the tanks (another committee to administer the tank-fund and see them in good condition), and those elected for the supervision of gardens. There were besides the great men in charge of the temples, charities, etc. The work of this assembly was subject to supervision by the imperial divisional officers (adhikārins), often associated with the divisional commanders of the forces (sēnāpatis). These officers moved through their divisions, asked for the accounts, examined them and made allotments out of the royal revenues, which had, however, to be appropriated for the special purposes by the assemblies themselves.

No. 49. at Tiruvallam[1] records that a certain Madhurāntakan Kaṇḍarādittan, Kaṇḍarādittan, son of Madhurāntaka, 'while he stood in the temple observed that the offerings presented to the Āḷvār (god) were reduced to two nāḷi of rice: the offerings of vegetables, ghee and curds had ceased and the perpetual lamps had been neglected.' He called the Ś'aiva Brahmans of the temple and the assembly of Tīkkālivallam and said: 'State the revenue and expenditure of the temple in accordance with the royal order and the royal letter.' The rest of the inscription is unfortunately built in.

SUPERVISION

No. 57. at Tiruvallam[2] records that two royal officers, the magistrate (adhikāri) Purān Ā'dittadēvanār *alias* Rājarājēndra Mūvendavēḷan, and the Sēnāpati, Rājarāja, Paranriparākshasan *alias* Vīra Sōḷa Iḷangō (probably a prince of the blood) met at Gangaikondān Sōḷan manṭapa to the east of the temple of Tirumayānamuḍayār (the lord of the crematorium, another name of god Śiva) at Kanchipuram in Eyil nāḍu sub-division of Eyil kōṭṭam and called for the accounts of the villages which were the dēvadānas (divine gifts) of the temple of the lord of Tiruvallam (Tiruvallamuḍayār). 'The magistrate Rājarājēndra Mūvendavēḷān ordered as follows:—(The incomes) from the villages which are the 'dēvadanas' of this temple, viz. ūrkaḷanju, kumārakachchānam, the fishing rent, the rent of the goldsmiths and other minor taxes and rents, the cloth

[1] *South Ind. Ins.*, vol. iii, pt. i.
[2] *I bid*, vol. iii, pt. i.

on the loom, vēlikkāśu, the tax on collecting rents (tanḍal), the sonship of the right-hand and the left-hand and the other internal revenue, which was being collected at the rate of twenty-five kaśu per 1,000 kalam (of paddy) had been entered in the register, and made over to this temple exclusively from the year which was opposite to (i.e. followed after) the seventh year of the reign of the Emperor Srī Vīrarajēndradēva. Accordingly Kukkanūr a 'dēvdāna' of this god in Tūynāḍu sub-division of Perumbānappāḍi has to pay thirty-eight and a quarter kāśu or at the rate of four kalam of paddy by the Standard-measure (Rājakēsari) per kāśu, 153 kalams of paddy; and Mandiram in the same nāḍu has to pay twenty-six and a quarter kāśu or 153 kalams of paddy; altogether sixty-five kāśu or 260 kalams of paddy were allotted to this temple for expenses not previously provided for and should be given from the third year (of the king's reign). A large committee then assembled and made allotments from this revenue for various heads of temple expenditure. This is the kind of supervision to which the assembly of a subdivision was subject. Otherwise in all matters of fiscal administration the village assemblies were practically supreme.

In a record of the time of Āditya II Karikāla, it is stated that the village of Siṟṟiyāṟṟūr had been granted as a dēvadhana and as a brahmadēya in the twenty-first year of Tonḍamānāṟṟūr-Tunjina-Uḍaiyar to the Sabha of Puduppākkam in the same nāḍu and kōṭṭam, on condition that the donee made over a certain quantity of the produce of the village and a fixed sum of money in gold every year to the temple of Mahādeva at Tirumālpēru. The next year the boundaries of the village were fixed and a document was drawn up. But the village was not entered in the accounts as a dēvadhana and brahmadēya. The mistake was rectified in the fourth year of Parāntaka the next ruler and the sabha were making over the stipulated produce and gold to the temple. In the thirty-sixth year of the same ruler an additional item was made payable from the village to the temple and entered in the accounts. The village assembly were misappropriating this item and the temple authorities made a complaint to the king while he was at Conjeevaram. The king sent for the parties and satisfying himself after inquiry, fined the assembly and restored the grant to the temple.

Justice: In the administration of justice the village assembly exercised equal power, if not even more. We have a few inscriptions in which such exercise of power is clearly on record. The normal punishment for causing death was, of course, death, as shown by some of the Chola inscriptions in Mysore territory;[1] but the punishment depended usually upon the merits of the case. In three instances on record, death was caused without intention on the part of the culprit and owing to pure accident. The Governor and the assembly which he convened for the purpose, in one instance, and the latter alone in the others sat in judgement and passed sentence that as death was caused unintentionally, the extreme penalty of the law should not be meted out to the culprit; all the same the accused should not go scot-free. He was, therefore, ordered to burn a perpetual lamp in the village temple for which he made over to the village assembly sixteen cows. This fine of sixteen cows, which would have been of the value of a quarter of a year's maintenance of an ordinary family, must have been rather heavy but would certainly have acted as a powerful deterrent against crimes caused by negligence. In all three cases on record death was due to shooting accidents.[2] A merchant had a

[1] *Haggadedēvanakōte* 18, *Epigraphica Carnātaka*, vol. iv.

[2] Sec. 26, Govt. *Epigraphist's Report* for 1900.

concubine on whom another attempted an outrage. The latter was stabbed to death by the merchant. He could not be prosecuted for murder and paid a fine like the others against whom the charge was neglect.[1] It is not out of place here to remark that the jury system which is believed to be the special birthright of Englishmen and spoken of generally as unknown in India, is found to have been in full swing. In the first instance above given, the governor, it was, that took cognizance of the case first; but he did not find himself competent to proceed without the assembly; whereas in the latter cases the assembly proceeded without even a reference to the governor.

Such were the powers of the village assemblies in those days. Considering the extent of the country and the want of rapid communication, and considering that the assemblies took great interest in the discharge of their manifold functions, (as the many references to the assembly having 'met without a vacancy' would show), there is no gainsaying the fact that the administration was efficient and well-suited to the times. The Assembly for each rural unit was constituted as follows:—

The constitution of the assembly: From certain inscriptions of the time of the Chola King Parāntaka[2] we are enabled to form an idea of the rural administration in those days not only, but even of earlier times. The particular records referred to are of the nature of instructions laid down by Parāntaka and explain how the system that had come down from ancient times was worked. The object of these regulations being that the 'wicked men might perish, while good men might prosper', we have to take it that they are of the nature of supplementary regulations.

[1] *Epigraphist's Report* for 1907, Sec. 42, this also contains seven other instances of accidents.

[2] *Epigraphist's Report* for 1899, Secs. 68-73.

Every unit, sometimes a single village, oftener a union had a general assembly to look after the affairs of the village or the union as the case may be. Under this general body whose number varied, perhaps, even up to five hundred, there were smaller bodies whose business it was to look after particular sections of the administration. These were the committees for tanks, for gardens, for justice, for general supervision, for the wards (kuḍumbu), for the fields, for supervising Udāsinas, etc. There are two others which are mentioned sometimes: (1) for gold supervision, and (2) pancha vāravāriyam. The latter probably refers to the committee of general management corresponding to the pancha pradhānas or aimberungulu. The former, of course, would refer to a currency committee.

Election Rule: Each union was divided into hamlets and wards, the former appears to have been geographical and the latter political. Uttaramallur the particular union under consideration, had twelve hamlets and thirty wards. First of all the names of men eligible in each ward were written on tickets and sent to the assembly with a covering ticket stating the number recommended. Secondly, these tickets were to be thrown into a pot and one chosen by lot. The following were eligible for the pot ticket:—

1. One with ¼ vēli of tax-paying land.

2. One with a house built on his own site.

3. Those who were below seventy-five and above thirty-five.

4. Those that knew Mantrabrāhmaṇa and were able to teach it.

5. 'Even if one owns only one-eighth vēli of land, he shall have his name written on a pot-ticket and put into the pot in case he has learnt one Veda and one of the four *Bhashyas* and can explain it.'

6. Among those possessing the foregoing qualifications:—

(1) Only such as are conversant with business and conduct themselves according to sacred rules shall be chosen;

(2) Those who have acquired their wealth by honest means, whose minds are pure and who have not been on any of these committees for the last three years shall also be chosen.

DISQUALIFICATIONS.

1. Those who have been on any of these committees but have not submitted their accounts and their relations specified below.

(1) The sons of the elder and younger sisters of mothers.
(2) The sons of their paternal aunts and maternal uncles.
(3) The brothers of their mothers.
(4) The brothers of their fathers.
(5) Their brothers.
(6) Their fathers-in-law.
(7) The brothers of their wives.
(8) The husbands of their sisters.
(9) The sons of their sisters.
(10) The sons-in-law.
(11) Their fathers.
(12) Their sons.

2. Those against whom illicit sexual intercourse or the first four of the five great sins are recorded, namely, killing a Brahman, drinking intoxicating liquors, theft, committing adultery with the wife of a spiritual teacher, and associating with any one guilty of those crimes.

All the various relations of these as specified in section 1.

3. Those that were excluded, perhaps personally:—

(1) Those who have been outcast for association (with low people) till they should have performed the expiatory ceremonies.

(2) Those who are foolhardy.

(3) Those who had stolen or plundered the property of others.

4. Those who were excluded for life:—

(1) Those who had taken forbidden dishes and become pure by expiation.

(2) Those who had committed . . . sins and have become pure by expiation.

(3) Those that had become village pests and similarly pure.

(4) Those guilty of sexual intercourse and purified likewise.

All these were excluded in the election, and the other qualified candidates had their names entered in the pot-tickets sent with a covering ticket stating the actual number from each ward. A full meeting of the village assembly, including the young and old, was then called for the purpose. All the temple priests, in the village on the day, were to attend without exception and be seated along with the assembly, in the village hall. In the midst of the temple priests one of them, the oldest, stood up and lifted an empty pot to be seen by all those present. Any young boy who knows nothing about the matter hands over one of the packets received from the wards. The contents of the packet are thrown into the empty pot and well shaken. From this packet one ticket is taken by the boy and handed over to the standing priest, the arbitrator. The latter receives it on the palm of his hand with his five fingers open. He then reads out the name on the ticket. This ticket is read again by all the priests in the hall. The name thus read is then put down and accepted. Similarly, one man was chosen for each of the wards.

'Of the thirty persons thus chosen, those who had previously been on the garden supervision (committee), and those who are advanced in learning and those who are advanced in age shall be chosen for the committee of annual supervision. Of the rest twelve shall be taken for the garden supervision and the remaining six shall form the tank supervision (committee). The last two committees shall be chosen after an oral expression of opinion. The great men who are members of these three committees shall hold office for full three hundred and sixty days and then retire. If any one who is on the committees is found guilty of any offence, he shall be removed (at once). For appointing the committees after these have retired, the members of the committee for the "supervision of justice" in the twelve hamlets (of Uttaramallur) shall convene a meeting with the help of the arbitrator. The selection shall be by drawing pot-tickets according to this order which lays down the rules (thereof).'

'For the Pancha-vāra-vāriyam and the (committee) for the "supervision of gold", names shall be written for the pot-tickets in the thirty wards, and thirty men shall be chosen as above. From these thirty tickets twelve men shall be chosen. Six out of these twelve (men) shall form the gold supervision (committee) and the remaining six constitute the pancha-vāra-vāriyam. When drawing pot-tickets for the appointment of these two committees next year, the wards that had already been represented (during the year in question) or the committees shall be excluded and the appointments made from the remaining wards by *an oral expression of opinion.* Those "who have ridden on asses" and those who have committed forgery shall not have (their names) written on the pot-tickets and put in the pot.'

'Arbitrators and those who have earned their wealth by honest means shall write the accounts (of the village). One who was writing the accounts shall not be appointed to that office again until he submits his accounts (for the period during which he was in office to the great men of the big committee (in charge) of the accounts, and is declared to have been honest. The accounts which one has been writing, he shall submit himself and other accountants shall not be brought to close his accounts.'

These were the rules promulgated by Parāntaka I to make rural administration more efficient. The rules show considerable anxiety to keep the wicked ones among the villagers out; but who the wicked ones were we are not informed. Failure to render accounts of the year appears to have been the chief trouble. It is not clear whether the accountants were honorary or paid and how they were elected. Offices seem to have been strictly annual, though this strictness itself would imply that the tendencies were the other way at the time, perhaps abnormally so. Both election and lot were, on the Athenian model, made use of for appointing the officials of the year. This strict rotation of offices would give every one of the villagers the chance of acquainting himself with the work of administration of the affairs of his village, and make the general committee of supervision very efficient in its control of the smaller committees. This and the committee for the supervision of justice appear to have been constituted in a way to command respect, but how they were constituted and in what manner they differed from the others we are not informed. In this fashion was the machinery provided for carrying on the various functions which fell to the lot of a rural unit.

That these rules were acted upon and enforced severely is in evidence in No. 583 of 1904 of date A. D. 1234-5 which records the dismissal of a village accountant and the debarring of his relations from holding the appointment for cheating.

Divisions of the Empire: A number of these rural units constituted a district (or nāḍu) and a number of these again formed a kōṭṭam (Sans. kōshṭaka,) elsewhere but a valanāḍu (fertile country) in the Chola country proper which, as far as could be made out, was divided into eight such divisions, namely (1) Arumoḻidēva vaḷanāḍu, (2) Kshatriyaśikhāmani vaḷanāḍu, (3) Uyyakoṇḍān vaḷanāḍu, (4) Rajēndrasimha vaḷanāḍu, (5) Keraḷāntaka vaḷanāḍu, (6) Rajāsraya vaḷanāḍu, (7) Pandyakulāśani vaḷanāḍu, (8) Nittavinōdha vaḷanāḍu. A number of these divisions went to make a province (manḍalam) which had originally been an independent kingdom gradually absorbed into the rising Empire of the Cholas. Each province was under a viceroy, who was either a scion of the dispossessed royal families or a prince of the blood. At any rate from the days of Rajādhirāja it became the fashion to confer viceroyalties upon near kinsmen such as uncles, brothers, sons, etc. This may have been on account of the general revolt of the frontier provinces. We find, however, several Pallavas in positions of influence and trust. The whole empire of the Cholas (except the Vengi country which occupied all along the position of a dependent ally was divided into six provinces, each of which had, at least, two alternative names: (1) its original name as an independent kingdom and (2) a new name derived generally from the titles of the emperor who conquered or from those of the viceroy whose rule over the province was specially distinguished. These provinces were: (1) the Tonḍamanḍalam or Jayaṃgonḍachōlamanḍalam (the Pallava country, embracing the coast districts between the rivers, the Southern Pennar and the North Pennar, if not the Krishna. (2) the Chōlamanḍalam itself (the Districts of Tanjore and Trichinopoly). (3) Rajarājamanḍalam comprising a part at least of the Pandya and the Kērala country, (Parts of Madura and the Travancore country). (4) The Kongu country or Adhirājarājamanḍalam, earlier Śōla-Kēralamanḍalam (districts of Salem and Coimbatore). (5) Gangaikonḍachōlamanḍalam (Districts of Mysore and Bangalore),—the western part of the Ganga country of Mysore. (6) The Nikharilichōlamaṇḍalam embracing the eastern part of the Ganga country of Mysore, the Bāṇa kingdom to the south-east and the Vaiṭumba country to the north-east (District of Kolar in Mysore, a part of North Arcot and Salem and the Maharājavāḍy part of the Cuddapah district).

Character of the Administration: That the administration of the Cholas was highly systematized early is amply proved by the fragments of their records that have come down to us on stones and copper. But the wonder is what could have happened to the records in the archives of the Government. Much earlier than the days of Rājarāja[1] or even Parāntaka, the Chola administration had been reduced to some sort of system and the title of the Chief Secretary 'Ōlaināyakam' shows that there were royal records on palmyra leaves (of which the epigraphical records were mere copies) kept at head-quarters. Besides these, as the inscriptions at Karuvūr and other places show, there were registers kept of the royal orders by each of the Mahāsabhas. Regret as we may the disappearance of these records, we have, thanks to the untiring industry of the epigraphical department, enough of material before us to gain an idea of the general character of the Chola administration.

We learn that the lands under cultivation were carefully surveyed and holdings registered at least a century before the famous Domesday record of William the Conqueror. The inscriptions of Rājarāja referring occasionally to 'the book' show that the survey was correct to $\frac{1}{52,428,800,000}$ of a veli of land which would

1 The machinery of the administration was the same even before. An inscription of the eighth year of Uttama Chola gives details which would make it clear that the administrative machinery was as complete before Rājarāja, as after. *Vide* Epigraphist's Report for 1910, sec. 18.

approximately be equivalent to $\frac{1}{50,000}$ of a square inch (a vēli being six and two-third acres). The unit of linear measure was the 'royal foot' Srīpātha of Kulōttunga), during the later period, from which was derived the unit measure of area. We find also graduated rods of sixteen and eighteen spans used in land measure earlier. Measured lands were entered either in kuḻi or in vēli in the Chola country proper; while the standard measure of other portions of the empire varied a little from that of this part. The royal dues, were taken either in kind or in gold or in both. These were fixed per kuḻi and the expressions 'calculated' (Kāṇikkāḍan) and 'settled' (Nichaiyitta) produce occur in some records which probably meant the revenue as entered against the particular holding by previous survey calculation and that founded on actual yield (during revision).[1]

[1] Here I beg leave most respectfully to differ from Dewan Bahadur Srinivasaragava Aiyangar, who surmises that these terms meant respectively the gross outturn and the Government share. He refers to an inscription of Kulōttunga, and finds that in some cases the revenue exceeds the outturn and in others it comes up to near two-thirds of the outturn. The former he explains away as due to errors of writing. A glance down the list given on the next page of his work shows, as do a number of Rajaraja's inscriptions in the Tanjore temple, that the Government demand came up to 100 kalams of paddy a vēli. Kulōttunga made a re-survey of the lands in A. D. 1086 (Epigraphist's report for 1900, section 25, page 10) and the record quoted is only a readjustment. Kulōttunga had the reputation of having abolished the tolls (Sungandavirtachola). Many of the figures quoted in the passage, as calculated produce, work up to a hundred kalams a vēli and in several there had been brought about a reduction. In others there was an enhancement, which would naturally follow a re-survey which was, as seems probable, undertaken to bring about an adjustment, as some lands might possibly have been over-assessed in consequence of the village assemblies receiving often the cost as well as the capitalized value of the revenue of lands made tax-free by themselves. One result of this might have been to enhance unduly the revenue payable by the tax-paying lands as the assemblies would have had to pay the same amount to Government, as would appear from the large number of extracts quoted above (*vide* Progress of Madras Presidency, appendix, sec. I. D. and E., pp. 17 to 20) *vide ante part of this* i. Chapter.

This latter must have been quite feasible as the revenues were collected by the village assemblies which could find out the actual yield to a nicety. If the Government dues were not paid the penalty was, of course, the taking over of the land by the village assembly to be disposed of otherwise; and the liability of the landholder ceased there. The person and the personalities of the man were not touched, as they are in our more civilized times. A record of the time of Vikrama Chola shows that the land revenue was not paid owing to floods and the villagers put the land up to sale by public auction and sold 2,000 kuḷi of wet land for twenty-five kāśu and another bit of 4,250 kuḷi of dry land for twenty kāśu. The same power was given to the sabhas over lands transferred to other proprietors by the circular order of Rājarāja above quoted.

The emperors and their work: The emperors whether they were in their capitals or out in their progress through their dominions did transact office business. In a number of inscriptions we find it stated that the emperor was seated in a particular part of the palace and issued orders which were committed to writing by the Royal Secretary (corresponding to the Private Secretaries of our days).[1] Whatever was the order it had to be approved of by the Chief Secretary (Olaināyakam) and by another high dignitary (Perundaram) Īrāyiravan Pallavaiyan in the days of Rājarāja and his son. Finally it was transmitted to the party concerned by the dispatching clerk (Viḍaiyadhikhāri) which again meeting with the approval of the viceroy or governor and the assemblies concerned was registered and sent into the record office. In illustration of how this was done I quote the following from an inscription of Vīrarājēndra:

[1] *Vikrama Chōlan Ulā.*, verse 50. *Indian Antiquary*, vol. xxii, p. 145.

'Being graciously seated in the royal bathing hall within the palace at Gangaikoṇḍa Sōḷapuram (the King) granted with libation of water, the village of Pākkūr in Vengāla nāḍu (a district) of Adhirājarāja manḍalam, (and) was pleased to order that this village, excluding the tax-paying lands in the possession of the ryots, should become tax-free temple land from (the year) which was opposite to the third year (of his reign) including revenue, taxes, small tolls, eḻuvai, ugavai, the three fines called manṟupāḍu, danḍam, kuṟṟam, everywhere where the iguana runs, the tortoise crawls, an ant-hill rises and sprouts grow, the grass for the calves and the lands enjoyed in full by the great village; that (this village) should pay to (the God) Mahādēva of Tiruvānilai (temple) at Karuvūr in the same nāḍu, the revenue hitherto paid by this village, namely 303½ kaḻanju and one and one-twentieths manjāḍi of gold; and 3,531 kalam, 1 tūni of paddy and that this village should be entered in the revenue register (vari) as tax-free temple land from this year forward.'

'Accordingly the Royal Secretary Vānavan Pallavaraiyan, the lord of Tāḻi Tiruppanangāḍu and the lord of Nērivāyil in Paṇiyūr nāḍu, a district of Kshatriya Śikhāmani, vaḷanāḍu, having written that the king had been pleased to order (thus), and the Chief Secretary Achchudan Rājarājan *alias* Tonḍamān, the citizen Uttamachōlan *alias* Rājarāja Brahmādhirajan, Araiyan Rājarājan *alias* Vīrarājēndra Jayamurināḍāḷvān, and Vīrarājēndra Mangaḷappēraraiyan having unanimously approved (of this document) Vīrabhadran Tillaiviḍangan *alias* Villavan Rājarājan ordered: "Let it be entered in our register in accordance with intimation received."' In accordance with this order there was a meeting of a number of members, but here the record of their deliberations is unfortunately obliterated. 'Our revenue officers having entered (this) in the revenue register in accordance with the royal order, let it be engraved upon copper and on stone (that this village was given) as tax-free temple land to the God Mahādēva of Tiruvānilai temple for the expenses of burnt-offerings, oblations and worship.'

Resources of the empire: This extract will give a far better idea of the administrative machinery of the Cholas than pages of description. I shall now proceed to a consideration of the resources of the empire and how they were spent. Quoted under is a part of an inscription of Tribhuvanachakravartin Kōnōrinmai-kondān, which enumerates in the fullest available detail the numerous fiscal items of the Chola rule. What detracts, however, from the full interest of the inscription is that at this distance of time we cannot understand the exact nature of any; nor even the general character of a few of these. The record is a gift of land free of taxes:[1] 'These seventy-seven, six-twentieths, and one hundred and sixtieths (vēli) of land, which may be more or less, we gave: including the trees over ground, the wells under ground, in the land and all other benefits (prāptis) of whatever kind, having first excluded the farmer owners and the hereditary proprietors, and having purchased (it) as tax-free property (Kāṇi) for the 106 Bhaṭṭas of this village and for the two shares (of the image) of Sāmanta-nārāyanaviṇṇagar Emberumān, from the rainy season of the thirty-fifth (year of our reign) as a meritorious gift (dharmadhāna) with libations of water, with the right to bestow mortgage or sell (it) as a tax-free grant of land to last as long as the moon and the sun.

(This grant) includes all kinds (vargas) of taxes, (kaḍamai) and rights (kuḍimai), namely, the right to cultivate kār (a kind of paddy), maruvu (a fragrant

[1] No. 22, vol. ii, pt. i, *South Ind. Inscriptions.*

plant, origanum majoranum), single flowers (oruppū) flowers for the market (kaḍaipū), lime trees, dry crops, red water-lilies, areca-palms, betel-vines, saffron, ginger, plantains, and all other crops (payir); all kinds of revenue (āya) including tax in money (kāśuk-kaḍamai), oḍukkuppaḍi, urainā̤li, the share of the village watchman who is placed over the veṭṭis (paths), the share of the karṇam who measures (paddy, etc.), the unripe fruit in kārtigai (month), the tax on looms (tari irai), the tax on oil-mills (śekkirai), the *tax on trade* (seṭṭirai),[1] taṭṭoli, the tax on goldsmiths (taṭṭārpāṭṭam), the dues on animals and tanks, the tax on water-courses (o̤lukkunīr pāṭṭam), tolls (va̤li āyam), inavari (appears to be a tax on caste); the tax on weights (iḍaivari), the fine for rotten drugs (a̤lugalśarakku), the tax on bazaars (angāḍipāṭṭam) and the salt tax (uppāyam); [what follows is different from either of the above groups; and the bearing of the items is not known; I set them down here in the hope that some one who has the means may explain the terms correctly: panjupili (பஞ்சுபிலி), Sandhivigrahappēru (ஸந்தி விக்கிரகப்பேறு), ilānjinaipēru (இலாஞ்சினைப்பேறு), vāśal-vinyōgam (வாசல்வினியோகம்), paḍaiyilārmuraimai (படையிலார்முறைமை), kūṟṟilakkai (கூற்றிலக்கை), kaḍaikkūṭṭilakki (கடைக்கூட்டிலக்கை), tanḍalilakkai தண்டலிலக்கை), viḍaippēr (விடைப்பேர், mādhappaḍi (மாதப்படி), araikkālvāśi (அரைக்கால்வாசி, ūśivāśi (ஊசிவாசி, vilaittunḍam (விலைத்துண்டம்), nīrāni (நீராணி),[2] kaverikkulai (காவிரிக்குலை), devakuḍimai (தேவகுடிமை), nāṭṭuppādi (நாட்டுப்பாதி), ānaikkūḍam (ஆனைக்கூடம்), kudiraippandi (குதிரைப்பந்தி).] Thus in accordance with this order (ōlai) it shall be engraved on stone and copper.'

This is a long list of taxes and would stand comparison with the list of seigniorial dues of Europe

[1] Rather on profits.

[2] Probably corresponding to the Nirganti, the official who controls tank sluices for irrigation.

before the French Revolution; but we are dealing with times about a thousand years ago. That there were so many imposts, and of such variety, points to the conclusion that these were so many devices for increasing the income of the Government. The chief source of this income was the land revenue; and if this were capable of direct increase, the state revenue could be easily raised by taking a greater proportion of the gross outturn of produce, without having recourse to the vexatious and roundabout way of gaining the same end. If the customary proportion could not be altered, the only other course would be to devise a number of petty imposts which, though not the most economical, is still an indirect way of increasing the revenue and, as such, less seen or understood. We may then take what is actually stated in one of the inscriptions of Rājādhirāja as true: that the portion of the produce demanded and taken by the Government was one-sixth of the gross outturn. He is said to have taken the sixth and assumed the title Jayaṃgoṇḍachola as though the sixth were the most usual proportion. The additional taxes (āyas) were divided into two classes: the internal (antarāya) and external (other oyas). The latter must have been of the character of tolls and octroi generally. The incidence of the former was chiefly on land as even handicraftsmen were paid often in land for their customary work. This, we find, was commuted into one-tenth,[1] in the inscription of Vīrarājēndra at Tiruvallam quoted above. The total demand upon land, therefore, would have come up to four-fifteenths of the gross outturn. From a number of inscriptions we find that the total revenue, on an average, from lands in the most fertile portions of the Tanjore and Trichinopoly districts was 100 kalams per

[1] Twenty-five Kāśu it is; but commuted into 100 Kalams at four Kalams per 1,000 Kalams. In the days of Rājarāja a Kāsu = two Kalams.

vēli by the Āḍavallan measure (equal to the Rājakēsari or Arumoḷidēvan, the standard measure of the days of Rājarāja) kept in possession of the temple authorities for safe custody. The Āḍavallan measure of paddy is found by the late Mr. Srinivasaraghava Aiyangar to have weighed 192 tolas while its modern counterpart weighs 240 tolas. This wou'd give the revenue per vēli of six acres and two-thirds (2,000 kuḻi) at eighty modern kalams of paddy (a kalam is about three maunds) and the gross outturn at 300 kalams, a very high yield, perhaps not impossible as the lands in question are those that pay the highest revenue situate in the most fertile parts of the Tanjore and Trichinopoly districts. All lands had not to pay the same revenue which varied from fifty to eighty modern kalams of paddy, or from four to nine kalanju of gold. The village assemblies[1] must have collected the royal dues with some elasticity as the order of Rājarāja quoted above would show.

The unspent part of this revenue was kept in up-country treasuries against demands from head-quarters. At a certain stage these revenue demands might have become so heavy that it must have been deemed necessary to abolish some at least of these dues.

One such act of clear-sighted statesmanship, it is, that got Kulōttunga, the first, the popular sobriquet of Śungandavirtachōla (the Chola who abolished the tolls), which is handed down to us in a suburb of that name in Tanjore town. In case of floods and

[1] The village assemblies often remitted taxes on certain pieces of land receiving its cost and the capitalized value of the revenues due. How they spent this money is not on record so far; but that the revenues might have been spread over the other lands is probable. Perhaps they applied the money for general improvements and making fresh clearings. In the latter case they began with a nominal revenue upon the lands in question gradually raising it through a term of years to the normal proportion. *South Ind. Ins.*, vol. i., 65.

other calamities remissions of taxes would appear to have been expected; but in one instance on record in Vikrama Chola's reign remissions were not granted in case of floods, and some of the village lands had to be put up to public sale by the villagers, a fact referred to above. This would not seem to be enough to warrant the inference that 'remissions were unknown' in those days.

Standards of measure, etc.: It has been already stated that the royal dues were paid either in kind or in gold, or partly in the one and partly in the other. Some of the minor taxes were paid in *kāśu*. The unit of land was a vēli of 2,000 kuḻis (six and two-thirds acres); of grain a kalam (about three maunds); of gold a kaḻanju (about one-sixth ounce Troy). The unit of currency was the gold *kāśu* (seven-twentieths of a kaḻanju or about twenty-eight grs. Troy). This coin appears to have passed for its metallic value, because the great Rajarāja got all gifts to the temple carefully weighed and appraised. All gold ornaments among these are entered with their weights alone but no value is given, while jewels set with brilliants, etc., are entered with their weights (by the standard Āḍvallān kāśukkallu) and their value in kāśu. We can safely infer that the kāśu passed for its weight in gold, although its value in grain and cattle might vary. Each kāśu was equivalent to two kalams of paddy in the days of Rājarāja and his son, though it exchanged for so much as four kalams about fifty years after: One buffalo, two cows, and six sheep exchanged for two kāśu in the former period. The total amount of revenue realized by the temple authorities was probably turned into cash, although it is possible that they kept a portion in grain alone. Much of the cash in the treasury, however, was lent out to village assemblies or even to individuals on the guarantee of the assemblies. Occasionally when they lent out to townsfolk, the loan was given on the joint responsibility of the relatives of the person or even the whole trade concerned. An interest of twelve and a half per cent was uniformly charged whether in grain or in kāśu. Several of these loans were given for providing the temple with the daily and periodical requirements; but often loans were made for purely agricultural purposes. In the former case the debtors had to pay interest in ghee, oil, camphor, or any other commodity agreed upon beforehand, while in the latter the interest was paid either in cash or in kind.

Expenditure: The main heads of expenditure of the royal revenues were the civil administration, the maintenance of armies, the building and beautifying of temples and cities, and the carrying out of useful public works on a scale beyond the capabilities of local revenues and administrations. The cost of civil administration was met from the rural revenues, the higher officers as well as the lower ones being rewarded by gifts of land or by assignments of revenue. Deducting this cost from the total revenue, the residue reached the royal treasury, to be spent on the other items.

The Cholas appear to have had a regular army, divided into sections according to the kind of arms they carried, and according as they were mounted or otherwise. We find reference to the 'chosen body of archers', the 'chosen foot-soldiers of the body-guard', the 'chosen', horsemen and the 'chosen' infantry of the 'right hand'.[1] I have not come across any reference to the infantry of the 'left hand'.[2] Some of the princes are referred to as 'ānaichēvagan' (perhaps commander of an elephant crops); 'Malaiyānai Oṛṛaichchēvagan' (the unequalled elephant man).

[1] Infantry recruited from the artisan class.

[2] The agricultural class is excluded from military service in the codes of law.

That they maintained an efficient fleet is borne out by references to the destruction of the Chera fleet at Kāndalūr, placed on the west coast by Dr. Hultzsch; the capture of Kaḍāram by Rājēndra after a sea-fight, and several invasions of Ceylon and Burmah. Besides this epigraphical evidence, ancient Tamil literature is full of details and descriptions of the sailing craft of those days. They also show abundant evidence of nautical experience by the figures and tropes made use of in the works. To give only one example in illustration; the author of the *Epic of the Anklet* refers to beacon lights being placed on the tops of palmyra trunks in lamps made of fresh clay at Puhār or Kaveryppūmbaṭṭinam on dark nights when the sea was rough. No clear reference is available as to the administration of the army.

Public Works: the Cholas were great builders: builders not only of cities and temples (sometimes for strategic purposes, sometimes in obedience to the dictates of their vanity), but also of useful irrigation works. These may be divided into major works and minor works. These latter were probably constructed, and certainly looked after, by the Public Works committee of the sabhas. The former were made and perhaps maintained by the Government. Passing over the ancient Chola Karikāla,[1] and his more modern namesake, reputed by tradition to have built the embankments on the Kavery, and to have cut the main channels for irrigation respectively, we find works of the kind undertaken by later rulers. The

[1] 'Madras can claim to have introduced, if not originated, a style of construction, which has been widely adopted within and without the empire, and to have established a plan of dealing with deltaic lands which has not been improved upon. A portion of the credit for these achievements belongs to the native engineers of the days preceding the British advent. They had conceived the idea of controlling a river at the head of its delta, and of thus securing the regular watering of their lands.'—*Irrigated India by Hon. Alfred Deakin.*

names[1] of most of the main channels of irrigation at present watering the Kavery Delta occur in the inscriptions of this dynasty of rulers. The following two instances should suffice to give us an idea of the importance attached to artificial irrigation works in those days. Driving across the town of Tanjore along the road to Trivadi, the first river we pass over is now known as Vaḍavāru (northern river). This river is called in the inscriptions Vīrachōla Vaḍavāru. (There is another Virachōlan river branching from the Kavery a few miles below the bridge at Kumbhakonam.) This was evidently cut out from the Veṇṇār by Vīrachōla to feed a big irrigation tank in the now postal town of Vaḍuvur in the Mannarguḍi taluq, which has no other feeder channel and which waters a large area, else unfit for cultivation. The other instance is the large artificial reservoir at Gangaikondaśōlapuram in the Woḍiarpaliam taluq of the Trichinopoly district. I take the following from Pharaoh's *Gazetteer of South India*[2]: 'It may also be mentioned that in Wodiarpalliam taluq there is an embankment sixteen miles long running north and south provided with several substantial sluices and of great strength, which in former times must have formed one of the largest reservoirs in India. . . The tank has been ruined and useless for many years and its bed is now almost wholly overgrown with high and thick jungle. It is said traditionally that its ruin was wilful and the act of an invading army. Near the northern extremity of the bund there is a village now

1 The Peruvaḷavōy Channel, in the district of Trichinopoly, The Arasalār, The Nāṭṭār, The Kaḍuvāyāru and the Pāndavāyaru should suffice. Of the last two, the first is a branch of the Veṭṭār and the next from the Veṇṇar (*vide* any irrigation map of the Kavery Delta).

2 pp. 338-9 of Mr. Kanakasabbai Pillai's 'The conquest of Bengal and Burma by the Tamils', *Madras Review* for August 1902, pp. 247, *et seq.*

surrounded by a jungle, called Gangaikondapuram; immediately in its vicinity is a pagoda of a very large size, and costly workmanship; and close by surrounded and overgrown with jungle are some remains of ancient buildings now resembling the mounds or "heaps" which indicated the site of ancient Babylon, but in which the village elders point out the various parts of an extensive and magnificent palace. When this palace was in existence Gangaikondapuram was the wealthy and flourishing capital of a small monarchy,[1] and the great tank spread fertility and industry over miles and miles of what is now trackless forest. . . . Speaking of the noble temple of Gangaikondapuram it must not be omitted that when the lower Coleroon Anicut was built, the structure was dismantled of a large part of the splendid granite sculptures which adorned it, and the enclosing wall was almost wholly destroyed in order to obtain material for the work.' This magnificent relic of lost greatness and a forgotten empire was the work of the great son of a still greater father who built the temple at, and fortified the city of, Tanjore. The temple at Gangaikondapuram measures 372 feet by 584 feet. The lingam made of a single block of polished granite is thirty feet now unfortunately split in twain by a stroke of lightning. The main tower of the Tanjore temple is about 200 feet high and the single block of granite which forms the minaret is twenty-five and a half feet square,[2] calculated to weigh about eighty tons. It was raised to its present position by an incline, which rested on the ground four miles away from the temple. These structures are believed to be the outcome of absolute power commanding

[1] Yes! Small indeed as it did embrace what is now the Madras Presidency and a part of Mysore. (For the extent of the Chola empire see *ante* p. 105.)

[2] Sewell's *List of Antiquities*, vol. i. p. 227.

unlimited labour.[1] There is a tradition current, however, of Karikālachola (it may be either the first or the second of the name, it does not matter for our purpose) that he paid the labourers on the Kavery embankment in depreciated coin (coins of leather it is said), in consequence of which there was a dust-storm which overwhelmed the capital and made him flee for his life. This story has its value alongside of the inference that, as these temples were years in building and of very great cost, they must have been the result of forced unpaid labour. The labour might have been forced or not, provided it had been paid. The builders of these structures ruled over what is now the Madras Presidency and half of Mysore. Their administration was not very expensive, and as great conquerors they must have brought from their wars much of the accumulated treasure of other powerful and prosperous kingdoms.[2]

Whether the labour was paid for or not (there are instances of slavery in the thirteenth century when five men and women were sold for 100 Kāsu[3]), we owe to these Cholas not only the grand structures, the temples, and palaces (indirectly useful, at least, as providing material for anicuts), but also the great part of the network of irrigation channels in the Tanjore district and a part of Trichinopoly.

We have ample evidence of the country's having been traversed by grand trunk roads. That armies could march to Kōṭṭāru near Cape Comorin at the one end, and the banks of the Mahanadi, if not the Ganges, at the other of the peninsula, and that trade was carried on largely by means of 'vessels' and 'vehicles'[4]

1 *Progress of Madras Presidency*, pp. 14 and 15.

2 Rājarāja's inscriptions of gifts to the Tanjore temple refer to the captured Chera Treasure.

3 *Epigraphist's Report* for 1905, sec. 20; date of record, A.D. 1239-40.

4 *Śilappadhikaram* and *Pattinappalai*.

are enough to prove their existence. If more proof be needed we have it in the fact that Kulōttunga planted agricultural colonies 'along the road to Kōṭṭāru'; and in the references in some of the inscriptions to roads of sixty-four spans, etc. There is besides mention of Vaḍugavaḻi road going to the Telugu country, Taḍigavaḻi road leading through Taḍigaināḍu, and what is more kīḻavaḻi eastern road in inscriptions. There appears to have been a regular service of ferries across rivers maintained either at public expense or by private charity.

Standard of Life: We can form an idea of the standard of life in those days from the following few facts gleaned from a number of inscriptions. Rājarāja made allotments from the temple revenue for the several officials in temple service and their annual salaries were fixed as follows. The officer in charge of the temple treasury is mentioned, but the figure opposite his name is obliterated. An accountant got 200 kalams of paddy by the Āḍavallan measure every year: and an under accountant seventy-five kalams. Bachelor Brahman servants of the temple got each sixty-one kalams and four kāśu, sixty-one kalams and five kāśu, and ninety-one kalams and four kāśu according to their work. These latter officials drew their pay at the city-treasury and the other officials above mentioned at up-country treasuries. Each temple watchman was paid 100 kalams a year, and each temple woman 100 kalams. An allowance of 120 kalams was made for the annual enacting of the Rājakēsarināṭakam. The offerings to a particular image, regulated probably by the requirements of a temple priest, are put down at 130 kalams a year. These allowances were probably fixed with reference to the requirements of the family of the class from which the official came. If this were really the case, we may take the 200 kalams of the Brahman accountant as representing the requirements of an average Brahman family (a temple priest has several perquisites over and above his salary); and the 100 kalams of the watchman, those of the Sudra family. If, with Adam Smith, we can believe over a long period of time the value of corn does not vary however much its price may, and assume that these represent the value of an equal quantity of grain to-day, the average income of a family per month would have been sixteen rupees and two-thirds, and eight rupees and one-third for a Brahman and a Sudra, respectively, on [1] the supposition of the average price of paddy at one rupee four annas per modern kalam. We cannot form any definite conclusion on the slender evidence we have; but if this represents at all the standard of life of those days we have all that is possible for us to know at present.

Religion: The Cholas were Śaivas by religion; but there is no evidence of the Vaishṇavas or of the Jains[2] having been persecuted as such, before the days of Kulōttunga, who appears to have driven out Rāmānuja from Srīrangam. Rājaraja and his son patronized the Śaivitic devotional works by providing for their recital in temples on stated occasions. We find references to gifts to Vaishṇava temples, and to provision made for the recital of portions of the *Nālāyiraprabhandam*. The great temple builder, Kōchchengan, appears to have been a builder of both classes of temples.[3] Appar, Sundarar, and Sambandar

[1] Mr. Srinivasaraghava Aiyangar's figures per head are Rs. 2-12-0 and Rs. 1-12-0 per month. The Government of India's Rs. 20 a year per head.

[2] The Jains had to pay a tax but the other Hindus also had to pay, such as the right-hand and left-hand castes. There is an 'inavari' which, if it means anything, ought to have been a tax on caste.

[3] Mr. Fergusson writes of the Tanjore temple: One of the peculiarities of the Tanjore temple is that all the sculptures in the gopuras belong to the religion of Vishṇu, while everything in the courtyard belongs to that of Śiva, an instance of the extreme tolerance that

are referred to in some of the inscriptions of Rājarāja, and somewhat later we find reference to the works of Kulasēkhara and Tirumangaiāḻvar, two of the twelve Vaishṇava Āḻvārs. The god at the temple of Ukkal is referred to by the name Tiruvōymoḻidēva. Dr. Hultzsch is of opinion that Nammāḻvār, the author of the *Tiruvōymoḻi*, must have lived 'centuries before A.D. 1000'. There is an inscription of Rajēndra, of the battle of Koppam fame, which makes provision for the enacting of the Rajakēsarināṭakam every year. Popular tradition makes Kulōttunga and some at least of his successors great patrons of literature. This dynasty of the Cholas encouraged Tamil literature, but for the date of composition of the great body of extant works we have to look much earlier.

prevailed in the age at which it was erected before these religions became antagonistic.

CHAPTER VII

SRĪ RĀMĀNUJĀCHARYA, HIS LIFE AND TIMES

To the religious history of India, the contributions that the southern half has had to make have been many. The south generally enjoyed more peaceful development, and was long out of the convulsions that threw the north into confusion, and all the internal revolutions and external attacks sent out the pulse of the impact almost spent out to the south. This has been of great advantage, and it is precisely in the dark ages of the north that often intercepted the brighter epochs, that the south sent out its light to relieve the darkness.

This general character of the history of the north of India from the first centuries of the Christian era onwards makes a continuous history impossible on certain lines; while in the south, during this period, there has been a continuity of development amidst all the din and clang of war and dynastic revolutions. Our concern here is about the Vaishṇava movement, and this has had a continuous history almost from the beginning of the Christian era.

There has been considerable mis-impression that the Vaishṇava movement originated in Rāmānuja, and that all those who claim to be Vaishṇavas (not including the disciples of Madhva who are Vaishṇava in a narrower sense), both in the north and the south, can trace their particular form of Vēdānta no earlier than

Rāmānuja. On the basis of this misimpression, theories have been built up, time and again, that the characteristic features of the special teachings of Rāmānuja have been borrowed from Christianity. The latest exponent of this theory is Dr. Grieson, though he would make a considerable distinction between the Vaishṇavas of modern times and those of the older, and, perhaps, set those of the north against the south. This no doubt is an error, which arises from not giving due weight to the indebtedness of Rāmānuja to those Tamil saints, who had gone before him long ere he came into the world. The hypothesis would be untenable, unless it could be proved that all these Tamil saints could be shown also to have visited the Christian shrine at Mylapore or elsewhere. Besides, even from the point of view of Sanskritic Vaishṇavaism, it cannot be said to have been proven that the peculiar features of Rāmānuja Vaishṇavaism are not traceable to earlier works and teachers. Hence a life of Rāmānuja based on historical material alone, and free from the legends that have gathered round it, as time wore on, would be of great advantage to clear away the wrong impressions that prevail regarding his life and teaching.

That Rāmānuja should have appeared in the eleventh century is quite as much of the mission's getting the man, as the advent of the Buddha in the sixth century before Christ. This century in the south of India was characterized by considerable religious ferment. It was then that each religious sect among the people felt the need for formulating a creed of its own, and for placing itself in a regularly organized religious body, so as to be able to hold its own in the midst of the disintegrating influences that gained dominance in society. That Rāmānuja appeared and did what is ascribed to him is just in the fitness of things, having regard to the circumstances of the times.

There has been a succession of devotees called in Vaishṇava parlance Āḻvārs in contradistinction to a similar Śaiva group called Aḍiyārs. These two classes had considerable similarity with characteristic distinctions. They both laid stress on the doctrine of Bhakti as a means to the attainment of salvation, the one through Vishṇu and the other through Śiva. The Vaishṇava tradition names twelve of the Āḻvārs while the Śaiva saints number sixty-three. The Tamil works of the former including a centum upon Rāmānuja himself, constitute the Prabhandam 4,000, while those of the Śaivas constitute a vaster collection of Tēvārams, etc.

The twelve Āḻvārs are in the traditional order.

I (1) Poygai Āḻvār.
(2) Bhūtattu Āḻvār.
(3) Pēy Āḻvār.

II (4) Tirumaḻiśai Āḻvār.

III (5) Nammāḻvār.
(6) Madhurakavi Āḻvār.

IV (7) Kulasēkharāḻvār.

V (8) Periyāḻvār.
(9) Āṇḍāḷ.

VI (10) Toṇḍaraḍippoḍi Āḻvār.
(11) Tiruppāṇāḻvār.
(12) Tirumangai Āḻvār.

The actual dates ascribed by the hagiologists to these Āḻvārs will not bear scrutiny, but the order in which they are mentioned is substantially correct. In order of importance, Nammāḻvār stands first, and it is his work that has the distinctive appellation Tiruvōymoḻi—'the word of the mouth'. They were all regarded by the generations that succeeded them as manifestations of divine wisdom to redeem the world from the perilous plights to which it had brought itself.

The next group that followed, as the hagiologists would have us believe, in unbroken succession, is known as Āchāryas (or preceptors) not so near to the divine, but still much raised above the ordinary man of the world. This orthodox succession of apostles include six names before Rāmānuja, of which the two most important are Nāthamuni and his grandson Āḷavandār. The great-grandson of this latter through one of his grand-daughters was Rāmānuja.

While Āḷavaṇḍār was still in occupation of the apostolic seat of the Vaishṇavas at Srīrangam, one of his grandsons requested permission of him to go and devote himself to the service of God on the Tirupati Hill. The permission was graciously accorded, and the young man went and settled there with his venerable father and two younger sisters. While there, two young men wishing to enter life as house-holders happened to go to the holy place and sought each the hand of one of the sisters. Of these two Āsūri Kēśava Bhaṭṭar of Srī Perumbūdūr wedded the elder, while Kamalanayana Bhaṭṭar of Maḻalaimangalam accepted the younger of the girls. Of the first pair in course of time was born a boy (in A.D. 1017), whom the maternal uncle named Lakshmaṇa (otherwise Rāmānuja or in Tamil, Iḷaya Perumāḷ).

Of the childhood of Rāmānuja, as of others in similar positions of life, very little is known. There appears to have been nothing extraordinary in his career, except that he appears to have lost his father while young. He received the kind of education ordinarily given to boys of his class and age along with his cousin (mother's sister's son), Govinda Bhaṭṭar, as he was called. The two young men had advanced sufficiently to seek a teacher in the Vēdānta to instruct them. They went to a teacher of reputation holding his classes in Conjeevaram, and this change marks the turning point in the career of the young men.

Under Yādavaprakāśa, then, the two cousins Rāmānuja and Govinda Bhaṭṭar were both studying the Vēdānta assiduously. The former made such progress, and his great-grandfather at Srīrangam heard such good reports of his remarkable advance, that he travelled all the way *incognito* to see the young man. This he did in the Dēva Raja shrine at Conjeevaram. Gratified with the look of the young man, he went back hoping that he might soon transfer the mantle of office to the youth of great promise that he had just seen. He did not wish to speak to Rāmānuja lest it should attract attention and disturb Rāmānuja's studies in any way. Rāmānuja went on with his studies yet a while, when he began to feel that at times Yādavaprakāśa's interpretations of Vedic passages were not quite up to his satisfaction. On one occasion, he even went the length of offering an explanation of his own, which struck those present, as more satisfactory than that of his master. This led to grave differences between master and disciple. Matters advanced a step further when, at the invitation of the ruler of the place, Yādavaprakāśa failed in an attempt at exorcising. The prince was possessed and the spirit declined to move at Yādava's bidding. It would, however, go away if it were Rāmānuja's pleasure that it should. Rāmānuja was pleased to give the order and the ghost was raised. This made Yādava more jealous of his pupil and the crisis was reached when interpreting another Upanishad. Yādava again rendered the passage in a somewhat absurdly disrespectful manner. Rāmānuja showed positive disapproval of what he considered a purposeful distortion of the texts. Yādavaprakāśa asked Rāmānuja to leave his academy. Indeed he was advised to get rid of Rāmānuja altogether.

At the instigation of some of his disciples Yādava organized a pilgrimage to Benares, and Rāmānuja and his cousin were among the party. The latter, having been more docile, stood in high favour with the master and was in the secrets of the plot to assassinate

Rāmānuja. It was arranged to kill him in the depths the forests, perhaps not very far from Kanchi. Information of this was given to Rāmānuja in time. He escaped at dead of night, and journeyed back to Kanchi under the guidance of a kind hunter and huntress. At daybreak the latter asked for a little water and, when Rāmānuja got down a well to fetch her some, the pair disappeared. Rāmānuja had not to travel much farther before he came in sight of the spires of the great temple at Kanchi.

Having reached Kanchi and intimated to his mother what had happened and how he escaped death by divine intervention, he settled down as a householder at the instance of his mother, and devoted himself to the service of the god Dēvaraja at Kanchi. Āḷavandār was drawing near his end in the meanwhile, and those about him despatched the eldest among his disciples to go and bring Rāmānuja to Srīrangam. Periyanambi, as this emissary was called, arrived at Kanchi and stood reciting one of the beautiful verses in praise of God (the Stōtraratna) composed by his master Āḷavandār. Rāmānuja's attention was drawn to the slōkas (verses) in spite of his single-minded devotion to his preparation for the morning service. Turning round he asked the stranger who the composer of the piece was. Periyanambi answered it was his great master Āḷavandār. The next question was necessarily, whether he could see him. 'If you would go with me now', said Periyanambi, 'I will take you to him' Rāmānuja hurried through his morning service and started with Periyanambi, having obtained permission of Dēvaraja for the journey.

They journeyed along till they reached the northern side of Srīrangam, when at a distance Rāmānuja descried a group of men on the south bank of the Koleroon River. Approaching closer Periyanambi and his younger companion discovered that Āḷavandār was no more, and the group, consisting of his disciples, came there with the remains of the departed great one for its final disposal. Rāmānuja was taken close to the body to take a first and final look at the great master, when lo! he saw three out of the five fingers of the right hand folded. Struck with this, he inquired whether the defect was noticed in life and the answer came that the defect was not physical and was not noticed in life. On further inquiry Rāmānuja was told that the master had three of his cherished objects unfulfilled, namely, an easily read and understood commentary upon the *Brahmasūtra*; the giving of the names of Parāśara and Shaḍagōpa to suitable persons who would make these names live among the people. Rāmānuja promised to see these fulfilled and the fingers straightened. Rāmānuja waited for the funeral ceremonies to be completed and returned to Kanchi to resume his duties of devotion to God.

Having passed days in his usual round of service, Rāmānuja felt that time was passing without any attempt on his part to perform what he had promised to do. Not knowing exactly what to do, he appealed to the elderly priest of the god Dēvaraja and wished him to ascertain the divine will regarding his own future. Tirukkachchinambi, as the priest was called, gave out the will of God, in the matter, in the following slōka:—

'Srīmān param-tatvam aham, matam mē bhēdah prapattirnirapāya hētuhu,

Nāvaśyakīcha smriti hiantyakālē mōkshaha, mahāpūrnaha iha āryavaryaha.'

'I am the supreme, my conviction is distinction, devotion is the unfailing cause of salvation, conscious volition not essential, release in the end; at present Periyanambi is the venerable preceptor.'

In these six phrases Rāmānuja was given the direction for his future work, whether the actual direction came from within himself or from without, or from those about him. He was to pin his faith to God and work out the qualified monistic system of Indian philosophy, accepting Periyanambi for his initiaton. He was to teach the doctrines of devotion to God, whose self-imposed duty it is to give salvation even without the conscious volition of the person wishing it. Rāmānuja felt the call and, with the permission of Dēvaraja, accorded through his priest, he started towards Srīrangam.

He halted at Madhurāntakam to pay his homage of worship to the god Rama in the temple there, situated on the tank bund. While in the act, he saw Periyanambi, who was on his way to Kanchi. They both inquired of each other the purpose of his journey, and found that each had in a way come to the end of it. Rāmānuja found the guru (preceptor) he sought, while Periyanambi's object was to take Rāmānuja to Srīrangam. In fact he had been sent on that special misson by the disciples of first degree of the late master Āḷavandār. At Rāmānuja's importunate entreaty Nambi initiated him into the mysteries of the hidden lore of the Vēdānta of those times, in presence of the god Rama in the temple. Both Nambi and Rāmānuja returned to Kanchi; master and disciple together lived there for sometime. But their separation came soon and gave a quicker turn to the whole career of Rāmānuja.

Nambi and Rāmānuja took up lodgings together and the two families lived amicably together for some time. Rāmānuja, however, does not appear to have been very happy in the choice of his wife. He did not find in her that ready sympathy and compliance to his own wishes he expected of her. On one occasion he had invited Tirukachchinambi to his house. The two sat down, and conversed together for a while. When the former went away Rāmānuja's wife quickly washed the seat occupied by him, the temple priest having been of a slightly inferior status in point of caste. Rāmānuja felt aggrieved and overlooked this offence with an admonition. Again one morning while he was still by the accustomed well preparing for the morning service at the temple, a poor man asked him for food. He directed him home with instructions to demand food of Rāmānuja's wife with the husband's permission. She said there was none available. The man returned telling Rāmānuja how he fared. Rāmānuja's inquiry on returning home proved that there was some food which might have been given to the person. Again he excused her. But the third offence proved to be the last straw, and was the most serious of all in Rāmānuja's estimation. Rāmānuja's wife and Periyanambi's both of them went to the same well to fetch water. It would appear that through the latter's carelessness some water from her vessel dropped into that of the other. This naturally led to some altercation in which the relative claims of the two families were rather too freely discussed by Rāmānuja's wife. The other lady reported the matter to her husband, who rather than offend the good man quietly broke up his establishment and returned to Srīrangam.

Rāmānuja soon found out the cause of Nambi's unceremonious departure, and resolved that the time had come for separating from his wife. He took advantage of an invitation from his father-in-law to send his wife away, and without further delay assumed the brown robes of a sannyasi (he who has renounced the world). This step at once added to the rising reputation of Rāmānuja, and disciples began to gather round him. It was now that disciples first appear round Yatirāja (king of hermits) as he came to be called. It was probably now also that the question assumed importance whether a sannyasi should be of the Ēkadanḍi or Tridanḍi (single rod or triple rod, as the symbol of office). The Vaishṇava version says that Yādavaprakāśa, his late master, became a convert to Rāmānuja under the name of Govindayōgi and wrote the work *Yatidharma Samuchchayam.* (The inquiry into the rules of conduct of a hermit).

While Rāmānuja was making progress in this manner, the disciples of Āḷavandār at Srīrangam wished to get him to live in their midst, and to occupy the seat of their late master which had remained unoccupied for lack of a suitable successor. This time they sent another of Āḷavandār's immediate disciples, his own son, by name Tiruvarangapperumāl Araiyar. Rāmānuja followed the Araiyar and settled down at Srīrangam. It was now that he set about seriously to acquire the qualifications, which alone would justify his accession to the high position to which he was looked upon by the public as the most worthy candidate. He had, therefore, to get himself initiated into every department of learning and philosophy, which then constituted the Vaishṇava lore. Periyanambi having become his *guru* (preceptor) in one part, he had to seek initiation of Tirukkōṭṭiyūrnambi for another (mantrārtham). He went six times in succession and on all these occasions the master was not satisfied with the earnestness of the disciple and declined to open his mind. Rāmānuja in despondency thought of giving up the business when he was asked to try another time. He succeeded in inducing the great one to unlock his secrets; after the customary promise not to publish except to a worthy disciple previously tried. Rāmānuja agreed and found the secrets of such efficacy for salvation that he taught all who were about him what he learnt. The guru summoned the disciple to his presence and asked him how it was that he had so flagrantly transgressed the injunctions of his master. Rāmānuja begged to be prescribed the punishment. The guru replied that the punishment would be 'eternal hell' hereafter, but nothing here. Rāmānuja replied with characteristic beneficence that he would gladly suffer hell himself, if by so doing he was instrumental in ministering to the attainment of salvation to the suffering millions of humanity. The master appreciated the spirit of the disciple's transgression, and said that the particular darśana (section of Vedānta) might hereafter be known as *Rāmānuja darśana*.

At this period Rāmānuja had to intervene in the affairs of his cousin and companion at school, Govinda Bhaṭṭar. This young man had continued his journey along with Yādavaprakāśa to the Ganges. It would appear that while he bathed in the holy waters of the river, a phallic emblem struck to the palm of his hand. Hence the name Uḷḷangai Gonarndanāyanār. From that time forward he became a staunch Śaiva and resided at Kāḷahasti not far from his maternal uncle at Tirupati. At Rāmānuja's request the uncle met the nephew, and brought him back to allegiance to the Vaishṇava persuasion under the new sacerdotal designation of Embār. Rāmānuja's name had begun to attract attention, and be felt that he should still acquire other qualifications before becoming every way the head of a darśana.

He began his studies in Tiruvōymoḷi first under Tiruvarangapperumāl Araiyar and then under Tirumālaiyāṇḍān. While with the latter, he had occasion to show his special acuteness of intellect in suggesting special interpretations of important texts, which on further discussion were found to have been in full agreement with the views of Āḷavandār. This new acquisition completed his round of qualifications and he became in fact a successor of Āḷavandār in every sense of the term.

Rāmānuja's fame had spread so wide and he came to be known so well that his little cousin at Tirupati (son of his maternal uncle) evinced a precocious desire to attach himself to Rāmānuja. The father sent the boy in charge of a nephew of his own, and the two arrived at Srīrangam, where Rāmānuja's life had been saved by the unlooked for intervention of a good woman. Rāmānuja, as a sannyasi had to go round at mid-day from house to house for food. One of the house-holders had instructed his wife to poison the food and serve it to him. The woman felt compelled to obey the husband, but, on giving the handful to Rāmānuja, could not bear the feeling that the good man would die of the food. She, therefore, prostrated herself before him while getting back into the house. It is recognized as a rule of practice that when a sannyasi goes out for alms (biksha), that no one should make the usual salutation. This strange conduct on the part of the lady struck Rāmānuja and he suspected foul play. On examination the poison was discovered, and ever after it was arranged that the elder of the two new arrivals should undertake the food supply of Rāmānuja. In spite of this attempt at assassination, all had so far gone smoothly; but the life of Rāmānuja becomes stormy hereafter. His fame had spread far and the few prominent conversions attracted attention. Whether he wished it or no, he had to make his position good against all comers and had to assume the rôle of a controversialist.

At this time there arrived at Srīrangam an Advaita sannyasi, by name Yegñamūrti, in the course of a controversial tour through India. Then there began between the two a great disputation regarding the relative superiority of their respective creeds. For sixteen days they went on with no decisive result either way, and Rāmānuja was somewhat anxious about his own position, when it struck him that he might derive some help from Ālavandār's works. He referred to the latter's Māyavādakandaṇanam (a refutation of the idealistic theory). Thus armed he overcame his adversary on the seventeenth day and, as a result, enlisted his rival among his followers under the Vaishṇava designation of Aruḷāḷapperumāl Emberumānār.

Sometime after Rāmānuja felt that he might conveniently pay the long-wished-for visit to his uncle, who sent word through his nephew that he very much wished to see him. Rāmānuja then set forward for Tirupati, one of the three 'holy of holies' of the Srī Vaishṇavas. He stayed a year receiving instruction in the Rāmāyana from his maternal uncle there, who at the end of the period made over to him his two sons. His preparations were now complete and as he was growing old, he set about fulfilling his undertaking to Āḷavandār. The first of his three promises was the writing out of such a commentary for the *Brahmasūtra* as would embody the views of the qualified monistic school of thought. It was absolutely essential for a due performance of this work that he should acquaint himself with the previous commentators, particularly of the *Bōdhāyanavritti*. This naturally was not easy of acquisition for one of his intentions explicit and implied. He had to go about much before he found access to a library in the north, containing the work, where he was allowed just to read it through. He felt that it was not enough when a quick disciple among his followers came to his rescue by saying that he had completely mastered the work and could give references whenever wanted. This was one among his first disciples, who lived to render yet greater services to his master. With the help of Kūrattaḻvān—for such was the name of this stout-hearted and quick-minded disciple—Rāmānuja wrote out the three works, the essence of the Vēdānta (*Vēdāntasāram*), a resume of the Vēdānta (*Vēdānta Sangraham*), the light of the Vēdānta (*Vēdāntadīpam*). He also wrote, or rather gave out, the commentaries on the *Brāhmāsūtra* and *Bhagavatgīta*.

This list of works redeemed Rāmānuja from his first promise.

But these must be accepted before Rāmānuja could feel he had done his duty to his master. He had, therefore, to start on a tour to different places to secure the approval of the learned. This tour naturally took him to the great seat of learning, Kāsmir. There at Sarasvatīpīṭa (the seat of learning) he read through the work in an assembly of philosophers and obtained from them the approval of no less an authority than 'Sarasvati' herself. As a token of her approval she presented Rāmānuja with the image of Hayagrīva (horse-necked, an aspect of Vishṇu) and said that his commentary might thereafter be known *Srī Bhāshya* (the commentary). It is because of this distinction that among his disciples Rāmānuja is known Bhāshyakārar (maker of *the* Bhāshya). The image of Hayagrīva has come down to the present generation and is believed to be that which is the object of worship at the Parakālamutt at Mysore.

Returning from the north he had to pass by way of Tirupati where matters had assumed a serious aspect on a dispute as to the nature of the deity there. The Śaivas claimed the shrine to be that of god Śiva while the Vaishṇavas claimed it as that of Vishṇu. The matter had, therefore, to be settled one way or the other, and they agreed to leave the decision to the god himself. It was arranged that one evening both parties should assemble and lock up the 'sanctum sanctorum' having placed the weapons peculiar to each deity. The shrine was to be that of Vishṇu or Śiva according as the one set or the other was assumed by god. It was found the next morning that the image had assumed the disc and conch characteristic of Vishṇu, and ever after the shrine appears to have been taken to be that of Vishṇu. Having settled this dispute Rāmānuja returned to Srīrangam and set about arranging matters for getting through the remaining items of work he had undertaken.

Rāmānuja's foremost disciple Kūrattāḻvān was for long childless. One night he had to go to bed without food, having had to fast the whole day for lack of provisions. The bell in the great temple pealed, indicating that the night-worship was going on. The devoted wife thought to herself that it was hardly fair that god Ranganātha should accept regular worship when the staunchest of his devotees lay starving. Soon after the temple priests brought a supply of food from the temple and knocked at the door of Kūrattāḻvan. The wife opened the door and delighted with the arrival of food, woke up the restless husband and fed him. As the direct outcome of this divine favour, she soon became mother of two sons to one of whom at the instance of Rāmānuja, the name Parāśara was given. This boy had grown up to man's state when Rāmānuja was looking out for some one through whom he might fulfil the second object. This young man Parāśara Bhaṭṭa was commissioned to write a commentary on the *Sahasranāma* (the thousand names of Vishṇu). This work of Parāśara Bhaṭṭa fulfilled the second of the desiderata of Āḷavandār.

There then remained the means of perpetuating the name of Nammāḻvār, the author of the Tiruvōymoḻi. Rāmānuja was perhaps thinking of a commentary himself. It would appear he was contemplating within a closed room a particular verse of the work attempting to realize its full significance when his cousin looked through a chink in the door. The young man, Piḻḻān by name, forthwith put the question whether the master was pondering the verse referring to the god at Tirumālirunjōlai. Rāmānuja was struck with the acuteness of the young man, and commissioned him to write out the 6000 commentary on the

Tiruvōymoḷi, giving him the name Tirukkuruhaippirān Piḷḷān, the first part of which being one of the many surnames of Nammāḷvār. This brought the third of Āḷavandār's desiderata to fulfilment. Rāmānuja could now feel his mission at an end and settle down to a life of quiet teaching. This way years rolled by.

He was not, however, altogether unmolested. A change of ruler, or a change in his surroundings brought about a change in the spirit of complete tolerance that as a rule characterised the administration. Be the cause what it may, the Chola ruler, for the time being, often given the name Kulōttunga, took it into his head to demand assent to the doctrine, 'Śivāt parataram nāsti'. 'There is no Being superior to Siva' This seems to have been aimed particularly against the Rāmānuja propagandists, perhaps because of a few prominent conversions. This challenge was openly thrown out, and naturally enough everybody pointed to Rāmānuja as the person whose assent ought to be obtained. Rāmānuja was summoned to appear in the royal presence.

Rāmānuja's friends feared danger, and to avoid it Kūrattāḷvān undertook to personate Rāmānuja. Assuming the robes of the sannyasi, Kūrattāḷvān went along with the venerable Periyanambi to the Chola Court, while Rāmānuja assuming the dress of a house-holder and at the head of a small body of adherents betook himself to the kingdom of the Hoysala Biṭṭi Dēva. Travelling along the banks of the Kaveri, Rāmānuja settled down at Sāḷigram where he lived for a period of twelve years, while Biṭṭi Dēva was just carving out for himself a kingdom here, along the southern marches of the Chāḷukya kingdom of Vikramāditya and the Chola frontier in the north-west.

A daughter of the king was possessed and after failing in all other attempts at exorcism Rāmānuja's aid was called in. Sure enough the ghost was raised, and Biṭṭi Dēva agreed to become the disciple of Rāmānuja. This could not, however, be without overcoming the Jains in controversy, as the king was reputed to have been a Jain. Rāmānuja had the best of it in the disputation and the bulk of the Jains either embraced the Rāmānuja darśana or were ordered to be ground down in oil mills. This latter threat, however, was not carried into effect through the intervention of Rāmānuja. Rāmānuja returned to Sāligram.

It was while here that Rāmānuja's stock of nāmam (the white earth which serves for the Vaishṇava caste mark on the forehead) ran out of stock and Rāmānuja was much concerned. He dreamt overnight that there was a hill of that material, not far from Toṇḍanūr, where he made the acquaintance with Biṭṭi Dēva. Following the clue he obtained, in his dream, and through the good offices of Viṭala Dēva (Biṭṭi Dēva) Rāmānuja got the spot marked out in his dream dug up; when lo! there appeared beneath a small shrine. He then got it consecrated as Tirunārāyaṇapuram (Mēlukōṭe of the maps). Thinking of a suitable image for this shrine, he dreamt of the image of Rāmaprya, which was at Delhi in possession of the daughter of the ruler at the time. He had to undertake a journey to northern India again. Having got possession of the image semewhat miraculously, he returned with it. As the princess proved inconsolable without her pet image, the king (whoever he was) sent a party of men to bring back Rāmānuja who found shelter in a Panchama village. It is out of gratitude for this protection that he ordained the admission of the latter into the temple on the car festival. The consecration of the image and the completion of the temple are placed in 1021 Śaka or A.D., 1099 which appears to antedate the event much. He had to make good his position here again as against everybody else, and held a successful disputation against the Bauddhas of Padmagiri (Śravana Beḷgoḷa). He then resided at Tirunārayaṇapuram expecting news from the south.

While Rāmānuja was busy doing the important things detailed above, Kūrattāḷvān and Periyanambi went to the Chola Court in obedience to the royal summons. There the question was put to them whether they subscribed to the statement 'Śivāt parataram nāsti'! Kūrattāḷvān subscribed with a reservation 'Drōṇamasti tatahparam'. 'There is Drōna above Śiva'!, taking Śiva in the sense of a measure, Drōna being a bigger measure. For this impertinence the angry king ordered the putting out of the eyes of the two Vaishṇavas. Periyanambi, a venerable old man, died on the way; but the sturdier Kūrattāḷvān, nothing daunted, returned and lived at Srīrangam. After a time the Chola ruler died of a carbuncle, which the Vaishṇavas put down to be the result of the ruler's cruelty to the devoted adherents of Rāmānuja. News of the death of the Chola was taken to Rāmānuja by the messenger whom he had sent to condole with Kūrattāḷvān in his misfortune. On receipt of this somewhat re-assuring news, Rāmānuja made up his mind to return.

Consoling his beneficent disciple as best he could, Rāmānuja had to set about arranging matters for the Adhyayanōtsava, an annual festival for the recitation of the works of the Tamil saints, for which it was the practice to fetch the image of Nammāḷvār from Āḷvār Tirunagari in the Tinnevelli District. This having been a year of heavy rainfall it was found impossible to bring the image of the Āḷvār all the way. Rāmānuja in consequence consecrated a shrine, and restored the image of the Āḷvār in Srīrangam itself, so that no similar difficulty might be experienced for the future. It was on the occasion of this festive celebration that one of the disciples of Kūrattāḷvān dedicated the centum in honour of Rāmānuja on the model of the decade of Madhurakavi on Nammāḻvār. Amudan of Arangam, the author of the centum, it would appear, was the Smārta manager of the temple at Srīrangam, and had been not over accommodating to the Vaishṇava apostle or his disciples. When his old mother was drawing near her end, the son dutifully inquired if she desired anything he might do for her. She wished that either Rāmānuja himself, or one of his nominees, might be invited to accept food from him on the occasion of her funeral ceremonies. Amudan had no alternative but to make the request of Rāmānuja, who advised that his indomitable disciple Kūrattāḻvān might be asked. The latter accepted the invitation and demanded for satisfaction the keys of the temple, which Amudan surrendered and became henceforward the disciple of Kūrattāḻvān. This Amudan in his new-born zeal composed the centum, and begged hard that it might be accepted. Rāmānuja accepted the dedication, and permitted its inclusion in the prabandha 4000 at the earnest pleadings of his first disciples. Having made provision for the regular annual recital of this 4000, Rāmānuja got images of the Āḻvārs and Āṇḍāḷ set up in Srīrangam and other important places, where also similar annual celebrations were ordained.

He then paid a visit to Āḻvār Tirunagari and, on his return, heard that his maternal uncle at Tirupati was no more. He then repaired thither and got the funeral ceremonies duly performed by the elder of the two cousins of his, the younger of whom he had long regarded as his son in apostolic succession. It was while he was yet here that he heard that the Govindaraja temple at Chidambaram had been overthrown and the image cast into the sea. He caused the image to be brought over, and housed it in the temple at the foot of the sacred hill where again he caused to be set up the images of the Āḷvārs and Āndāḷ as elsewhere. He then returned to Srīrangam by way of Kanchi and Madhurāntakam. After this he went to Tirumālirunjōlai and Srīvilliputtūr to complete his round of pilgrimage to the sacred shrines of Vishṇu in the south. Having thus established his influence throughout South India, and having organized and popularized the teachings of Visishṭādvaita-vēdānta he could now think that his mission was at an end. He arranged for the continuance of his teaching by nominating seventy-four from among the worthiest of his followers. Of this number four had special custody of the *Bhāshya*, one among whom had the *Prabhanda* teaching also. This one was no other than his cousin-son Piḷḷān, who became the actual successor of Rāmānuja.

While he was preparing to depart from this world, he found the most indomitable among his companions anticipate him in this as well. Having got his funeral rites duly performed, Rāmānuja felt that he had arrived at the end of his mission, when again, at the importunate entreaty of his disciples, he had to permit three of his own images to be consecrated and set up in Srīrangam, Srīperumbūthūr, and Tirunārāyaṇapuram. This example has been followed later on, and now every Vishṇu temple in the south has, as a necessary adjunct to it, a little shrine for Rāmānuja Consoling his sorrowing disciples and companions, Rāmānuja felt the call and so passed away quietly, having completed the one hundred and twentieth year of his age.

The above, in brief, is an outline of the life of Rāmānuja, according to the most authoritative tradition. This tradition has a tendency to gather volume, as time passes, and there have been as many varieties of this biography as there have been those interested in hagiologists. But this account relies particularly on two contemporary works, which have special claims for our acceptance Neither of them is a professed biography, and both of them were written for the acceptance of contemporaries. One of them had been read before Rāmānuja and obtained his imprimatur. This is the work of Amudan of Arangam. It consists of one hundred stanzas in Tamil, included in the *Prabandha* of the Tamil part of the Vaishṇava lore. The other is the work of a disciple also, by name Vaḍuhanambi (or in Sanskrit Āndhrapūrṇa), probably because he was a Telugu man. This is called *Yatirāja Vaibhavam* and consists of 114 slokas. This work describes in a way quite free from exaggeration all that Rāmānuja did. It strikes one as being particularly reliable. The name of the author occurs among the seventy-four successors of first degree of Rāmānuja, and his obligation to the master is indicated in the sloka which is now quoted:—

'Kāmschid Kasminschid arthē pratiniyatatayā sanniyōjyāntarangān, tatra kshīrārtha krityē pratiniyatamahō dāsamapyatyanarham, Kurvan srīmān yatīndrassvapatavinata tatdāsānudāsam māmapyatyantabhaktam svahitamiva sadā gōpayan sōpi jīyāt.'

Having ordered his most trusted disciples to accept particular offices, Rāmānuja 'who protected his worthless servant, servant of his servants, entrusted with the service of providing milk, may he prosper.'

It now remains to examine from available historical material what truth there is in the above account, and how far certain impressions that prevail regarding Rāmānuja and his teachings find justification from his life and times. Having already recounted the incidents in the life of Rāmānuja, we shall now proceed to examine critically, whether the main incidents of his life are what his disciples claim them to have been, and whether recent research, so far as it bears upon these, lends any support to these as a whole. The following incidents will be examined seriatim, as they appear to be arranged in chronological order:—

1. Rāmānuja's conversion of Yādavaprakāśa, his preceptor.

2. His conversion of Yegñamūrti, an advaita sannyasin.

3. Settlement of the Śaiva Vaishṇava dispute about the god at Tirupati.

4. The Chola persecution of Rāmānuja.

5. The Hoysala Vishṇuvardhana's conversion.

6. Foundation of the temple at Tirunārāyaṇapuram (Mēlukōṭe).

7. The conversion of Amudan of Arangam, the author of *Rāmānuja Nūṟṟandhādhi*.

8. The consecration of the Govinda temple at the foot of the Tirupati Hill.

For the purposes of this again we shall, as far as possible, have recourse to such works of reliable authority, as those of Rāmānuja's contemporaries and immediate successors only.

1. Yādavaprakāśa was an advaitic teacher of reputation at Conjeevaram. He was also a writer of authority in his philosophy; and in his days, and after, he was a leader of a school of thought; that Vēdānta Dēśika quotes him, as the best representative of advaitic exposition, and disputes his position. He is the reputed author of *Yatidharma Samuchchayam* and of the *Yādava Nikaṇḍu*. According to others the two works are from separate persons. At any rate the Yādava of the former work is in all probability, the philosophical expounder of the advaitic system. In the face of these facts, it would appear impossible that he should have been the first convert to the teachings of his ex-disciple Rāmānuja, whom he did not love overmuch as a disciple. I have long thought that the story was a pious fabrication. There is no

reference at all in the *Yatidharma Samuchchayam* to his conversion. This is a work which undertakes to examine what the duties of a sannyasi are according to the best authority; and the author seems to hold that there is good authority for both classes of sannyasins—those with the sacred thread and tuft of hair on the head (the Vaishṇava), and those without these adjuncts (the Śaiva). Except a reference to the '*Prabhandas* in the invocatory verse and to the invocation itself being addressed to Vishṇu as Dattatrēya, the work is non-committing in this particular. But the work, *Rāmānuja Nāṟṟandhādhi* of Amudan of Arangam, one of his own converts, refers often to success in disputation against great controversialists; but does not mention names though the references are such, as would warrant the inference that they were in particular Yādavaprakāśa and the sannyasin Yegñamūrti (stanzas 58, 64, and 88). But in two works of Vēdānta Dēśika coming just three generations after, or say about a century, we have direct references to the purpose. The first half of verse thirteen of *Yatirája Saptati* refers to' 'Svabhalāt uddhrita Yādavaprakāśa', or he that had up-rooted with his own strength Yādavaprakāśa. This need not necessarily mean conversion, but that such was actually the case is clearly stated in one of his other works, *Satadhūshaṇi*.[1]

[1] I am obliged for this reference to the late lamented Tarkatīrtha Punḍitaratnam Kastūrirangāchar of Mysore.

असमीक्षितदशापरित्यक्तब्रह्मसूत्रैश्च यादवप्रकाशैः समीक्ष्य संजातानुशयैः स्ववेषप्रमाणमनुयुक्ता वासुदेवयात्रोत्सवसमागता नानादिगन्तवास्तव्यशिष्टाश्च प्रायश्चित्तमेव उत्तरंददुः । भ्रष्टस्तर्हि असावितिचेन्न । प्रायश्चित्तात् पूर्वमेव तथात्वस्य प्राचीनैर्निश्चितत्वात् । तत्समुच्चितस्यैव यतिधर्मस्याद्यापि मानवादिवदविगानात्. — ।

शतदूषणी—यतिलिङ्गभेदभङ्गम् 64

Vēdānta Dēśika followed Rāmānuja at an interval of three generations only, and we may take him as sufficient authority for the fact, as he takes Yādava's opinions and seriously controverts them in other parts of his works.

2. As to Yegñamūrti's conversion we are not in a position to say anything, as nothing more is known of him than the fact of his having been a sannyasin Ēkadandi).

3. The question about Tirupati is of far greater importance, the more so as there has recently been a lively controversy about the same subject in the columns of the journals and papers, consequent on Mr. Venkyya's reference in his official report to the temple being a Śaiva one. It will be seen that the Vaishṇava account says that the god on the hill had just lent his characteristic weapons, the disc and the conch, to the Tonḍamān Chakravarti. This evidently refers to the conquest of Kalingam by Karuṇākara Tonḍamān about A. D. 1111. Messrs. M. Narayanasami Iyer, B.A., B.L. and T. A. Gopinatha Rau, M.A., have both written concerning this in the *Sen Tamil*. The former inclines to the Vaishṇava view and the latter to the Śaiva. The question, therefore, needs to be examined with care. The following facts concerning the point appear to be agreed upon. The authors of the *Tēvāram* have not at all celebrated the shrine; the Vaishṇava Āḻvārs have. The Tamil epic *Śilappadhikāram* has explicitly given the temple a Vaishṇava character, and there is no possibility of mistake here. On this account, therefore,

ततश्च परित्यक्तयज्ञोपवीतादिकेषु एकदण्डिकेष्वपि – अद्यापि आयुष्मतो विप्रतिपत्तिः भास्करयादवप्रकाशादि ग्रन्थरसायन सेवया–निवर्तते ॥

शतदूषणी—अश्लेपकमतभङ्गम् 65

Mr. Gopinatha Rau would place the Śilappadhikāram after Poygai Āḻvār. Whether he puts it also after Rāmānuja is not quite clear, though he shows a wish to bring it to the middle of the twelfth century. This gentleman holds that the original god was Subrahmaṇya as the place is called Iḷangoil, and the god is referred to once or twice as Kumara, though not without other adjuncts. The latter is quite decisive according to him. So it would be, if the premises were quite as they are represented to be. One fundamental defect here is the taking out of words without reference to their context. Mr. Gopinatha Rau refers to the god being known as Bālājee among the northerners. This may be so, but Bālājee is not exclusively applied to Subrahmaṇya, if applied to him at all. There are numbers of persons known as Bālājee, but the word stands for Bālakrishna. This is equally sound. There is something more. The early Āḻvārs, Poygai Āḻvār, Bhūtattār and Pēy Āḻvār delight in referring to God in one of his aspects as a child, either as Rama or Krishna, preferably the latter. One has only to look through the writings of these to be convinced of this. Why they do so is beside the point. It is this Bālakrishna—he is not so named in the work—that has given rise to the name Bālājee[1], since Krishna, as Viṭōba, is very popular in the Mahrata country. Anyhow this interpretation of Bālājee is in keeping with the writings of those Āḻvārs who had bestowed their best thoughts upon God's manifestation at Tirupati. Pēy Āḻvār lends the greatest support to this contention as to the nature of the deity. He refers to the God as இளங்குமாரன் றண்விண்ணகர் (61); விளங்கனிக்குக் கன்றெறிந்தோன் வெற்பு (68); இளங்குமாரர் கோமா

[1] One at least of the explanations for this designation is that, when the northerners first had a look of the image, they were so struck with the softly beautiful look that they exclaimed in surprise Bālā (Damsel). This was the account given by the people in the locality.

னிடம் (72) *நான் முகத்தோன் நன்குறங்கில், வாய்ந்த குழவியாய்* (77). It will thus be seen that he refers to the same deity in four different ways as above. They are, of course, to be taken synonymously. References one and three may be doubtful, but the other two must be used to help us in the interpretation. Reference two clearly indicates one of the acts of young Krishna, and reference four, though not equally clearly, to an achievement of Vishṇu, when Brahma was about to grant the boons sought of him by Rāvaṇa. If a more direct indication be needed, the stanza sixty-two makes it clear to any unprejudiced mind. There are a number of places sacred to Vishṇu and the names given are Vaishṇava names, e.g. Tiruvarangam and Tirukuḍandhai (Kumbhakonam). There is thus nothing to bear out the contention that the god there was ever meant to be Subrahmaṇya. Stanza sixty-three of the same third *Tiruvandādi* states clearly that the manifestation of God there is in the united form of Śiva and Vishṇu. This is borne out by the stanzas five and ninety-eight of the first *Tiruvandādi*. This would, therefore, make it clear that the god was of the 'harihara' type. Then the question arises why it is that Iḷangō speaks of it as a Vishṇu temple in such clear terms. The explanation, perhaps, would be that the temple had been known only as a Vishṇu temple, though there was the duplex character in the idol. This would be noticed only by a devotee, who was in close touch with the temple, and this Iḷangō could not pretend to have been. It is not strange if most people in these days do not know this. Its established reputation as a Vishṇu temple accounts for the omission of Tirupati by the Nāyanmārs of the Śaivas. How then was it that the Śaivas laid claim to it in the days of Rāmānuja? Rāmānuja's time was remarkable for the revival of the *Prabhandam*, which was being taught much more widely than before. Besides this Rāmānuja's cousin's conversion must have made the Śaivas alive to the danger of this Vaishṇava neighbourhood. So on the old grounds of the dual form of the image they revived their claims, particularly as the ruling sovereign was likely to lean to the Śaiva side. Naturally enough Rāmānuja appealed to a trial by ordeal of some sort. Ever after, there appears to have been no dispute as to the character of the deity. This must have taken place sometime after A. D. 1111–2, the probable date of the conquest of Kalingam.

4. The next item of importance in the life of Rāmānuja is the Chola persecution. The Chola ruler at the time was Kulōttunga, the Chāḷukya-Chola (A. D. 1070 to 1118). Most of the Cholas were Śaivas, but they were tolerant of other religions as well, while some of them even went the length of endowing Vishṇu temples. This Kulōttunga was not particularly narrow-minded, as he made a grant even to the Bauddha settlement at Negapatam. But as the Vaishṇava account itself states he was persuaded by others into compelling all to assent to the doctrine of the supremacy of Śiva. This is not at all improbable, considering that this was the period of great Śaiva activity and the ruler was the special patron of Śēkkiḻār. The general body of Vaishṇavas were not ill-treated, but Rāmānuja's active work at Srīrangam attracted attention and ended in the blinding of Kūrattāḻvār and the old preceptor of Rāmānuja himself. This must have taken placc about the nineties of the eleventh century. Rāmānuja was compelled to leave the country. His immigration into the Mysore country brings us to the next important incident in his life.

5 and 6. He moved up the Kavery and settled at Sāḷigram, from which place he was invited to the headquarters of Viṭala Dēva Rāya or Biṭṭi Dēva. This latter could not have been the ruling sovereign at the time, as his brother lived to the end of the century and a few

years later. During the last years of the century he was still active in the Gangavāḍi frontier, and it was while here that he must have met Rāmānuja. His elder brother 'had for his god Īśa', which probably meant that he was a Śaiva. Biṭṭi Dēva was converted and helped Rāmānuja in the restoration of the temple of Nārāyaṇa at Mēlukōṭe. I have elsewhere[1] shown that the persecution of the Jains ascribed to Vishṇuvardhana is hardly supported by facts. The consecration of the temple at Mēlukōṭe is placed in the year A.D. 1099, twelve years after Rāmānuja's arrival at Sāḷigrām. This may have been the case, as Rāmānuja would have taken care not to provoke the hostility of the ruler of his new domicile. Vishṇuvardhana thenceforward supported the cause of Rāmānuja and encouraged Vishṇavaism. He went on building temples and endowing them, not without supporting the other temples and creeds as well, though not perhaps to the same extent. This activity culminated in the building and consecration of the temple at Bēlur in (or about) A.D. 1117.[2] There is nothing improbable in the date, as it was in this year that he could claim to have become master of the Gangavāḍi. So Rāmānuja must have lived in Mysore for nearly a quarter of a century. It was the death of the Chola Kulōttunga in A.D. 1118 that enabled him to return. But then there is an inconsistency with respect to dates. As the *Guruparamparai* states, it appears that the Chola died soon after the blinding of the two friends of Rāmānuja; but in actual fact the death of the persecuting Chola came many years after, if the date A.D. 1099 be taken as correct for the Mēlukōṭe incident, which appears too early to be true. It would be too much to expect this kind of accuracy in such an account and in one of its professed character.

[1] Chapter IX. Vishṇuvardhana, following.

[2] Hassan volume of the *Epigraphia Carnāṭaka Ins. Belur* 58 and 71.

7. The next incident of importance is the conversion of Amudan of Arangam, the manager of the temple at Srīrangam, a non-Vaishṇava. For this we have evidence of the convert himself. He is the author of the *Rāmānuja Nūṟṟandādi* and in verses three, four and seven of the work he makes it clear that he was a convert by favour of Rāmānuja and Kūrattāḻvār. In verses eight and twenty-one, he clearly describes Rāmānuja's relation to the Āḻvārs and Nāḍhamuni and Āḷavandār (Yamunaitturaivar), in spite of opinions to the contrary by scholars who implicitly believe in the opinion of Dr. Caldwell. Not only this. The centum (in fact 108) of his stanzas gives in a small span, mostly allusively but none the less clearly, the main achievements of Rāmānuja, and thus becomes the contemporary authority for most of the facts of Rāmānuja's life as detailed above. The moderation of tone and sobriety of language commend its authority the more, for otherwise Rāmānuja would not have been persuaded to include it among the *Prabhandam* 4000.

8. Lastly comes the construction and consecration of the Govinda shrine at the foot of the Tirupati hill. This affords the best clue to the date of Rāmānuja. The *Guruparamparai* gives this as the last act of a busy life under circumstances which, thanks to the researches of Brahma Sri R. Raghava Iyengar, Court Pandit of Ramnad and Editor of the *Sen Tamil*, the organ of the Madura Tamil Śangam, prove to be quite historical. The story, it will be remembered, is that the Govinda Raja temple at Chidambaram having been removed from the premises of the great Śiva temple, Rāmānuja and his disciples got the idol enshrined in a new temple at Tirupati. In a number of historical works relating to the period, particularly in the *Kulōttunga Chōḻan Ulā* of Oṭṭakūttan,[1] this achievement is ascribed to Kulōt-

[1] *Śen Tamil*, vol. III, part. v, pp. 166-7.

tunga II, the son and successor of Vikrama Chola and one of the patrons of Kūttan himself. There it is said that he renovated the Śaiva temple and plated the roofing with gold—incidentally mentioning that the 'God Vishṇu had been sent back to his original shrine —the sea.'[1] This would mean not only the removal but the throwing of the image into the sea. In another, there is a reference to Kulōttunga's having rooted out the minor gods from the great shrine. This must have taken place in the reign of Kulōttunga II (*circa* 1123 to 1146). That the Vaishṇavas were enabled to enshrine the god at Tirupati shows the limitation of the Chola authority at the time, or their indifference to the fact, provided the obnoxious god had been removed from the hallowed presence of their 'Holy of Holies', a place full of the most narrow-minded of the Śaivas. That the Vishṇu shrine was previously in the temple at Chidambaram is borne out by a reference in the works of Māṇikka Vāśagar (*Tiruchchiṟṟambalakkōvai, 86*). There is absolutely no reason to doubt the authority of these works about this particular, and this gives us the ultimate limit of Rāmānuja's active life. According to the traditional account, Rāmānuja lived for 120 years from A. D. 1017 to 1137. Some object to this length, and regard it as a fabrication just to give the reformer the Mahādaśa as it is called. It is a matter of very small consequence to us whether he lived the 120 years or not. What is more important for our purposes is that his was a long and active life, and covered three reigns of the Cholas: Kulōttunga I (A. D. 1070 to 1118), Vikramachola (A. D. 1118 to 1135), Kulōttunga II (A. D. 1123 to 1146). Rāmānuja's active life may, therefore, be safely referred to the last quarter of the eleventh and the first half of the twelfth century A. D.

[1] *Śen Tamil*, vol. III, part viii, pp. 301–2.

CHAPTER VIII

THE MAKING OF MYSORE

MYSORE, the modern State, is a product of the nineteenth century. The country actually included in the term got united under one ruler, only under the vigorous rule of the Musalmán usurper, Haidar 'Alī. Through much of its history before, the State was parcelled out into a number of States of varying extent and importance. It will, therefore, be profitable to inquire whether, at any time before the last quarter of the eighteenth century, the whole State was brought under one rule.

Adjusting our time-telescope, if we look through it, as far as we can see at all, into the dim vistas of the early centuries of the Christian era, we are able to see but little. The sources of information available are the most meagre of hints from early Tamil literature. We have references leading to the location in Mysore territory of some petty chieftains, among whom may be mentioned one whom the Tamilians call 'Erumaiyūrān' (the chief of the Buffalo country) among the seven petty chiefs. Passing from this time, we come unto the period of the Gangas, a race of rulers whose domain in the south of Mysore embraced the southern portions of the modern Ashṭagram and Nandidrug divisions. This dynasty was at times powerful enough to make its influence felt in South Indian politics, but at no time of its history did it make good its claim to having passed beyond the lead of another power, generally the sovereigns of the Dekhan. Before passing on further, it will be well to look back upon the disposition of the Powers north and south in order to better understand the rôle that Mysore played in the history of South India.

To begin again at the beginning of history so far as is known at present, we find that India throughout historical times is divisible for purposes of history into three geographical parts: Hindustan, the Dekhan and the Farther South. When the Āndhra successors of the Mauryan dynasty were overthrown, a dynasty of rulers, the Āndhrabhrityas of the Puranas, fastened themselves upon the Dekhan. It is this dynasty (100 B.C.–A.D. 300) that, from the second line of defence of peninsular India, withstood successfully and beat back the incursions of the foreigners—the Scythians of Central Asia, who had established themselves in the north-west of India. The territories of these Sātavāhanas (vulgo Sālivāhana), or Āndhrabhrityas, embraced the whole of the Dekhan extending from coast to coast. They had to maintain two capitals, one in the south-east and another in the north-west, and occasionally two rulers, the father and son, or brother and brother, holding each his Court. This division of authority betrays the need for protection against two powerful neighbours, always on the alert to take advantage of any opportunity that might offer itself for cutting off a slice of territory. The north-west capital was at Paiṭān (Plithāna of the Greeks) on the upper waters of the Godavery, and the south-east one at Dhanakaṭaka (Dharnikōṭ) in the Guntur taluq, the Amarāvati of Buddhist fame. This must have been the period when the three crowned rulers of the Farther South laid claim to having defeated 'the Aryan Army', and to having planted their respective, emblemson the Himalayas (which may be an eastern figure of speech for extensive conquests in the northern Dekhan). There is a hiatus now and we lose the thread. The Āndhrabhritya Power breaks up, perhaps because of the simultaneous attacks of the Guzerat and Mālva Kshētrapas, after about three centuries of existence, and then other Powers are forming. The Guptas assume imperial responsibilities, and from the central Indian bastion beat back the Kshētrapas on the one side and the Hūṇas on the other, thus giving time to the Dekhan States to settle down to the normal condition from the amorphous state to which they had been reduced after the fall of the Sātavāhaṇas. The Pallavas are erecting themselves in the north of the Tamil country, with their head-quarters moving south till they reach the ancient Chola town of Kanchi, the head-quarters of the Toṇḍamān Rajas. Before this, we hear of them at Amarāvati, Palakka and other places further north. Perhaps these Pallavas were feudatory wardens of the marches of the Sātavāhanas in the south, and when the latter Power broke up the Pallavas made themselves, as was often the case, paramount. When, therefore, we come to the period of Samudragupta (*circa* A. D. 400) the great Gupta Emperor of the north, we find Vishṇugōpa of Kanchi, already an important ruler, whose dominion lay beyond the sphere of influence of the Gupta emperor. Simultaneously with this Power rises that of the Chāḷukyas of Vātāpi (Badami in the Bijāpur taluq). These were, or must have been again, the wardens of the marches in the south-west under the Āndhrabhrityas. So that when Yuwan Chwang (Hiuen Thsang) travelled through the country in A.D. 640, we find India marked out into three clearly defined political divisions. Śīlāditya or Harshavardhana of Kanouj was, in succession to the Guptas, ruling over Hindustan to the frontiers of Assam; Pulikēsin II of the Mahārāshtra at Badami, with his younger brother Kubja Vishṇuvardhana at Rajamahēndri (Jananāthāpura); and Narasimhavarman Pallava or Mahāmalla at Kanchi. This division continues under all the vicissitudes of families and dynasties till the overthrow of Vijayanagar. The Chāḷukyas were succeeded by the

Rāshṭrakūṭas of Mānyakhēta (Malkhed in the Nizam's Dominions) and by the later Chāḷukyas of Kalyāṇi (near Bidar); while the country north of the Vindhyas had passed on to the Gūrjaras and then to the Rajaput dynasties. The Pallavas had been succeeded by the Cholas, so that about A. D. 1000 the following were the positions of the Powers, drawing in their breath for a grand struggle for supremacy which, with varying success, had been going on all the time.

The western Chālukyas of Kalyāṇi were ruling over Raṭṭappāḍi seven and a half lac country (the Bombay Presidency south of the Vindhyas), and more than half of the Nizam's dominions with portions of the Central Provinces. Their cousins of the east at Rajamahēndri held sway over the Madras Presidency as far as Nellore, and were already getting under the influence of the powerful Chola Rājarāja. These two occupy the Dekhan. South of the Krishna in its lower course and the Tungabhadra from its confluence to its source was the territory either directly under the Chola, or just falling into his power. It will be seen at once that Mysore occupies a convenient angle between the two Powers, and this position proved of advantage sometimes.

Early in the century ending A. D. 1000 the Gangas were playing an important part under their rulers, Perumānaḍi Būtuga and Mārasimha. The Cholas, having already conquered the Pallava territories and the Kongu country, were advancing upon the Gangas, who were feudatory to Krishna III of the Rāshṭrakūṭas and his successors. About the middle of the century the Ganga on behalf of his suzerain defeated the Chola ruler Rajāditya at Takkōlam. This set back the tide of Chola aggression for a while; but his more indomitable successors, Rājarāja and his son, effected the conquest of Gangavāḍi. Before this event happened, and while the Rāshṭrakūṭas were busy fighting against the later Chāḷukyas in a vain attempt at holding out for a while longer, the Gangas absorbed the Noḷambavāḍi 32,000, the modern Tumkur and Chitaldrug districts, under their ruler Mārasimha II. The Rāshṭrakūṭas were overthrown in A. D. 972, and the Chāḷukyas had to establish themselves in their stead, when the southern Chola took his opportunity to push his arms northwards. By A. D. 1000 the Chola had gained a footing in Mysore, and the Gangavāḍi had been made Chola. Since this conquest Mysore had become the battle ground of the contending nations, the Kannaḍa Chāḷukyas and the Tamil Cholas. The wars were long and tiresome and the results changing and doubtful. At one time we hear of the Cholas being beaten back to the Palar; again they press back the enemy. In A. D. 1052, an epoch-making battle was fought at Koppam on the Pērār (Tungabhadra). The elder Chola brother Rājādhirāja loses his head; but his younger brother Rājēndra retrieves the honour of the Cholas and victory rests with them. Āhavamalla Sōmēsvara of the Chāḷukyas has to content himself with the Tungabhadra for the frontier. With the death of these mighty rulers, the affairs of their empires get into confusion and the opportunity for Mysore arrives. Here begins, then, the carving out of a kingdom of Mysore and the carvers were skilful artists indeed. Āhavamalla died leaving behind a number of sons. The eldest son Sōmēsvara succeeded, as was natural, but the second Vikramāditya found it convenient to rebel, after having carefully gauged the temper of the Mahāmanḍalēsvarās (or viceroys of provinces). Vikramāditya, the hero of Bilhaṇa's Vikramānkadēva Charitam, started on a progress through his brother's dominions, under the pretext of going to stop the advance of the then Chola ruler Vīrarājēndra, a brother of the two who distinguished themselves in the battle of Koppam, and he himself was victor over the

Kuntaḷas (western Chāḷukyas) at Kūḍal Sangamam. Somehow or other, these two enemies enter into an agreement, the terms of which are not forthcoming, which was sealed by the marriage of prince Chāḷukya with the daughter of the reigning Chola. This must have been brought about in the interests of both. Vikramāditya found a valuable ally for his project, which now definitely had formed itself in his mind, of overthrowing his brother Sōmēsvara. Vīrarājēndra found that Vikrama's alliance would be of great value to him, as his position was threatened by his sister's son Kulōttunga Chola, who was certainly heir to, at least, his paternal dominions of the Vengi country (eastern Chāḷukya dominions). After the treaty on the banks of the Tungabhadra, Vīrarājēndra marches into the eastern Chāḷukya dominions, and one of his inscriptions claims that he appointed Vijayāditya, the paternal uncle of Kulōttunga, as the Chola viceroy of the newly conquered territories. Kulōttunga Chola and Sōmēsvara naturally combined against the allies, but the result proves favourable ultimately to Vikramāditya and his father-in-law. But Vīrarājēndra dies and his son is installed by Vikramāditya, only to lose his head along with the crown. Kulōttunga instals himself ruler of the eastern Chāḷukya and the Chola dominions. Kulōttunga's reign lasts very nearly half a century (A. D. 1070 to 1118), while his rival contemporary comes to the throne a few years later. He also has as long a reign (A. D. 1076 to 1128). Among the Mahāmanḍalēsvarās of this Vikramāditya, we see one name, Vishṇuvardhana Hoysala, and the sequel will clearly show to us that he laid the foundations of the kingdom of Mysore for the first time in history.

In the far off recesses of the western ghats, there is a place called Angaḍi (mart) in the Mudegere taluq of the Kadur district. Its situation, where the road over the ghats from Mangalore meets two others leading to Saklēśpur in the south-west and Bēlur in the south-east, must have been the cause of the name. This place has the honour of having been the cradle of this dynasty of rulers of Mysore. The name Angaḍi was given to it under the rule of Vijayanagar, the earliest epigraphical use of this name being in an inscription of Achyuta Rāya. Before this time, the place bore the name Śaśakāpura, or Sośevūr (rabbit town), and the inscriptions in the village temple call the goddess Vāsāntikā Dēvi, the Vasantamma of modern times. It was here that the Hoysalas had their origin, and several inscriptions account for the name by an achievement of Sala, the eponymous ancestor of the Hoysalas. Once upon a time there happened to be a Jain Muni (ascetic) in the Vāsāntikā temple absorbed in contemplation. A tiger sprang upon the saint, who noticed it too late to save himself. In sheer helplessness he cried out: 'strike Sala' (Poy Sala), addressing the humble but valiant lay-worshipper who was at the time before the goddess. With no more formidable weapon than a stick, Sala killed the tiger and got the name Hoysala for himself and his posterity. This, with the usual variation of detail, is the origin of the dynasty as given by the inscriptions. But one point in connexion with this deserves to be noticed. This legend, which may be based on some actual feat of one of the dynasty, appears in the records of the later Hoysalas only, while those of the earlier ones show them to have been quite commonplace mortals struggling out of obscurity in the most ordinary way. This view is borne out by the story recorded in one of the Mackenzie manuscripts, which says that an actual tiger was committing ravages in that part of the country. One of the ancestors of the Hoysalas having killed it, was voted a 'pana' per head of population, which provided the sinews of war, for organizing a small force and forming a small State for himself by conquering the neighbouring chiefs. (*Vide* Rice's *Gazetteer*, vol. i. p. 335.)

There is a similar tradition connected with another Malayamān chief of some repute in Tamil literature, Irungōvēḷ of Arayam. He is described as the forty-ninth in descent from a king of Dvāraka, who appeared from the sacrificial fire of a Rishi. His head-quarters was Arayam, composed of the small and the big cities, which, according to Kapilar the poet, was burnt on account of the insult an ancestor of the chief offered to an older poet Kaḷāthalaiyār. This Irungōvēḷ is addressed by Kapilar, 'Puli Kaḍimāl', the slayer of the tiger; and the localities would agree fairly: but there is such a great distance of time between the two, that it would perhaps be too much to filiate the one upon the other.

Be this as it may, the Hoysalas were a number of petty hill chiefs whose domain lay along the western ghats. That this was actually the case, and that they had no higher origin, is shown by the sign manual of these 'Royalties', Malaparōḷ Gaṇḍa (the man among the Malapas or hill-chiefs), which figures even in the grants of the Hoysala 'emperors of the south'. The earliest epigraphical mention of them is found in a Chola inscription of A.D. 1007. The Chola viceroy Appramēya claims to have killed a number of chiefs in the battle of Kaḷavūr; the Hoysalas Manjiga, Kaliga, Nagavaramma and others falling in the battle. Appramēya, the lord of Kottamanḍala, in consequence, styles himself 'Death to the family of the hill-chiefs' (Malapa kula kāla).

The next record referring to them is dated A.D. 1022 and shows the Hoysalas, now under Nripakāma, fighting against the Tamil Kongāḷva chiefs of Coorg and of the adjoining parts of Mysore. In one of the records of Nripakāma's time he is called the base (munḍa) Hoysala; but no reason for this is given. Another record of his shows him as helping the ruler of Banavasi (Nagar division), against his enemies whoever they were. Here, then, is the first historical Hoysala struggling out of obscurity, but his achievements are against chiefs of his own level. His resources could not have been very great, if he was in danger of losing his life, as he is said to have been, in his wars against the petty chief Rājēndra Chola Prithvi Kongāḷva, who claims a victory over him at Mannē in the record of A. D. 1026. Curiously enough an inscription (Mg. 19) of the seventh year of this very Kāma Hoysala at Uggihalli, a place situated near Angaḍi, refers to him as 'Kāma Hoysala called Rajamalla Perumānaḍi' (Rajamalla Perumānaḍi Yenipa Kāma Hoysala). This Mr. Rice considers a clearly Ganga title and so it is; but he thinks that this could not be given to the Hoysala unless he were the son of a Ganga prince. Could it not be that he was a Ganga feudatory and bore his over-lord's title, just as the Kongāḷvas about the same region gave themselves Chola titles? (e. g. Rājēndra Chola Prithvi Kongāḷva). The successor of Nripakāma is his son Vinayāditya; but strange to say the former's name is omitted in inscriptions of later years, which give elaborate genealogies. This omission was perhaps due to the agnomen 'base' having had some historical basis. Whether this was so or not, it is Tribhuvana Hoysala Vinayāditya who brought the dynasty into some prominence. He had his headquarters at Śaśakāpura, but his successor, his grandson Beḷḷāḷa, rules from Bēlur as his capital. Vinayāditya's time is coeval with the death grapple between the Cholas and the Chāḷukyas. Among the Mahāmanḍalēsvarās of Sōmēsvara Āhavamalla, the name Vinayāditya is associated with the Gangavāḍi 96000; but this very province was divided by the Cholas into three governorships, under a viceroy at Talakāḍ, Muḍikonḍa

Choḷamaṇḍalam, Vikrama Choḷamaṇḍalam and Nikharili Choḷamaṇḍalam running from west to north-east along southern Mysore. Thus it is clear that the Cholas were in actual possession of the territory, while the Chāḷukya asserted his right to the same by the appointment of a viceroy, with head-quarters far beyond the province itself. It is from this struggle that the Hoysalas emerge more important than ever before, but what part the Hoysala actually played is not clear from the inscriptions, though there is no room for doubt that they rendered yeoman's service to their liege lords, the Chāḷukyas.

To go back to general South Indian history for a while, Rājēndra, the Gangaikoṇḍa Chola, died in A. D. 1042, and was succeeded by his son Rājādhirāja (A. D. 1018 to 1052) already associated with him from A. D. 1018. Natural and undisputed though the succession was, there was a general attempt, in the frontier provinces, to throw off the yoke so recently imposed upon them. Rājādhirāja had to strike first at Ceylon, then at Travancore and again at Mysore, in order to bring these new provinces back into allegiance. This he did with great success, ably seconded as he was by his younger brother Rājēndra. About the middle of his reign, the Chāḷukya dominions passed on to Āhavamalla Sōmēsvara (A. D. 1044 to 1068). Rājādhirāja's inscriptions claim several victories for him in the Mysore country and the claim seems to be based on fact. At last the time had come for a decisive battle to settle once for all, who was to be the master of the province under dispute. At Koppam on the Pērār (Tungabhadra) the battle was fought in A. D. 1052. Rājādhirāja was defeated and fell fighting. His younger brother Rājēndra came up with reinforcements, and, having retrieved the honour of the Cholas and the fortunes of the day, was then crowned on the field of battle.

One of Āhavamalla's inscriptions states that the Chola lost his head, having sacrilegiously burnt the Jain temples, which the Perumānaḍi (a Ganga chief or perhaps the Chāḷukya) had built in the Beḷuvoḷa 300, situated in the Bellary district. In the course of the series of wars, which culminated in the epoch-making battle of Koppam, the Hoysala must have had opportunities of making himself more powerful than his father; nay, even of creating himself one of those wardens of the marches, who have at all times proved king-makers. Vinayāditya is credited by the inscriptions of his successors with having ruled over the country bounded by Konkaṇa, Āḷvakheḍa, Bayalunāḍu, Talakāḍ, and Savimale. This would mean the country enclosed by the Kanaras, Talakāḍ on the Cauvery in the south of Mysore, and the regions about the river Krishna or Tungabhadra. This must be the extent of territory under his successor Vishṇuvardhana, which has been given to him, as Dr. Fleet thinks. All through his time and almost to the end of the century, he is associated with his son Eṛēyanga (the red-bodied), as Yuva Raja or heir apparent.

Before taking up the successor of Vinayāditya in the Hoysala lineage, it is necessary again to consider their surroundings. In A.D. 1062 or 1063 Rājēndra Chola, the second of the name, died and was succeeded by his younger brother Vīrarājēndra, while at the same time Rājarāja the eastern Chāḷukya also died. His son, Rājēndra Chola, better known by his later title Kulōttunga Chola, succeeded though not at Rajamahēndri. This latter prince was the son of Ammangadēvi, sister of the three Chola emperors ending with Vīrarājēndra and daughter of the Gangaikoṇḍa Chola. Kulōttunga appears to have aspired to the throne of the Cholas, and this fact introduced a disturbing element in what would otherwise have been a quiet succession. While Vīrarājēndra was doing all he could to make his position secure, Āhavamalla Sōmēsvara of the western Chāḷukyas died in A. D. 1069 and was succeeded by his eldest son Sōmēsvara (II) Bhuvanaikamalla. Unfortunately for the history of South India, he had a talented brother Vikramāditya. This latter was waiting for an opportunity to overthrow his elder brother and occupy the throne himself. Vikramāditya appears to have had a better hold upon the affections of the Mahāmanḍalēsvarās than Sōmēsvara. This posture of affairs led to much diplomatic activity and military demonstration, which culminated in the alliance between Prince Vikramāditya and the emperor Vīrarājēndra, after the latter had defeated the Kannaḍa armies in the battles of Kūḍal Sangaman, at the junction of the Tungabhadra and the Krishna. This treaty was sealed by the marriage of the designing prince with the daughter of the Chola. Sōmēsvara appears so far to have relied entirely upon his younger brother's loyalty, and all the campaigns against the indomitable Cholas were conducted by him. When Sōmēsvara discovered later on the designs of his brother and the success the latter had obtained with the Chola, he entered as a counter-move into a treaty with Kulōttunga, who was now ruling, at least, the southern part of his ancestral dominions (i. e. the districts round Madras). Vīrarājēndra proved too strong even for this combination. He invaded the eastern Chāḷukya dominions and appointed Kulōttunga's uncle Vijayāditya, viceroy of the eastern Chāḷukya territories. Vīrarājēndra died soon after in A.D. 1070. Vikramāditya installed his brother-in-law Adhirājarāja; but Kulōttunga found his opportunity now and occupied the Chola throne, Adhirājarāja falling a victim to this usurpation. Hemmed in by this powerful Chola, the Chālukya usurper, Vikramāditya, had to bide his time and completed (A. D. 1076) his project of overthrowing his brother and making himself emperor.

During all these transactions, both diplomatic and warlike, between the Cholas and the Chāḷukyas, the Mahāmanḍalēsvaras of Gangavāḍi and Noḷambavāḍi must have had their share. While, on the one hand, the inscriptions of Vīrarājēndra claim for him the credit of having granted to Vikramāditya, the 'Youvvarājya' or the position of heir apparent, Hoysala inscriptions of about A.D. 1100 claim for Eṛēyanga and his father-in-law, the Nolamba Chief's brother, the credit of having rendered valuable service in the same cause. Eṛēyanga caused Thribhuvanamalla's (Vikramāditya's) elder brother to sheathe his sword, while his father-in-law, Irukkapāla, defeated Bhuvanaikamalla and gave the kingdom to Vikramāditya, whose right hand Eṛēyanga is described to have been. This makes it clear that, in spite of Bilhaṇa's Vikramānkadēva Charitam, Vikramāditya was helped in his machinations against his brother by the Mysore chiefs. While these chiefs proved his strength then, they were later on to contribute mightily also to the overthrow of his empire. Eṛēyanga was ruling the Gangavāḍi 96,000, that is the little of it that was not under the Cholas. As a trusty lieutenant of the Chāḷukya, he took part in the distant expeditions to the north; for Eṛēyanga lays claim to a victory at Dhāra in Mālva, the kingdom of the Pramāras. He must have died before his father, leaving behind three sons by his wife Ēchaladēvi who might, or might not, have been the Mahādēvi, the daughter of the Noḷamba above referred to.

Vinayāditya was succeeded by his eldest grandson Beḷḷaḷa I in A.D. 1101. This ruler had his capital at Bēlur with which the Hoysalas were associated, though Dvārasamudra was an alternative capital. His province is given the same boundaries as that of his grandfather, and he is said to have paid a visit to Sośevūr. In A.D. 1103 he made a regrant of Sindagere to Mariaṇē Dhanḍanāyaka as the wages for the 'wet nursing' of his three daughters, whom Beḷḷaḷa married in the same pavilion at Bēlur. In A.D. 1104, he led an expedition against the Changāḷvas, whose domain lay in the Hoḷē Narasipur taluq. In the same year, with his younger brother Vishṇu, he conducted a successful expedition into the neighbouring Pandya dominions of Noḷambavāḍi, and had to repulse an invader Jagaddeva, probably the Sāntara prince of Humcha in Nagar taluq, who had penetrated as far as Dvārasamudra (Haḷēbīd). It is a significant fact that an inscription of Beḷḷaḷa's time is dated in Chāḷukya Vikramakāla (Kp. 35).

Beḷḷaḷa I was succeeded by his younger brother Biṭṭi Dēva, better known by his later title Vishṇuvardhana. He is the real founder of Hoysala greatness, and many even of the titles of his successors and predecessors (in inscriptions) are borrowed from his. The first mention of his name is found in a record of A.D. 1100 associated with his brother Beḷḷaḷa. The records of the latter do not go further than the year A.D. 1106, at which date or soon after Biṭṭi Dēva must have ascended the throne. But all inscriptions agree in ascribing his real exploits to, at least, ten years later. Hence it is possible that Beḷḷaḷa continued to rule even after A.D. 1106. Despite all the claims put forward by his predecessors, he has to undertake the conquests on the one side of Noḷambavāḍi and on the other of Gangavāḍi, which two conquests constitute his claims to the title of one of the greatest of Vikramāditya's Mahāmanḍalēsvarās. The elaborate accounts of the conquest of Gangavāḍi, and the great credit claimed for it show the firmness of the hold the Cholas had upon the country. The conquest is claimed separately by a number of Vishṇuvardhana's generals among whom prominence must be given to Gangaraja a dispossessed scion of the Ganga dynasty. Other generals who distinguished themselves in the taking of Talakāḍ were Kētayya Daṇḍanāyaka and Puṇīsa. After this conquest, Biṭṭi Dēva assumes the titles Vīra Ganga and Talakāḍugoṇḍa. Kulōttunga Chola seems to have acquiesced in the conquest, after his generals Adiyama, Damōdara and Narasimhavarma were overthrown; for we see Vishṇuvardhana making a progress through Gangavāḍi, in the course of which, at Vijayādityamangala (the modern Bētmangala), his niece, the daughter of his younger brother Udayāditya, died. About the same time, or soon after, he invaded Noḷambavāḍi, and at Dumme on the border between Shimoga and Chitaldroog won a victory over the Pandya ruler of the country, who had his capital at Uchchangidoorga. This conquest was only temporary, and his grandson had to do it over again.

The year A.D. 1117 marks an epoch in the advance of the Hoysala power. Vishṇuvardhana by this year had become master of Gangavāḍi 96,000 and had made himself felt in Noḷambavāḍi. I now give the history of his conquests, as they are recorded in many of his inscriptions, chiefly the one at Bēlur, which was inscribed on the occasion of the dedication of the temple, after he had adopted the teachings of Rāmānuja, the Vaishṇava reformer, and assumed the Vaishṇava title of Vishṇuvardhana. 'First taking into his arms the fortune of the Poysala kingdom, which he had inherited, he brought all points of the compass under his command, and was capturing Talakāḍ, became the first ruler to the Ganga kingdom. . . . He made the earth tremble with the tramp of his Kambōja horse, was lord of Gaṇḍagiri, split the great rock Pandya, burst the hearts of the Tuḷu kings, destroyed the army of Jagaddēva, devoured the fierce elephant Sōmēsvara, displayed his valour before Māṇikyadēvi of the Chakrakūṭa throne, brought down the pride of Adiyama, overthrew the tree Narasimha Varma, split the skull of king Kāla, destroyed the serpent Chengiri, broke down the plantain stems the spears of the Irungoḷas, shook the mountain Cheṅgiri Perumala, set up Paṭṭi Perumala, made Talakāḍ his own, took the Kongu country, protected Noḷambavāḍi, expanded Nīlaparvata, extended Kōlālapura, uprooted Kovatūr, shook Terēyūr, crossed over Vaḷḷūr, unchained Nangalipura, pulled up the door of the Ghats, and made Kānchipura tremble.' The boundaries of his kingdom at the time were—east, the lower ghat of Nangali; south, Kongu, Cheram and Ānamalai; west, Barakanur and other ghats of the Konkana; north, Śavimale.

This list of conquests has to be carefully considered in order to ascertain what measure of truth there is in it, and how much of it has to be put down to the panegyrist. Biṭṭi Dēva succeeded to his ancestral dominions, which clearly did not include Gangavāḍi, the claims to the province of his father and grandfather notwithstanding. His capture of Talakāḍ is the crucial achievement which entitles him to the rule of Gangavāḍi 96,000. This achievement takes away the province from the Tamilians once for all, and Rājēndra Kulōttunga evidently acquiesced in the conquest. Gaṇḍagiri has not yet been identified. He is said to have split the rock Pandya. This perhaps means no more than the Pandya defeat at Dumme (on the frontier between Shimoga and Chitaldroog districts). The achievement against Jagaddeva may be the same as that of his brother Beḷḷāḷa against the Sāntara prince of Humcha (Paṭṭi Pombuchāpura). The achievement against Sōmēsvara is put down against the Chāḷukya king by Mr. Rice. The Chāḷukya king at the time was Vikramāditya, who had a son Sōmēsvara who may have acted in the name of his father, as was often the case, as the governor of Banavase, a province, which was regarded of sufficient importance to require a prince of the blood often for its viceroy. No information is forthcoming about the Māṇikyadevi of the

Chakrakūṭa throne. Adiyama and Narasimha Varma were Chola feudatories in the south of Mysore. Kāla was a ruler of the Nīlagiris; Chengiri might have been Tiruchengōḍe in the Salem district (rather than Gingee as Mr. Rice surmises), formerly part of the Kongu kingdom. Irungōḷa was a Tamil chief of Niḍugal in the Pavagada taluq, and Terēyur was again a place of some consequence in the north-east of Tumkur. Nangali is the frontier town between Mysore and North Arcot in the Mulbagal taluq. Thus this narration would entitle Biṭṭi Dēva to the conquest of southern and south-eastern Mysore. That he effected the conquest of Gangavāḍi finally is borne out by the specific mention of his rule over the two capitals, Talakāḍ and Kolar. In A.D. 1118, he is said to have been in residence at Talakāḍ. This completes his conquests. The boundaries given to his dominions in the north appear to be more questionable. Śāvimale, somewhere in the upper reaches of the Krishna, is too near his liege lord's head-quarters, and he had to effect the conquests of other chiefs before he could extend his dominions so far. This no doubt he did, but not as yet.

The year 1121 finds him again at his head-quarters at Dvārasamudra, and it was in this year that a certain Kētamalla, probably a merchant, built a temple, dedicated to Śiva under the name Vishṇuvardhana-Hoyasalēsvara, the great temple at Halebīḍ. A record at Virupākshapura in the Channarāyapaṭna taluq of A.D. 1121 shows that 'Malēparoḷ Ganḍa-Srīmāt Tribhuvanamalla, Talakāḍ-Kongu-Nangali-Noḷambavāḍi, Uchchangi-Banavase-Hanungaḷam Gonḍa Bhujabala Vira Ganga Hoysala Dēva' made a grant with his Paṭṭa Mahādēvi (queen-consort) and the Pancha Pradhānas (five ministers) to the god Jayangonḍēsvara. These titles of Biṭṭi Dēva would show clearly his object, but several of these were mere attempts at acquisition as yet. The five ministers ought to have been, although Mr. Rice passes over them with a 'whoever they were', the heir-apparent, the commander-in-chief, the priest, the senior Sandhi Vigrahim (minister for foreign affairs) and the chief secretary. Sāntala Dēvi was the queen-consort. It is remarkable that with these, most of whom were Jains, the king made a grant for a Śiva temple Jayangonḍēsvara, the name of which indicates that it was of Chola foundation, Jayaṃkonḍa having been one of the titles of Rājādhirāja.

In A.D. 1123, he is again on the banks of the Kavery, while his northern boundary is described as the Pērddore or Krishna. Here he hears of the death of his younger brother Udayāditya and makes a grant. It was in the same year that he made a grant of the village Grāma to the east of Hassan to his Jaina wife who divided it among 220 Brahmins. It is even now one of the most flourishing of Brahmin villages. The same year Sāntala Dēvi built the Gandhavāraṇa Basti in Sravaṇa Beḷugoaḷ. In A.D. 1125, he is again at Talakāḍ and makes a grant to the great Jain teacher and controversialist Srī Pāla, who claimed the titles 'Shaḍ Tarka Shaṇmukha', 'Vādhiba Simha' and 'Tārkika Chakravarti'. The king is at Yādhavapura (Mēlukōṭe) in A.D. 1128, and from his royal residence there he makes a grant to Mārbala īrtha, apparently a part of the Śaiva shrine on the Chāmunḍi hill. By this time the emperor Vikramāditya had died and was succeeded by his son Sōmēsvara Bhūlōkamalla. Kulōttunga Chola had died a few years earlier, but was succeeded by his son Vikrama Chola. The Hoysala aggression southwards appears to have been checked so carefully, that Vishṇuvardhana's attention was entirely devoted to conquest in the north. In a record of A.D. 1129, the boundaries of the Hoysala territories are thus defined—east, Nangali ghat; south, Kongu, Cheram and Ānamale; west, Barakanur ghat (north-west of Śhimoga); and north, Sāvimale. He is said to have terrified Sōmēsvara. Long before this, Vishṇuvardhana's activity, after the conquest of Gangavāḍi and the attack on Noḷambavāḍi, seems to have attracted the attention of the emperor Vikramāditya. He, therefore, sent a number of Mahāmanḍalēsvarās, among whom figure the Kaḍambas of Goa. But the most trusted chiefs appear to have been of the Sinda chieftains of Yelburga, one of whom, Achugi II, claimed like Eṛēyanga to have rendered great services to Vikramāditya in his usurpation. Though Biṭṭi Dēva's general Ganga Raja claims to have defeated these loyalists, the fact that the former still recognized, even nominally, the liege lordship of the emperor, would warrant the conclusion that he received a check in his onward career towards independence. On Vikramāditya's death, however, he resumes his activity in the north and this is what terrified Sōmēsvara. At this time he was helped by his son Kumāra Beḷḷāḷa, and had a number of daughters, the eldest of whom was Hariyāḷē. The fact that she was Jain would lead one to regard her and her brother and sisters as the children of Śāntala Dēvi; but this is not a necessary inference, considering the religious condition of the Hoysalas and of these times.

In A. D. 1130, then, we find the Hoysala power practically supreme over Kongu, Nangali, Talakāḍ, Gangavāḍi, (though very much less so here) Banavase, Hanungal and Huligere. Of these provinces and cities, except the two last, the rest comprise the modern Mysore province. Hanungal is the modern Hangal in Dharwar, and Puligere is Lakshmēswar about the same locality. But that among his enemies are still found the Kongāḷva and Chengāḷva petty chiefs is significant of the fact that he had not as yet attained to unquestioning obedience to his authority within the province. This explains why he is found constantly moving about in his province. It is in this year that he assumes the titles Noḷambavāḍi Gonḍa which appears on some of his coins.

An inscription in the Śiva temple at Maddur of the year A. D. 1131 (Saka 1053) presents Biṭṭi Dēva thus: 'The Mahāmanḍalēsvara the capturer of Talakāḍ, Kongu, Nangali, Banavase, Uchchangi, the strong armed Vīra Ganga, Vishṇuvardhana Hoysala Dēva, was ruling the kingdom of the world, in his residence in the royal city of Dvārasamudra, punishing the evil and protecting the good in Gangavāḍi 96,000, the Noḷambavādi 32,000, the Banavase 12,000, and the Hanungal 500.' The record mentions a grant made by the king to Swāyambhu Vaijyanātha of the Śivapura of Maddur *alias* Narasimha Chaturvēdimangalam. What is most interesting in this record is, that Piḷḷayānḍa claimed certain lands, as having been granted by the Ganga king Śivamāra and showed a copper plate grant. His claim was allowed after the plates had been examined.

It was in this year that his queen-consort Śāntala Dēvi died. A couple of years later another great champion of the Jainas died, and one who had contributed largely to the greatness of his master. This was Ganga Raja, the capturer of Talakād and the restorer of the Jain temples destroyed by the Cholas. By this latter act he is said to have made Mysore shine like Kōpaṇa (Koppal in the Nizam's Dominions). On his death Ganga Raja's son Boppa built a Jīnālaya in memory of his father at Halēbīḍ, called Drohagharaṭṭa Jīnālaya. Having it consecrated by Nayakīrti, the sacred food was sent to the king who was then at Bankāpura, the northern frontier of the Hoysala kingdom. This reached Vishṇuvardhana just as he was returning victorious from an expedition against Maśaṇa, and while his queen Lakshmi Dēvi had just borne him a son and heir. The Jain priests were, therefore, received with favour, and the king pleased with the auspicious arrival of the priests named his son Vijaya Narasimha, and

16

wished that the Jīna in the new temple should be called Vijaya Pārsvanātha. It is this Jain Basadi that is still an object of sight to travellers. It is situated a couple of furlongs from the great Hoysalēsvara temple. From this period onward, Vishṇuvardhana was chiefly engaged in the north against the chiefs on the frontier for the acquisition of Banavase and Noḷambavāḍi for himself; for in spite of the Mysore records the inscriptions of Sōmēsvara III show a series of Manḍalēsvaras in charge of Banavase, and a certain Vīra Pandya is said to have been ruling from Uchchangidurga over the Noḷambavāḍi 32,000. It is only in the year A.D. 1137 that Vishṇuvardhana is shown by those records to be the Mahāmanḍalēsvara in charge of Gangavāḍi, Noḷambavāḍi, and Banavase (i. e. the modern State of Mysore). All the interim must have been a period of struggle. Ever since he was beaten back by the loyal Sinda chieftain, Achugi II, on behalf of Vikramāditya, he must have acquiesced in the merely subordinate rôle of the Mahāmanḍalesvara of Gangavāḍi, which may actually have been more than the province itself. At no time, however, could he have extended his boundaries permanently further north than Bankāpur in Dharwar, for he was hemmed in by the powerful and loyal Sindas on the east and the Kaḍambas on the west. Thus Krishnavēṇi for the northern boundary of Vishṇuvardhana must have been about as real as Ramēswaram in the south. This year A.D. 1137, or the year after, marks another stage in the advance of the Hoysala power. Here is a record of the year 1137, which sets down his conquests, while another Jain record of the same date recognizes clearly the subordinate position of Vishṇuvardhana as a feudatory, however powerful he be, of Somēsvara III, Bhūlōkamalla. The first part of the record is gone and the meaning of the first few sentences is not clear. It reads: 'On his deserting his queens, forsaking his kingdom, and dying in the country near Cheṅgiri, he took possession of the company of Narasinga's wives, put down Angara, trampled on Singalika and, turning in the direction of the Ganges, slew the kings of the northern countries—the son of King Eṛēyanga. Having succeeded in this expedition to the north, his elephant trampled down the army of the Pandya king, ashamed of so easy a victory, having defeated Chola and Gauḷa in terrible great wars. And pursuing Pandya he seized Noḷambavāḍi, capturing Uchchangi in a moment, and tossing it up as if playing at ball—Kānchi-Gonḍa. Vikrama-Ganga. After that, marching to the Telinga country, he captured Indra . . . together with his elephants, the wealth gained by his victories and the inherited wealth of his family. After that, destroying root and branch Maśana, who was a torment to the country, he wrote down the Banavase 12,000 in his Kaḍitha (account-book). When the King Vishṇu was playing as if at tirikal, a kind of pitch and toss, with the great Sahya mountains, Nīlagiri and . . of what account are the others; and what wonder is it that he took Pānungal in half a second with the flip of his finger . . killing only with a glance . . another who was taking Kiśukāḍ, he pursued after Jayakēsi and gained possession of the Palāśigē 12,000 and the . . . 500. Turning and turning he entered hill-forts going farther and farther away as far as the ocean . . . attacking them again and again, he sought out the bravest in the north and slew them—Vishṇuvardhana Dēva. Whatever countries are considered famous, whatever hill-forts are specially described, whatever kings are worthy of being reckoned, he subdued and added to his fame throughout the world as far as the limits of the four oceans—the glory of the Kshatriya race, the brave king Vishṇu.

When that great Kshatriya, entitled to the five great drums, Mahāmanḍalēsvara (with numerous other titles), a Bhairava of the last deluge to the Chola race, a royal lion to the elephant Chera, a submarine fire to the ocean the Pandya race, a wild fire to the sprouts of the creeper the fame of the Pallava, a sārdūla to the lion Narasimhavarma, his unshaken fame a lamp into which Kālapāla and other kings fall like winged white ants, the twang of whose bow, putting to flight the Anga, Vanga, Kalinga and Simhaḷa Kings, Kānchipura, resounding with his orders as with the sharp sounds of drums (named), the wives of hostile kings employed in his house as female servants, squeezing in his hands the southern Madhurāpura, having destroyed Jananāthāpura by his General, Kanchi-Gonḍa-Vikrama-Ganga, Vīra Vishṇu-vardhana Dēva, protecting under his sole umbrella the Gangavāḍi 96,000, Noḷambavāḍi 32,000, and Banavase 12,000, was ruling the Kingdom in peace and wisdom.'

This long recital of his deeds shows where Vishṇuvardhana had to be most active, and what a long struggle it must have cost him before he could have united the three separate provinces into one united whole. The first portion of this quotation appears quite historical, while by the time the composer of the record reached the second portion he seems to have worked himself up to a high pitch of hyperbole. His activities were all required in the north against the more powerful Mahāmanḍalēsvaras Jayakēsi II, the Kaḍamba ruler of Goa and Hangal, against the Noḷambas of Uchchangi, as Vīra Pandya is said to be ruling from the same hill-fort his hereditary province of Noḷambavāḍi thirty-two thousand in A.D. 1139, and the Sinda chieftains of Yelburga, particularly Achugi II. Thus it would appear impossible that he ever reached, much less conquered, either Kanchi, or Madhura, or Jananāthāpura (Rajamahēndri not Mahābalipuram, or Mālingi near Talakāḍ). The conquests of Anga, Vanga, and Kalinga are much more remote from the actual. By the year

1137, then, Vishṇuvardhana had so far succeeded in uniting, not beyond dispute as yet, though recognized at head-quarters, the whole of the modern Mysore State under his rule. But he did not feel his position sure enough to assume the royal dignity. The remaining six or seven years of his life he devotes himself to securing himself in the northern frontier, where things were moving fast towards disruption.

In the year A.D. 1137 Vishṇuvardhana's capitals were respectively Talakāḍ in the south, and Bankāpur in Dharwar in the north—two fortified places on either frontier against the two emperors, one on either side. This same year he performed the royal act of tulāpurusha, i.e. he weighed himself against gold and distributed it among Brahmins and other deserving recipients of gifts of charity. About the end of the year 1138, he crossed the Tungabhadra and laid siege to Hangal, notwithstanding so many previous statements as to the conquest of it. This and the fight next year at Dvārasamudra with Jagaddeva indicates that his advance in the north was not acquiesced in.

It must be remembered here that in the year 1138 Sōmēsvara Bhūlōkamalla died, and was succeeded by Jagadēkamalla in the Chāḷukya empire. Vishṇuvardhana must have repeated his attempt to profit by a succession. This time again he was foiled by the loyal Mahāmanḍalēsvaras, helped by the Sāntara prince Jagaddēva. In 1140 Biṭṭi Dēva is again at Bankāpura ruling the following provinces: Gangavāḍi 96,000, Banavase 12,000, Sānthaḷige 1,000, Hanungal 500. Halāsige 12,000, Mogelle 300, and the Haive 12. Having given away his own country to Brahmins and temples and ruling only the foreign countries he had won, he was in residence at Bankāpura with the Krishna and the three oceans as the boundaries of his dominions. Here he died in the year A.D. 1141, having fallen short of his ambition only in not having been able to assume the titles of royalty, though he was in undoubted enjoyment of the substance of it. Vishṇuvardhana was succeeded by his son Vijaya Narasimha, who was born in the year 1133, and crowned at his birth, probably because his father lost all his other sons, or, at any rate, the son who was already old enough to help him in the great work of building up a kingdom.

While through the constant endeavours, often successful though occasionally foiled, of Vishṇuvardhana, Mysore was rising into a kingdom, the empire of which it formed an integral part for centuries was fast moving towards disintegration. It is, therefore, necessary, before taking up the tale of Narasimha's conquests, of his attempts at the conservation of his inheritance, to glance at the history of the Chāḷukya empire and the causes which led to its disintegration. Vikramāditya's long reign of fifty-two years was one of peace essentially, except for an invasion of the Chola dominions and for the check he had to administer to the rising ambition of his Hoysala feudatory, about the end of his reign. Like his predecessors, the early Chāḷukya Pulikēsin II and the Śātvahana Gōtamīputra Śātakarni, he had often to carry on war across the Narbudda, but even this he does not appear to have had to do very often. His empire extended in diagonal lines from Broach to Erode and from Mangalore to Sitabaldi. This vast territory was parcelled out into a number of viceroyalties; among the viceroys may be mentioned in order from the north-west—The Sēuṇas or Yādavas with capitals at Sinnar (near Nasik) and later at Deogiri; the Silāharas of Northern and Southern Konkan and of Kolhapur; next come the Kadambas of Goa and Hangal; east of these are the Sindas of Yelburga, the Guṭṭas of Guṭṭal in Dharwar and Raṭṭas of Saundatti in Belgaum; then come the dominions under the head-quarters, namely, all the Nizam's Dominions except the most easterly part, the Khamamet division; and lastly the viceroyalty with head-quarters at Sitabaldi. This leaves out Banevase, Noḷambavādi and Gangavāḍi more or less under the Hoysalas, although to the end of Vishṇuvardhana's life other viceroys continued to be appointed for the two former. This vast empire passed on to his son Sōmēsvara Bhūlōkamalla in A.D. 1128, thanks to the loyal exertions of the Sinda chieftains against the southern viceroys. Sōmēsvara died in 1138 and the empire passed again to his son, Pērma Jagadēkamalla, who ruled till A.D. 1150. In this reign comes into notice a young man of promise, whose father was governor of Tārdawāḍi 1,000, the district round Bijapur, an alternative capital of the Chāḷukyas. This was Bijjala. He was governor of the same province as his father, but later on he becomes sufficiently important to be appointed viceroy of Noḷambavāḍi and Banavase, governing these provinces by deputies, himself keeping at head-quarters, like the Saiyid brothers under the Moghul emperor Muḥammad Shāh. This change in the position of Bijjala is noticeable under Jagadēkamalla, but when the latter was succeeded by his brother Taila III, he keeps growing in power, till in 1156 he becomes virtually ruler, though Taila continues nominally emperor till A.D. 1163. There is only one explanation for this. He is seen named in grants as the commander-in-chief of all the forces, an officer never heard of before. There was probably a rising of all the more powerful viceroys or an anticipation of such a rising, which would naturally require a masterhand to deal with the situation. That masterhand not being found on the throne, a wire-puller would naturally enough come in. If Bijjala did this, nothing else is needed to explain his own appointment to the provinces most under dispute.

About this time on the eastern frontier another enterprising ruler was rising on the horizon of history. Since the accession of Vikrama Chola, the eastern Chāḷukya dominions happened to be neglected somehow, and an enterprising chief between the two Chāḷukya empires had his opportunity. Just within the frontier is the hamlet of Anamkoṇḍa, the ancestral capital of Bēta, the founder of the family of the Kākatīyas, who was to become famous as the Kākatīyas of Warangal, which his son Prōḷa founded and whither he had shifted the capital. This Prōla claims to have defeated Tailappa sometime in his reign, and it is very likely that this event occurred about A.D. 1155. This external shock, combined with the internal loss of hold on the Mahāmaṇḍalēsvaras, must have thrown Tailappa into the arms of Bijjala, who for the while proved the saviour. This saviour usurped first the power and then the position and paraphernalia of the empire. Bijjala, however, was not allowed to effect his usurpation undisputed. The Sindas were loyal as usual in spite of a close family alliance with Bijjala, and the Pandyas were equally so. Bijjala and his sons continued in the empire from 1163 to 1183, when a general of Bijjala, by name Kāma Dēva or Kāvana, had a son Bomma or Brahma. This latter restored the son of Taila III under the imperial title of Sōmēsvara IV in 1183, using for the purpose the army under his father, who appears to have been to the Kalachūrya ruler much what Bijjala himself was to Tailappa. Sōmēsvara ruled till A. D. 1189, and his rule was confined to the southern and south-western part of his dominions. A combination of some of his chiefs against him and his loyal feudatories the Sindas made him retire to the north-west frontier of his dominions, and nothing more was heard of him. In the scramble for territory that followed, not in an orderly Congress of Vienna but by appeal to arms, two Powers stood out heirs to the empire, the Yādavas of Deogiri and the Hoysalas of Dvārasamudra, the Kākaīyas of Warangal taking their humble share of the spoil, and the history of the latter will now be resumed.

Narasimha, a tender boy of eight years, supported by the remnant of his father's veteran generals and ministers, succeeded to the difficult position of his father. He ruled from A.D. 1141 to 1173, a period of thirty-two years during which all his exertions were required to conserve the dominions bequeathed to him. His reign is coeval with those of Jagadēkamalla and Taila III, and runs into a part of even the Kalachūrya usurper, Bijjala's reign. It has been already remarked that, although Vishṇuvardhana's title to Banavase and Noḷambavāḍi had been recognized in 1137 to 1138 under Sōmēsvara III, other imperial officers continued to be appointed for the viceroyalty of each of these provinces. That the hold of the Hoysalas over these provinces was of the slightest is proved by the fact that in these localities the earliest Hoysala inscriptions are those of Narasimha's son Vīra Beḷḷāḷa. Noḷambavāḍi under two powerful brothers, Vīra Pandya and Vijaya Pandya, after its recovery, and Banavase under a series of viceroys, first of the Kaḍamba family and then of others, the last of whom was Bijjala, continued their allegiance to the empire. Except an invasion or two into these provinces, Narasimha was able to do but little; but in one direction his arms were victorious. His general Bōkkimayya, or Bōkaṇa (the Garuḍa of Vishṇu), brought under subjection to him the Tuḷu, the Changāḷva, the Kongāḷva, and Bayalnāḍu in 1155. In 1161, he marched upon Bankāpura, which was occupied by the Kaḍambas, and defeated them. It was between these dates that Bijjala was carrying through his scheme of usurpation, and in consequence there was a struggle among the southern Powers. At first Narasimha seems to have had the better of it against the other viceroys, and then against Bijjala himself. It is this opposition to Bijjala on the part of the Sindas and the Pandyas of Noḷambavāḍi that led to the final conquest and absorption by Beḷḷāḷa of Nolambavadi and Banavase. By the year 1165, he had a son Kumāra Beḷḷāḷa and continued to rule till 1173, when he is described as 'a royal swan sporting in the lake of the Āndhra women, a sun to the lotus faces of the Simhaḷa (Ceylonese) women, a golden zone to the waist of the Karnāṭaka women, an ornament stamped with musk of the Lāṭa (Gujarāti) women, the saffron paste on the goblets (the breasts) of the Chola women, a moon to the water lilies (the eyes) of Gauḷa women (a part of Bengal), the wave on the . . . of the beauty of the Bengāḷa women, a bee to the lotuses, the faces of the Māḷavas.' In addition to the queens Chēngala Dēvi, Echalā Dēvi (mother of Beḷḷāḷa) and Gujjalā Dēvi, he is described as maintaining a harem of 384 women of good birth. It is no wonder then that he died at the early age of forty in the year 1173 unlike his father and others of his family, who had been trained in a hardier school of discipline than the inner apartments of a royal palace.

Narasimha was succeeded by his son Vīra Beḷḷāḷa, whose reign was a comparatively long and vigorous one of forty-seven years, A.D. 1173 to 1220. Vīra Bellala II is the actual maker of Mysore, although his grandfather deserves credit not only for having laid the foundation but also for having carried his project much farther than that. Circumstances, however, combined to put off the realization of his ideas to the time of his grandson, who was quite worthy of such a noble mission. Bijjala in the full flush of his power had created opposition to himself in the south, which was the opportunity for the Hoysala. Bijjala continued to rule till 1167, when he abdicated in favour of his eldest son, who and his three brothers ruled the empire till 1183, in succession, when Bamma restored the Chāḷukya, Sōmēsvara IV.

Vīra Beḷḷāḷa is found associated with his father's general Tantrapāla Hemmāḍi in the conquest of the malē chiefs, Kongāḷva, Changāḷva and others, who were brought into subjection in A.D. 1168. With the year 1174 the references to Chāḷukya supremacy completely disappear, probably, because it then appeared to the Hoysalas that there was no chance of the Chāḷukyas regaining their power, as they well might have done, under the Kalachūrya Bijjala and his sons. This fact notwithstanding, it is remarkable that Vīra Beḷḷāḷa did not assume the titles and designations of royalty. He even recognized the over-lordship (in A.D. 1178) of Sankama, the third son of Bijjala. It was either in this year, or a little before it, that he besieged and took possession of Uchchangi Droog, the capital of the Pandyas. He appears, however, to have restored Vijaya Pandya on his submission to the Hoysala authority. This event must have happened when the loyal Sindas and the Pandyas were hard pressed in the north. Against these the Kalachūrya usurpers and the powerful southern feudatory Hoysala must have come to an understanding as between themselves. This would account for the invasions of the Hoysala dominions by Bamma or Brahma, who restored Sōmēsvara IV, the last Chāḷukya, to his ancestral throne in A.D. 1183. This last Chāḷukya had to betake himself to the south-west of his dominions under the increasing pressure put upon him by the powerful Yādavas under Billama his own feudatory on the north-west, and the rising power of Warangal under Prōḷa and his son Pratāpa Rudra Dēva I. The Yādava extension from the north-west and the Hoysala extension from the south bring them face to face on the banks of the Malprabha and the Krishna. In this neighbourhood a battle was fought at Soraṭūr near Gadag, where Bhillama Yādhava was finally defeated, and the fort of Lokkuṇḍi in Dharwar occupied by

Vīra Beḷḷāḷa in A.D. 1190. The fortified places he rapidly took this year or before it were—Virāṭa's city (Hangal), Kurugōḍu, the Matanga Hill, Doravādi, Guṭṭi, Guṭṭavolalu, Uddare, Haḷadi, Bandaṇike, Baḷḷare, Soraṭūr, Eremberege (Yelburga), Halawe. Manuve, and Lokkigundi itself (all in the region between the present Mysore frontier and the Krishna). Before this in 1189 Sōmēsvara IV was defeated probably by the Yādavas and no more is heard of him. The time was now ripe for Beḷḷāḷa to assume formal independence of any suzerain, for there was none, except the Yādava Jaitugi who had been defeated with his father. The Sindas having been overcome already there was no one between the two. Hence, the Malprabha, and after its junction the Krishna, became the parting line between the Hoysalas in the south and the Yādavas of Deogiri in the north, and this division continued till both were overthrown in succession by Mālik Kāfúr in A. D. 1310. Vīra Beḷḷāḷa in A. D. 1191–2, assumed the following paramount epithets and titles—'Samasta Bhuvanāśraya, Srī Prithvīvallabha, Mahārājādhirāja, Paramēsvara and Parama Bhaṭṭaraka', and the style of 'Pratāpachakravartin Bhujabala Pratāpa Chakravartin, Hoysala Chakravartin, Bhujabala Pratāpa Chakravartin, and Yādava Chakravartin, and started an era in his name. This completes the independence of the Hoysalas, although the claim to the whole of Kuntaḷa appears mere extravagance. By A. D. 1191–2 Mysore as an independent State had been made, and the rest of the Hoysala story belongs to another chapter of South Indian history.

We have thus seen the stages by which a petty chief and his descendants in the south-west corner of the Kaḍūr district worked their way up to the establishment of a powerful State, which made its influence felt in the history of South India. In this work the chiefs displayed not only military ability, but also great diplomatic shrewdness by which, without in the least giving cause for the suspicion of disloyalty, they turned every circumstance to their advantage and waited till they could, without fear of being charged with treachery and disloyalty, assume the regal position. In this work, political circumstances of the times combined with personal skill, and this happy conjunction it was that made their course uniformly successful; for otherwise they would have been overthrown beyond recovery by Vikramāditya. Vinayāditya was perhaps a more active chieftain than his peers, but it was the valuable services of his son to the rising sun of the Chāḷukyas that established his claim to the emperor's gratitude. His son Vishṇu rendered an even more valuable service to the empire—not emperor only—by stopping the advancing tide of the Chola conquest. Through a long period of activity he was able to gain imperial recognition to the rule of modern Mysore. This, however, had to be made good as against other ambitious but loyal chieftains, who were overthrown during the usurpation in the empire. This was taken advantage of by Vīra Beḻḻāḷa, as has been pointed out already, who gave the *coup de grâce* and stood in the plenitude of power as the 'Emperor of the south'—merely the south of the western Chāḷukya empire and nothing more as yet. There is still the expansion of the Hoysala empire, which goes so far as to establish an alternative capital near Srīrangam, and then comes the fall, not in the usual course, but through the intervention of a disturbing element, the Muḥammadan invasion of the Dekhan. That is a century hence and falls in the reign of an *ill-fated Vīra Beḻḻāḷa.*

CHAPTER IX

VISHṆUVARDHANA

In the 'Making of Mysore' I have dwelt somewhat fully upon the aspect of this great ruler of Mysore as an empire-builder. I have, however, hardly touched upon the great change that came over him in the course of his royal career, which led to his conversion from Jainism to Vaishṇavaism. I propose in this chapter to deal with this side of his character, and thus describe the religious condition of Mysore in his days.

Before proceeding to deal with this question, one or two common heresies regarding the particular form of worship followed by the disciples of Rāmānuja have to be disposed of. It was Bishop Caldwell who gave currency to the idea that Rāmānuja was the founder of Vishṇu worship and that the Āḻvārs were his disciples. Caldwell could be pardoned readily, if the late professor Seshagiri Sastriar of the Presidency college, with much of the results of research that Caldwell had not before him, could hold the same opinion and identify the Vallabha Dēva of the days of Periyāḻvār with Ati Vīra Rāma Pandyan, A. D. 1563, and bring other Āḻvārs later in point of time. Professor Julien Vinson of Paris, following in the wake of these, with much more reasonable excuse in his favour than the late Professor, believes that Vaishṇavism began about the fifteenth or the sixteenth centuries. The Chola inscriptions published by Dr. Hultzsch in his latest volume (Vol. III. P. II.,) effectively dispose of Caldwell's contention and *a fortiori* of those that follow in his footsteps. Mr. Venkayya, in his report to the Government last year (1904), refers to one inscription in the Triplicane temple of the time of the Pallavas, thereby proving the existence of the temple in Pallava times. If further proofs were wanted in this matter one has but to look for them. The Śilappadhikāram, a Tamil Kavya of the second century of the Christian Era (the most unfavourable estimate of its antiquity placing it in the seventh century A. D.), refers to the Vishṇu temples at Srirangam, Triuppati and Tirumālirunajōlai. Coming up from them, Paramēsvara Varman Pallava (regarded by Dr. Hultzsch as the second of the name) built the temple Paramēsvara Viṇṇagaram (Ulagaḷandha Permāl Koil) in Conjevaram. The period of the Pallava ascendency in Southern India must have been the period of great Hindu activity in religion, as against the rival faiths of the Jīna and the Buddha. This was exactly the period of the great temple builders, and several temples dedicated alike to Śiva and Vishṇu in South India owe their existence to this dynasty. Simha Vishṇu or Narasimha Varman, otherwise Mahāmalla, was the builder of the rock-cut temples at Mahābalipuram (the Seven Pagodas) and he was the rival contemporary of Pulikesin II, whose court Ywan Chwang (Hiuen Thsang) visited in his travels through India. Kōchengan, a Chola who must have preceded the Pallavas, built temples to Vishṇu and Śiva in close proximity often, so that from the seventh century onward Śaivaism and Vaishṇavaism developed side by side and were alike patronized by the royalties of those days.

Through all this time, however, Mysore remained generally Jain. The Ganga rulers appear to have been Jains, although the Kongu chronicle states that the great Ranganātha temple at Srirangapatam was built in the days of the later Ganga rulers. There are records.

however, of the existence of Śiva and Vishṇu temples, endowed by individual sovereigns of the Ganga dynasty. In the days of Vishṇuvardhana a temple manager of the Śiva temple at Maddur (*alias* Śivapura) claimed a plot of land on the strength of a copper-plate grant of Śiva Māra II. (*Circ.* A. D. 750). There are similar references to Vishṇu temples. This Śivamara's father, Srī Purusha Muttarasa, is referred to as a worshipper at the feet of Nārāyaṇa. Thus then we see Vaishṇavaism as a religion was in existence long before the days of Rāmānuja, however much he may have reformed, altered or added to it.

The advance of the Chola Power in South India marks the advance also of the Śaiva religion, as most of the sovereigns were of the Śaiva persuasion and richly endowed the temples, which either they themselves built or which were already in existence, although occasional grants were made and existing grants confirmed to the Vaishṇava temples. About A. D. 1000, therefore, there was fresh vigour in religious development, partly because the struggle against the Jains had become somewhat keener, and partly because the work of the saints, Śaiva and Vaishṇava, had borne fruit in the increased attention to religion. It was while this religious ferment was beginning to operate that the Chola conquest of Mysore began. This conquest, which gradually gave the Gangavāḍi 96,000 and the great part of Noḷambavāḍi 32,000 to the Cholas, brought the Śaivism of the Cholas and the Jainism of the Chāḷukyas face to face in the Mysore country. Noḷambavāḍi had been lost practically to the Chāḷukyas before the days of Āhavamalla Somēsvara, so that the continual wars in this part of the frontier had also a religious element in it. When Vishuṇvardhana, therefore, came to take part in the politics of Mysore, the country was in the unsettled state of religious debate. Jainism was generally in the ascendant, while there was a considerable following for the Śaivas and Vaishṇavas as well.

It was while matters were in this state that the Brahman youth of Conjevaram succeeded to the Vaishṇava apostolic seat at Srīrangam of his great grand-father Āḷavandār. This young man was Rāmānuja, who, born in the year 937 Saka, was to become the great reformer of India, and whose disciples hold much of the country south and north. Having put away his wife and assumed the robes of an ascetic, he spent the best part of his days in teaching the Vaishṇavas of Srīrangam. In his vedantic teachings he had often to criticize other schools of thought in religion which naturally made him a few enemies, though, if we can judge of the man by his works, he must have been far from a militant preacher. An impertinent and half-blasphemous remark of one of his disciples in reply to a challenge sent out by a doughty Śaiva champion jeopardized Rāmānuja's position in Srīrangam. The erring disciple placed himself in the position of the inoffensive preceptor and sent the latter for asylum into the Mysore country—the land of toleration. Here Rāmānuja spent, according to the *Guruparamparai*, twelve years before he was brought to the notice of Biṭṭi Dēva, then gradually becoming master of the Gangavāḍi 96,000. The sincere piety and the persuasive eloquence of Rāmānuja's teaching must have prevailed with the king, for he became a convert to the Vaishṇava faith about A. D. 1116. Biṭṭi Dēva thenceforward continued in the same persuasion under the title Vishṇuvardhana.

The account of this apparently simple incident has come down to us in a variety of ways. The Vaishṇava accounts say that while at Saligram Rāmānuja's stock of Nāmam (the kaolin-clay used as the face mark by the Vaishṇavas) was spent, and that he was in difficulties as to what to do, when he dreamt of a hill

17

of that earth near Mēlukōṭe. Thither he went and on his way he found Biṭṭi Dēva (Viṭala Dēvaraya) in camp at Tonḍanūr. This latter had a daughter, who was possessed by evil spirits, and all Jain incantations having failed to lay the ghost, Rāmānuja brought about a successful exorcism, which convinced Biṭṭi Dēva of his superiority. He became a Vaishṇava and after successful disputation in Biṭṭi Dēva's presence Rāmānuja had a whole body of Jain ascetics and laymen ground in an oil mill, which is even now pointed out at Moti Talab (Tonḍanūr).

The Jain account states that the king was influenced by Rāmānuja through one of his queens to become a Vaishṇava. He resisted the temptation for a long time; but when, owing to the loss of a finger of his right hand in war, the Jain ascetics declined to dine with him, he forthwith became a Vaishṇava.

Of these two versions the latter must be stamped as false entirely, because Vishṇuvardhana was an eminently sensible man, treated his Jain wife, ministers and subjects with great consideration. His wife, the first at least, who after his conversion was a Jain to the day of her death, and her Basadi, the Savati Ghanḍavāraṇa Basti at Sravana Belgoḷa, is evidence of her religion. His daughter Hariaḷe was a Jain. More than this, his right-hand man in the work of founding a kingdom, the great General Gangaraja in whose memory was built the Drohagharaṭṭa Jīnālaya at Halebid, was also a Jain of eminence; for the inscriptions say that, by restoring Jain temples in the kingdom, he made it resemble Kōpaṇa or Koppal in the Nizam's Dominions. It could not, therefore, be that he became a Vaishṇava by any underhand dealing, nor could he have had any particular dislike of Jainism as such.

The other version simply brings in a miracle to explain an ordinary event in the life of a great man.

In those days it was the custom for eminent divines, Jain, Hindu or Buddhist, to discourse upon religious topics under the presidency of the great laymen—kings or rulers of provinces. We have numbers of references to it in the Shimoga inscriptions. Very probably Rāmānuja held such a discourse, and ground down in the mill of his logic the arguments of his rivals. The oil mill affair could have been no more than this, for even if Rāmānuja should have been so minded, Biṭṭi Dēva could hardly have permitted it, if not out of clemency, at least out of policy. With his wife, and his generals, and councillors all Jains, it would have been the height of folly in him to have done so. It is, therefore, nothing more nor less than a boastful assertion of triumphant success on the part of the Vaishṇavas of a succeeding generation. Nor were they—the only sinners in this particular.

We read in an inscription of about A. D. 1128 at Sravana Beḷgoḷa that the Jain Akaḷanka achieved a similar feat. The Bauddhs of Kanchi to get rid of the Jains, challenged their great teacher Akaḷanka, from Sudhapura or Sōḍe in North Kanara, to a disputation under Himasītala A. D. 855. Having once before defeated the Buddhists on behalf of the Vīra Śaivas, he went forth confidently and having, after days of argumentation had the better of the debate, Himasītala ordered them to be ground in oil mills. Akaḷanka, true to his character, as the preceptor of the Ājivakas interceded, and got them banished to Ceylon and other distant islands. Strangely enough after this general destruction of the Buddhists by the Jains, we hear of Buddhists as governors of provinces even; to wit Buddhamitra, governor of Ponpaṟṟi near Ramanad in the reign of Kulōttunga II.

The oil mill incident was an accepted embellishment in handing down the accounts of these disputations, of which there must have been a number going on at different places simultaneously. That it is impossible that either Vishṇuvardhana or his successors could have sanctioned any such thing, is borne out by a number of incidents in their history. It was from the royal residence at Mēlkote that Vishṇuvardhana makes a grant to the Śaiva temple, at Chāmund Hill. He does receive the 'holy food' presented by the Jains after the consecration of the Jīnālaya at Haḷēbiḍ, and directs the image to be named Vijaya Pārśvanātha in honour of his victory. He honours Srī Pāla Trividya Dēva (the Jain controversialist) and even appoints him tutor to his children. It was about this time that the Vīra Śaiva (the so-called Lingayat) sect comes into prominence, so that in the course of the century Jainism was subjected to the simultaneous attacks of the Vaishṇavas from the south and the Vīra Śaivas from the north. The manner in which the Hoyasals—rulers and ministers alike—dealt with these rival sects is a supreme instance of their religious policy from which more modern rulers might learn lessons of wisdom. Here is the historical account of the foundation of the temple at Harihar: 'The great minister, the setter up of the Chola, Vīra Narasimha Dēva Pōlāḷvadanḍanātha caused to be made a temple for the god Harihara, shining with one hundred and fifteen golden Kalasas.' The object of building the shrine was to reconcile the opposing sects of the Śaivas and the Vaishṇavas. 'Some saying that beside Hari there is no god on earth, and some saying that besides Hara there is no god in the earth, in order to remove the doubts of mankind, was assumed with glory in Kūḍalūr the one form of Harihara. May he with affection preserve us. The celebrated Śiva acquired the form of Vishṇu, Vishṇu acquired the great and famous form of Śiva, in order that this saying of the Veda might be fully established, in Kūḍal there stood forth in a single form, praised by the world Harihara—may he protect the earth' 'The renowned Vaishṇava Chakravarti, this celebrated Pōlāḷvadaṇḍadēva, is the only one who obtained success with the collyrium of merit; if not how could he successfully acquire the treasure to create the lofty mansion of Harihara, shining with a hundred golden Kalaśas? Formerly Hermmaḍi Raja wanted to make a temple for Harihara, but stopping him in a dream, saying: "A faithful one will be born hereafter who will make my abode, you stop," and Harihara having with affection said: "you only make my temple in a suitable manner, Polāḷva," he made it.' This achievement of a Vaishṇava minister in reconciling the two opposing sects is a unique instance of a breadth of view in religion, which is hard to find elsewhere at the time.

This was the feat of one of a class of persons, rulers and ministers, who have been devoted Vaishṇavas. Vishṇuvardhana after his conversion, perhaps through the course of his career, built temples dedicated to Nārāyaṇa—at any rate endowed them richly—such as Vīra Nārāyaṇa at Talakāḍ, Vījaya Nārāyaṇa at Belur, Kīrti Nārāyaṇa at Baṇṇūr. In his progress through his dominions he had taken pains to inquire into the condition of these and other foundations, and saw that they were restored to their former position of eminence as places of worship. He did not in this show any partiality to one sect or the other. His general Gangaraja endowed Jain temples equally with the sanction of his master, as the several donations to Jain temples by this general and other Jain devotees would show. This example was followed by his successors, equally well whether they were Vaishṇava or Śaiva for some of them were of the latter persuasion also.

Thus then it is clear that in the matter of religion, this Vaishṇava Constantine, Vishṇuvardhana, as the disciples of Rāmānuja took delight in calling him, was far from being a sectarian. No attempt was made at any uniformity of religious belief, and the policy of the rulers was the most liberal that could be imagined. If other states and rulers had maintained this neutrality in religion the world over, the world would have been saved many bloody wars. Had Vishṇuvardhana and his successors adopted any other policy in religion, they would have shown a fatuity which might have ruined them. That they deliberately adopted this policy of religious neutrality speaks much for their statesmanship.

CHAPTER X

BIJJALA

It has been pointed out in the chapter on the making of Mysore that the kingdom could be regarded as such only after A.D. 1193, almost in the middle of the reign of Vīra-Beḷḷāḷa. Vishṇuvardhana had made it in a way; but it required the energy and enterprise of his grandson before his rule could be regarded as complete. The credit of consolidation belongs to Vīra-Beḷḷāḷa, who succeeded his father on the twenty-second July A.D. 1173.

The Karnāṭaka, or the Chāḷukya Empire, stretched out southwards from the Sātpura mountains to the end of the Dekhan plateau, and had been divided into a number of governorships, each under a Mahāmanḍalēsvara, with more or less of other authority vested in him, according to the character of the official and the degree of favour enjoyed by him at court. Of these potentates those round about the head-quarters of the emperor were more under imperial authority, and were usually loyal, as a virtue, perhaps, of necessity. Whether this was actually so or not, we have references to a southern treasury of the empire and by inference other treasuries likewise. Each of these larger divisions appears to have had a common fisc and included a number of provinces. An attempt had evidently been made to bring the frontier viceroys under the direct control of the head-quarters officers by the appointment of a board of control, whose chief functions appear to have been financial, thus bringing the sinews of war beyond the absolute disposal of the viceroys. This, we see, was the practice under the usurper Bijjala, and it lets us thus into the secret of his elevation to the empire.

Bijjala's father, Pērmmāḍi, was governor of Tārdavādi 1,000 district round Bijāpur under Somēsvara III Bhūlōkamalla (A. D. 1128). His son was Bijjala, who may have succeeded to his father's estate of governor of the Tārdavādi 1,000. Whether he did so or not, he is heard of about the end of the reign of the emperor Jagadēkamalla II (1138–49) with no official titles; but 'his servant' Vijaya Panḍya was ruling the Noḷambavāḍi 32,000. As inscriptions of Vīra Panḍya are met with up to A. D. 1148, the inscriptions referred to above must be about the end of Jagadēkamalla's reign. It is in his reign that Bijjala rises into importance, and what is more he is found busy on the very frontier which was fast passing out of the emperor's hands. The Hoysalas had madc themselves masters of the Gangavāḍi (which is not included in the 'Southern Treasury,') for some time; but their claims to the provinces of Banavase and Noḷambavāḍi were very strongly contested by the Muhāmanḍalēsvaras themselves and by the emperor. It was against these two sets of rivals that Vīra Beḷḷāḷa had to make good his claim.

Of these Noḷambavāḍi had surely fallen under the Chola power. The fact that Chāḷukya inscriptions of an earlier period are absent, and the Chola inscriptions are found in the province shows the Chola hold upon the province. The Panḍyas of Noḷambavāḍi were as forward as the Hoysalas to render service against the Cholas and had earned the gratitude of Vikramāditya—no less than their compeers and relatives, the Hoysalas. Thenceforward the dynasty of viceroys, the Panḍyas of Uchchangi ruled from their hill-fort the province so recently recovered from the Cholas. When we come to the reign of Vīra Beḷḷaḷa, two generations of Panḍyas had ruled after the brother of Irukkapāla the father-in-law of Vishṇuvardhana's father Eṛēyanga. When Bijjala appears on the scene, Vīra-Panḍya, one of the most powerful of the dynasty, was in power, which was about to pass to his younger brother Vijaya Panḍya.

The neighbouring province of Banavase had long been under the empire. Vikramāditya had himself been viceroy under his father, and when he became emperor, his younger brother Jayasimha was viceroy. So that this had come to be regarded as the premier province of his empire. Whatever was the reason for it, upon the loyalty of the viceroy of this province depended the imperial authority over the provinces belonging to the southern treasury. When Bijjala emerges into the full light of history, we hear of him as the viceroy of the two provinces, ruling by deputies. This must have come about somewhat in this wise: Bijjala must have shown great administrative capacity which included in it great military ability, as governor of his hereditary province of Tārdāwaḍi, which must have been too narrow a sphere for the full display of his faculties. Either to put them to the best use or to get rid of them, he was entrusted with the duty first of all of watching and counteracting the machinations of the southern viceroys—perhaps as the fiscal officer sent out by the emperor. This would explain why, while claiming the Panḍya for his servant, he appears without official titles of his own. This superior position he was able to turn to account, when later on Jagadēkamalla was succeeded in the empire by his brother Taila III. Under the latter he grew to be so useful and loyal that he was called to the head-quarters to help the emperor, governing Banavase and Noḷambavāḍi by deputies. These deputies, whatever their loyalty, he subordinates and keeps under the eyes of the emperor, and that is himself by sending out five commissioners to control ostensibly the finances of the southern treasury. By so doing he keeps the most turbulent of these viceroys well in hand.

Unfortunately for the empire there arises the new power of the Kākatīyas of Wārangal, and Bijjala's activity, so successful in the south, is wanted in the north-east, the more so, as the new power under Prōḷa inflicted a defeat upon the empire in A. D. 1155. Bijjala's name has been handed down to us with the stigma of cruelty and persecution attached to it; first, because of his usurpation, and next because of his persecution of the so-called Lingayets and their founders. Both these charges against him have to be carefully examined in the dry-light of history before the verdict is pronounced by the historian. Bijjala does not appear to have used any cruelty in his ascent to power, though no doubt he made a very skilful use of the advantage of his position and the adverse circumstances of the empire. He was not alone in this. Every viceroy tried to take advantage of the troubles into which the empire was thrown, while Bijjala ought to be given credit for having early observed the trend of affairs and for having made a successful attempt to stop the flowing tide of disruption. Exposed as it was to simultaneous attacks of the powerful Cholas in the south and the Chāḷukyas in the east, the empire was preserved from dismemberment through the genius of Vikramāditya. If it did not break up immediately after his death, it was because the enemy's powers were otherwise engaged, and the Mahāmanḍalēsvaras of Vikramāditya remembered with gratitude his services to them. Nevertheless, the tendencies were there and, with each advance of the viceroys, other powers were rising on the horizon. The Hoysala activity in the south and the Kākatīya exertions in the east were kept under control by Bijjala taking advantage of the counteracting forces. This naturally led him on to the pinnacle of power, and it was only when he found that there was no possibility of keeping up the phantom of an emperor that he assumed imperial state. In one sense, therefore, he might be regarded as the benefactor of the empire, not emperor of course, in keeping it half a century longer than its appointed time. To him also probably belongs the credit of organizing the imperial resources and of bringing the viceroys under control by placing them under financial control from head-quarters. For it is in his reign that we see the five Karaṇams being sent out to keep a watch over the doings of the viceroys of Banavase and probably of other troublesome provinces as well.

In the religious aspect of the question again Bijjala had been brought to the notice of posterity only by the religious literature of the Vira-Śaivas, mostly composed centuries after the time they treat of. In these he is held up naturally enough to execration. But inscriptions of his time in the Shimoga district—particularly at Baḷagamvé—throw a curious light upon the much-abused man and the ruler. On the one hand the inscriptions point to a far greater control over the viceroys, as grants have to be made with permission from head-quarters or at least obtain sanction when made. On the other hand, the lands and other grants made to Śaiva, Vaishṇava and Jain shrines are all placed under the control of the leading men of all persuasions. The place was sacred alike to all three of these. In A.D. 1162, while Bijjala had made himself supreme, his viceroy was Kāśyapa, with whom no one can be compared 'in taking sole charge of a country ruined by the administration of others and bringing it into prosperity'. 'With the permission of that great one, Barmmarasa was governing the Banavasenāḍ.'

'The royal inspectors were the five Karaṇams—Sridhara Nāyaka, Achaṇa Nāyaka, Chaṭṭimayya Nāyaka, Malliyaṇa Nāyaka and Ṭikkamayya Nāyaka:—these shone like the five senses to king Bijjala Deva'—all 'benevolent to others, powerful as the ocean, in ministerial skill unmatched, bold as fierce lions, able in detecting frauds, superior to all opposition, their great fame like the sound of the tūrya (a musical instrument), strengthened with all manner of self-acquired merit, devoted to the faith of the Īśvara,—these Karaṇams were great.' Barmmarasa's great minister was Ravidēva.

'While all these, united in the enjoyment of peace and wisdom, were one day discoursing on Dharmma, Bijjala Maharaja having come there, in order to subdue the southern region, encamped in Baḷagamvé, Kaśappya Nāyaka rising and standing in front of his Mahāraja, folding his lotus hands said, "Dēva, a petition", and spoke as follows: "The southern Kēdāra is the means of the absolution of sin, the very presence of Śiva manifested to all the citizens, visibly displaying all the glory of the Krita Yuga. Besides this, its maṭha is like the ancient Kamaṭha (tortoise) a support of all the world."

'Descended in the line of the gurus of that Maṭha, the disciple of Gautamachārya, is Vāma Sakti Munīsvarāchārya.' 'Therefore were the Dēva to perform in that Maṭha some work of merit, it will endure as long as the sun and moon.'

'On his saying thus, the King Bijjala taking it to mind—for the decoration of the God Dakshiṇa Kēdārēsvara, for gifts of food to the ascetics, for gifts of learning, for repairs to the temple, and for satisfying the good and the beloved,—in his sixth year, etc., at the time of the sun's eclipse, washing the feet of Gautamāchārya's disciple Vāma Sākti Paṇḍita Dēva, made a grant.'[1] On the same day as this he made grants to other Śiva temples as well.

Several others of his viceroys and governors were staunch Śaivas and Vaishṇavas who built and endowed Śiva and Vishṇu temples, the greatest among the latter having been Kēśava Daṇḍanāyaka. A ruler who could not merely tolerate, but also actively participate in benefactions to the religious institutions of the rival sects could not be charged with persecution without ample evidence. It does not matter for the question, whether this was out of sincere toleration or as a matter of policy to keep the viceroys well disposed towards him. This would appear the more remarkable in Bijjala, when it is remembered that the time was one of great religious activity. The Vaishṇavaism of Rāmānuja was gaining strength in the south and on the border of Mysore some of the sects, the Pāśupata, Kāpālika, Kāḷāmukha, etc., of the Śaivas were strong. What was more, Vāmadēva Paṇḍita, the disciple of Gautamāchārya, was the most important figure, often called in inscriptions the Rājaguru, and in the inscriptions at Baḷḷigamvē, he is shown up as a prominent teacher in whom is placed so much faith by Government and people alike, that the endowments to temples, Śaiva, Vaishṇava, Jaina, etc., are placed in his charge. While Bijjala was strengthening the imperial hold upon the viceroys, local governments appear to have been working with great vigour as well—the paṭṭaṇaswamis or town mayors playing a very important part at the head of their town councils. The fact which Mr. Rice notices of Jīna images having been pared down into Lingams must have been of a later time when the so-called Lingayets or Vīra Śaivas, got the upper hand in those regions; for we see that in the next generation the struggle on

1 102 of Shikarpūr, *Epigraphia Carnātaka*, vol. vii.

the border land is not between the Jains and the Śaivas but between the Vaishṇavas and the latter. In this struggle again the rulers showed a commendable spirit not merely of toleration, but also of an attempt at reconciliation, the direct outcome of which policy is the Harihara temple at Harihar.

Thus in religion and equally so in administration, Bijjala and his sons, who followed in succession, pursued a conciliatory policy which kept the turbulent viceroys under control and their administration, strong and popular. Āhavamalla, the last of them, charged his viceroys of treasuries thus: 'Govern the country which is the treasury of the south like a father.' One Kēsava Nāyaka ruled so well under his Government, that none was conceited, none conspicuous in splendour, none in opposition, none clamouring for influence, none creating a disturbance, none who was in suffering, no enemies filled with anger, and none who receiving titles had his head turned by the songs of poets! Though a usurper Bijjala was able to retire in favour of his sons and let them succeed peacefully, a contingency very often not met with in rulers even of the most undoubted succession. His assassination which appears to have been a fact must have been brought about by some private misunderstanding and, if such scandal could be believed in, had been brought about by a liason with the minister Basava's sister who is credited with an immaculate conception, by the Basava and Channa Basava Puranas, the outcome of which was the Younger Basava or Channa Basava. This would also account for the main plank of reform of the Lingayats—the re-marriage of widows.

During all this period of usurpation in the empire, the Hoysala activity appears to have been carefully checked; and through much of this period, Narasimha, ably seconded as he was by his father's viceroys and his son Kumāra Beḷḷaḷa, had to be content with the

Gangavāḍi 96,000. Any activity, noticeable at all, was against the petty chiefs, the Kongālvas and other hill-chiefs of the western frontier. When Vīra-Beḷḷaḷa came to the throne in A.D. 1173, he had to begin to work on the lines of his grandfather Vishṇuvardhana, while the empire had passed to Rāyamurāri Sōvi-Deva.

CHAPTER XI

MYSORE UNDER THE WOḌEYĀRS

THIS chapter is an historical outline of the origin and growth of the State of Mysore under the present dynasty up to the time of Ḥaidar 'Alī. This period of the history[1] of Mysore is hardly touched at all in any history except in that by Colonel Wilks, who was not in possession of the historical material now available to the student of history. The errors he has fallen into are rather serious but quite excusable in one who wrote so early in the century as he did, and who obtained all the information then possible. The publication of the volumes of inscriptions in Mysore by Mr. Rice is likely to throw a flood of light upon Mysore history and that of some other contemporary kingdoms. This and the lately published works of Minister Tirumala Iyengar are the main authorities on which this paper rests for its information. The history of Mysore in Kannaḍa prose compiled at the direction of his late Highness, though not of much value as an historical composition, is still of use as supplying fuller information on what is otherwise found to be the truth. It is not as an

[1] I refer to two works—The *Palace History* and Wilks' *History*.

The *Palace History* is a Canarese compilation from the *Vamśāvali* and other MS records in the palace. It was compiled at the instance of His late lamented Highness Śrī Channarajendra Woḍēyār. It is based on traditions of a more or less reliable character.

The Historical Sketches of South India by Wilks is referred to in the chapter as Wilks' *History*.

authoritative composition that I write this chapter on Mysore. It is only a small contribution, which may eventually lead to the writing of a good history of Mysore, of which this is but an imperfect sketch of a period covering nearly two centuries.

In the epoch making battle of Talikoṭa, in which the Musalmáns and the Hindus contended for supremacy in southern India, and which ended in the complete victory of the Muḥammadan coalition, the emperor Rama Raja, the last real one, fell. His only surviving brother Hiri Timmaraja fled with the wreck of the army to Vijayanagar, and finding it impossible to sustain himself any longer there against the conquerors, he shifted his capital to Ghanagiri (Penukoṇḍa). Here he died leaving three sons, Sriranga Rayal, Rama Raja, and Venkaṭapati Rāya. The division of the empire was made during the father's lifetime in accordance with which, Sriranga Rayal ruled from Penukoṇḍa, nominally at least, the whole of the Telugu country; Rama Raja had for his share the Kannaḍa country with his capital at Srirangapatna; Venkaṭapati Rāya ruled from Chandragiri[1] over the largest portion as would appear, namely, over the Toṇḍa, Chola, and Pandya Manḍalams. But that this rule was anything more than nominal is matter for doubt as will appear from the sequel. As it was, however, the Vijayanagar empire extended from the banks of the northern Pennar, if not the Tungabhadra to Cape Comorin, and was divided in 1597 into the viceroyalties of Penukoṇḍa, Ginjee, Tanjore, Madura, Channapatna, and Srirangapatna, the first one and perhaps nominally the whole under Sriranga Rayal, the next three under Venkaṭapati Rāya, and the last two under Rama Raja.[2]

[1] *Chikka Deva Raja Vamśāvaḷi*, pp. 1-16.
[2] Wilks' *History*, vol. i, p. 59.

About this time, Sriranga Rayal died without issue, and Rama Raja also followed leaving Tirumal Rāya, his son, a minor; so that the whole empire devolved upon Venkaṭapati Rāya. Tirumal Rāya lived with his uncle, leaving at Srirangapatna as vice-regent Remati Revati, or Timati Venkaṭa the general of Rama Raja. The viceroys, aware of the weakness of the central authority, bore the yoke rather lightly and waited for an opportunity to shake it off, when an incident happened to accelerate the natural tendencies to disruption. This incident is reported by Tirumala Aiyangar, who lived in the latter half of the seventeenth and the earlier half of the eighteenth centuries, occupying all along a commanding position in the courts of successive rulers of Mysore as follows: 'The Madura Naik revolted and Venkaṭapati Rāya sent his nephew (probably now a major) to put down the revolt. Instead of doing this, his plain duty, Tirumala Rāya received bribes from the rebellious satrap and marched with all his army to Srirangapatna, thereby bringing on himself a deserved retribution and showing to onlookers the hollowness of the empire.'[1] It was under these circumstances that there arose a particularly clever ruler in Mysore, who turned them all to his advantage and laid the foundation of the present Mysore State.

We shall now proceed to inquire who this personage was and what his position. There seems to have been in use in the territory of Mysore (and even outside it) ever since the dawn of history the designation of Woḍeyars signifying a certain feudal status. What the amount of the land was, the possession of which gave this honorific title to the possessor, is very hard to determine now. There have been Woḍeyars whose possessions varied from a village or two to thirty

[1] *Chikka Deva Raja Vijayam*, 2nd Canto; *Chikka Deva Raja Vamśāvaḷi*, pp. 1–16.

or forty. The Woḍeyar of Karoogahally[1] owns himself master of only one village; and Raja Woḍeyar of Mysore about the same time was lord of twenty-three villages.[2] But the term Woḍeyar is also largely used in another sense being merely equivalent to 'lord'. This is the term used in addressing priests among the Lingayets. It may be a combination of both when applied to the members of the ruling family. But Yadu Rāya is said to have been requested by his wife to assume this title as a mark of gratitude to a Lingayet priest who helped him in taking possession of Mysore from the usurper Daḷawāy Māranāyaka.[3] Whatever may be the value of this story, the title seems to have retained both the above meanings as applied to the Mysore family.

This family traces its descent from a certain Yadu Rāya who is believed to have reigned from 1399 to 1423. He is said to have come to this province from Dwāraka. The object of his journey to Mysore with his brother Krishna is differently given by different authorities; some giving the worship of god Nārāyaṇa of Mēlukōṭe as the object, and others that of the goddess Chamunḍi of the Mysore Hill. Whatever the motive of these brothers, they appear to have been fugitive princes of the lately overthrown Hoysala family which had its capital at Dwārāvati (the modern Haḷebíd), or of that of the Kākatíyas of Warangal which claimed to belong to the Chandra Vamśa as well.[4] But Wilks mentions them as Yadava fugitives from the court of Vijayanagar, which seems very likely. They came to Mysore where circumstances favoured

[1] *Chikka Deva Raja Vamśāvaḷi*, p. 16.

[2] Thirty-three villages according to Wilks (*vide* vol. i, p. 21, footnote).

[3] *Palace History*, p. 16.

[4] This view seems to receive support from the author of copper plate No. 64 of Srirangapatna.

Vide page 23 translation.

Epigraphia Carnāṭaka, vol. i, part 1.

their founding a family. Here again accounts differ, but the one given in the *Palace History* looks more probable than that of Wilks. A certain Chama Raja Woḍeyar of Mysore died leaving behind him his widow and an only daughter. The Daḷawāy Māranāyaka assumed the regency which he tried eventually to convert into royalty. The widow and her daughter seem to have been helpless in his hands.[1] Perhaps, he would have married the daughter and thus given an appearance of legality to his usurpation; but his unpopularity and the discontent among his officers came to a head in a conspiracy against him. The palace party seems to have had the sympathy of the people and the conspiracy against the usurper had gained in strength, when Yadu Rāya was ready to play his part by heading the conspiracy. Success attending the conspiracy, Yadu won the hand of the Woḍeyar's daughter, and he succeeded to her father's estate as was agreed to before. It was a 'jungam' priest that negotiated the treaty, and hence the title Woḍeyar attached to the princes of the family as mentioned above.

This is the historical founder of the family, and he ruled over Mysore town and a few villages about it. What the actual extent of this small State was we have no means of ascertaining now. He settled upon his brother an estate, which he took from one of his father-in-law's relatives, and died in 1423.

His son Hiri Beṭad Chama Raja Woḍeyar succeeded him in 1423. Nothing is known of this personage except his name. He was in turn succeeded by his son Timma Raja Woḍeyar in the year 1458. His son Hiri Chama Raja Woḍeyar ascended the throne of the little kingdom, if we may call it a kingdom at all, in the year 1478. This ruler's son was Beṭad Chama

[1] *Palace History*, p. 9, et seq.

Raja[1] whose reign began in the year 1513, and it is this person who has the honour of being mentioned in the inscriptions and copper plates next to Yadu, the intervening names being omitted. Beṭad Chama Raja is credited by the *Palace History* with having constructed a big tank in Mysore, and by Wilks with having repaired the fort of Mysore 'till then known as Puragēry.[2] He is also said by the same authority to have removed the capital to Mysore, probably from Hadana, the place conquered by Yadu. This account, of course, differs from what is stated above. All the authorities referred to agree in giving this person three sons, Timma Raja, Krishna Raja, and Chama Raja 'the bald'. During his lifetime, he arranged, according to custom, to settle Hēmanalli upon Timma Raja, and Kembala upon Krishna Raja. Timma Raja was, however, to succeed his father,[3] Chama Raja 'the bald', ruling after him. This is probably what is referred to by Wilks as the partition of the estate. But it is better to regard it as a settlement only, since all the other parties appear to have been subject to the ruler at Mysore. This is borne out by the settlement made at his death by Raja Woḍeyar. Before leaving Beṭad Chama Raja,[4] it ought to be mentioned that this was the person who is regarded as having, by his prowess, earned the title of 'Birudantembara Ganḍa' (the man of those that say they are so and so) mentioned in the inscriptions.

This ruler was succeeded in 1552 by his son Timma Raja according to the testament of his father. Timma Raja is reputed to have acquired the undoubted and sole right to the title of 'Birudantembara Ganḍa'

[1] *Vide* Srirangapatna, 64, 100 and others (*Epi. Car.*).

[2] Wilks' *History*, vol. i, p. 22.

[3] *Palace History*, pp. 18, 99.

[4] *Chikka Deva Raja Vamśāvaḷi*, p. 56, et seq.

by defeating other Woḍeyars who laid claim to it likewise during a visit to Nanjanagūḍu. He followed up this victory by the conquest of Ummatur and Sinduvalli.[1] During his time, Mysore territory must have been very small in extent, as he had to get permission from other independent Woḍeyars to pass through their territory to Nanjanagūḍu.

This ruler was succeeded by his youngest brother Bōḷe[2] Chama Raja or Chama Raja 'the bald'. This was no doubt the wish of the father, but why his elder brother Krishna Raja was passed over is not quite clear. Can it be that he died before 1571? This Chama Raja then ruled for five years 1571–6, and is credited by Wilks with having evaded the tribute due to the viceroy at Srirangapatna.[3] It is now not ten years after the battle of Talikoṭa which took place in 1565. The viceroy is said to have besieged the fort of Mysore, and it is recorded that his Daḷawāy[4] Revati Remati, or Timati Venkaṭa, was defeated and forced to cede Kottagala. This shows the want of efficiency in the viceregal government.

About this time, also, Akbar had made himself almost master of Hindustan, and was turning his attention to the southern side of the Vindhyas. This new element of disturbance, and the resistance which it provoked in the Musalmán Powers of the Dekhan, gave to the further south comparative peace, even the Bijapur and Golconda princes having had to divide their attention. It was only the imbecility of the Vijayanagar rulers that gave these petty Woḍeyars an opportunity for rising to greatness. Rama Raja, the

[1] Wilks' *History*, vol. i, p. 22 ; *Palace History*, p. 19.

[2] Hiri Chama Raja of Wilks and Doḍ Chama Raja of Srirangapatna, 157. Page 36, translation (*Epi. Car.*).

[3] Vol. i, pp. 12-13.

[4] *Chikka Deva Raja Vamśāvaḷi*, p. 45, et seq. Srirangapatna 64 and others.

viceroy, was dead leaving behind him the minor Tirumal Rāya mentioned above, whose treason cost him his viceroyalty.

Bōḷe Chama Raja left at his death four sons, Rājādhi Raja, Beṭad Chama Raja, Muppim Deva Raja and Chama Raja.[1] Here there is a disagreement among the authorities which appears hard to reconcile. There is a confusion in Wilks' *History* between Beṭad Woḍeyar, Timma Raja's son, and Beṭad Chama Raja Woḍeyar, Bōḷe Chama Raja's son. Wilks makes Raja Woḍeyar, the son of Timma Raja, in opposition to all the other authorities. He is evidently wrong, as there is an inscription,[2] dated 1614 (Raja Woḍeyar died in 1617), which represents him as the son of Doḍḍa Chama Raja Woḍeyar of Mysore. But before going to Raja Woḍeyar, we have to dispose of a Beṭad Chama Raja Woḍeyar, who ruled for two years (1576–8). The *Palace History* makes him the eldest son of Chama Raja 'the bald'. But the inscriptions and other works referred to, make him the younger brother of Raja Woḍeyar. Wilks,[3] on the other hand, makes the successor of Bōḷe Chama Raja, a Beṭad Woḍeyar, his nephew. He seems to be in the right, because the inscriptions and the works of Tirumala Aiyangar, above referred to, make no mention of this ruler. Besides, since both the cousins bore nearly the same name there is room for confusion, and the short duration of the rule of Beṭad Woḍeyar has a suspicious air of forced abdication rather than of voluntary retirement. The idea of a younger brother superseding the elder to get over financial embarrassment, or of the compulsory retirement of the latter by the elders of the land, seems not to be very common in the traditions of Indian rulers. The father Timma Raja having ruled,

1 *Vide* Genealogical table No. 3.

2 Srirangapatna, p. 36. Translation (*Epi. Car.*).

3 Wilks' *History*, vol. i, p. 21.

Beṭad Woḍeyar naturally wished to succeed him, but his uncle came in the way with the authority of the testament above mentioned. At his uncle's death, he succeeded in the absence of a previous arrangement, and was probably persuaded to retire in favour of his cousin Raja Woḍeyar on the ground of the settlement of Hēmanalli upon his father, Mysore falling to the lot of Chama Raja 'the bald.'[1] According to Wilks, there is nothing strange in Beṭad Woḍeyar's quiet retirement, or in his accepting the office of Daḷawāy under Raja Woḍeyar. There is nothing worthy of mention in this reign of two years.[2]

In 1578, there came to the throne of Mysore a ruler, at once capable and politic, who laid the foundations of its greatness and consolidated, to a certain extent, the disintegrating viceroyalty of Srirangapatna; this was Raja Woḍeyar who, for reasons given above, may be considered the eldest son of Bōḷe Chama Raja of Mysore. The minority of Tirumal Rāya of Srirangapatna gave ample scope to the aggrandizement of the Woḍeyars generally,[3] and Raja Woḍeyar benefited most of all. A glance at the lists of his conquests shows that there were many powerful Woḍeyars along with him under the nominal suzerainty of the viceroy at Srirangapatna. These Woḍeyars can be roughly divided into two classes with respect to Raja Woḍeyar. Many of them were connected with him by marriages or otherwise; while there were others who, having suffered at his hands, kept aloof from him and intrigued at the viceroy's court. To the former class belonged the Woḍeyars of Kalale, Biḷuguḷa, Biḷikere, Hura, Hullanahalli, Mūgur, etc. To the latter class belonged the Woḍeyars of Amma-

[1] *Vide* Genealogical tables i and iv.

[2] *Palace History*, pp. 474–8.

[3] *Ibid.*, pp. 22–3. Wilks' *History*, p. 28.

chavadi, Kanniambadi, Talakāḍ, Karoogahalli, etc.[1] Each member of these two classes seems to have been independent and did not always look up to the viceroy for help, as is evidenced by the alliances and treaties entered into independently. Each one seems to have thought only of making what use the name and prestige of the viceroy could afford him. At the commencement of his reign, Raja Woḍeyar is said to have been master of twenty-three and a half 'townships'[2] with a revenue of three thousand honnus (a honnu is a rupee and a half). This territory was divided among 300 jagirdars, each with a head-quarter town of his own. The principal sources of revenue were taxes derived from this estate, plunder got from war, and tributes paid by other Woḍeyars. With these means at his disposal, he seems to have been a troublesome neighbour, first attacking the Woḍeyars of the Channapatna viceroyalty, and latterly under some pretext or other those of Srirangapatna itself. For all the conquests thus made, he appears to have sought the authority, at least after conquest, of his suzerain. But the suzerainty was at this time divided between the traitorous Tirumal Rāya and his uncle Venkaṭapati Rāya. Raja Woḍeyar, in his aggressive conduct against the viceroy of Srirangapatna, received the moral support of Venkaṭapati Rāya, the nominal ruler of the Vijayanagar empire. Venkaṭapati Rāya, about this time, made a number of grants to Raja Woḍeyar which appear to have been conquests rather than grants.[3] This growth of power and territory of the Woḍeyar naturally alarmed the viceroy at

[1] *Chikka Deva Raja Vamśāvaḷi*, pp. 15–26.

[2] *Ibid.*, p. 26, et seq.

[3] Srirangapatna 157. Tirumakuḍlu Narsipur 116. Compare *Chikka Deva Raja Vamśāvaḷi*, pp. 17–20.

Chikka Deva Raja Vamśāvaḷi, pp. 17 and 20; Wilks' *History*, vol. i, p. 25.

Srirangapatna, who tried to bring about the death of Raja Woḍeyar. War was thought of, but stratagems were voted better by his vassal councillors. A general muster of the viceregal army was ordered under pretence of a review for the Dussarah, and Raja Woḍeyar was invited to pay a friendly visit. Raja Woḍeyar, in his turn, and on the advice of his brothers, Beṭad Chama Raja and Deva Raja, assembled his army, having been previously informed by his spies of the real state of feeling at Srirangapatna. He thought it better, however, to leave the army under Beṭad Chama Raja and paid his visit to the viceroy with his brother Deva Raja and a faithful body of followers.[1] The viceroy received him with apparent cordiality, having previously arranged an ambuscade to take Raja Woḍeyar prisoner while going out for a ride. But, luckily for Raja Woḍeyar, a petty incident thwarted the project. As soon as Tirumal Rāya turned his back on Raja Woḍeyar's quarters after his visit, the Woḍeyar's attendants began, as usual on all public occasions, to repeat his titles, among them 'Birudantembara Gaṇḍa' so fruitful of quarrels in Mysore history. Tirumal Rāya sent word that this one of all the titles might be given up by both parties, as neither of them could lay claim to it as a hereditary title. This was resented. Raja Woḍeyar with his faithful retainers marched through the army of the viceroy which was described as follows: 'The contingents of Baḷḷapur, Koḷatala, Bangalore, Magadi, Punganoor and other Morasa countries were twenty elephants, two thousand horse, twenty thousand foot; of Talakāḍ, Yelandur, Ammachavadi, Tirukanambi and other interior nāḍs (states), ten elephants, five hundred horse, ten thousand foot; of Kaḷale, Belur, Keḷadi, and other Malnāḍs (hill-states), twenty elephants, two thousand

[1] *Chikka Deva Raja Vamśāvaḷi*, p. 33, et seq.

horse, twenty thousand foot; of Chintanakal, Chikkanāyakanahalli, Banavara, Basavāpatna, Sira and other Beḍar nāḍs (hunter states), five elephants, five hundred horse, ten thousand foot.' Rāna Jaga Deva Rayal, Kereyoor Timma Naika and other 'Ravuta Payakas' (cavalry and infantry officers) supplied contingent of fifteen elephants, four thousand horse, twenty-four thousand foot. With the reserve force of thirty elephants, three thousand horse, thirty thousand foot, the total runs up to a hundred elephants, twelve thousand horse and one hundred and fourteen thousand foot.[1] This is really Napoleonic indeed for an army that was defeated by Raja Woḍeyar! It is not probable that these were the actual numbers in the field; but the above computation shows the miscellaneous composition of the army, and what little common interest they could have had in fighting for the viceroy. The viceroy resolved after due deliberation to lay siege to the fort of Kesaregonṭe and not, as originally proposed, to Mysore. The first seems to have been, at the time, unfit for standing a siege. It was situated between Srirangapatna and Mysore. Beṭad Chama Raja Woḍeyar held out till a relieving force approached from Mysore, and the miscellaneous viceregal army was then put to flight easily. Tirumal Rāya, the viceroy, was already meditating flight from Srirangapatna, when some of the Woḍeyars who had formerly counselled the advance of the army, now persuaded him to stand a siege, and encamped with their forces on the northern side of the fort. These were again defeated by Narasa Raja, the eldest son of Raja Woḍeyar, and Tirumal Rāya now fled to Talakāḍ

[1] *Chikka Deva Raja Vamśāvaḷi*, pp. 26–33.

In the States depending on Bijapur and Golconda were maintained 200,000 horse.

Footnote 2 at p. 58, vol. i of Wilks' *History*.

leaving his family behind.[1] This event is generally regarded as having taken place in 1610. But it is recorded that Raja Woḍeyar received Srirangapatna as a grant from Venkaṭapati Rāya in 1612.[2] It would thus appear that Raja Woḍeyar obtained the sanction of Venkaṭapati Rāya for keeping possession of what he actually conquered. On the flight of Tirumal Rāya, the treatment accorded by Raja Woḍeyar to the wife of the ex-viceroy is variously related. According to Tirumala [3] Aiyangar, Raja Woḍeyar pointed out to her the desirability of accompanying her husband and provided her with an escort to go to Talakāḍ, and this authority calls her Sriranganāyaki. But the *Palace History* (pp. 31–2), gives a different version which appears to be nearer to the truth. The lady is named Alamēḷumanga, and she went to Mālangi after her husband. Raja Woḍeyar, at the instance of the priest of Ranganāyaki, the goddess, sent for some jewels belonging to the goddess in the possession of the viceroy's wife at the time, with a threat that the jewels would be taken from her by force if she did not surrender them at once. She refused to surrender them all on the score that they were her own, though she very often lent them for the decoration of the goddess. Having said this, and being afraid of her own safety, she drowned herself in a well at Mālangi. But the popular tradition is that Raja Woḍeyar hounded her to death for the sake of her jewels and perhaps of her person too. She is said to have pronounced a curse at her death which may be rendered as follows: 'May Mālangi be no more than a tank; may Talakāḍ be buried under sand; may the Raja of Mysore have no issue left.'

1 Wilks' *History*, vol. i, p. 26.

2 Tirumakuḍlu Narasipura 62 (A.D. 1622, actual date Saka year 1534, the year of cycle paridhāvi).

3 *Chikka Deva Raja Vamśāvaḷi*, pp. 31–2.

And Raja Woḍeyar is believed to have lost all his four grown-up sons on account of this. It is customary even now in the royal family to perform an expiatory ceremony on the ninth day of the Dussarah to appease the angry spirit of this injured lady. From this custom it would appear that, whatever may have been the cause of her death, Raja Woḍeyar, in having arranged for this ceremony, thought himself responsible for her tragic end. Thus was Srirangapatna mastered once and for all; but Raja Woḍeyar, in spite of the grant of Venkaṭapati Rāya in 1612, did not assume full sovereignty. In all the inscriptions[1] of his and of his grandson's reigns, the Vijayanagar emperor is introduced as the ruling sovereign, the grants being made in his time. The first inscription, in which this kind of introduction is dispensed with, is one dated 1646, during the reign of Kanṭīrava Narasa Raja Woḍeyar,[2] while another of the first year of this ruler duly acknowledges the suzerainty of the Vijayanagar ruler.

On the overthrow of the viceroy at Srirangapatna Raja Woḍeyar received an ambassador,[3] named Gambhīra Raja Virupanna, from Venkaṭapati Rāya, who conveyed his master's congratulations to the Raja Woḍeyar on his victory over the viceroy. Raja Woḍeyar was probably then appointed by the emperor to succeed Tirumal Rāya, thus making the appointment a virtue of necessity. Raja Woḍeyar then ruled for a period of five or six years, nominally as viceroy, but actually as sovereign in his territory, which, with the additions he made to it, embraced nearly the whole of the present Mysore district and a part of Hassan.

But before closing his history, a word must be said as to his administration. He appears to have

[1] Srirangapatna 103, pp. 29-30, Translation (*Epi. Car.*).

[2] Nanjanagūḍu 198, pp. 115-6, Translation (*Epi. Car.*).

[3] *Chikka Deva Raja Vaṁśāvaḷi*, pp. 55-6.

been careful to take the actual administration of the conquered territories into his own hands and to appoint his own officers. He is also reputed to have celebrated the Dussarah festival on a grand scale and made the rule that, in future, the death even of the closest relatives of the royal family should not interfere with the festivities. This question had to be discussed by experts in his reign on account of the death of his eldest son Narasa Raja. The appointment of a Daḷawāy, discontinued ever since the usurpation of Māranāyaka, was now revived owing, as Raja Woḍeyar is made to say, to the vast additions to his estates. The first appointment was unsatisfactory, as indeed many of them were throughout. The first Daḷawāy under the present dynasty was Raja Woḍeyar's nephew, Karikala Mallarajayya of Kaḷalē, of the same family as the Daḷawāy brothers, who brought about the downfall of the ruling dynasty and the rise of Ḥaidar 'Alī. Mallarajayya resigned shortly after his appointment and was succeeded by Beṭad Woḍeyar.[1] This Beṭad Woḍeyar must have been the same as Raja Woḍeyar's cousin who was superseded by him. This act of trust on the part of the latter flattered the feelings of the former who had quietly abdicated the royal position. Previous to the appointment of a Daḷawāy, Raja Woḍeyar's army appears to have been uniformly led by his brother Beṭad Chama Raja Woḍeyar; and, therefore, he could not have been the new Daḷawāy. Raja Woḍeyar, by this time, had lost all the four of his grown-up sons and his youngest brother Chama Raja. He settled the succession, therefore, in consultation with his two surviving younger brothers, Beṭad Chama Raja and Deva Raja, on Chama Raja Woḍeyar, his grandson by Narasa Raja. He is said by some

[1] *Palace History*, p. 45.

authorities to have left to the infant Immaḍi Raja the Jagir of West Daṇṇayakanakōṭe,[1] but Immaḍi Raja is generally regarded a posthumous son. The sons of Beṭad Chama Raja and Deva Raja received the Jagirs, Rangasamudra and Nullur Vijayapura and Arikere and Yelandūrumangala respectively[2] Having made these settlements, he retired with his brothers to Melkōṭē where he died in 1617.

Raja Woḍeyar accordingly was succeeded by his grandson, Chama Raja Woḍeyar, who ruled from 1617 to 1637. It has been mentioned that, under Raja Woḍeyar, the office of Daḷawāy was revived to meet the exigencies of increased territory and administration. This office combined in itself the offices of Prime Minister and Commander-in-Chief. At the accession of Chama Raja Woḍeyar, Beṭad Woḍeyar held this important office and exercised his authority not so much as the Daḷawāy, but as guardian to the young Raja. The Raja and the Daḷawāy very soon fell out on a small matter, the one having been as tenacious of his authority as the other of his dignity. Beṭad Woḍeyar, it would appear, dismissed a few servants near the person of the Raja who were found to be abusing the trust. This was resented and consequently an attempt was made by Beṭad, Woḍeyar's son, to poison the Raja. Beṭad Woḍeyar fled for his life which was granted him at the cost of his eyes. The office of Daḷawāy always appears to have been unfortunate in Mysore, for the officers were ready to misbehave, whenever the ruler was not strong enough to keep them under control. There were four Daḷawāys in this reign, the last of whom was Vikrama Rāya, the natural son of Beṭad Chama Rāja, brother of Raja Woḍeyar. Chama Raja Woḍeyar

[1] *Chikka Deva Raja Vamśāvaḷi*, p. 57, et seq.

[2] Wilks' *History*, vol. i, p. 29. *Palace History*, p. 49, makes Raja Woḍeyar prophesy the birth of a male child to his pregnant wife.

entrusted the whole administration to the Daḷawāys in order to have time enough to discharge his domestic duties.[1] So long as the Daḷawāys were men unconnected with the ruling family, they valued their position too much to intrigue, as was the case with the second and the third Daḷawāys of this reign.[2] These Daḷawāys, however, made a number of conquests and annexations and extended Chama Raja's inheritance in all directions. It is during this reign that the viceroyalty of Jagadeva Rayal was reduced to nothing by the capture of Channapatna and Nagamangala, and by the siege of Hoskote.[3] It is evident that Chama Raja persevered in carrying on the administration according to the lines laid down by his grandfather by keeping down the Woḍeyars, by conciliating the ryots and by not increasing the rents.[4] He is said to have collected a great deal of war material and to have established a dépôt at Srirangapatna.[5] He is also credited with having written a commentary on the Ramayana and the Mahabharata. He died without issue in 1637, and was succeeded by his boy uncle, Immaḍi Raja Woḍeyar. Daḷawāy Vikrama Rāya lorded it over the new ruler, whom he found to be not the nominal one that he would have him, and so he had him poisoned in the year 1638.

Who was to be the next ruler? At the time of Raja Woḍeyar's death his brother's children were provided with jagirs as became their dignity. Though nothing is recorded about Deva Raja, Beṭad Chama Raja is said to have been living in retirement at Rangasamudra not without exercising a wholesome influence at court. Now

[1] In one of the inscriptions Vikrama Rāya is referred as the natural son of Raja Woḍeyar.

[2] Nanjangūḍu 9, p. 96, Translation *Epi. Car.*

[3] *Palace History*, p. 51. Wilks' *History*, vol. i, p. 29.

[4] *Chikka Deva Raja Vaṁśāvaḷi*, p. 60, et seq.

[5] *Palace History*, p. 61.

that Raja Woḍeyar's line failed of male issue, people naturally looked up to the children of his next younger brother Beṭad Chama Raja. From the palace genealogical[1] tree, it appears that Beṭad Chama Raja had only one son living at the time and that was Kanṭīrava Narasa Raja Woḍeyar. This person cannot have been the mere nominee of Vikrama Rāya, who was the natural son of Beṭad Chama Raja, as Beṭad Chama Raja was himself living, and as Kanṭīrava Narasa would have suited ill the ambitious schemes of the Daḷavāy. The *Palace History* (p. 65) besides makes Kanṭīrava Narasa the adopted son of Raja Woḍeyar, and, as such, he was invited and crowned by one of his widows. The adoption seems likely enough, as Raja Woḍeyar must have had reasons to fear that the direct line would fail. It must also have been the interest of the palace party not to have a nominee of the Daḷavāy for the ruler. The subsequent insolent behaviour of the Daḷavāy would also support this view. However nominated, Kanṭīrava Narasa began his rule in A. D. 1638. It is this personage that first made grants in his own name,[2] even his predecessor Chama Raja having owned the nominal suzerainty of the phantom ruler at Ghanagiri. The first inscription in which an elaborate genealogy of the Mysore rulers alone is given, without reference to the ruler at Penukonda, is dated A. D. 1646, and is a grant by Kanṭīrava Narasa.

The reign of Kanṭīrava Narasa commences the glorious period of the present dynasty, and the three successive rulers, himself and his two successors, may be called the makers of modern Mysore. The first act of this reign is the dismissal from service of Daḷavāy Vikrama Rāya[3], and the infliction on him of the condign punishment

[1] *Vide* Genealogical table No. 4.

[2] Srirangapatna 103, pp. 29–30 (*Epi. Car.*).

[3] *Palace History*, p. 67.

for his treason against the former ruler. The *Palace History* states that the Daḷawāy was punished after due inquiry and confession by himself; but Wilks appears to be right in saying that he was despatched by the hand of the assassin.[1] For the Daḷawāy was not only a natural son of Beṭad Chama Raja,[2] but also the first officer in the State. As such, he must have been too powerful and perhaps too popular to be punished like an ordinary servant. This seems to have taught Kanṭīrava Narasa a good lesson, and we see him throughout his reign making vigorous and rather successful attempts to curb the power of the Daḷawāys, so that we see the office changing hands a little too often. This ruler is credited by Wilks with having celebrated the Dussarah festival on a grand scale and for the first time. Whatever the scale of the celebration, he was not the first to celebrate the festival, Raja Woḍeyar having done it many times during his life.[3] Kanṭīrava Narasa, finding it inconvenient to have a number of different coins in circulation, asserted his sovereignty over other Woḍeyars by establishing a mint and coining in his own name.[4] This is the first step at unifying the loose conglomerate of the petty chieftaincies he inherited, and his coins seem to have had currency in other parts of South India as well. He is also given credit for having made an elaborate survey of the lands under the Woḍeyars, and, having found the purse-proud ryots too troublesome, he took away all that they had over and above what was necessary for their bare living and occupation.[5] This had the desired effect, and not only cowed the refractory Woḍeyars and

1 Wilks' *History*, vol. i, p. 31.

2 *Palace History*, p. 59. Nanjangūḍ 9, dated 1643, makes him the son of Raja Woḍeyar.

3 *Vide ante* p. 286.

4 *Palace History*, p. 34; Wilks' *History*, vol. i, p. 32.

5 Wilks' *History*, vol. i, p. 32; *Palace History*, p. 20.

other landlords, but enriched Kanṭīrava Narasa beyond all expectation. This act of public plunder was not questioned in those days, as the people had no other means of asserting their rights than that of taking arms against the ruler. This latter measure must clearly have been to their own ruin, for, in the place of one strong master, however unjustifiable his measures, they would have had many more plunderers without the advantage of protection which the former offered. The next step Kanṭīrava Narasa took was to keep the Daḷawāys in check. There were in all ten Daḷawāys in this reign, all of whom, excepting one, held the office but for a brief space of time. Under a strong ruler, the Daḷawāys had only to play a subordinate part, and, whenever they attempted to make themselves something more, they earned their dismissal. This office, the first in importance in the State, had always been given to a person intimately connected with the ruler either in blood or by association. Whenever the choice fell on relatives, the appointment did not prove happy, as they attempted to assume all power and to turn the attention of the sovereign solely to the enjoyment of home life. Whenever the appointment fell to the lot of some one outside the circle of relations, the choice proved happier, because they had not the same influence in the palace as the others had, and so could be easily dealt with by the ruler. Kanṭīrava Narasa appears to have made a discovery of this fact, and, therefore, deviated from the principle of choice inaugurated by Raja Woḍeyar whose Daḷawāys were near connexions in blood. Perhaps Raja Woḍeyar could not as yet have trusted others outside his family, but Kanṭīrava was much too strong for fear of that kind. So, after the fall of his half-brother, Daḷaway Vikrama Rāya, he appointed Thimmappa Nāyaka and six others in succession who were, if at all connected, very distant relatives. Thus we see that Kanṭīrava Narasa always kept all real power in his own hands, and so did his two successors. Hence the vigour of the administration during the three reigns.

This ruler seems besides to have paid much attention to public works. He rebuilt the forts of Srirangapatna and Mysore when they got damaged during the siege by Ranadhoola Khān. The details given of these forts are not of much importance. With the money he obtained, as above mentioned, he provided the forts with all that was needful to protect them from assault, and appears to have mounted a large number of guns over the ramparts. He is said to have constructed several tanks, and also the canal which runs over the bridge on the southern arm of the Kavery bringing fresh water into the fort. He also made rich endowments to the temples in the province, particularly to those of Sriranganātha and of god Narasimha at Srirangapatna. He seems to have commanded armies in person, rather than trust them into the hands of the Daḷawāys. He is known to have been very remarkable for his strength and courage, and his first exploit was the defeat of a remarkable prize-fighter at Trichinopoly. Having gone there incognito, he returned, after killing the man, without waiting to receive the prize. This gave rise to one or two unsuccessful conspiracies against his life which may be passed over here. But the most important military act of the reign was the defence of Srirangapatna against Ranadhoola Khān, the general of Bijapur.[1] The siege was brought about as follows: Kanṭīrava Narasa incited Kenge Hanuma of Basavapatna and other Woḍeyars of Ikkēri against their liege lord, Veerabhadra Nāyaka. The disturbance was promptly quelled by the Ikkēri Nāyaka.

1 Wilks' *History*, vol. i, p. 31.

Kenge Hanuma went to Bijapur to solicit the aid of the Padisha there.[1] At this time, there was also another fugitive Woḍeyar, Channīāh of Nagamangala, lately conquered by Chama Raja Woḍeyar. The Padisha sent his most reputed general, Ranadhoola Khān, at the head of an army of forty thousand men to reinstate Kenge Hanuma and to take Srirangapatna if possible. The general having easily succeeded in doing the first, was very near accomplishing the second as well. Having taken possession of Ikkēri, Sira, and Bangalore on his way, he laid siege to Mysore and Srirangapatna simultaneously. Besiegers and defenders seem to have fought well, but the loss of the former must have been immense, considering that, even after having effected a breach, they were not able to effect an entry into the fort of Srirangapatna. They were not more successful in Mysore either; and the double victory is ascribed to divine intervention on behalf of the defenders, thus indicating that the Mysoreans were hopeless of victory in spite of their stubborn defence. Despite this failure to take the forts, Kanṭīrava Narasa found it impossible, either to stand another siege or to fight his enemy in the open field. So, through the mediation of Kenge Hanuma, a peace was concluded which left to the Mysoreans all the country[2] south of the Kavery, that on the north of the river being made over to Bijapur. But the administration of the Bijapur portion was still left in the hands of Kanṭīrava Narasa himself, on condition of paying over to Bijapur all the surplus revenue after meeting the cost of administration. This took place in the year of his

[1] *Chikka Deva Raja Vamśāvaḷi*, pp. 67-8, et seq.
Chikka Deva Raja Vijayam, 2nd Canto.

[2] *Chikka Deva Raja Vamśāvaḷi*, pp. 67-8, et seq.
Chikka Deva Raja Vijayam, 2nd Canto.
Palace History, p. 75.

accession 1638–9. Though Kanṭīrava Narasa agreed to this treaty in his helplessness, he does not seem to have thought seriously of fulfilling his promise. Ranadhoola Khān, on the other hand, leaving Kenge Hanuma as the Bijapur agent, returned to Bijapur, his head-quarters. Veerabhadra Nāyaka of Ikkēri availed himself of this opportunity to avenge his wrongs on Ranadhoola Khān, and sent an embassy to Bijapur to expose to the Padishah the hollowness of the agreement, and the unreliable character of the agent. Ranadhoola Khān was suspected, and a royal commission was sent to inquire into the affairs of Kenge Hanuma, of which Nagamangla Channīāh was a member. Kenge Hanuma faltered and Kanṭīrava Narasa grew defiant. To add to this, Channīāh was murdered by Kenge Hanuma, as he was the only member of the commission conversant with the details of the administration.[1] Ranadhoola Khān was, in consequence, superseded by Khān Khān. This general and his successor, Mustafa Khān, were sent in succession to take possession of Srirangapatna, the fort of which had been completely rebuilt since the first invasion, but they fared no better than their predecessor. A plundering raid undertaken by Hemaji Pundit of Bijapur and 'Abdu'llāh Khān, a general, effected nothing of importance except the temporary occupation of Turuvekere. Having thus far been on the defensive, Kanṭīrava Narasa could now take the offensive. In his aggressive march eastward, he defeated the Bijapur forces and took possession of its late conquests. Having defeated the Vaṇangāmuḍi Mudaliar of Kongu, he took Samballi, Bomballi, and Satyamangala, having previously worsted the Madura Nāyaka, his liege lord. On the west, he defeated Nanja Raja Woḍeyar of Coorg, and after hunting him from place to place,

[1] *Palace History*, pp. 77. 79.

took possession of Periapatam, his capital, and six other districts (Ghadis).[1] In the north, he extended his conquests to the frontiers of Ikkēri, Chitaldroog and Sira. After such an eventful reign he died in 1659 leaving no male issue to succeed him.

The descendants of Muppin Deva Raja, the third brother of Raja Woḍeyar, came in for their share of rule now. This Deva Raja had four children, one of whom succeeded Kanṭīrava Narasa. But, as to which of these four sons succeeded, there is considerable difference of opinion among the authorities. The *Palace History* (p. 91) makes the successor the third son, Wilks[2] the fourth, and Tirumala Aiyangar, a contemporary, the first. In all the inscriptions of this ruler's and his successor's time, the latter is recorded as the nephew of the former. Tirumala Aiyangar himself makes Doḍ Deva Raja succeed nominally only, while Kempa Deviah, his third brother, was carrying on the administration in fact.[3] The truth appears to be, that Kempa Deviah, the third son, was the successor ruling for a short time in the name of his eldest brother who must have been old, and then in his own name, on condition that the said brother's son should succeed him. Wilks and the *Palace History* alike seem to have gone wrong in certain particulars about this ruler, and the mistake is accounted for by all the four brothers bearing the same name, Deva Raja, with a qualifying epithet. Besides the fact that Chikka Deva Raja and his father were in prison at Tirukanamby is not borne out by any other authority. It is, however, mentioned that Chikka

[1] *Chikka Deva Raja Vamśāvaḷi*, pp. 68, et seq.; Wilks' *History*, vol. i, pp. 33-5: *Palace History*, pp. 67, 69.

[2] Wilks' *History*, vol. i, pp. 35-6.

[3] *Chikka Deva Raja Vamśāvaḷi*, pp. 18, et seq., and *Chikka Deva Raja Vijayam*, iv Canto, Stanzas 170, et seq. Srirangapatna 14, 64 and others. *Vide* Genealogical table No. iii.

Deva Raja was sent away as a youth with his two wives to Gundlu, remote from Court, to keep him from profligate ways into which he was falling.[1] His father, on the other hand, lived with his younger brother at Srirangapatna and then retired to a village where he died soon after. Besides, Chikka Deva Raja is recorded to have offered his services against the confederacy of rulers besieging Erode, and was well nigh entrusted with the command of the army. Besides this, Chikka Deva Raja was a mere youth, being only twelve years old, when his uncle, a grown-up man, succeeded to the throne.[2] Thus, then, Kanṭīrava Narasa was succeeded by his cousin Kempa Deviah, who became Doḍ Deva Raja Woḍeyar of Mysore. At the accession of this ruler to full sovereignty, he was the legal successor, his next elder brother having died. Chikka Deva Raja, then a youth, was recognized heir-apparent and each of them, the ruler and the heir, was guardian to his younger brother.

The two remarkable events of this reign were, the invasion of the country by Chokkalinga Nāyaka of Madura, and the siege of Srirangapatna by Śivappa Nāyaka of Ikkēri, who had but lately overthrown his master and established himself in his place. In both these events Sriranga Rayal, the fugitive ruler of Vijayanagar, was put forth as the leader. Chokkalinga Nāyaka, having made himself independent ruler of Madura, wanted to make the most of the imperial fugitive then with him, and advanced in the latter's name to Erode, on the south-east frontier of Mysore, assisted by Anantoji of Tanjore, Vedoji of Bijapur, Golconda, Gingee, and Iyyappah Nāyaka (a jagirdar). Perplexed by the magnitude of the invading army, Doḍḍa Deva Raja wished to try diplomacy, when Chikka Deva Raja offered his services to lead the

[1] *Chikka Deva Raja Vijayam*, Canto v.

[2] *Palace History*, p. 100.

Mysore forces to victory over the disunited mass of the invading army. Chokkalinga Nāyaka, however, on the advice of his ambassador at Srirangapatna retired to Trichinopoly, leaving his allies to take care of themselves. It was, perhaps, true, as Chikka Deva Raja is made to say, that the allied army, though large in number, was wanting in discipline; but one cannot but suspect that the ambassador was bribed into effectually detaching his master from the coalition. Chokkalinga Nāyaka apart, the others were easily defeated by the Daḷawāys, the superior generalship of Chikka Deva Raja having been found unnecessary. Iyyappa Nāyaka was slain, and among those defeated was the Brahmin Nāyaka of Ginjee.[1] The Mysore general took the elephant Kulasēkhara and its mate as spoils of war, and made the permanent conquests of Ōmalūru, Erode and Dārāpuram. Thus ended the formidable coalition in the name of the last scion of the Vijayanagar family, who now betook himself to Bednore.

Śivappah Nāyaka, immediately after his accession to power, sent an embassy to Mysore professing friendship to the ruler. This seems to have been refused acceptance as beneath the ruler's dignity, coming as it did from a usurper. This gave offence, and Śivappah Nāyaka prepared to lay siege to Srirangapatna. Sriranga Rayal was now with Śivappah Nāyaka, who extended his frontiers in the name of the fugitive. This invasion was successfully repelled, the Bednore Nāyaka having been compelled to cede the fortresses of Hassan and Sakkarēpatna. Nothing more was heard of Sriranga Rayal, and thus came to an end the once glorious dynasty of Vijayanagar.

Doḍḍa Deva Raja never appears to have led an army in person. He was generally peacefully inclined. He

[1] Srirangapatna 14, p. 10, Translation (*Epi. Car.*).

devoted a great deal of attention to works of charity. He is said to have established a number of agraharas (villages for Brahmins) and built way-side choultries, at short intervals of distance throughout his dominions. He constructed several tanks, one of those at Mysore among them. His devotion to the goddess Chāmuṇḍi led to the construction of the steps up the hill, and to the Basavanandi (a gigantic bull in stone) half way up.[1]

His principal items of expenditure of the money gained in wars are naïvely said by the historian[2] to have been three: providing (1) ornaments to his queens; (2) endowments to his Brahmin friends; and (3) rewards to servants for meritorious services.

After a reign of thirteen years, he died in 1672 in a progress through his dominions at Chikkanaikanahalli. He was succeeded by his nephew, Chikka Deva Raja Woḍeyar, as had been previously agreed upon. The reigns of Doḍḍa Deva Raja and his successor are coeval with that of Aurangzeb in Hindustan, and when it is borne in mind that Chikka Deva's reign coincided in time with the rise of Sivaji and the difficulties of the Moghul emperor in the south, it will not be difficult to understand how this ruler consolidated his State in comparative peace. The Musalmān power of Bijapur was the most aggressive and troublesome neighbour of Mysore. Bijapur expeditions into Mysore have been for one reason or other frequent, and this Power very often interfered in the affairs of the Woḍeyars. But now, this and the other Musalmān Powers of South India had to turn their attention, and to devote it all against the advance of Moghul arms in the south, and the rise of a more dangerous enemy from amongst their own servants, the Maharattas.[3] Even the line

1 *Palace History*, pp. 94, et seq.
Wilks' *History*, vol. i, pp. 35-6.

2 *Chikka Deva Raja Vijayam*, end of the v canto.

3 Wilks' *History*, vol., p. 56.

of conquests of Shaji and his son Sivaji went round the Mysore territory and did not go past Bangalore, thus leaving Mysore at the angle between their northern and southern possessions. At this time it was that Chikka Deva Raja came to the throne of Srirangapatna, and worked unostentatiously and cleverly at the unification of the petty States which he had inherited.

During the first twenty years of his reign, he gradually consolidated the conquests of his predecessors and, after reconquering those places which had been taken back, he extended his conquests principally in two directions. To the south-east he extended his conquests as far as Trichinopoly, while to the north-west he pushed his frontiers far into the territories of his neighbours. Thus he added a large part of Tumkur and Kadur districts and a portion of Chitaldroog to his own dominions. The powerful gaud of Magadi was gradually giving way before the onsets of more powerful neighbours, and by the acquisition of Bangalore in 1687–8, by purchase from Ekoji, the half brother of Sivaji, Chikka Deva Raja Woḍeyar reduced him to an insignificant position, till later on he was completely overthrown during Doḍḍa Krishna Raja Woḍeyar's reign. His conquests before 1679 are detailed as follows[1]: 'In the east, having conquered the Pandya king Chokka in battle, he captured Tripura (Trichinopoly) and the wealthy Anandhāpuri. In the west he subdued the Keladi kings, who came against him with the Yavanas, and gained Sakalespura and Arakalgūḍu. In the north, having conquered Ranadhoola Khān, he took Ketasamudra together with Kanhikere, Handalageri, Gulur, Tumkur and Honnavalli. Victorious in battle over Mushṭika who came with Moraśas and Kiratas, he seized Jatakanadurga

[1] Srirangapatna 157, p. 35, Translation (*Epi. Car.*).

and changed its name to Chikka Deva Rāya Durga.[1] The Varāha at Srīmushṇa, which had been broken in the Yavana invasion, he brought to Srirangapatna out of devotion to Vishṇu. He took Maddagiri, Midagesi, Bijjavara and Chennarayadurga, having conquered Thimmappa Gauda and Ramappa Gauda.' By 1686[2] Vishṇu, incarnate as Chikka Deva, did subdue in Panchavaṭi, Dadoji, Jaitaji and others in the form of Maharattas. Sambhu lost his valour, Kutub Shāh failed in his purpose, Ikkēri Basava was disgraced, Ekoji was deserted by all when the mighty Chikka Deva Raja, having cut off all the limbs and slit the noses of Jaitaji and Jesvata, set forth for war.' Chikka Deva Raja, however, is more remembered for the administrative reforms he introduced into the government of his State. His first minister was the Jain Visha Lakshaṇa Pandit of Yelandur, who exercised great influence over the Raja. He was his companion, or his tutor, when, as a prince, he was sent to Guṇḍlu near Tirukanambi in order to keep the Raja from evil ways. When the prince succeeded his uncle, he appointed the Pundit to be his chief minister and, under his guidance, he began to reform every department of the administration. It has been already mentioned that, in Kaṇṭīrava's reign, there was a great variety in the currency of the realm, and that this was put an end to by the introduction of the Kaṇṭīrava coins as the sole currency. There was also a great deal of variety in the details of all the departments of the administration. This was all done away with, and uniformity was introduced by Chikka Deva Raja. The first reform was a revision of taxes which cost the life of the Jain Pundit, the responsible author of the revision. This affront to the dignity of the ruler

[1] *Vide* map at the commencement of Wilks' *History*, vol. i, map.

[2] Srirangapatna 14, p. 11, Translation (*Epi. Car.*).

was more than avenged by a wholesale massacre of the fanatical Jungam priests, who were suspected of being the authors, or the instigators of the murder.

From time immemorial the rent of land remained fixed, and whatever extra revenue was needed was raised by means of taxes. In the reign of Raja Woḍeyar, the only sources of revenue, as mentioned above, were rents of land, plunder from enemies, and tribute from other Woḍeyars. Kanṭīrava Narasa is said to have taken an extraordinary contribution of almost all the movables under some pretext or other. Thus we see that, though extraordinary contributions were demanded, there was nothing like a regular system of taxation. In the absence of any precedent for enhancing the rent of land, Chikka Deva Raja Woḍeyar deemed it necessary to legalize and systematize the extra demands by instituting a number of taxes. These taxes were none of them the creation of Chikka Deva, but old ones which had fallen out of use during the disturbed times that intervened. In one of the inscriptions, dated A. D. 1290, we find incidentally a list of taxes collected under Perumāḷa Daṇḍa Nāyaka, the prime minister of Narasimha Deva of the Hoysala dynasty. On a comparison of this list with those given in Wilks' *History of Mysore* and in the *Palace History*, it will be found that there is a close agreement, thus showing that they were only old taxes revived.

When all this was done, Chikka Deva Raja Woḍeyar turned his attention to the administrative divisions of his territory, and divided the whole State, as it then existed, into eighty-four ghadis (divisions) each under a subahdar. Some such division appears to have already existed, but Chikka Deva Raja equalized their extent. The central administration was divided into eighteen departments on the model of the Moghul administration. This must have been the result of the embassy to the imperial Court during the closing years of the century, when the Great Moghul, in his difficulties, condescended to receive 'a Vakil from the Zemindar of Mysore'. This arrangement still survives in the public offices, which are popularly known as the 'Eighteen Cutcheries'. Chikka Deva Raja Woḍeyar kept down the Woḍeyars with an iron hand, and reduced them to complete dependence on the central authority. This was done by means of one of his departments, which combined the postal and the spy system, and which informed him of all that took place even at great distances from Court.[1] He is said to have introduced a kind of militia police system, each hobli, or sub-division of a ghadi, maintaining a certain number of men in its service, who were to be policemen in ordinary times and soldiers in times of war.[2] In one word, then, Chikka Deva introduced order and system where confusion had reigned. One other matter should be mentioned here. Having introduced uniformity in measures, weights, etc., he next introduced the system of paying his officials half their salary in money and the other half in kind. The convenience of this arrangement in those days was beyond a doubt. After all these reforms, the total revenue derived by Chikka Deva Raja Woḍeyar from his territories is said to have been seven hundred and twenty thousand pagodas. The method of the collection of this amount was somewhat peculiar. It was arranged to bring in two thousand pagodas every day to the royal treasury at Srirangapatna, and unless this daily instalment came in Chikka Deva Raja refused to take breakfast. Thus he ensured the collection of the revenue, but how this daily amount was raised and what was the actual

[1] Wilks' *History*, vol. i, p. 31.
[2] *Palace History*, pp. 184-7.

amount paid by the ryots, it is not possible now to determine. This revenue, at three rupees a pagoda, would amount to twenty-one lakhs and sixty thousand rupees, the present revenue of the State (in 1898) being one crore and seventy lakhs approximately.[1] There are not data enough available to institute any real comparison between the revenues of the State now and those of two centuries ago.

Chikka Deva Raja divided the whole class of Woḍeyars into two sections of thirteen and eighteen families. The first of these sections included the royal family itself, which was known to have preserved its blood free from any admixture. This class was prohibited from giving away their girls to members of the other class, though permitted to take the girls of the latter for junior wives. The second section was charged with having contracted marriage alliances with people of lower classes, and thus they were treated as being inferior to the other.[2] This classification was really due to the fact that the second class of Woḍeyars comprised the recently conquered Woḍeyars. Their poverty and caste distinctions may also have called for this classification. Nowadays, however, no such distinction is kept up, and all classes of arasus are regarded as one.

During the reign of Chikka Deva Raja, the Daḷawāys do not seem to have made themselves prominent. He was guided by the counsels of a few friends, who were unconnected with the royal family, although they held high offices. These ministers sometimes advised conjointly but very often singly. The chief of these, after the murder of the Jain pundit Visha Lakshaṇa of Yelandur, was Tirumala Aiyangar, the companion of the Raja from his boyhood. He is

[1] *Palace History*, pp. 124-5.
Wilks' *History*, vol. i, p. 63.
[2] *Palace History*, p. 127.

the author of the Kannada works already, referred to but he unfortunately breaks off his narrative when he comes to the reign of Chikka Deva Raja, thus leaving his works incomplete.

Chikka Deva Raja Woḍeyar, in his later days, was a staunch follower of the principles of Rāmānuja. The Vijayanagar viceroys of Srirangapatna were all of them Vaishṇavas, and Raja Woḍeyar seems to have been of the same creed, either out of policy or of faith, but it cannot, also, be said that all his successors were consistently such. Chama Raja and Doḍḍa Deva Raja do not appear to have been very zealous about the sect. Kanṭīrava Narasa devoted himself heart and soul to Vishṇu. Chikka Deva Raja, probably through the influence of Tirumal Aiyangar, became a Vaishṇava, perhaps after adopting the principles of his first minister the Jain Pundit[1] for some time. In his zeal for the Vaishṇavas, he is said to have commanded all the Woḍeyars to become Vaishṇavas too. This order was withdrawn on the strong representation of a number of Woḍeyars[2]. His devotion to Vishṇu led to the construction of a temple at Mysore, dedicated to the god Swēta Varāha (white boar) of Srīmushṇa. The idol seems to have been roughly handled by the Muḥammadans in one of their incursions into the far south, and was in consequence brought by Chikka Deva to Mysore.[3]

Thus having consolidated his dominions and introduced a settled form of administration, he bequeathed his kingdom to his dumb son, Kanṭīrava Narasa, in 1704, just three years before the death of the great Moghul Aurangzeb. From the death of Chikka Deva Raja dates the decline of prosperity of the Woḍeyars,

[1] Wilks' *History*, vol. i, p. 124.
[2] *Palace History*, p. 132.
[3] *Vide* ante p. 300 (quotation).

just as that of his imperial contemporary marks the turning point in the history of the Moghuls.

The succession of a dumb ruler, impossible under a less settled government, was brought about to suit the father's wish by his friend Tirumala Aiyangar under the pretence of a supernatural intervention.[1] The ruler could not have done anything, and thus in this reign alone, the reins of government slipped perceptibly out of the hands of the sovereign into the hands of the Daḷawāys. These latter officers gradually usurped the real power in the State. The Daḷawāys of this reign are Kanthia and his son Nanjaraja; his son Basavaraj and his son Nanja Raja. The last was succeeded by the Kaḷale Veerajiah, the son of Doḍḍa Raja, and the father of the brothers Daḷawāy Deva Raja and Nanja Raja of the later reigns. Under the first Daḷawāy and his son and grandson, the Mysore people conquered the two Baḷḷapurs, Miḍigesi, and Sira. It is also during this reign that the Nawab of Arcot makes his appearance in Mysore, levying the 'contribution war'.[2] Thus having reigned, rather than ruled, for nine years he passed away, leaving the succession to Doḍḍa Krishna Raja Woḍeyar, who was more remarkable for reckless charity than for any administrative qualities.

This Krishna Raja Woḍeyar is, in contradistinction to one of his successors of the same name, known as Doḍḍa Krishna Raja. He is celebrated in some of the inscriptions of his times for large and numerous gifts to Srī Vaishṇava Brahmans in particular. This reign is remarkable for giving the best of opportunities to the Daḷawāy brothers for their ascent to power. They eventually became the king-makers of the province. It is, however, worth noting here that the

[1] *Palace History*, pp. 145–6.

[2] Wilks' *History*, vol. i, p. 140.

time itself was rich in producing usurpers and king-makers. This is seen in Delhi, Poona and Mysore. The last Daḷawāy of Kanṭīrava Narasa was Veerajiah of Kaḷale. The elder of the two sons of this Daḷawāy was Deva Raja who, in his turn, became Daḷawāy and retained the office almost till the usurpation of Ḥaidar 'Alī. This Daḷawāy, whose sister was one of the wives of the Raja, soon contrived to fill up important offices with his own people, and, by pampering the king with all conceivable luxuries, managed to concentrate all real power in the State in his own hands. The rise of this person into prominence ultimately brought about the downfall of the dynasty, though for the time being it made the administration somewhat vigorous. The most important events of this reign, other than the above, are two invasions of the province ending in the siege of Srirangapatna and the final overthrow of the Gauḍ of Magadi. The first of these two invasions was undertaken by a confederacy of newly created Nawabs. The Mysore territory was surrounded by the dominions of Nawab Sa'adatu'llāh of the Karnatic Páenghat and Ameenkhan of the Karanatic Bālaghat. Besides these, there were the Nawabs of Kurpa, Kurnool, and Sāvandi. There was also a Maharatta neighbour Siddoji Ghorepara of Gooti. Srirangapatna was laid siege to by all these six together, and Krishna Raja bought them all off by the payment of seventy-two lakhs of rupees to be equally divided among them, and twenty-eight lakhs in addition given to the negotiator of the peace,[1] Sa'adatu'llāh Khān, though the *Palace History* claims a victory to Mysore in this case as in the next. But the elaborate copperplate grants which dwell at great length on the other virtues of Krishna Raja make no mention of any such victory, and a victory

1 Wilks' *History*, vol. i, pp. 141-2.

is the last thing to be silently passed over by the panegyrist.[1] Besides this, the victories of the other sovereigns are carefully mentioned in the same grants, one of which makes mention of the victories of Daḷawāy Deva Raja.[2] The author of one of the grants referred to is Tirumala Aiyangar, who must, at least, have lived up to 1729, whereas the dates of these two invasions, as given by the *Palace History*, are 1725 for the confederate invasion, and 1727 for the Maharatta invasion. So in both these the Mysoreans must have had the worst of it.[3] The second expedition was undertaken by Baji Rao at the head of the Maharattas, and the Peshwa was likewise bought off by Krishna Raja. To redeem these failures Daḷawāy Deva Raja succeeded in taking possession of the impregnable rock of Savandroog, the stronghold of the Gauḍ of Magadi. The Gauḍ himself was taken prisoner and allowed to die in the state prison of Srirangapatna.[4] In spite of this, however, the weakness of the Mysore State to defend itself against foreign invaders was proved beyond a doubt by the two invasions mentioned above, and this discovery led to a great deal of foreign complications, which facilitated the upward course, first of the Daḷawāy brothers and secondly of Ḥaidar 'Alí. Having reigned for eighteen years Doḍḍa Krishna Raja died without an heir in 1731. Daḷawāy Deva Raja, with the consent of the widow of Krishna Raja, who, however, was not his sister, placed a certain Chama Raja, connected but remotely with the ruling family, on the throne. The legitimate line of rulers thus came to an end here, and Chama Raja had no more claim to the throne than what he derived from the nomination of the

1 Srirangapatna 64 and 100.

2 Tirumakuḍlu Narasipur 63, pp. 79-80 (Translation).

3 Srirangapatna 64, p. 24 (Translation *Epi. Car.*).

4 Wilks' *History*, vol. i., pp. 140–3.

widow and the Daḷawāy. This personage was not long in showing himself to be very far from being the docile instrument of the Daḷawāy that he had agreed to become, when he was nominated ruler. He was, herefore, made the victim of an intrigue and sent to Kabbaladroog with his family. This time the Daḷawāy was careful to place an infant three years old on the throne to avoid the recurrence of the difficulties. This nomination was in perfect keeping with the projects of king-makers generally, the real rulers of Mysore now being Daḷawāy Deva Raja and Sarvādhikāri, Nanja Raja, the Daḷawāy's uncle. On the retirement of this latter officer, the appointment was conferred upon Kara Chūri Nanja Rajiah (the brother of the Daḷawāy), who, later on, became the father-in-law of the infant ruler Immaḍi Krishna Raja Woḍeyar. The administration was carried on by these two brothers with the nominal Pradhan Venkaṭapati of Canniambadi, with considerable vigour till, owing to the advanced age of Deva Raja, the brothers exchanged offices. This change led to a misunderstanding between the brothers, which eventually proved fatal to their power, and thus paved the way for the rise of Ḥaidar 'Alí, who became the *de facto* ruler in A.D. 1761. Thus was brought to an end the rule of the Woḍeyars in Mysore, till it was revived under the ægis of the British power after the fall of Srirangapatna in A.D. 1799. The power of the Woḍeyars thus passed through all the stages of decay that the Moghul rule underwent, but it had the good fortune to be revived which was denied to the other.

We have now traced the gradual growth of the small principality of Raja Woḍeyar until it became a compact and powerful State under Chikka Deva Raja. We have also made a rapid survey of the decline of fortune of the ruling family, until the State passed out of its hands into those of a foreigner.

I.—WILKS' GENEALOGICAL TABLE.

- Vijaya. (Hadana and Kārugahalli.)
  - Chama Raja. (Arberaḷ = Six-fingered.)
    - Beṭad Chama Raja. ,, ,, (1507.)
      - Appan Timmaraj Hemanhalli.
        - Beṭad Woḍeyar (1576 to 1578).
          - Kanṭīrava Narasa (1638 to 1659).
        - Raja Woḍeyar (1578 to 1617).
          - Narasa.
            - Chamaraja (1617 to 1637).
          - Immadi Raja (Posthumous) (1637–8).
      - Krishna (Kembala).
      - Boḷe Chamaraj (Mysore.)
        - Muppin Devaraj.
          - Doḍ Devayya.
            - Chikka Devaraj (1672 to 1674).
              - Kanṭīravaraj (1704 to 1714).
                - Doḍ Krishnaraj (1714 to 1731).
                  - Two usurpers Chamaraj (1731 to 1734).
                    - Chikka Krishnaraj (1734 to 1766).
          - 2nd
          - 3rd
          - Kempa Devayya (1659 to 1672).
            - Doḍ Devayya.
        - Here Chamaraj.

—Daḷawāy Grant No. 63, Tirumakuḍlu Narsipur

(*Epi-Karnāṭaka.*)

- Chamaraja.
  - Timmaraja.
  - Krishnaraja.
  - Beṭad Chamaraja.
    - Raja Woḍeyar.
      - Narasa Raja.
        - Chamaraja.
          - Immaḍi Raja.
            - Kanṭīrava Narasa.
              - Devarajendra.
                - Chikka Devaraj.
                  - Kanṭīrava Narasa.
                    - Krishna Raja Nripathi.
                      - Krishna Raja.

III.—Srirangapatam, Nos. 64 and 100 of Epigraphia Karnāṭaka.

(*Copperplate 64 and inscription 100 of Srirangapatam.*)

Yadu.

Beṭad Chamaraj (Anthembara Gaṇḍa).

Timmaraj. Krishna Bhūpati. Chama Nripati. (Victor over Revati Venkaṭa).

Rājādhi Raja. Beṭad Chamaraja. Devarajendra. Chamaraja.

Amrithamba = Dod Devaraj. Chikka Devarajendra. Devaraj. Mari Deva.

Devamamba = Chikka Devendra. Kanṭīrava Mahīpati.

Kanṭīrava Narasa = Cheluvajamamba.

Krishnaraj = Devajammah and eight others (Hence the eight names of eight tanks at Melnkote).

IV.—PALACE HISTORY.

Yadu Raja (1399 to 1423).

Here Beṭad Chamaraja Woḍeyar (1423 to 1458). Chamaraja Wodeyar.

Timmaraja Woḍeyar (1458 to 1478).

Here Chamaraja Woḍeyar (1478 to 1513).

Beṭad Chamaraja (1513 to 1552).

Timmaraja (1552 to 1571). Krishna Raja. Boḷe Chamaraja (1571 to 1576).

Beṭad Chamaraja (1576 to 1578). Raja Woḍeyar. (1578 to 1617). Muppin Devaraj. Chamaraj.

Raja Woḍeyar. Kanṭīrava Narasa (1638 to 1659). 1st. 2nd. Doḍḍa Devaraja (1659 to 1672).

Narasa Raja. Beṭad Woḍeyar Nanjraja Chama Raja. Immaḍi Raja (1617 to 1638). Chikka Devaraja (1672 to 1704). Kanṭīraya Narasa

Chama Raja (1617 to 1637).

Kanṭirava Narasa (1704 to 1713).

Dod Krishna Raja (1713 to 1731).

Both of these adopted by the widow of Doḍ Krishna Raja. { Chama Raja (1731 to 1734). Chikka Krishna Raja (1734 to 1761).

V.—THE GENEALOGICAL TREE ADOPTED IN THIS CHAPTER.

- Yadu (1399 to 1423).
  - Here Beṭad Chamaraj (1423 to 1458).
    - Timmaraja Woḍeyar (1458 to 1478).
      - Hero Chamarajarasa (1478 to 1513).
        - Beṭad Chamaraj (1513 to 1552).
          - Timmaraj (1552 to 1571).
            - Beṭad Woḍeyar (1576 to 1578).
          - Krishnaraj
          - Boḷe Chamaraja (1571 to 1576).
            - Rājādhi Raja (1578 to 1617).
              - Narasa Raja.
                - Chamaraja Woḍeyar (1617 to 1678).
              - Beṭad Wodeyar.
              - Nanjraj.
              - Chamaraj.
              - Immaḍi Raja (1637-8).
            - Beṭad Chamaraja.
              - Raja Woḍeyar (died young).
              - Kanṭīrava Narasa (1638 to 1659).
            - Muppin Devaraj.
              - Doḍ Devaraj.
                - Chikka Devaraj (1672 to 1704).
                  - Kanṭīrava Narasa (1704 to 1713).
                    - Doḍ Krishna Raj (1713 to 1731).
                      - Chamaraja (1731 to 1734).
                      - Chikka Krishnaraja (1734 to 1761).
                - Kanṭīrava Narasa.
              - Chikka Devarajendra.
              - Kempa Devayya (1659 to 1672).
              - Mari Deva
  - Chamaraja.

CHAPTER XII

THE VALUE OF LITERATURE IN THE CONSTRUCTION OF INDIAN HISTORY

IT is a notorious fact that Indian literature has few professed histories, and the inference seems warranted that the historical faculty received no development in the country. History, as we understand it, is entirely a product of the nineteenth century even in Europe. Works which constitute good material for history have been many, whatever their shortcomings from the point of view of the modern historian. It is in the sense of professed histories, which may be subjected to criticism and used as material, that histories are wanting in India.

So the problem of constructing the history of India, as a whole, or of any part of it, is subject to this additional defect. Defective it may be and much more so than in European countries. Still there is ample material yet left, despite much vandalism which may yield good results if exploited systematically. Historical material in India as elsewhere, may be grouped into three classes:—

1. Archæological (including architecture).
2. Epigraphical (including numismatics).
3. Literature.

Of these the first goes back to the earliest times reached in this country by historical research. What can be gathered from this source is, however, scanty, though reaching to the earliest antiquity. The second does not go beyond the period of the Asoka Inscriptions. For periods anterior to this, we are thrown upon literature only, both Vedic and Buddhistic. With respect to South India also archæological evidence may take us farther back, but the epigraphical does not go back beyond the beginning of the Christian Era except for a few Asoka and Sātavāhana records. Whether literature will take us beyond this limit may well be regarded doubtful as we are at present, but careful research in this direction may take us past this limit and may yield us results beyond our expectations. I have not set myself to inquire here whether it is so, nor whether all literary evidence has been brought to bear on historical research. I shall only try to show that the inquiry will not be in vain if it is made.

This inquiry necessarily leads us to the question of languages. For any work of research concerning India, Sanskrit is indispensable. This is clear from what we know of the pre-Buddhistic period of Indian history. When we come to deal with South India, Tamil becomes equally essential. Of the other Dravidian languages, Telugu does not take its available literature much anterior to the eleventh century A. D., and this literature seems to be modelled upon Sanskrit entirely. Kanarese has certainly a more ancient literature. A work of the ninth century undoubtedly is the Kavirājamārga of Nripatunga. If a work of poetry like this had been written in the ninth century, we might presume that there was an amount of anterior literature to require this. Malayalam seems to have grown out of Tamil in the early centuries of the Christian Era. But Tamil which, according to some, is the mother of these three, goes back to a far greater antiquity. It has a wealth of literature for particular periods which is worth study on scientific lines. This body of literature, independent of Sanskrit and yet so closely interwoven with it, deserves well of those who wish to be among the educated of their country's sons. It may not be all who can afford to study it, but those who can ought not to neglect to do so. How is this vast literature, both Sanskrit and Dravidian, to be exploited to any purpose, and what is likely to be the utility of such exploitation for history?

I began with the statement that history depends upon archæology, epigraphy and literature for its materials. The work on the first two has been considered to belong to the province of Government, for it is beyond the resources of private work, though private agency may do much if facilities are provided. Work upon the third is so far left entirely to the patriotic lovers of literature. It is not literature as literature that is my concern here, but literature so far as it can be of use for the making of history.

That literature can provide for history needs no proof now. The study of the literature of Pāḷi, the vernacular of Northern India in the centuries before Christ, opened to us a fresh vista into the domain of the history of ancient India. Will the Dravidian languages similarly open another vista? It is this question I shall attempt to answer here, confining my observations to Tamil literature, the oldest and the most voluminous of these southern tongues, as they are at present. That a systematic study of this literature will yield results of great value even where one least expects it, I can illustrate from the following incident in the life of Rāmānuja, the Vaishṇava apostle.

Tradition states, and the *Guruparamparais* record, that Rāmānuja constructed the temple at the town of Tirupati, and enshrined the image of Govindaraja there. This image was believed to have been the image of Govindaraja at Chidambaram, pulled out of the temple and cast into the sea by a certain Chola king, called

Krimikanṭa by the Vaishṇavas, a persecuting Chola. So far as I know at present, there seems to be no inscription bearing upon this question, and the matter was believed to be traditional and nothing more. It was asserted in a court of law that the existence of the Vishṇu shrine at Chidambaram was due to the pious fraud of a Vaishṇava Brahman, who planted the image of Vishṇu overnight, and duped the people, who woke up one morning to find the image of Vishṇu in the Śaiva Holy of Holies. If the witness himself believed in it, as in honesty we are bound to grant he did, he must have been a credulous person indeed. We are not concerned with his credulity or otherwise, but we are with the credibility of the tale. Stanza 86 of the *Tiruchchiṟṟambalakkōvai* of Māṇikkavāśagar runs as follows:—

புரங்கடந் தானடி காண்பான் புவிவிண்டு புக்கறியா
திரங்கிடென் ரூடென் றிரப்பத்தன் னீரடிக் கென்னிரண்டு
கரங்கடந் தானொன்று காட்ட மற்றுங்கதுங் காட்டிடென்று
வரங்கிடந் தான்றில்லை யம்பல முன்றிலம் மாயவனே.

The above stanza states in the words of the devotee that Vishṇu was lying in the court yard of the temple at Chidambaram supplicating Śiva, when, in response to Vishṇu's prayer, after fruitlessly penetrating the earth to discover the feet of Śiva, he displayed one foot, that he might show the other as well. This is a clever description of the relative positions and postures of the two deities in the temple. Naṭēsa is in his self-forgetful dance with his right foot lifted up. Govindaraja is in his bhōgaśayana (reclining posture).

Kulasēkhara Āḻvār states regarding the same Govindaraja as follows:—

செந்தளிர்வாய் மலர்நகைசேர் செழுந்தண் சோலைத்
தில்லைநகர்த் திருச்சித்ர கூடந் தன்னு
ளந்தணர்க ளொருமூவா யிரவ ரேத்த
வணிமணியா சனத்தமர்ந்த வம்மான் றானே.

The statement here is that Vishṇu was recumbent on a throne, with the three thousand Brahmans chanting his praise in the Chitrakūṭa of Thillai city, surrounded by cool and shady gardens, smiling with flowers and tender shoots.

Next comes what Tirumangai Āḻvār says about the same :—

பைம்பொன்னு முத்தும் மணியுங் கொணர்ந்து
  படைமன்னவர் பல்லவர் கோன்ப ணிந்த
செம்பொன்மணி மாடங்கள் சூழ்ந்த தில்லைத்
  திருச்சித்ர கூடஞ்சென்று சேர்மின்களே.
ஒருமா கடலுட் கிடந்தா னுவந்து
  கவைநா வரவி னணைப்பள்ளி யின்மேல்
திருமால் திருமங்கை யோடாடு தில்லைத்
  திருச்சித்ர கூடம்
மூவா யிரநான் மறையாளர் நாளும்
  முறையால் வணங்கவ் வணங்காய சோதித்
தேவாதி தேவன் திகழ்கின்ற தில்லைத்
  திருச்சித்ர கூடம்

The first extract simply indicates that a Pallava king made some costly dedications to the temple. The second that Vishṇu was in a lying posture on his serpent couch. The third that the three thousand of Thillai worshipped according to orthodox rights the God of Gods.

Thus, then, in the days of the two Āḻvārs and Māṇikkavāśagar, the Vishṇu shrine occupied the position that it does now. Let us proceed then to a later period, the period of the later Cholas. The Chola decline may be dated as commencing with the death of Kulōttunga Chola I. He was succeeded by his son Vikramachola; and he by his son Kulōttunga II, who was succeeded by Rāja Rāja II. The poet called Oṭṭakkūttan, there are reasons for believing, was a contemporary of all the three. Among the works ascribed to him are three ulās, as they are called, pieces of conventional composition celebrating a patron as he passes in triumph through the streets of his capital, appealing to his vanity by elaborate descriptions of the effects produced upon the lady folk of the city. I take the following extracts from the *Kulōttungachōḷanulā* and *Rājarājanulā* regarding the Vishṇu shrine at Chidambaram :—

புவனி முழுதுடைய பொற்றொடியுந் தானும்
அவனி சுரர்சுருதி யார்ப்ப—நவநிதிதோய்ந்
தேத்தற் கருங்கடவு ளெல்லையிலா னந்தக்
கூத்தைக் களிகூரக் கும்பிட்டுப்—போற்றினமேற்
றில்லைத் திருமன்றின் முன்றிற்—சிறுதெய்வத்
தொல்லைக் குறும்பு தொகுத்தெடுத்து
திருவே திருமாலை
சூட்டத் திருமகுடஞ் சூட்டியபின்—னோட்டு
பொன்னிற் குயிற்றிப் புறம்பிற் குறும்பனைத்து
முன்னிற் கடல்களில் மூழ்குவித்த—சென்னி
திருமகன் சீராஜ ராஜன்

These two passages indicate in no uncertain terms that, in carrying out the renovation of the temple, Kulōttunga found the opportunity to get rid of the Vishṇu image which was obnoxious to his piety. That the Vishṇu shrine was what was particularly offensive to this pious devotee is clear from the expression *முன்னிற் கடலில் மூழ்குவித்த*, which means 'submerging in the sea, the former house'. This very idea of the author and the same act of his zealous patron find expression in another work, the *Takkayāgapparaṇi* :—

முன்றிற் கிடந்த கருங்கடல் போய் முன்னைக் கடல்
[புகப்பின்னைத் தில்லை
மன்றுக் கிடங்கண்ட கொண்டல் பெற்ற மரகத
மேருவை வாழ்த்துவனே—

It is clear then that Kulōttunga II, the grandson of the first of that name, perpetrated this act of pious hostility to the Govindaraja shrine, which led to the establishment by Rāmānuja of the shrine at Tirupati town.

Last of all is a Sanskrit extract which lets us know how the Govindaraja temple came to be again where it is at present. It is a quotation from the *Prapannāmritram* of a certain Anantārya, a descendent of Āndrapūrṇa who was a contemporary of Rāmānuja. It is a life of Rāmānuja at the end of which the author of the life gives his own genealogy. In the course of this pedigree occurs the following passage:—

श्रीरामदेवरायाख्यः कृष्णरायादनन्तरम् ।
शशास राज्यं धर्मेण गुरुभक्तिपरायणः ॥
सभापतिर्महातेजा ययौ चन्द्रगिरिं प्रति ।
गुरुं ताताख्यमादाय रामरायाभिधस्तदा ॥
तस्मिन्काले महाचार्य सर्व शास्त्रविदां वरः ।
अवर्तताप्रतिद्वन्द्वो वाधूलो घटिकाचले ॥
किलीकृतं चित्रकूटं क्रिमिकण्ठेन यत्पुरा ।
तत्प्रतिष्ठापितुं सम्यक् तदा मेने महागुरुः ॥
रामरायसहायेन महाचार्यो महायशाः ।
दुर्जयानपि निर्जित्य शैवां शास्त्रविदुत्तमः ॥
स सम्यक् स्थापयामास गोविन्दं चित्रकूटके ॥
गोविंदराजो भगवान् महाचार्यप्रतिष्ठितः ।
महोच्छ्रायश्चित्रकटे ह्यद्यापि परिदृश्यते ॥

Freely rendered, it means that Rāmarāya, who came after Krishnarāya, once went to Chandragiri taking with him his Guru Tatārya. Mahācharya (Doḍḍayācharya as he is popularly called) of the Vādūlagōtra at the height of fame for learning, was then in residence at Ghaṭikāchallam (Sholingar). He wished to restore the temple of Govindaraja at Chidambaram (Chitrakūṭa), which had been uprooted by the Chola Krimikanṭa. Overcoming in argument the invincible

Śaivas, this great one in learning restored the Govindaraja temple at Chitrakūṭa with the assistance of Ramarāya. This Govindaraja thus established by Mahācharya is even yet to be seen at Chidambaram.

These are isolated facts gathered from a number of works, showing no obvious connexion with each other. How are they to be brought together and used to serve the purposes of history?

The first essential to history is chronology. If the facts are not placed in the order in which I have placed them, they will be unintelligible; and to place them in this order more is required than mere individual ingenuity. If the last fact of the above series could only be placed before its predecessor, the contention of the recent litigants would find some justification. Unfortunately, however, for them I am not marshalling here facts in law for a judge and jury, but facts of history for a critical student. The investigation of the historian ought first of all to be chronological.

The date of Māṇikkavāśagar cannot yet be regarded as a settled fact of history. Varying dates are ascribed to him, as often with as without evidence. Some refer him to the fifth century A.D.; others to the ninth century; others again to an antiquity not definitely ascertainable. That Sundaramūrtināyanār does not include him among the Tiruttoṇḍar is one fact all are agreed upon; and that he was a contemporary of a Varaguṇapāṇḍyan is also tradition accepted on all hands. The epigraphist would keep him to the Varaguṇa of the eighth century after Christ. The literary critic sees quotations and adaptation from Māṇikkavāśagar in the works of the earlier aḍiyārs of the Śaiva hagiology. That his works were well known in the thirteenth century, and the work that readily challenged comparison with those of Māṇikkavāśagar was the *Tiruvōymoḻi* of Nammāḻvār are in evidence in the following lines of the *Saṭagoparandādi*, ascribed to Kamban, who, there are good reasons for believing, lived in the twelfth century A. D.

துறவா தவர்க்குந் துறந்தவர்க் குஞ்சொல்லவே சுரக்கும்
அறவா விலையிங் கோராயிரம் நிற்கவந் தோசிலர்போய்
மறவா தியர்சொன்ன வாசக மாமலட் டாவைப்பற்றிக்
கறவாக் இடப்பரங் கென்பெற வோதங்கள் கைவலிப்பே—

In this, as is evident, Kamban compares the thousand of Nammāḻvār to a thousand milch-cows, both to the renounced and the worldly; and the *Tiruvaśagam* to cows which give no milk. We are not concerned with the judgement here, but only with the fact of the case, although it must be said in passing that this prince of poets in Tamil is far from being a fanatical sectarian; for he says in the *Ramayana*:—

அரனதிக னுலகளந்த வரியதிகன் எனவுரைக்கு
மறிவி லார்க்குப்
பரகதிசென் றடைவரிய பரிசேபோல்

As it is impossible to attain salvation for those who dispute in ignorance that Hara is the greater or the world measuring Hari, etc.'

Regarding the two Āḻvārs the dates are no more fixed than for Māṇikkavāśagar. They are both of them anterior to the middle of the eleventh century A.D., inscriptions of which date refer to the works of these Āḻvārs as having been held in high esteem. One of the decades of Tirumangaiāḻvār refers to the occupation of Kanchi by a king called Vairamēghan :—

மன்னவன் றொண்டையர்கோன் வணங்குநீள்
[முடிமாலை வயிரமேகன்
தன்வலிதன் புகழ்சூழ்ந்த கச்சியட்ட புயகரத்தாதி—

The first being, that is in Aṭṭabhuyagaram in Kanchi, that was surrounded by the forces and fame of Vairamēghan of long garland and high crown, entitled to the respectful submission of the Pallava, the ruler of the Tonḍas (people of Tonḍamanḍalam).

The only date so far known for Vairamēgha Dantidurga of the Rāshṭrakūṭa dynasty is A. D. 754. The latter half of the eighth century A.D. may, therefore, be taken as the age of Tirumangaiāḻvār.[1] The earlier quotations would then refer us to the eighth and ninth centuries A.D. at the latest for the existence of the Govindaraja temple at Chidambaram.

The next batch of references leads to the inference that it was Kulōttunga II, the son of Vikramachola and the father of Rājarāja II A.D. (*circa*) 1133 to 1150, who uprooted the shrine in his pious work of renovation of the great Śaiva temple. This is clear from the quotations themselves which are from the works of a contemporary author.

Lastly, the Sanskrit quotation refers the reconstruction to Doḍḍayāchārya through the good offices of a Rāmarāja who ruled after Krishnarāya. It was in this connexion that this āchārya came in contact with Appaiya Dīkshita, the great South Indian scholar and philosopher. In his commentary on Vēdānta Dēsika's *Yādavābhyudaya*, this scholar says that he took up the work of a commentary on this kavya at the instance of Pinna Thimma, grandson of Rāmarāja. The Rāmarāja referred to is clearly the one that fell at Talikōṭa. There is nothing very improbable in Appaiya Dīkshita's having been contemporaneous with Doḍḍayāchārya or Rāmarāja on the one hand, and with Pinna Timmarāya on the other. Besides the writer of the *Prapannamritam* itself was a disciple of Kumāratātārya, popularly Kōṭikanyakādanam Tātāchar, whose patron was Vankaṭapatirāya, who ruled till A. D. 1614. It must therefore be sometime before A. D. 1565 that the temple was restored.

We are thus able to obtain an account of the vicissitudes of this temple for about five centuries at least.

[1] *Vide* Chapter XIX.

I have taken this as a simple illustration of what historical information can be gained even from apparently unconnected literature. The facts here are all the more reliable, even including the last, as they are mere incidental references. It will now appear that there can be no history without chronology, and the attempts to fix the dates of works and authors, which to many appear absurd, is of the essence of historical research.

What is wanted, therefore, now for historical research is a systematic and organized study of literature, both vernacular and Sanskrit, in a way that will facilitate work both literary and historical. This work cannot be done by one man all through for his own requirements. He will require the collaboration of a number of others. A student engaged in historical research has to keep himself in close touch with the archaeological, epigraphical and literary work that may be going on, and must be something of an archaeologist and epigraphist himself; but that any one should be all the three by himself is beyond human possibility in most cases. This is very often recognized, and the two branches are held to be distinct. In point of literature also—I am concerned with literature only as an auxiliary to history—the collection of manuscripts and documents, and the bringing out of good and critical editions of works ought to be regarded as quite a distinct branch. Most editions of the classics published in India till quite recently, both in Sanskrit and the vernaculars, were uncritical editions. It is the Bombay Sanskrit Series, that set the fashion for Sanskrit. Our esteemed countryman, Mahāmahōpadyaya Swaminathaiyar, has given us a number of remarkably well-edited texts of important Tamil works. The advantage of this kind of editing is quite apparent. The various readings are given for the reader to choose from; the variety of comments are also noted. When this is well and accurately done the text editor has rendered good service to the historian. What then is the utility of such editions? To give only an example or two. The learned editor of the *Śilappadhikāram*, Pundit Swaminathaiyer, has taken care to give in a footnote thirteen lines at the beginning of the second canto, found only in one manuscript among those he consulted. He remarks in another place that manuscripts found in the same quarter have been the most reliable in many particulars. These thirteen lines refer to Karikāla as the ruler at the time, and state that the *Paṭṭinappālai* had been dedicated to him by the author. There are references to the same incident in other works but far later in point of time.

Similarly in stanza fourteen of Kāḷidāsa's *Mēghadūta*, where there is the reference to Diṅnāga, it struck me that the interpretation of the whole, as applied to Diṅnāgācharya, was forced, for in the alternative interpretation the commentator Mallinātha has to omit a part of a compound word. The pundits whom I consulted consider that that is no bar to the slēsha. I understand now from a Bombay edition of the text and commentary that Hēmādri does not countenance the interpretation. The result is that the estimate of Kāḷidāsa's age, based on his contemporaneity with Diṅnāga, falls to the ground so far. Hēmādri may be right or Mallinātha; but those who read with a view to building up a hypothesis in history ought to have an opportunity of knowing both the commentaries. Then he formulates his hypothesis at his own risk.

Further down Mallinātha lays down that the three slokas which he comments on are interpolations. He does not choose to tell us why he thinks so, though his reasons would have been valuable. There is a great and important amount of work to be done, in the way of examining critically the texts with a view to distinguish the genuine from the spurious part of it. Associations and private organizations may well pay some attention to this line of work. The Government have organized their archaeological department for work in archaeology and epigraphy. They are also devoting some attention to the collection and cataloguing of manuscripts. Associations, like the South Indian, may well supplement the work of Government by directing some of its energies both material and mental to critical work upon these materials. The initiative may be taken by the Association; but the result depends entirely upon the support and encouragement it receives at the hands of the more intelligent and enlightened of our countrymen. The South Indian Association at Madras ought to take in this particular the place of the Asiatic Societies elsewhere; and if those of us who are in a position to do something for our country make up our minds to contribute towards the fulfilment of this laudable ambition, it will not be long before the South Indian Association will achieve it.

It is alleged, often with truth, that the historian reads his thoughts and feelings into the writings of the past. This no doubt is a defect that he has to guard himself against. If the record of the past is placed in his hands in an accurate form he ought to have no excuse for making such mistakes. The defect arises from an insufficiency of information which would enable him to form a complete idea of the men and of the period he is dealing with. This is a point that the late Professor Maitland seems to have laid great stress on in the course of his lectures. It is in regard to oaths and the influence that they exercised on truthfulness that the Professor took occasion to make the remark. This defective appreciation is considerably in evidence among a class of scholars engaged in research work. It is traceable to the importing of our own ideas and the circumstances about us to periods of which we have either no, or have no means of having, full information. To illustrate the position I go back to the *Brihatkathā*. The work was written in Paisāchi and appears to have been held in high esteem by successive writers of note in Sanskrit literature, at least from the days of Daṇḍi to the age of the Kāsmirian Sōmadēva. We have four different versions of it as our only source of knowledge of the work. The *Kathāsarithsāgara* of Sōmadēva, is professedly a translation; *Brihatkathāmanjari* is a collection of stories from the *Brihatkathā*; a third version or collection was obtained from Nepal; and lastly a Tamil translation of it, which is of an antiquity prior to that of the now known Śangam works. Professor Speyer, a Dutch scholar, who has made a critical study of the *Kathāsarithsāgara* has, on the strength of the supernatural powers ascribed to Nāgārjuna in the work, referred the *Brihatkathā* to a period between the third and the fifth century A. D. This is because the Professor thinks that people would hardly have believed in supernatural power unless a considerable interval had elapsed. The inference would certainly be warranted, if all people were rational and sceptical to an equal degree at all periods of history. All the world over, and in regard to all religions, miracles play an important part at a particular stage of development; and people are not wanting in the enlightened twentieth century who have full faith in occultism and spiritualism. This it is that makes several Indian works seem ridiculously absurd to European scholars. If they could appreciate the influence a belief in transmigration exerts upon the minds of simple people, and how closely interwoven it is in all the varying belief of the people in India, they would see that what strikes them as absurd is quite obviously believable even by contemporaries. That this has, as a matter of course, been the case could be proved, if Tamil literature and literary tradition were called into requisition.

There are several works in Tamil called mahākāvyas. The translation of the *Brihatkathā*, a sirukāppyam or a minor kāvya called *Udayanan kadai* or *Peruṅgadai* or even simply *kadai*, is believed to be the work which gave the authority for the use of the word kāvya. This work is ascribed to the period of the middle Śaṅgam, that is, anterior to the third Śaṅgam, the works of which we have in some number. I have put forward my arguments for referring the third Śaṅgam to the earlier centuries of the Christian era; hence this work ought to be referable to a period coeval with the beginning of the era of Christ. If only this could be established beyond a doubt, the history of Vikramāditya and Kanishka, about which there is yet considerable divergence of scholarly opinion, would become settled to a degree not dreamt of by any yet; because, Sōmadēva, the translator of the Brihatkathā, says in so many clear words that he makes no change in the matter of the original beyond the mere change of language and the necessary abbreviation. It would be hyper-criticism to dispute the assertion of the author without establishing a clear motive as an essential prerequisite. This has not always been conceded to him.

There is work to be done, therefore, in the co-ordination of the study of the two languages, Sanskrit and Tamil, in the interest of both. In the absence of the original, if the Sanskrit translation could be collated and compared with the Tamil, the result would go far towards solving one of the most important problems of ancient Indian History; namely, the origin of the Samvat era which has had to be accounted for in so many fanciful ways by great scholars. There are references in both the *Kathāsarithsāgara* and the *Brihatkathāmanjari* to a Vikramāditya-Vishamaśīla, who got rid of the Mlēcha trouble, and came to be regarded an incarnation of the divine energy of Vishṇu or Śiva, it does not matter which to us. This question is too long for discussion here.

My object is not to settle disputed questions or to formulate a new historical hypothesis. Now that archaeological and epigraphical work have made some advance, I appeal for a better, more rational, and systematic study of the literature of the country, with a view to making them yield the results that they are capable of. Inscriptions and archaeological research can after all provide the dry bones only. All else will have to be got from literature. Besides, there is a period to which inscriptions do not lead us. For such periods we have to depend upon literary evidence alone, if this is available, either from Sanskrit or the vernaculars. It is a duty that every one owes to his country to do all in his power to advance the study of this literature. In addition to the discharging of a duty, this study of literature will be a source of pleasure even to busy people. Here individual effort can take us only a small way. But if these efforts were made to flow into one channel, the volume would be the greater and the work turned out the larger.

CHAPTER XIII

THE THIRD TAMIL ŚAṄGAM

In a learned article on the age of Māṇikkavāśagar in the *Asiatic Quarterly Review* for April, 1902, Mr. L. C. Innes arrives at the conclusion that, if the Śaṅgam existed at all, it must have come into existence about A. D. 1100 'just prior to or coincident with the time of Kambar', the author of the Tamil *Ramayanam*. The *Epic of the Anklet* or *Śilappadikāram*, an admittedly Śaṅgam work, was written by Iḷangōvaḍigaḷ, a younger brother of Śenguṭṭuvan Śēra, at whose court resided also another Śaṅgam Poet Śīttalai Śāttanār, otherwise Kūlavāṇihan Śāttan, the author of the companion work the *Jewel Belt* or *Maṇimēkalai*. Tiruvaḷḷuvar's *Kuraḷ* again is quoted by these two authors and acknowledged to be a Śaṅgam work also. There is another group of Śaṅgam poets, the authors of the *Ten Poems* or the *Pattuppāṭṭu*, of which two by Rudirāngaṇṇanār celebrate respectively Chola Karikāla and Tonḍaimān Iḷandiraiyan. From the *Śilappadikāram* we learn that the Chola king at the time of its composition was Karikāla, with his capital at Puhār, Kōḻi or Uraiyūr being also an important city; the Pandya king Neḍumśeḻiyan with his capital Madura and the Ceylon king Gajabāhu. There were according to the same work two northern kings at the Court of Śenguṭṭuvan, Kanaka and Vijaya. Of these personages the *Mahāvamśa* of Ceylon mentions two Gajabāhus, one about 133 B. C. and the other about A. D. 1142. One of these two kings is said to have invaded the

Chola country in revenge for a past conquest or occupation of Ceylon by the Cholas. This conquest Mr. Innes thinks impossible for the Cholas, so long as the Pandyas were powerful, for strategic and geographical reasons. He thinks it would have been imprudent on the part of the Cholas, and, therefore, unlikely that they should expose their flank undefended against their sworn enemies. The invasion of Ceylon by the Cholas cannot have taken place before the reign of Kulōttunga Chola I, who ascended the throne in A. D. 1070 and in whose reign the Pandyas were overthrown. Even a part of the Pandya country was colonized along the road to Kōṭṭāru near Cape Comorin. Had it not been so they would have had to pass through the Pandya country. These two reasons cannot stand, as we know in fact that Ceylon was invaded many times before the time of Kulōttunga, whose father-in-law Rājēndra's inscriptions are found in the country. Rājēndra Chola, who ruled from A. D. 1001 to 1042, captured after a sea-fight Kaḍāram and other places in the Ramnad Zemindari,[1] and even his father Rājarāja (A. D. 984 to 1016) had a fleet with which he defeated the Śeras at Kānduḷūr. An invasion of Ceylon would have been a naval invasion and the Pandyas would have been always on the flank. The Cholas were engaged in wars in the distant Kalingam, on the banks of the Tungabhadra and even on the Malabar Coast, before the Pandyas were subjugated by Kulōttunga I. So there is no difficulty in the way of our accepting the account of the Mahāvamśa about the occupation of Ceylon in the first century B. C. or so. If the chronicle cannot be relied on for the period earlier than the middle of the fifth century A. D. it may be sound to infer that the earlier Gajabāhu's date may be somewhat later than

[1] Now proved to be in Burma.

it actually is stated to be, and that the Tamil occupation of Ceylon may have taken place later than the first century B.C., say about the first century A.D. It thus appears quite possible that the first Gajabāhu might as well have invaded the Chola country as the second. About the year A.D. 1142 the Chola ruler must have been Rājarāja II, and from the published inscriptions of him and of his predecessor nothing can be traced as to an invasion of the Chola country by the Ceylonese. Rājarāja II's successor Kulōttunga III claims to have conquered the Ceylonese, Madura, etc.; but Kulōttunga III ruled from A.D. 1178 to probably A.D. 1216.

The next personage of importance who figures in the *Śilappadikāram* is a Karikāla Chola. Mr. Innes is of opinion that this need not be the earliest Chola of the name that we know of. This is very true. Whether we have to take him to be the earliest or the latest must be settled on good grounds. So far as we know the history of the Cholas, we know four Cholas of this name. The first is Karikāla of the poems *Śilappadikāram*, *Paṭṭinappālai* and *Porunarāṟṟuppaḍai*; the next in chronological order is Āditya II, Karikāla, the elder brother of Rājarāja the Great, (A.D. 984 to 1016); the third is not a Chola sovereign, but only a viceroy and younger brother of Rājēndra, who is the father-in-law of Kulōttunga I; and lastly Kulōttunga I himself. Karikāla, the contemporary of Śenguṭṭuvan, of the Śaṅgam fame, must be one of these four. As I understand the article, Mr. Innes consider him to be the last. The Srīvaishṇava saint Rāmānuja at Srīrangam gave offence to a Śaiva ruler Karikāla and in consequence had to flee the country. He went into the Mysore country and converted the the Jain king Biṭṭi Dēva *alias* Vishṇuvardhana of Dvārasamudra to the Vaishṇava faith. Subsequent to this, he founded the temple at Melukōṭe, which event is placed by the Guruparamparāi in Śaka A.D. 1021 or 1099. In this work it is not stated that the Karikāla was the Chola sovereign himself and Rāmānuja is stated to have stayed a number of years at Sāligrāma in Mysore before meeting Vishṇuvardhana. It would stand more to reason to identify his enemy Karikāla with the younger brother of Rājēndra, as he is definitely stated to be the viceroy of Kōḷi or Uraiyūr. But it matters little to our present purpose even if he be Kulōttunga I himself, but it is unlikely, as the latter's capital was either Gangaikoṇḍa Choḷapuram or Kanchi. Again the same Guruparamparāi makes mention of a Toṇḍaimān Chakravarti, who could be no other than Karuṇākara Toṇḍaiman, the general of Kulōttunga I, and the real hero of Jayaṃkoṇḍān's *Kalingattupparani*. These two were undoubtedly contemporaneous with Rāmānuja. Mr. Innes would identify these worthies with the heroes of Rudirānganṇanār's *Pattinappalai* and *Permabāṇāṛṛuppaḍai*. This cannot possibly be. Jayaṃkoṇḍān above mentioned is professedly a contemporary of Kulōttunga Chola I, and celebrates in his poem, the *Kalingattupparani*, the conquest of Kalingam by Karunākara Toṇḍaimān of Vanḍai (Vanḍalūr) for his master Kulōttunga I. In the canto of the poem dealing with the royal genealogy he states explicitly that the two poems in praise of Karikāla were sung in praise of the earliest of the name. The *Perumbāṇāṛṛuppaḍai* of Rudirānganṇanār celebrates a Toṇḍaimān indeed ; but a Toṇḍaimān Iḷandirayan, the son of the ancient Chola king Kōkiḷḷi by the Nāga Princess of Negapatam, as expressly stated in the poem itself. In the face of this, it is a feat of boldness to identify the two groups of personages. This is not all. Karikāla of these poems is closely associated with Puhār or Kaverippūmbaṭṭinam as his capital with a possible alternative of Kōḷi or Uraiyūr or Urandai. But in all the published inscriptions of the later Cholas I have not come across any reference to Puhār at all.

The Pandya king at the time of the events narrated in the *Śilappadikāram* is Neḍumśeḻiyan who was succeeded by Iḷamśeḻiyan, the viceroy, probably, of Korkai, another Pandya capital. At about A. D. 1175 we come upon a line of Pandya rulers with the alternating titles of Kulasēkhara and Sundara. With the rise of these rulers the Pandyas also rise into prominence, but till then the Pandyas were in no condition for an 'academy' at Madura. Ever since the days of Rājarāja I the Pandya country had been so much harassed by the Cholas that they had to maintain a perpetual struggle. This culminated in the complete subjugation of the country by Kulōttunga, who marched through the Pandya country and planted colonies in agricultural parts along the road to Kōṭṭāru in the Travancore country near Cape Comorin. This would hardly be the time for the Śaṅgam which admittedly flourished in the Pandya country.

The Śaṅgam, therefore, ought to have existed at a time when the Chola country was ruled by Karikāla and his successor Perunarkiḷḷi at Puhār and Uraiyūr; when the Pandya country was ruled by Neḍunśeḻiyan of *Muduraikkānji* and *Neḍunalvāḍai* fame at Madura and Korkai; when Śenguṭṭuvan Śēra was ruling at Vanji; when Gajabāhu was ruling in Ceylon. As far as is known at present the earlier Gajabāhu's time would answer better than the reign of Gajabāhu II. If it could be proved beyond doubt that the alphabet was not known in South India before the third century A. D., we may have to bring Gajabāhu I up to within living memory of the time of the author of the *Mahāvamśa* written about the middle of the fifth century A. D.

Kambar might not have lived even so early as A. D. 886. It is clear from his reference to Rāmānuja that he must have followed the latter. The popular account which would bring together Kambar, Oṭṭakkūttar, Pugaḻēndi, etc., and place them in the court of Kulōttunga may be correct in so far as these authors are concerned, but none of these had anything to do with the Śaṅgam. Kambar, we are told, went from place to place to gain the approval of the learned for his *Ramayanam*, but he is not said, like Tiruvaḷḷuvar, to have gone to the Śaṅgam, whose imprimatur would at once have stamped his work with authority. Kambar therefore could not have been a contemporary of the Śaṅgam, and there is nothing against his having been to the Śaṅgam *proximus sed longo intervallo* (next but at a long interval).

CHAPTER XIV

THE AUGUSTAN AGE OF TAMIL LITERATURE

DREARY as the prospect may well appear to the earnest student of Tamil literary history, as in fact does early South Indian history in general, there has, of late, been brought to light a considerable body of Tamil literature which throws a flood of light upon the much-doubted, though often debated, period when literary activity in Tamil reached its high watermark. Scholars are much divided in opinion as to the Śaṅgam having ever existed at all, except in the active imagination of later poets and the idle tongue of tradition. This is not strange, considering how much truth is generally overgrown and interwoven with fable and legend. Whether wantonly or otherwise, the truth is very often hidden almost beyond recognition in later literature; and early scholars in modern Indian research have unwittingly contributed their own quota to the very same end. Much has, therefore, even to be unlearnt before making an attempt to learn something about this distant past of the oldest of the Dravidian languages of South India. Even in the traditions handed down to us, much distorted though they are, there are certain cardinal facts and characters standing clearly marked out from the rubbish outgrowths. It will not, therefore, be without interest to attempt to place these facts in the light in which they appear on an unbiased and impartial inquiry.

An attempt therefore will be made in this chapter to set forth the available evidence, literary and historical, which tends towards the following conclusions :—

(1) That there was an age of great literary activity in Tamil to warrant the existence of a body like the traditional Śaṅgam.

(2) That the period of the greatest Śaṅgam activity was the age when Śeṅguṭṭuvan Śēra was a prominent character in politics.

(3) That this age of Śeṅguṭṭuvan was the second century of the Christian era.

(4) That these conclusions are in accordance with what is known of the later history of South India.

There are a number of works in Tamil literature of a semi-historical character of a later and of an earlier age. These alone will be relied upon here, without altogether eschewing tradition of a reliable character. So far as tradition is concerned, there were three Tamil Śaṅgams[1] that flourished at or about Madura, and of these, the third is all that we can presume to speak about. This Śaṅgam had, for its members, forty-nine critics and poets who constituted a board of censors. There were forty-nine Pandya rulers, among whom were Muḍattirumāran and Ugra-Peruvaḻudhi, who actively patronized the Śaṅgam. This last personage is the sovereign before whom the *Kuṛaḷ* of Tiruvaḷḷuvar received the Śaṅgam imprimatur. It is not out of place to remark here that the author of the *Kuṛaḷ* was not among the Śaṅgam members, and there were a large number like him at different places, as will appear in the sequel.

Taking this Ugra-Pandyan for reference, a number of poets and kings can be grouped around him from internal evidence of contemporaneity without having recourse to any legends concerning them. But it

[1] The poem quoted in the note at page 2. *Śilappadhikāram.*

is first of all necessary to show that it is probable that Tiruvaḷḷuvar was a contemporary of Ugra-Pandyan. Apart from the verse in praise of the *Kuṛaḷ* ascribed to him, it is a well-known fact that Tiruvaḷḷuvar had a sister by name, or rather title, Avvaiyār. This poetess sings of this same Pandyan and his two friends the Chola Kiḷḷi, who performed the *Rājasūya*, and the Chēramān Māvaṇkō, although the names of these personages are not mentioned as such in the poem 367 of the *Puranānūṛu*. But poem twenty-one of the same collection by Iyūr Mūlangiḻār specifies his victory over Vēngaimārban and the taking of the 'great fortress of the forest (Kānappēreyil).' It also refers to the fame of this Pandyan as transcending the skill of poets. This Ugra-Pandyan is credited with having caused the collection *Ahanānūṛu* to be made. Certain mythical achievements are ascribed to one Ugravarma Pandyan in the *Madura Sthalapurana* and the *Hālāsya* or *Tiruviḷayāḍal*, which achievements are alluded to in the *Epic of the Anklet.*[1]

Leaving aside Ugra-Pandyan for a while, the greatest of Avvaiyār's patrons—in fact, almost the patrons—were Adiyamān Neḍumān Anji and his son, Pohuṭṭeḻini. Their territories were in the modern Mysoṛe province and in the Salem district, with the capital at Tagaḍūr,[2] identified with Dharmapuri in the latter district, though there was another Tagaḍūr of some consequence in later history in the Mysore district, not far from Nanjanagūḍu near Mysore town. There was an Adiyamān about the same region who,

[1] *Śilappadhikāram*, Canto xi, ll. 26-31.

[2] Mr. Kanakasabhai Pillai identifies this place with Dharmapuri, Salem district. *Vide Epigraphia Indica*, VI, No. 34, and *ante*, XXII, pp. 66 and 143. Mr. F. J. Richards, M.A., I.C.S., informs me that a hill overhanging the town Atur goes by the name Avvaimalai, the hill of Avvai.

as the Chola viceroy, was driven across the Kaveri when Talakāḍu was captured by the famous Ganga Raja, the general of Vishṇuvardhana Hoyśāla before A. D. 1117. Of the many poems in the *Puṛanā-nūṛu* collection ascribed to Avvaiyār, the great majority celebrate Anji, one of the last 'seven patrons of letters', as patronage went in those days. Several of these mention the hero and his son by name. Poem ninety-one gives the hero's name and refers to the gift to Avvaiyār of the black gooseberry supposed to confer immortality on the lucky eater thereof. The same incident is referred to, with the name of Avvaiyār put in it, in the poem *Siṛu-pāṇāṛṛuppaḍai*[1] of Nallūr Nattattanār included in the *Ten Tamil Idylls*, another Śaṅgam collection. The poem has for its special object the celebration of Eṛumānāṭṭu Nalliyakkōn, a petty chief over Vellore Amur and other places near about, as the most liberal among the liberal patrons of those days, namely, the Chēra, the Chola, and the Pandya, and the seven last patrons. Poem ninety-nine of the *Puṛanānūṛu* is of importance, as giving us another clue to a different synchronism of the utmost consequence. This poem celebrates Anji's conquest of Tirukkōvilūr, and states that the hero's fame transcended the capacity of the poets of an older generation, and yet the poet Paraṇar 'sings to-day of the glory of your conquest of Tirukkōvilūr '.

This mention of Paraṇar is of very great importance to literary history. He was a poet among the Śaṅgam members and is credited with a large number of the *Puṛanānūṛu* collection. But Paraṇar's fame should have been greater, had he really enjoyed the patronage of Śeṅguṭṭuvan Śēra, whom he celebrated in the fifth division of another Śaṅgam

[1] ll. pp. 99–103.

collection, the *Ten Tens* (*Padirruppattu*). The parentage ascribed to Śeṅguṭṭuvan there agrees word for word almost with that given by the author of the *Epic of the Anklet*, a brother of the king, and is even fuller of particulars. The last verse,[1] the *Padigam*, written either by a friendly contemporary or disciple or some one else in a similar position, explicitly gives us the names of the hero and the author, and thus leaves us in little doubt as to the correctness of the connexion. It is on these two accounts that the commentator of the latter work relies for his fuller account of the Chēra's history. From the reference to the *Śiṛupāṇ* made above, it is clear that Avvaiyār enjoyed the patronage of Adiyamān Neḍumān Anji. Poem ninety-nine of *Puṛanānūṛu* refers to Paraṇar as having celebrated the same patron. The last verse of the fifth division of the *Ten Tens* connects unmistakably Śeṅguṭṭuvan with Paraṇar. Thus then it is clear that Śeṅguṭṭuvan Śēra, Adiyamān Anji, Avvaiyār and Paraṇar must have lived, if not actually at the same time, at least in the same generation. Śeṅguṭṭuvan was a remarkably great ruler, and thanks to the efforts of our modern 'Nachchinārkiniyar', Mahāmahōpadhyāya Pandit Saminatha Iyer of the Madras Presidency College, we have two great works composed at his court and in his time, which shed a flood of light on contemporary history and which would go a long way in settling many a knotty point in the literary history of South India. These are the *Epic of the Anklet* (*Śilappadhikāram*) and the *Jewel-Belt* (*Maṇimēkhalai*). The first is the work of Iḷango, the younger brother of Śeṅguṭṭuvan, who, after renouncing civil life, resided at Kuṇavāyil near Karūr

[1] *Vide* p. 10, footnote on p. 11, and canto xxix. Pandit Saminatha Iyer's edition recently published, pp. 78-6. *Śilappadhikāram.*

[2] *Śilappadhikāram*, canto xi, ll. 20-31.

(Vanji), the ancient capital of the Chēra; and the second, the companion and supplement, though the earlier composed, from the pen of (rather the style of) Madurai Kūlavāṇigan Śāttan, otherwise known as Sītthalaichchāttanār, the corn merchant of Madura. (His head was believed to have been exuding matter on account of the blows dealt by himself whenever he detected errors in other's composition, considering it a misfortune to have to read or listen to such blunders; so uncompromising was he as a critic.) Before proceeding to a consideration of these great works, it is better to dispose of a few other important characters.

Of the last seven patrons celebrated in the *Śiṟupāṇāṟṟuppaḍai* of Nallūr Nattattanār (believed to be one of the Śangam forty-nine), there is one Pēhan (otherwise Vaiyāvikkōn Pērumbēhan) who was so liberal (inconsiderately so) as to give a warm covering to a peacock. This same incident is referred to in poem 145 of the *Puṟanānūṟu* ascribed to Paraṇar. This personage sometime in his life transferred his affections from his wife Kaṇṇahi (to be carefully distinguished from the heroine of the epic) and several poets, among whom Paraṇar, made poetical appeals on her behalf. The others were Kapilar, Ariśil Kiḻār and Perumkuṉṟūr Kiḻār (poems 43–7 both inclusive of the *Puṟanānūṟu*). There is considerable similarity of sentiment in these. Poem 343 of the same work is also ascribed to Paraṇar, and it refers to a Kuṭṭuvan very liberal in the donation of wealth 'brought down hill-country and from oversea'.

Passing on to Kapilar, another Śaṅgam celebrity reputed by tradition[1] to be the younger brother of Tiruvaḷḷuvar, it is found that he had for his patron and friend a chieftain, Vēḷ Pāri, whose demesne Paṟambunāḍu comprised 300 villages and who was master

[1] The actual story connecting these is regarded as a fabrication by some scholars.

of Paṛambu Hill. Kapilar is credited with having composed the *kuṟinji* section of the *Aiṅguṟunūṟu*, the seventh of the *Ten Tens*, the *Kuṟinjippāṭṭu* of the *Ten Idylls* (all Śaṇgam works) and the *Iṇṇā* (that which is bad and therefore to be avoided), *Forty*. When Pāri fell a victim to the treachery of the three Powers, who made a futile attack on him jointly, Kapilar as his chief friend took his two girls with him to be given away in marriage to some person worthy of them, and thus do his last duty to his departed friend. Poems 200, 201 and 202 of the *Puṛanāṉūṟu* refer to the incident[1] of Pāri's giving a car to the creeper *mullai* and to Kapilar's offering the girls to Vichchikkōn and Pulikaḍimāl[2] Iruṇgōvēḷ of Malaināḍu. Both of them refused to marry the girls, and some insult offered as to the social standing of his patron's family the poet resents in poem 202. Poem 201 refers to Iruṇgōvēḷ, said to have been a descendant in the forty-ninth generation from the ruler of 'Tuvarai'[3] who was born from a sacrificial fire. The title Pulikaḍimāl has considerable similarity in its origin to a story which is given as explaining the origin of the Hoyśālas in inscriptions of a later time. The following poem resents Iruṇgōvēḷ's refusal to marry the girls, and refers to the destruction of Aṛayam city, the head-quarters of this family, in consequence of an insult offered to the poet Kaḷāthalaiyar[4] by an ancestor of Iruṇgōvēḷ's. The poet further begs, with biting sarcasm, to be pardoned for having introduced the girls as the daughters of Pāri, instead of as the descendants of Evvi, a chief in the Pandya country.

[1] *Vide Siṟupāṇ.*

[2] He that killed a tiger.

[3] Tuvarai may be either Dwāraka in Guzerat or Dwāravati or Dwārasamudra of the Hoyśālas.

[4] Another poet who celebrates Karikāla, and his Chēra contemporary, Perumśeralādhan. (Poem 65, *Puṛanāṉūṟu.*)

Kapilar himself is connected with the Chēra Māntharam Śēral Irumporai and is spoken of with great regard as a poet by another poet, Porundhil Iḷangīranār. Poem 126 by Marōkkattu Nappaśalaiyār refers to his praise of Malaiyamān Tirumuḍikkāri, who was in possession of Muḷḷūr Hill. It incidentally refers to the naval strength of the Śēra, likening the futility of the author's attempt at celebrating Kāri, after Kapilar had done so, to the endeavour to sail a ship in the face of the Chēra fleet. Poem 174 by the same author refers incidentally to Muḷḷūr Hill, celebrated by Kapilar, and directly to Śoḷiyavēnādhi Tirukkaṇṇan (otherwise Tirukkiḷḷi), who rendered yeoman's service to Peruviraṟkiḷḷi while in hiding at Muḷḷūr. The poem further credits the Malayamān Śoḷiyavēnadhi Tirukkaṇṇan with having restored the Chola to his position. Another person that Kapilar celebrates is Tirumuḍikkāri, ruler of Malaināḍu, with his capital at Tirukkōvilūr and with the hill Muḷḷūr. Poems 122 and 123 refer to his having been sought in alliance by the three powers.

Beginning with a consideration of what little is known of these three personages, Avvaiyār, Paraṇar and Kapilar, we have been introduced to a number of poets and potentates living within a generation of one another. Before proceeding to a consideration of the chief rulers of the age and their geographical location, let us turn aside to glean what we can of contemporary history from the two epics of the age of Śeṇguṭṭuvan, who was by far the most important character of the period and about whom we could gather an amount of information from the above works.

The *Epic of the Anklet* is the story of Kōvalan (Gopala, and his wife Kaṇṇahi), both of the mercantile community of Puhār (Kaverippūmbaṭṭinam), and has, for its moral, the triumph of the wife's chastity and the vindication of the husband's innocence. The story is as follows in brief outline: Kōvalan, the son of Māśāttuvan of Puhār, was early married to Kaṇṇahi, the beautiful daughter of Mānāygan of the same place and community. The marriage was celebrated with great pomp and becoming circumstance, as the two parties were of high social standing. After a while, the mother-in-law set her daughter-in-law up independently in a different house in the same city, provided with all that the young couple might need for conducting a successful and virtuous life, as householder and housewife. Sometime after, Kōvalan took a fancy for a highly accomplished and exceedingly lovable professional dancing-woman, whose skill in her art was unsurpassed, nay even unsurpassable. The lover and mistress led a happy life and had a daughter, the only offspring of their affection. Disconsolate as Kaṇṇahi was, she never lost her affection for the husband who had thus given her up, and was quite as faithful to him as she would have been under ordinary circumstances. At the conclusion of the annual festival to the god Indra, the usual bathing in the sea brought the festivities to a close. This was a day of enjoyment for all and the whole elegant society of Puhār turned out to the beach to spend the day in music, dancing, and other such amusements. The happy lovers singing to the accompaniment of the yāḻ, a Tamil musical instrument now gone out of use, by turns, suspected, from the tenor of the songs, each the other of having changed his or her affection. Stung by this imagined bad faith on the part of his sweetheart Mādhavī, Kōvalan went home to his house, instead of to hers as usual, and felt quite ashamed of himself for his treatment of the wife, who redoubled her attentions to him since she had seen that something ailed her lord. Overcome with remorse, Kōvalan confessed to his wife his position with respect to Mādhavī and communicated to her his resolution to make amends for his past misconduct by entering into business in Madura on his own account, asking her if she would follow him, should he act upon his resolution. Kaṇṇahi signified a ready assent and gave her husband the pair of anklets (śilambu), the only thing valuable he had not as yet given away to Mādhavī, for providing the capital necessary for him to become a merchant in Madura. That very night the repentant and admiring husband with his faithful spouse unknown to anyone, started away before dawn and took his way along the northern bank of the Kaveri. Picking up the nun Dēvandhi, a few miles above Puhār, they continued their journey to Srīrangam and Uraiyūr. Thence taking one of the three roads indicated by the Malainādu Brāhmaṇ from Māngāḍu (Alavāy in Travancore), who was returning from Madura on a pilgrimage to the shrines of Vishṇu, they reached the outskirt of the capital city of the Pandyans. Leaving his tender wife in charge of a hospitable shepherdess and her daughter, he entered Madura city the next day to sell one of the pair of anklets. Not finding a ready sale, as the jewel was of very high value, he wandered long before he was accosted by a goldsmith, who was going towards the palace at the head of a number of his apprentices. On Kōvalan's offering the jewel for sale, the wily smith promised to get it sold, with a request that he would keep the jewel with him and wait there till he should send for him from the palace whither he was then going. Proceeding gleefully to the royal residence, he reported to the king that the thief who had stolen the queen's anklet had been caught with the jewel in his possession and had been kept waiting under promise of purchase. The king who was much distressed at the loss of the jewel and the pain it caused the queen, said that the jewel should be brought, having killed the thief. He actually meant that he required the man and the jewel to be brought, in order to kill the man, if guilty. The plot of the goldsmith, the real culprit, succeeded so well that the king was deluded and the innocent hero was murdered, after transacting a pathetic scene much like the one in Shakespeare's Richard III. News of this calamity reached Kaṇṇahi who, in great anger, forgot her usual modesty, and bent upon establishing her husband's innocence and the power of her chastity, walked boldly forth, quite, unlike her ordinary self, with the other anklet in her hand and rang the bell of justice in the great gate of the palace. This alarm, quite unheard of in the reign of the then Pandyan ruler, made the hall-porter suspect that something seriously wrong had taken place. The unusual apparition of a young injured woman with an anklet in one of her hands, with anger and grief on her countenance, was immediately announced to the king. Admitted without delay into the royal presence, Kaṇṇahi proved that the anklet for which her husband suffered death was hers and not the queen's, demonstrating that the jewel in dispute was filled with rubies. The queen affirmed hers was filled with pearls. Kaṇṇahi invoked a curse that Madura should be consumed by fire for this remissness of her king, who, rather than survive the disgrace he had brought upon a line of illustrious rulers, died immediately. The queen followed her consort, and Kaṇṇahi left the city by the western gate towards the hill-country, where she was to join her husband in a fortnight, as promised by the goddess of Madura. This union of the wife and the husband was seen by the hill-tribes, who duly reported the matter to their king, then in camp on the hills with his queen and retinue. At the request of the good queen, the king built a temple and consecrated it to the chaste lady (Pattinī Dēvi) who had undergone so recent an apotheosis.

This is, in the merest outline, the story of the first epic, and the second is a sequel to this. Information of all the proceedings at Madura was given at Puhār by a Brāhmaṇ friend of Kōvalan, who, having bathed at Kumāri (Cape Comorin, near which was once a river), was baiting at Madura on his homeward journey. The mother and mother-in-law of Kaṇṇahi died of grief. The father and father-in-law renounced life and became Buddhistic monks. Mādhavī, disconsolate at Kōvalan's sudden disappearance, sent him an importunate appeal to return, while he was yet on his outward journey to Madura. Finding it of no avail, she had been overcome with grief, and when news of Kōvalan's death reached her, she gave up life and all its pleasures to become a lay disciple of a Buddhistic monk; while her daughter just blooming into a woman of rare beauty and womanly grace, entered the Buddhistic cloister. *Jewel-Belt* (*Maṇimēkhalai*) was her name. Her renunciation forms the subject of the epic called by her name. The heir-apparent of Puhār is very deeply in love with her, but she is taken care of by a goddess, who plays the guardian angel, much like the Ariel of Shakespeare. To save her from the loving prince's ardour, she is removed to an island by the goddess while asleep; and there she is initiated into the Buddhist mysteries. Having understood her past life, she returns to Puhār with a begging-bowl of extraordinary virtue. The prince still prosecuting his hopeless love, falls a victim to the jealousy of an angel, whose wife's disguise the heroine assumed to keep out her importunate lover, her own husband in a previous life. Consoling the queen and the king in their sorrow for the loss of their son, she leaves Puhār (at the mouth of the Kaveri) and proceeds to Vanji (not far from Kranganūr at the mouth of the Periyār), where she learns all that the teachers of different religious systems have to teach her. Not satisfied with their philosophy of religion, she is directed to Kānchī by her grandfather, who had betaken himself to Vanji in anticipation of Puhār being overwhelmed by the sea. Maṇimēkhalai proceeds to Kānchī and relieves the place from famine by the use of her begging-bowl. Learning the true philosophy of the Buddha from a saintly monk, she stopped there. This is the merest outline of the two poems, forming a single epic, which is of a dramatic-epic character with something of the narrative in it. Containing, as they do, a great deal of the supernatural, there is yet much that must be regarded as historical. In one word, the setting is poetical, but the background is historical.

The *Epic of the Anklet* has much to say about the 'three great kings of the south' and its companion concerns itself with three likewise; but the place of the Pandyan is taken by the ruler of Kānchī. To begin with the Chola kings celebrated by the poets, two names stand out; those of Karikāla and Kiḷḷi, called indifferently Neḍumuḍikkiḷḷi, Velvērkiḷḷi, Mavaṇkiḷḷi, etc. Of these two, Dr. Hultzsch has the following in his South Indian Inscriptions[1]: 'It will be observed that each of the four documents, which record the names and achievements of these ancient Chola kings, enumerates them in a different order. One of the four kings, Kōkkiḷḷi can hardly be considered a historical person, as he is credited with having entered a subterraneous cave and there to have contracted a marriage with a serpent princess, and as the *Vikkirama Śoḷan Ulā*, places him before the two mythical kings, Sibi and

[1] Vol. ii, part iii, pp. 377-8.

Kavera.' . . . Of Karikāla and Kō-chchengaṇ here follows what the same authority has to say: 'A comparison of these conflicting statements shows that at the time of the composition of the three documents referred to, no tradition remained regarding the order in which Kō-chchengaṇ and Karikāla succeeded each other. Probably their names were only known from ancient Tamil panegyrics of the same type as Kaḷavaḷi and Paṭṭinappālai. It would be a mistake to treat them as actual ancestors of that Chola dynasty, whose epigraphical records have come down to us. They must rather be considered as representatives of extinct dynasties of the Chola country, whose names had survived in Tamil literature either by chance or by specially-marked achievements.

'To Karikāla the Leyden grant attributes the building of embankments along the Kaveri river. The same act is alluded to in the *Kalingattupparaṇi* and *Vikkirama Śoḷan Ulā*. The *Kalingattupparaṇi* adds that he paid 1,600,000 gold pieces to the author of the *Paṭṭinappālai*. According to *Porunarāṟṟuppaḍai* of Muḍathāma Kaṇṇiyār the name of the king's father was Iḷanjētchenni. The king himself is there called Karigāl or blackleg or the elephant-leg; while the Sanskritized form of his name Karikāla would mean "death to elephants". He is said to have defeated the Chēra and Pandya kings in battle fought at Veṇṇil. According to the *Śilappadhikāram* his capital was Kaverippūmbaṭṭinam. In one of his interesting contributions to the history of ancient Tamil literature, the Hon'ble P. Coomarasami allots Karikāla to the first century A. D. This opinion is based on the fact that the commentaries on the *Śilappadhikāram* represent Karikāla as the maternal grandfather of the Chēra king, Śeṅguṭṭuvan, a contemporary of Gajabāhu of Ceylon. Mr. Coomarasami identifies the latter with Gajabāhu I, who, according to the *Mahavamśa*, reigned from A. D. 135. With due respect to Mr. Coomarasami's sagacity, I am not prepared to accept this view, unless the identity of the two Gajabāhus is not only supported by the mere identity of name but proved by internal reasons, and until the chronology of the early history of Ceylon has been subjected to a critical examination.'

A careful examination of the first book of the *Epic of the Anklet* shows that during the early part of the life of the hero, the king of Puhār was Karikāla Chola. Apart from the fact that the commentator invariably interprets all references to the ruling king as applying to Karikāla (and this in itself is much, as the commentator was one who was thoroughly qualified for the task and can, as such, be expected to embody nothing but correct tradition in his commentaries), there are a number of direct references to him, either by name or by the fact that the erection of the tiger-emblem on the Himalayas was attributed to him. The last four lines of canto i blesses the ruler 'who erected the tiger-emblem on the crest of the Himalayas.' There is direct mention of Karikāla's name and of his rewarding the poet of the *Pālai* [*Paṭṭinappālai*][1] in one of the manuscripts consulted by the editor; further down, lines 158–60 of canto vi, mention as clearly as one could wish Karikāla as ruling at the time, and the commentator explains it as such by giving the passage the necessary expansion, not to mention the allusive but undoubted reference to the same personage in lines 95-8 of canto v. Of the three kings praised in canto xvii, there is reference to Karikāla's Himalayan exploit in the last stanza in page 400, and this is the last Chola ruler referred to. Canto xxi, lines 11 et seq., clearly state

[1] Pages 44–5—Pandit Saminatha Iyer's edition of *Śilappadhikāram*. There is nothing in the lines to lead one to regard them as later interpolations.

that Karikāla's daughter had married the then Chēra king, whom she joined when he lost[1] his life in the sea. These would undoubtedly point to Karikāla as having ruled at Kaverippūmbaṭṭinam till Kōvalan's departure for Madura. The supernatual achievements are clearly nothing more than the fanciful way in which these Buddhistic authors attempt to explain even the most ordinary occurrences. The most cursory examination will discover that it is so, and the faith of these authors in the doctrine of *karma* comes in for much that would otherwise be inexplicable in the story.

To return to Karikāla. He was the son of Uruvappaharēr-Iḷanjētchenni and had married among the Nāngūr Vēḷ class. It is said that he assumed the form of an old judge in order to satisfy the scruples of the parties, who were afraid that, being a youth, he could not bring mature experience to bear upon the question coming up for decision. His name is actually accounted for as having been due to an accident by fire[2] while yet a baby. He is the hero of the two poems in the *Ten Tamil Idylls*, *Porunarāṛṛuppaḍai* of Muḍathāma Kaṇṇiyār and the *Paṭṭinappālai* of Rudirānganṇanār, for which latter the author received the sixteen lakhs of gold pieces mentioned above. He defeated the Chēra by name Perumśeraladhan and a Pandyan whose name is not mentioned, in the battle of Veṇṇil.[3] This Chēra wounded in the back in battle died of disgrace.[4] Rudirānganṇanār celebrates another hero, the Toṇḍamān

[1] The text has it that when he was drowned she called out for him. The waves showed him to her when she joined him and both disappeared, much like Kaṇṇahi's union with her husband.

[2] The 3rd stanza from the *Palamoḻi* quoted at the end of the *Porunarāṛṛuppaḍai*.

[3] Lines 143-8. *Porunarāṛṛuppaḍai*. Veṇṇil is Kovil Veṇṇi in the Tanjore district.

[4] *Puṛanānūṛu*, poems 65-6.

Iḷandirayan of Kānchī whom tradition traces to the Chola Kiḷḷi by a Naga princess, as stated by Dr. Hultzsch, in the quotation above. This Kiḷḷi, otherwise Neḍumuḍi Kiḷḷi, is the ill-fated successor of Karikāla, in whose reign a catastrophe befell Puhār and brought the Chola fortunes very low indeed. While luckily there are but a few Karikālas among South Indian rulers, there are a number of Kiḷḷis,[1] among whom it is a matter of great difficulty indeed to fasten upon the individual here mentioned. Fortunately for us, there are certain distinguishing features which give us the clue. One of the exploits of Śeṅguṭṭuvan Śēra is the victory at Nērivāyil, a village near Uraiyūr (Trichinopoly), where he defeated the nine Kiḷḷis of the Chola family and thus restored his cousin (brother-in-law) to power. From the *Epic of the Anklet* and the *Jewel-Belt* we learn he was the last ruler in Puhār and it was in his reign that the ancient Chola capital was overwhelmed by the sea. It is this Kiḷḷi, whatever his distinguishing epithet, that is the father of the Tonḍamān referred to by Dr. Hultzsch. While in the *Perumbāṇāṟṟuppaḍai*, the commentator Nachchinārkiniyar (who must have lived in the thirteenth century A.D. or thereabouts)[2] makes the Tonḍamān the son of a Naga princess with whom the Chola lived in a cave, which is generally, taken to mean the nether-world. The *Jewel-Belt* gives the following much less romantic version of the story, which agrees in all details except the cave, so far as it goes, while accounting for the destruction of Puhār. Without relegating them actually to Hades, we find reference to Naga rulers in India and Ceylon, between whom a war once took place for the possession of some Budha-relic, according,

[1] Twelve in *Puṟanāṉūṟu*, and nine in *Śilappadhikāram*.

[2] Mr. Anavaradha Vinayagam Pillai allots him to the ninth century A.D. (*Christian College Magazine* xvii), 1900.

to the *Jewel-Belt.*[1] The same also refers to another race of the Nagas as naked cannibals. The story goes on to state that Kiḷḷi fell in love with a Naga princess, who appeared before him all alone like a damsel from the fairy-land, in what is called the 'Kaḻi Kānal'[2] (the grove by the back-water) at Puhār. After a month of happy life, she left him (and this is explained away by preordination), when she had taken her residence in an island near the coast,[3] 300 miles away from Puhār. Sometime after she had become the mother of a beautiful son, she sent the child to the father through a merchant, whose ship called at the island on its homeward journey. While nearing Puhār, the ship got wrecked off the coast and the baby's fate was not known for certain. On hearing of this disaster, the king ordered a thorough search to be made, and in his paternal anxiety forgot his duty to the god Indra, whose annual festival had been forgotten. The wrath of the god showed itself, very likely, in a storm-wave which destroyed Puhār completely.[4] This account taken from the *Jewel-Belt* of the birth of the Toṇḍamān makes Dr. Hultzsch's objection as to the myth, lose edge, and therefore it is quite possible—nay even historical—that there was a human ruler by name Kiḷḷi, who ruled at Puhār after Karikāla.[5] The destruction of Puhār accounts

1 We find reference to such wars in the *Mahāvamśa*, in the earlier chapters of the work.

2 This Kaḻi Kānal is referred to in canto vii as the place of resort of pleasure-seekers—nay, a veritable 'lover's arbour' in Puhār.

3 *Vide Maṇimēkhalai* note, pp. 97-8. The island of Ceylon, in which is Adam's Peak, is sacred to the Buddhists. This hill is now known as Samantakūṭam and Samanelai, but referred to in the work as Samantam and Samanoḷi.

4 There is a story of similar import with respect to a Ceylonese king, whose wife was abducted by a Chola king under similar circumstances. There are no grounds to connect the two at present, at any rate.

5 The descent into Hades, therefore, will have to be regarded as an eastern figure of speech and nothing more. There are other incidents

for the association of Kiḷḷi with Uraiyūr at the end of the *Epic of the Anklet*, in the course of which the catastrophe to Puhār must have happened. The ruler at Kānchī during the period, according to the *Jewel-Belt*, was an Iḷam Kiḷḷi, the brother of Kaḻar Kiḷḷi.

This last ruler of Puhār is referred to in the *Jewel-Belt* with the following adjuncts indifferently, namely, Vaḍivērkiḷḷi, Velvērkiḷḷi, Māvaṇkiḷḷi, and Neḍumuḍikiḷḷi. With the help of his younger brother, Iḷangō (perhaps Iḷamkiḷḷi of Kānchī), who was probably the heir-apparent as the term would indicate, he defeated the Chēras and the Pandyas on the banks of the river Kāri.[1] The three poems concerning this personage in the *Puṟanānūṟu* refer to his having been besieged at Uraiyūr and Āmūr by Nalamkiḷḷi. After the destruction of Puhār he must have been reduced to the woeful plight from which Śeṅguṭṭuvan Śēra, it is clear, relieved him by his victory at Nērivāyil[2] over the nine Chola princes who forgot their allegiance to the Kiḷḷi. This is borne out by the enmity between Neḍumuḍikiḷḷi and Nalamkiḷḷi indicated in poems 44, 45, and 47 of *Puṟanānūṟu*. There are besides a number more of

throughout these epics, which interpreted literally would be quite as absurd; and these are easily accounted for by the author's belief in the doctrines of Karma and re-births, the main pillars of the Buddhistic faith, as also to a modified extent of the Brahmanic. It is this that makes them attempt to account for actual phenomena by causes supernatural. This, modern European critics fail to bear in mind, and hence all appears grotesquely legendary and absurdly fabulous. These remarks find their full application in the *Jewel-Belt*, though there is hardly any Indian work of a quasi-religious or ethical character in criticising which one could afford to forget them.

1 Pandit Saminatha Iyer's edition of *Maṇimēkhalai*, page 741, canto xix, lines 124, 130.

2 Nērivāyil in later history belonged to the Kshatriya Sikhāmaṇi Vaḷanāḍu, i.e., the region round Uraiyūr, and the royal secretary of Vīrarājēndra as the owner of this village as also of Tāli Tiruppanangāḍu. *South Indian Inscriptions*, vol iii.

Kiḷḷis, each with a distinguishing epithet which would support the existence of the nine Kiḷḷis (Kiḷḷi being a generic name of the Cholas like Śenni, etc.) The author of these poems, Kōvil Kiḻār, celebrates another Kiḷḷi who died at Kuḷamuṛṛam. None of these Kiḷḷis is associated with Puhār. In fact neither in the *Puṛanānūṛu* nor in the *Śiṛupāṇāṛṛuppaḍai* do we find the city of Puhār associated with these Cholas.

Leaving aside the Cholas, we find the whole time, during which the incidents narrated in the two epics, took place, taken up by Śeṅguṭṭuvan Śēra, whose capital was at Vanji (Karūr) at the mouth of the Periyār on the west coast. His exploits are recorded in some detail in these works and the others referred to already. His father and uncle are celebrated in the two preceding sections of the *Ten Tens*. His chief achievements were a naval victory over the 'Kaḍambu,' two invasions of the north with victories on the banks of the Ganges over Kanaka and Vijaya, sons of Bālakumāra and the victories at Nērivāyil and Viyalūr (there is a Viyalūr connected with Nannan, an ancestor of Vichchikkōn, whom Kapilar celebrates in poem 200 of the *Puṛanānūṛu*). Like his father, Śeṅguṭṭuvan also claims to have cut out the bow-emblem on the Himalayas.

Coming to the Pandyas of Madura, we have two names in the *Epic of the Anklet*, namely, Neḍum Cheḻiyan, victor over the Aryan army; and Ilam Cheḻiyan, who was viceroy at Korkai when Neḍum Cheḻiyan died at Madura. Before discussing these names we have to dispose of one other Pandyan of importance in literary history. When Tiruvaḷḷuvar submitted the *Kuṛaḷ* to the Śaṅgam critics, the king was Ugra-Pandyan, victor over the 'big forest fort (Kānappēreyil) under the chief Vēngaimārban.' The *Tiruviḷaiyāḍal Purāṇam* ascribes to him some achievements which are of a legendary character, though some might have been possible. These are the very achievements [1] ascribed to a Pandya ruler by the Malaināḍu (hill-country) Brāhman from Māngāḍu (Ālangāḍu or Ālavāy), then at Uraiyūr in the course of a pilgrimage to the shrines of Vishṇu, who directed Kōvalan to Madura from Uraiyūr. This praise would lose all point unless it referred to the ruling Pandyan when the Brāhman pilgrim sojourned at Madura, on his visit to Tirumāliruṅjōlai. The author of the epic clearly designates him the Pandyan Neḍum Cheḻiyan 'victor over the Aryan forces', whatever these forces might have been. There are a number of references throughout the work to the erecting of the fish-emblem on the Himalayas. It is the boast of Karikāla Chola, Ugra-Pandyan, and Neḍumśēralādhan (father of Śeṅguṭṭuvan) that they cut out their respective emblems on the Himalayas. These achievements are clearly ascribed to the reigning Pandyan in the commencing and the concluding lines of canto xvii. Thus then the Ugra-Pandyan [2] of the *Purāṇas* and tradition could not have been any other than the ill-starred Pandyan Neḍum Cheḻiyan of the *Epic of the Anklet.* Avvaiyār's reference to Paraṇar referred to above would agree quite well with this identification, as in accordance with that reference, Paraṇar should have been the earlier of the two.

The successor of the Pandyan, apparently his son, Pandyan Iḷam Cheḻiyan, otherwise Veṟṟivēr-Cheḻiyan, was in Korkai when his father died, and succeeded to his father's estate in the course of the story. We are

[1] Canto xi, lines 23–31. There are besides references to his achievements in connexion with the ruling Pandyan in many places throughout the work.

[2] Stanza 4, bottom of page 400. Mr. Kanakasabhai Pillai in his interesting papers on *The Tamils 1800 Years Ago*, makes Ugra-Pandyan the contemporary of the successor of the Kiḻḻi, the grandson of Karikāla. This would bring Tiruvaḷḷuvar's *Kuṟaḷ* too late for quotation by the friendly authors of the two epics, as the *Kuṟaḷ* received the Śaṅgam approval under Ugra-Pandyan. [*Madras Review*, vol. ii, No. 6.]

vouchsafed no other information, except that he propitiated the manes of the injured lady, Kaṇṇahi, by the sacrifice of one-hundred goldsmiths. This may have been a massacre of that class of artisans. Probably, his reign was short and uneventful. He must have been succeeded by Pandyan Neḍum Cheḻiyan, victor at Talayālaṅgānam[1] over the two other kings and seven chiefs. Kapilar is connected with prince Māntharam Śēralirumporai of the 'Elephant-look' by Porundhil Iḷam Kīranār in poem fifty-three of *Puṛanānūṛu.* This Chēra was ruling over Toṇḍi (Quilandy, and not the Śoḻaṅ Toṇḍi, on the east coast now in the Rāmanād zamīndarī), and was the master of Kolli Malai,[2] which is a hill in the Salem district quite on the border of Trichinopoly. His position in this region would have been possible only in the light of Śeṅguṭṭuvan's victories over the Kongus at Seṅgaḷam (red-field), at Viyalūr, about the same region, and over the nine Cholas at Nērivāyil, near Trichinopoly. This personage was taken prisoner by the Pandyan Neḍum Cheḻiyan[3] of Talayālaṅgānam fame. At this latter place, the young Pandyan overthrew the 'Tamil army' under the two kings and 'seven chiefs'. This Pandyan was a great celebrity in literature and in his reign flourished a number of poets of the Śaṅgam fame. He is the hero of Māṅguḍi Marudanār's *Maduraikkānji* and Narkīrar's *Neḍunalvāḍai* among the *Ten Tamil Idylls.* He was himself, like several other rulers of those days including his grandfather, a poet. There are a number of poems relating to him in the *Puṛanānūṛu* collection.

[1] He must have been particularly young when he came to the throne, *Puṛam*, 7.

[2] The last lines of canto xiv, the *Epic of the Anklet*, refer to the reigning Chēra as the ruler over the country between the Himalayas with the bow-emblem and Kolli Malai.

[3] *S. A.*, canto xxviii, lines 115–25. Seliyan is again a generic name like Pandyan, and the father or the son have the adjunct 'big', 'young', much as 'Smith, senior or junior.'

Thus we see that during the course of the story, the rulers of Puhār were Karikāla and his grandson Kōkkiḷḷi [1], of Madura Neḍum Cheḻiyan, identified with Ugra-Pandyan, and Iḷam Cheḻiyan followed later by Neḍum Cheḻiyan, victor over the Tamil army at Talayālaṅgānam ; the Chēra ruler all the time at Karūr (Vañji) was Śeṅguṭṭuvan Śēra, the brother of the author of the epic and the patron of the author of the *Jewel-Belt,* the father and the uncle of this personage having been the heroes of the second and third sections of the *Ten Tens.* Chēra (prince) of the 'elephant-look' must have been his son and viceroy of the newly-conquered territories.

These were the sovereigns of the three kingdoms who flourished in the generation of the literary celebrities headed by the names chosen at the commencement, namely, Avvaiyār, Paraṇar and Kapilar. These were the three stars of the first magnitude in the literary firmament, as those in the political, of South India. Other poets there were and patrons likewise. Of the latter, mention has already been made of Pāri of Paṛambunāḍu and Paṛambu Hill; Kāri of Tirukkōvilūr in Malaināḍu and Muḷḷur Hill; Irungōvēḷ of Arayam in the western hill-country of the Tuvarai [2] family with the special distinction of having killed a tiger to save a saint absorbed in contemplation; Pēhan of Naḷḷūr in Malaināḍu (hill-country) : and Adiyamān Anji of Tagaḍūr and Horse-hill, overthrown according to the eighth section of the *Ten Tens* by the Perum Śēral who overthrew Tagaḍūr. These are all mentioned by name as well as by distinguishing achievements, most of them in a somewhat fabulous

[1] Mr. Kanakasabhai Pillai places a Nalamkiḷḷi between these two. [*Madras Review*, vol. ii, No. 7.]

[2] Tuvarai might have been either Dvāraka in Guzerat or Dvārāvatī or Halebid in Mysore; but the latter does not appear till much later, and the name Tuvarai in classical works is always taken to mean Dvāraka.

garb in the *Śirupāṇāṟṟuppaḍai* of Nallūr Nattattanār. Besides these, we have already mentioned the prince Chēra of the 'elephant look', ruler of Tonḍi and master of Kolli Hill. To come to the poets, in addition, to the three already referred to, we must mention here only a few of the more important, such as Tiruvaḷḷuvar, Iḷangōvaḍigal, Śīththalai Śāttanār, Rudirānganṇanār Muḍathāmakkāṇṇiyār, Māngudi Marudanār, Narkīrar and others, whose works are held even to-day in high esteem by the Tamil world as masterpieces in their respective departments. Some of the rulers were themselves poets of some merit, and Avvaiyār was not the only poetess. The two young daughters of Pāri could compose verses and the elegiacs ascribed to them is proof of their ability in this direction. There is besides a poem in *Puṟanānūṟu* ascribed to the wife of Bhūta Pandyan, who performed sati on the funeral pyre of her husband. These names raise a strong presumption in favour of the view that, as the age of Śeṅguṭṭuvan, including in it a generation either way, was one of great literary activity, it might have been the time when the Śaṅgam activity was at its height.[1] This was the age when the creed of the Buddha was in the ascendant, which, like all other reform movements of a later time, gave a powerful impetus to the development of the vernaculars of the country. Although the Śaṅgam is not mentioned as such in these early works, we find the cultivation of Tamil specially associated with Madura, which is often referred to as 'Tamil Kūḍal',[2] despite the fact that a

[1] It will be clear from the above that the author of the *Kuṟaḷ* could not have been much earlier than the friendly authors of the epics. Still they quote with great respect from the *Kuṟaḷ*. This could only be if the *Kuṟaḷ* were authoritatively approved of after being read out before the Śaṅgam, Śīththalai Śāttan being one of the august body. Iḷangō, however, was not among this body, although he quotes from the *Kuṟaḷ* likewise.

[2] *Śiṟupāṇ* and *Puṟanānūṟu*, and *Kalingattupparaṇi*, of a later age.

large number of poets mentioned above flourished in other courts. In the traditional lists of Śaṅgam celebrities we find mention of the names of most of the authors referred to above. It is not improbable, therefore, that a board of censors like the Śaṅgam existed about this age at Madura.

Without pausing to examine what other literary men can be grouped along with those spoken of already, we may pass on to the consideration of the more important question of the probable age of this great literary activity in South India. The two chief epics, the *Epic of the Anklet* and the *Jewel-Belt*, were Buddhistic, the latter more so than the former; and the other works of the age show considerable Buddhistic influence and follow in this order with regard to dates of composition. The *Kuṛaḷ* is the earliest of the major works, as there are quotations from this work in the companion epics, which even acknowledge the quotations. The two epics must have been composed about the same period. The *Jewel-Belt* precedes the *Epic*. The *Ahanānūṛu* miscellany is ascribed to Ugra-Pandyan, before whom the *Kuṛaḷ* received the Śaṅgam imprimatur. The *Kuṇḍalakēśi* is another Buddhistic work and, so far as we know it at present of a controversial character, much like the *Jewel-Belt* in plan. This was followed by the *Nīlakēsitteruṭṭu*, which attempts a refutation of the *Kuṇḍalakēśi* and must, therefore, be of a later age. If this general course of literary activity is correctly indicated by the editor of the *Śeṅ Tamil*, whose account is relied on here, and if we can fix the probable period of this literary activity, this will prove the sheet anchor in the literary chronology of South India.

In the midst of the confused tangle of mere names and names of similar sound and meaning, we have, fortunately just a few distinct characters and characteristics that make the attempt not altogether hopeless, provided the question be approached in the spirit of unbiassed inquiry. Although Killi is quite a common name among the Chola rulers, Karikāla is somewhat uncommon. Śeṅguṭṭuvan is definite enough and his Ceylon contemporary Gajabāhu's name occurs, luckily for students of Tamil history, but twice among 174 names unlike Vikramabāhu for instance. The *Kalingattupparaṇi*, a work composed between A. D. 1111–35 refers to Karikāla and Kō-kiḷḷi in the reverse order, Kiḷḷi being followed by Kōcheṅgaṅ, Karikāla following both. There appears, from the *Puṟanānūṟu*, to have been a Kiḷḷi in the third generation before Karikāla; but the Chola succession is fixed as follows: with respect to this—taking only such names as are specifically mentioned in the following order—Iḷanjētchenni, his son Karikāla, his grandson Neḍumuḍikiḷḷi. The *Kalingattupparaṇi*, like the great commentator who must have lived after Jayamkonḍān, the author of this work, ascribes to Kiḷḷi the descent into Hades. It is just possible that there was a mistake made, as to the particular Kiḷḷi whose union with the Naga princess was thus described by later writers. If this were so, the Karikāla of the Himalayan fame could not have been Kullōttunga I A. D. 1070 to 1118 certainly, nor the viceroy of Kōḷi (Uraiyūr) in the reign of his father-in-law Rājēndra A. D. 1053–60. There is one other Karikāla of the later dynasty[1] whose epigraphical records are available to us—Āditya Karikāla, *circa* A. D. 950–85 who killed Vīra Pandyan in battle, as if in sport. But the author of the *Kalingattupparaṇi* places Karikāla three names before Vīranārāyana or Parāntaka I, while Āditya was the eldest son of Parāntaka, a grandson of the first of

[1] For a list of this dynasty of kings, see the table prefixed to my article, 'The Chola Ascendency in South India' (*Madras Review*) for November, 1902, or the *South Indian Inscription*, vol. iii, part II, recently published. Chap. vi. Pt. I, *supra*.

that name. So then, we are driven to the necessity of looking for this Karikāla far earlier than A.D. 900.

It has been shown above that the works themselves point to an age when the religion of the Buddha was in the ascendant as the probable period when the works under consideration at least the greatest of them were composed. Buddhism was overthrown about the seventh century A.D. when Hiuen Thsang was travelling through India, and when Tirujñānasambhanda flourished. About A.D. 862, a battle was fought between Varaguṇa Pandyan [1] and the western Ganga king Sivamara, at Sri Parambi (Tirupparambiyam near Kumbhakōnam). This would not have been possible had the Cholas been at all powerful. Nor do the works of the age under review mention the Gangas as so powerful. We are at this period (A.D. 750 to 850) passing out of the Pallava ascendency in South India which must have begun about A.D. 500, if not earlier with Vishṇugōpa of Kānchī, the contemporary of Samudragupta. There is no reference in the works under notice to such premier position of the Pallavas or even the Toṇḍamān rājās—the only Toṇḍamān of the period figuring as a minor chief, and Kānchī was a Chola viceroyalty. In the Rayakoṭṭa [2] plates, a Pallava king, by name Skandaśishya, who must have been earlier than Vishṇugōpa claims descent from Aśvattāman through a Naga princess. Perhaps by this time the origin of Iḷandirayan had been so far forgotten as to make this credible. These considerations lead us to assume an earlier period for Karikāla. This personage is associated with Puhār even in tradition, and the *Jewel-Belt* tells us in unmistakable language that Puhār was submerged in Kiḷḷi's reign. All the poems in the *Puṛanāṉūṛu* about Kiḷḷi, a number

[1] *Annual Report for Epigraphy*, 1905-06, part II, p. 25, and *Epigraphia Indica*, vol. viii, pp. 295 and 319.

[2] No. 8, *Epigraphia Indica*, vol. v.

of them with distinguishing epithets, connect them with Uraiyūr, and none of them is connected with Puhār. Uraiyūr figures as a considerable town in the *Epic of the Anklet.* Even the Śiṟupāṇāṟṟuppaḍai does not mention Puhār. This is a very important circumstance as will appear presently.

When Śenguṭṭuvan performed an elaborate sacrifice on the occasion of the consecration of the temple to Pattinī Dēvi, the heroine of the *Anklet,* there was present, among others, Gajabāhu of Lanka surrounded by sea [as opposed to Māvilangai of Ērumānāṭṭu Nalliyakkōn.] This Gajabāhu of Ceylon, Iḷam Cheḷiyan of Madura, and Kiḷḷi of Uraiyūr, built temples to the same deity, following the lead of the Chēra. The question now is whether this Gajabāhu is the first or the second of the name. The first Gajabāhu ruled as monarch of all Ceylon from A.D. 113–35; the second as one of three from A.D. 1142–64 as in the list appended to Miss Duff's *Chronology of India.* Dr. Hultzsch's challenge to the Hon'ble Mr. Coomarasamy is to establish by internal evidence that the Gajabāhu mentioned was the first and not the second of the name. As to the other part of his objection, it must have become clear from the above that for the myth about Kiḷḷi, later writers alone are responsible; and enough direct evidence has been adduced to show that Karikāla was ruling at Puhār when Kōvalan began life as a married man, and that his daughter was the wife of the Chēra king then reigning. To return to Gajabāhu; let us for the sake of argument take him to be the second of the name. We know something of the history of South India in the middle of the twelfth century and the geographical distribution of the Powers. The Chola rulers ought to have been either Vikrama or Kulōttunga; the rulers of Madura either Vīra Pandyan or Vikrama Pandyan; the sovereigns of the Chēra country were Vīra Kēraḷa Varman and

Vīra Ravi Varman; of the Mysore country, Vishṇuvardhana and his son, Narasimha. There were no separate rulers at Kānchī, except in the sense that it was an alternative capital of the Cholas. There was an Adiyamān, no doubt, about this period (somewhat earlier), but he was the Chola viceroy at Talakāḍ (not connected with Tagaḍūr), who was driven across the Kaveri by Ganga Raja, the famous general of Vishṇuvardhana. There were no Kongu rulers such as are mentioned in the *Epic of the Anklet*. Gajabāhu himself was in no plight to come to Vanji[1] (Karūr) at the mouth of the Pērār, not far from the modern Kranganur (Koḍungalūr). Gajabāhu was fighting his own battles nearer home with his two neighbours, Mānābharaṇa and Parākramabāhu, and it was all he could do to keep himself from being permanently overwhelmed.

The first Gajabāhu invaded the Chola country to bring back the inhabitants of Ceylon, carried off by the Chola army on a previous invasion of the island during his father's reign; they were then in bondage at 'the city of Kaveri in the country of Soḷi'. He brought back besides the relics and the begging-bowl of the Buddha, 'which aforetime had been carried away by the Dhamilas'. The *Rājaratnākari* while ascribing the same achievements to him, states that the Ceylonese went of their own accord 'to serve at the river Kaveri.'[2] He is there said to have brought a number of the Tamils and settled them in Ceylon. In the *Rājāvaḷi*, however, there is an even more elaborate version. The ruler is there called Rājabāhu,

[1] Vanji itself was not the capital of the Chēra at the time. The capital of Kerala was then Quilon, and during the period of the Chola ascendency (A. D. 900-1300).

[2] Vol. II, pages 57-8. This mention of the river instead of the town would show that when the *Rājaratnākari* was compiled the existence of the town was passing into oblivion.

which may be due to a miselection. He was accustomed to make solitary night-rounds; when he heard the wailings of a widow in her house, for her two sons had been taken captive by the king of 'Soḷi Raṭṭa'. The Adigars (officers) failing to discover anything wrong, the king sent for the woman and learnt from her that 12,000 families had been carried away, 'when the king of Soḷi Raṭṭa made his descent upon the island'. The same achievements as in the previous account are recorded, with the addition 'that the king of Ceylon also, upon that occasion, brought away the foot ornaments of Pattinī Dēvī[1] and also the four arms of the gods.' This Pattinī Dēvī could have been no other than the heroine of the epic, who was known as Pattinī Dēvī or Pattinī Kaḍavul. This must have been regarded as a valuable relic in those days, when relics played such a prominent part in religion. As to the begging-bowl of the Buddha, a bowl of extraordinary virtue had been brought by Maṇimēkhala from an island south of Puhār, where there was a Buddha-seat as well, which had the divine quality of letting people into the secrets of their former existence, a belief in which was one of the cardinal doctrines of Buddhism. The *Jewel-Belt* also states that two Naga kings fought for the possession of this Buddha-seat. These then are the native accounts of the Ceylonese chronicles with respect to Gajabāhu I; but, unfortunately, the reference to Pattinī Dēvī does not occur in the earlier compilations. This is matter for great regret. It must, however, be noticed that all these works were compiled from earlier writings and living tradition. Here follows what the learned

1 The distinction between the Chola country and other parts of South India is not carefully made in the *Mahāvamśa*. Sometimes they specially talk of Soḷi Raṭṭa, at others of Malabar generally, meaning not the Malabar Coast necessarily, but India generally.

translator of the works has to say about them : 'so carefully has the text been handed down that the discrepancies found to exist between the more ancient and modern copies are very slight indeed. The *Rājāvaḷi* is a work of different hands and compiled from local histories; it is used as a corollary or addition to the two preceding works, continuing the narrative through the struggles between the Portuguese and their rivals, the Dutch.'

All tradition, therefore, and the historical circumstances attending the stories of these epics point to the first Gajabāhu, as the Ceylon ruler who was present at the celebration of the sacrifice by Śeṅguṭṭuvan Śēra and if the *Rājāvaḷi* could be relied on, the conclusion would be forced upon us. As it is, however, there is but little ground to connect these events with the second Gajabāhu, as some scholars would have it.

As to the date of the first Gajabāhu, the chronicle gives A.D. 113–35 as the period of his reign. Whatever be the real worth of this actual date, we have little reason to regard that of his successor namesake as inaccurate. It has been pointed out that the middle of the twelfth century could not possibly be the time when the poets flourished. There is the *Kalingattupparaṇi*, the date of composition of which could not have been much later than A. D. 1111, certainly not later than A. D. 1118. Sundaramūrti Nāyanār, whom the late Mr. Sundaram Pillai placed in the eighth century A.D. refers to Pāri,[1] the patron of Kapilar, and the general tenor of the epic points to Buddhistic times, which the twelfth century was not. Taking

[1] The reference is to the complaint which the devotee makes in respect to the lack of liberality in people in his days, although one should choose to describe a miser as a patron liberal as 'Pāri', much as Bacon complains of learned men turning Faustina into Lucretia.

the Buddha Nirvāna, at 487 B.C., instead of 543 B.C., as accepted by most authorities now, the dates for Gajabāhu I go up to A.D. 162–91. Until it is proved that the earlier dates of the *Mahāvamśa* are unreliable[1] (except for this error), these dates will have to stand, and the period of the greatest literary activity in Tamil must thus be put down as the second and third centuries of the Christian era at the latest. This would be quite consistent with the power of the Tamils in the centuries preceding the Christian era, when they several times invaded Ceylon and imposed themselves on the Ceylonese as usurpers, about the middle of the first century B.C. These facts coupled with the emperor Asoka's reference to these Tamil powers, along with the five Hellenistic potentates, warrants great probability with respect to the high state of civilization of the Tamils.

Besides the mention of Gajabāhu, we find mention of a number of other rulers in the course of the *Epic of the Anklet,* who were some of them friendly and others hostile. The friendly kings were the 'hundred karṇas', who provided Śeṅguṭṭuvan with a fleet of ships with which to cross the Ganges, when he invaded the northern country to punish Kanaka and Vijaya, sons of Bālakumāra who spoke disparagingly of the Tamil rulers. These brothers were helped by Uttara, Vichitra, Rudra, Bhairava, Chitra, Singa, Dhanuttara and Śvēta.[2] Mr. Kanakasabhai takes the 'hundred karṇas' as equal to Sātakarṇin of the *Matsyapurāṇa.* But against this, there is the objection that the Tamil poet mentions 'the hundred persons, the karṇas';[3] and in one place the

[1] Prof. Rhys Davids finds the chronicle borne out in important details by the inscriptions among the finds of the Sanchi Tope, etc. (*Buddhist India*, pp. 299–300); page 1 et seq., *J. R. A. S.*, 1908; *Indian Review*, May, 1908: the *Date of the Buddha* by Mr. Gopala Iyer.

[2] *S. A.*, canto xxvi, ll. 180–5.

[3] *S. A.*, canto xxvi, l. 149.

author even speaks of 'the karṇas' without the hundred.[1]

Besides, as would appear from Dr. Bhandarkar's *Dekhan*, the name Sātakarṇin was that of a dynasty and not of only one ruler. The name Sātakarṇi alone appears in the early part of the list and the date is 40 B.C. to A.D. 16 (see 166, *Bombay Gazetteer*, vol. i, part II). The word itself could be taken to mean 'keen-eared' (rather than hundred-eared), figuratively. It is hard to understand how a contemporary could have rendered it with the number attached not to the ears but to men. Besides, these were ruling in southern India, although Magadha was included in their dominions. So then, even if the 'hundred karṇas' meant Sātakarṇin, the particular sovereign might have been Yajña Śrī who ruled from A.D. 154–74 in the Mahārāshṭra, and A.D. 172 to 202 in Telingana. If this be so, we have also a Vijaya, mentioned in all the purāṇas, who was in Telingana from A.D. 202–8 but as against this, there is the objection that Śeṅguṭṭuvan crossed the Ganges and fought with Vijaya and his brother on the northern bank of the Ganges. This, notwithstanding, that Śeṅguṭṭuvan must have flourished about this time, could be inferred from the fact that Śeṅguṭṭuvan's father, Pandyan Neḍum Cheḻiyan and Karikāla all claim victory over the Aryan forces. It is very likely that the Tamil forces helped in the overthrow of the foreigners by Gōtamīputra Sātakarṇi[2] and the direct mention of gifts to Karikāla

1 *S. A.*, canto xxvii, p. 177.

2 This is the more likely, as the Saka Nahapana and his successor, Rishabadata, ruled over the Mahārāshṭra, with Junnār for their capital, and their territory extended up to Malabar. This dynasty, together with that of Chashṭana in Mālva, was overthrown by Gōtamīputra Sātakarṇi and his son, Pulimāyi, among whose possessions we find 'the regions of the Malaya and the Sahya.' These Āndhrabhrityas came from Dhanakaṭaka near Guntur, and driving back the usurpers, recovered their ancestral dominions. (Introduction to *Literary Remains of Dr. Bhau Dhaji*, page 25, and Dr. Bhandarkar's *Dekhan*, secs. iv, v, vi.)

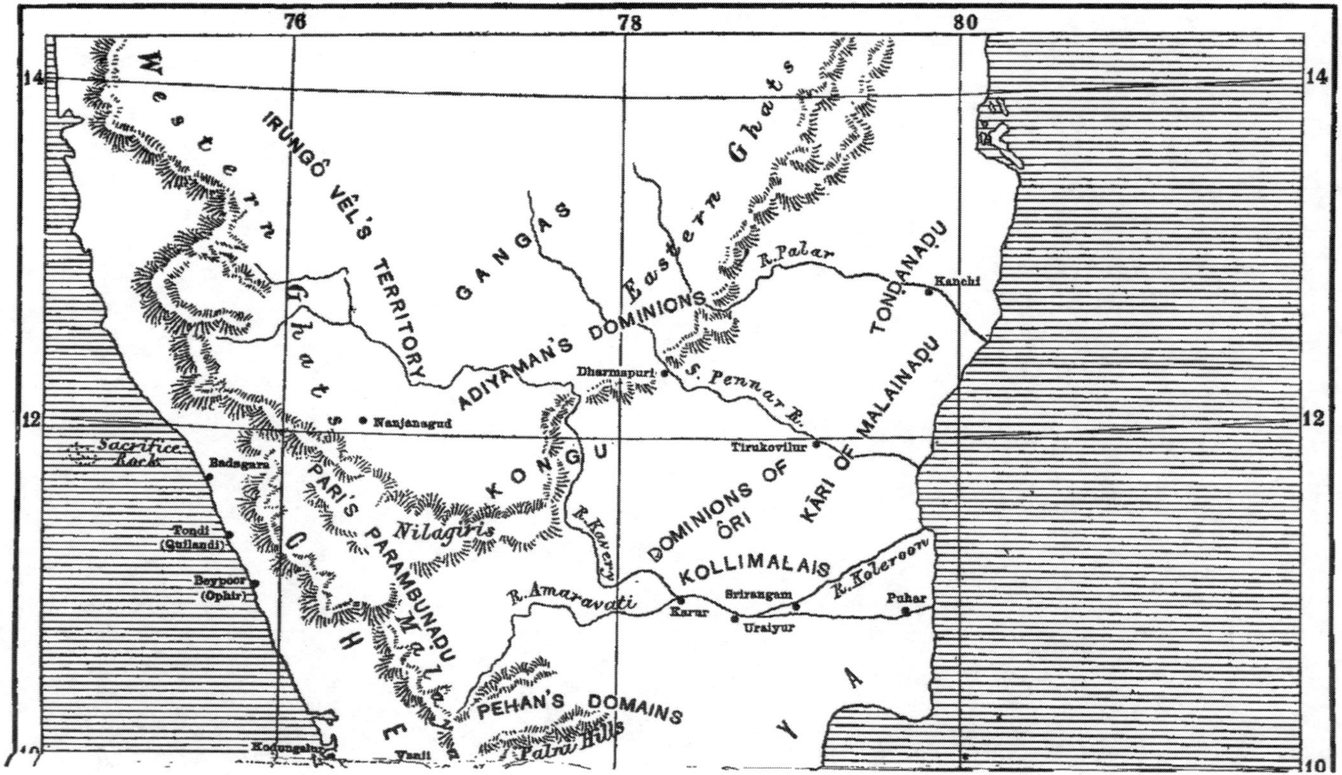
76
78
80
14
12
10
Western Ghats
IRUNGÔ VÊL'S TERRITORY
GANGAS
Eastern Ghats
R. Palar
TONDANADU
Kanchi
ADIYAMAN'S DOMINIONS
Dharmapuri
S. Pennar R.
MALAINADU
Nanjanagud
Sacrifice Rock
Badagara
KONGU
Tirukovilur
KĀRI OF
DOMINIONS OF ŌRI
PARI'S PARAMBUNADU
Nilagiris
R. Kavery
Tondi (Gulandi)
KOLLIMALAIS
R. Koleroon
Beypoor (Ophir)
R. Amaravati
Karur
Srirangam
Uraiyur
Puhar
CHERA
Mala
PEHAN'S DOMAINS
Palni Hills
Kodungalur
Vanji

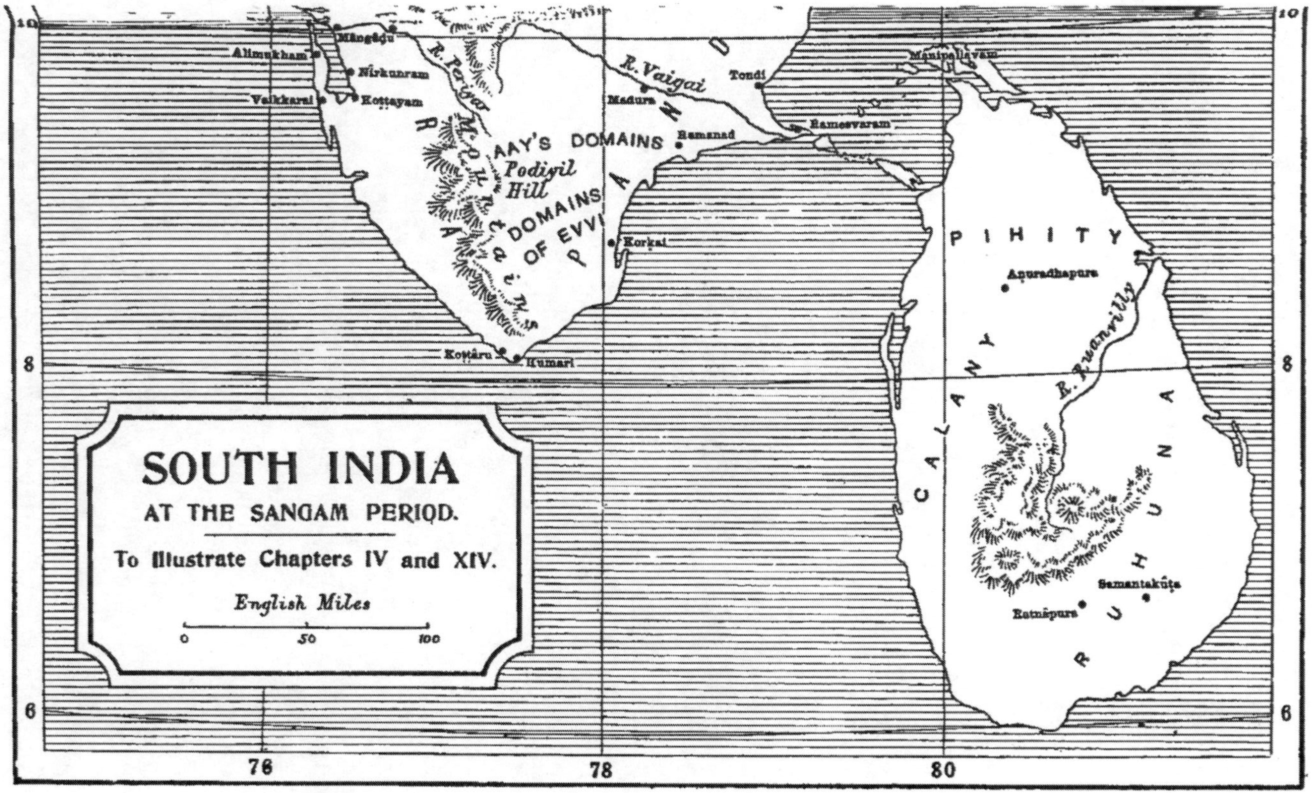
SOUTH INDIA
AT THE SANGAM PERIOD.
To Illustrate Chapters IV and XIV.
English Miles
0
50
100
Alimukham
Māngāḍu
Nirkunram
Valkkarai
Koṭṭayam
R. Periyar
Mountains
AAY'S DOMAINS
Podiyil Hill
& DOMAINS OF EVVI
R. Vaigai
Madura
Ramanad
Tondi
Rameswaram
Korkai
Koṭṭāru
Kumari
Manipallavam
PIHITY
Anuradhapura
R. Kuanvilly
CALANY
RUHUNA
Samantakūṭa
Ratnāpura
76
78
80
10
8
6

by the Rājas of Bundelkhand (Vajranāḍu), Magadha and Māḷava (Avanti) could not be altogether a figment of the imagination, since it is so very definite. All circumstances attending point to the second century A.D. as the era of Śeṅguṭṭuvan; and the era of the greatest literary activity may be taken to be the second and third centuries after Christ.

Buddhism was introduced into South India during the last quarter of the third century B.C. It must have taken some time to strike root, and in those days must have been somewhat slow in spreading. Judging from the exposition of it, as shown in the *Jewel-Belt*, we might take it that it was as yet so free from any element of corruption as to evoke the admiration of even Christian scholars, like the learned translator of the Ceylonese chronicles. The early centuries after Christ may, therefore, be regarded as the age of Buddhistic ascendency in South India. When Fa Hian was travelling in India, there were already the early signs of revulsion, and Brahmanism returned to the fray. In the next two or three centuries Buddhism was swept off the country and the restoration of Brahmanism was completed when Hiuen Thsang came to India, chiefly through the agency in the Tamil country of the earlier Śaiva devotees and some among the Vaishṇava. From this time the struggle is not so much between Buddhism and Brahmanism, as between the latter and Jainism.

In the first centuries of the Christian era, then, we find India south of the Tungabhadra thus politically divided. If we start at the source of the Kaveri and follow its course till it meets the Amarāvati near Karūr, and then go up the latter river continuing our journey till we reach the Palnis and the Western Ghauts, we shall have marked the land-boundary of the Chēra sphere of influence. If we take a straight south-easterly line from Karūr till we reach the sea, east of the Zamindari of Sivaganga and south of the old Chola town of Tondi, the south of this line would be the Pandya, and north of it the Chola sphere of influence. It must not be understood that the territory allotted to each power was always directly under it. The frontier regions were always of doubtful allegiance, as could be seen from the care with which rulers in those days fortified and strengthened frontier towns. So far as the Cholas were concerned, they had always prominently before them the strategical advantages of Uraiyūr on the west and Kānchī on the north, although their chief city was Puhār on the sea-coast. Karūr was the meeting place of the three powers and its neighbourhood was the scene of many a hard-fought battle. This central region, particularly the hilly portion, was therefore filled with petty chieftaincies owning allegiance, so long as it could be enforced, to one or other of these powers, and constituting a group of frontier 'buffer-states'. Thus there was Irungōvēḷ north of the Mysore district and on the frontiers of Coorg. Next to him was the Adiyamān in the southern-half of the Mysore district and part of Salem with his head-quarters at Tagaḍūr. He belonged to the Chēra family. South of this must have been the territory of Pēhan with Nallūr for his head-quarters, the country round the Palnis; between the two last was probably Paṛambunāḍu of Pāri. Next follows the Kongu country, which we might put down as including a part of the Coimbatore and Salem districts. In a line east of this is the hill-country of Kāri with its head-qurates, Tirukkōvilūr. South of this is the Chola country proper, and north the province or kingdom, according to circumstances, of Kānchī. South of the Pālghāt gap and in the Pandya country was the chieftaincy of Ā'ay round Podiyil Hill in the Western Ghauts. On the opposite side round Korkai were the territories of Evvi. During the latter part of the reign of Śenguṭṭuvan there was a Chēra, probably only a viceroy holding a tract of country extending from the Kolli Mal'ais[1] to Toṇḍi on the coast, with the Chola and the Pandya countries on either side. This was the prince Chēra of the 'elephant-look' (probably he had small deep-set eyes). The above appears to have been the geographical division of the country. This kaleidoscopic arrangement vanished and another pattern presented itself with every turn that affairs took.

If we call the age under consideration the age of the Chēra ascendency, as Śenguṭṭuvan Śēra appears to have been at one time in his life the arbiter of the destinies of this part of the country, we pass on gradually from this into a struggle, the Chēra supremacy being shaken by the Pandyan. Here we lose the thread till we come to about A.D. 400, when the Pallavas rise into importance. The Pallava ascendency begins with Vishṇugōpa of Kānchī, the contemporary of Samudragupta, and reaches its grand climacteric under Narasimhavarman, the destroyer of Badami (Vātāpi), the Chālukya capital about A. D. 640. Over a century hence we find the Gangas and Pandyas fighting near Kumbhakonam. This *rōle* the Pandyas play several times in history. Their position at the farthest end of the peninsula gives them safety. It is only when the frontier powers fall, that we see the Pandyas asserting themselves. Throughout history the South Indian powers had to oppose the incursion of the Dekhan powers, and from the period of the rise of the Pallavas we can have a clear idea of the general position of the South Indian powers. Varguṇa Pandyan succeeded in chasing the Gangas back into their territory. In another century a new dynasty of the Cholas rise into

1 This was the tract taken from O'ri by his enemy Kāri and given to the Chēra.

eminence and achieve an ascendency, matched only by that of the later empire of Vijayanagar in its best days. The decline of the Cholas again brings into prominence, the Pandya in the south and the Hoyśalas in the north. Both alike of these powers are overwhelmed in that great wave of Muslim invasion under Malik Kāfūr. The Muḥammadan is beaten back by the heroic efforts of a number of chiefs and this movement culminates in the establishment of the Vijayanagar empire in the middle of the fourteenth century. The fall of this empire brings the history of Hindu rule in South India practically to a close, and the Mahrāttā Empire belongs to a different chapter of Indian history.

CHAPTER XV

SOME POINTS IN TAMIL LITERARY HISTORY

IN the *Malabar Quarterly* for March 1904, Mr. K. B. Ramanatha Iyer draws attention to a work of the French savant, Professor Julien Vinson, who offers some remarks on the history of Tamil literature. Mr. Iyer has thus rendered valuable service to the Tamil public, the majority of whom cannot have read the French original. The Professor divides Tamil literary history into three periods: The Jain period the Buddhistic period and the Brahmanic revival in, chronological order. The first period falls between the ninth and the twelfth or the thirteenth centuries; the second between the twelfth and the sixteenth centuries; the third, the period contemporaneous with Vallabha Dēva, *alias* Atī Vīra Rama Pandyan of Madura, and his followers. He ascribes the *Kamba Rāmāyaṇam*, Villiputūrar's *Bhāratam* and the *Sthala Purāṇas* to the third period, namely, that of the Śaiva ascendency. The grammarian Pavaṇandi and the lexicographers, Śēnden and Manḍalapurusha, are given a later date. The most important of all his conclusions in this line is the period ascribed to the *Mahākāvyas* of Tamil, namely, *Chintāmaṇi*, *Śilappadhikāram* and *Maṇimēkhalai*. He is of opinion that the second of these is the earliest in point of time. The first comes next in order; no dates or periods are ascribed to these, and the third is placed later than *Vīraśōḻiyam* of Buddhamitra (end of the eleventh and beginning of the twelfth centuries) because '*Maṇimēkhalai* is not referred to in the work'.

Before proceeding to examine these conclusions in the light of recent research, we might draw attention to another authority in the same line whose conclusions are no less important. Dr. Reinhold Rost's article in the *Encyclopædia Britannica*[1] though seventeen years old now, was not deemed worthy of revision in issuing the supplementary volumes to the same monumental work. It is, therefore, to be presumed that those concerned are of opinion that the conclusions arrived at in the article still hold good. These are its main conclusions in the department of literary history :—

'But practically the earliest extant records of the Tamil language do not ascend higher than the middle of the eighth century of the Christian era, the grants in possession of the Israelites at Cochin being assigned by the late Dr. Burnell to about A. D. 750, a period when Malayalam did not exist yet as a separate language. There is every probability that about the same time a number of Tamil works sprang up, which are mentioned by a writer of the eleventh century as representing old literature.' The article further mentions that the earlier of these might have been Śaiva books, the more important of the others being 'decidedly Jain'. Admitting traces of northern influence, Tamil works are believed to show a spirit of independence of Sanskrit influence. The *Tolkāppiyam*, the oldest Tamil grammar, is ascribed on the authority of Dr. Burnell to the eighth century, the *Vīraśōḻiyam* to the eleventh, and the *Nannūl* which superseded both, to the fifteenth century. 'The period of prevalence of the Jainas in the Pandya kingdom, from the ninth or tenth to the

[1] Vol. xxv.

thirteenth century, is justly termed the Augustan Age of Tamil literature. To its early doings is ascribed the *Nālaḍiyār*, which is supposed to have preceded the *Kuṛaḷ*.' . . *Chintāmaṇi* and the *Divākaram* are also both ascribed to this early Jain period. Kamban's *Rāmāyaṇam* (about A.D. 1100) is the only other Tamil epic which comes up to the *Chintāmaṇi* in poetical beauty. The most brilliant of the poetical productions which appeared in the period of the Śaiva revival (thirteenth and fourteenth centuries) are two collections of hymns addressed to Śiva, the one called *Tiruvāśakam* by Māṇikkavāśagar, and a later and larger work called *Tēvāram* by Sambandar, and two other devotees Sundarar and Appar. 'The *Nālāyiraprabandham* is a collection of Vaishṇava hymns contemporaneous with the former. After a period of literary torpor, which lasted nearly two centuries, king Vallabha Dēva, better known by his assumed name of Atī Vīra Rama Pandyan (second half of the sixteenth century) ,endeavoured to revive the love of poetry, by compositions of his own, the most celebrated of which is *Naiḍadam*. Atī Vīra Raman was followed by a number of imitators, etc. . .'

This, in brief, is the substance of the part of Dr. Reinhold Rost's article dealing with the history of Tamil literature. We shall now proceed to examine the conclusions of these savants, with due deference to the high positions of the authors and with all gratitude for their having led the way in this line of inquiry.

The researches and astronomical calculations of Professor Kielhorn[1] have assigned A.D. 1562-3 as the date of the accession of Atī Vīra Rama Pandyan. If then he marks an era in Tamil literature (he does mark the end of the period of decadence, and the revival under him and his followers may

1 *Epigraphia Indica*, vol. vii, p. 17.

be called the classical period—a period when poetical compositions were made by rule of thumb), it must have begun at the earliest about A.D. 1600. In this there is no cause for dissent. Going back from this date through the two centuries of decadence or literary torpor, we arrive at A.D. 1300. This torpor is to be accounted for by the disturbed state of the country owing to the overthrow of Hindu kingdoms by two waves of Mussalman invasion. According to Dr. Rost then, A.D. 1300 would mark the latter end of the Śaiva revival. And to this period, extending over perhaps a century or more, are ascribed the works of the *Tēvāram* hymners, the Āḻvārs and even Māṇikkavāśagar. Professor Vinson would place the *Maṇimēkhalai* also in this period. *Maṇimēkhalai*, as admitted by the Professor himself, is a Buddhistic work, and we should rather feel inclined not to include it in the Śaiva revival, if there had been such at the period. But of *Maṇimēkhalai* later on. With respect to the others, Māṇikkavāśagar has not yet lent himself to any definite period. Mr. Ḷ. C. Innes[1] placed him in the ninth century, Pundit Vēdanāyagam Pillai[2] in the third century, and Mr. Tirumalaikkoḻundu to a period different from either. But of the *Tēvāram* hymners, Sambandar and Appar were contemporaries; and Sambandar paid a visit to Śiṛuttoṇḍar, another of the sixty-three Śaiva saints. This latter played an important part in the burning of Vātāpi by the Pallavas, which event has been ascribed to Narasimhavarman Pallava in the middle of the seventh century A.D.[3] Therefore it is as good as certain now that Sambandar and Appar lived in the seventh century A.D. As to Sundarar, he was a contemporary of Chēramān, the

[1] *Imperial and Asiatic Quarterly Review*, April, 1902.

[2] *Christian College Magazine*, 1904.

[3] *Epigraphia Indica*, vol. iii, pp. 277 et seq., and other references in page 52, of Miss Duff's *Chronology of India*.

last Perumāḷ, the end of whose reign marks, according to some, at least, the beginning of the Kollam Era, A.D. 825. Whether this date be correct or not, he was certainly prior to Nambi Āṇḍār Nambi, a contemporary of Rājarāja Abhaya Kulasēkhara, *alias* Rāja Kēsarivarman Rāja Rāja A.D. 985-1013.[1] As to the Āḻvār's, all of them were anterior to Rāmānuja, in spite of Dr. Caldwell's statement to the contrary. A glance down the first twenty stanzas of the *Rāmānuja Nūṟṟandādi* (included in the 4000 *Prabandhams*) will show the relation between Rāmānuja and the Āḻvārs. Rāmānuja's date is A.D. 1017–1137 and no grounds have been as yet shown anywhere that I know of, to regard this period as at all improbable, while the evidence in its favour is accumulating. Not only were they merely anterior, but some of them had also been deified generations before him. Nāthamuni, in the fifth generation before him, revived the chanting of Nammāḻvār's *Tiruvāymoḻi* already practised and forgotten.[2] In addition to these considerations, there is forthcoming epigraphical evidence of an unimpeachable character to place the Vaishṇava Āḻvārs and the Śaiva Aḍiyārs much anterior to A.D. 1000. Rājarāja made provision for the recital of the *Tēvāram* in the Tanjore temple.[3] His grandson—a viceroy, of Kongu, made provision for the recital of the works of two of the latest Āḻvārs.[4] About A.D. 1000 images of gods in temples were named after *Tiruvāymoḻi*,[5] the work of Nammaḻvār. The theory of a Śaiva revival from the tenth to the thirteenth centuries will definitely have to be given up.

1 The late Professor Sundaram Pillai's article in the *Christian College Magazine* for 1891.

2 *Srīvaishṇava Guruparamparai* (a chronicle of Vaishṇava high priests).

3 Inscriptions of Rājarāja. Dr. Hultzsch's *South Indian Inscriptions*.

4 Government *Epigraphist's Report* for 1900. Sec. 21.

5 Vol. iii, p. 1, *South Indian Inscriptions*.

This is the period of commentaries and commentators rather than of writers. The revival which these works and their authors mark is a Hindu as opposed a Śaiva revival. And its period is the seventh to the tenth century. It is in the following centuries—under the great Chola ascendency—that the antagonism between the two sects (Śaivas and Vaishṇavas) was getting pronounced. There were even in this period Jains and Buddhists, the former more than the latter, and these were not prevented from composing or writing works. This literary period is, therefore, coeval with the period of the Pallava supremacy in South India, and there is ample internal evidence in the works in support of this conclusion.

As to the date of Kamban's *Rāmāyaṇam* being A.D. 1100, this conclusion appears to be based on the old belief that it was published while a Rājēndra Chola was ruling. This ruler was identified with Kulōttunga Chola I (A.D. 1063–1118). For this statement of contemporaneity there is no authority, and so far as the known circumstances of the author's history go, the date 807 Saka (or A.D. 885) does not appear to be far beside the mark. Here, it may be observed in passing, that in regard to such inquiries it has hitherto been the fashion to discard all local and traditional evidence and accept nothing that has no epigraphical basis. It ought to be remembered in this connexion, that all tradition is not necessarily false. If tradition is interpreted with care and other evidence duly brought to bear upon it, the result will be far from disappointing, and so it is with respect to Kamban. This is not to be understood to mean that all tradition is of equal value and is quite credible. Kamban, I have pointed out elsewhere,[1] could have had no royal

[1] *Christian College Magazine*, 1902. This line of argument for Kamban is not warranted by later research. His date is probably the middle of the twelfth century A.D.

patron, for he celebrates none, while he had a patron in a lesser mortal Saḍaiappa Mudaliar. He was a contemporary of Nāthamuni who lived five generations before Rāmānuja in point of lineage. The time occupied by these five generations, if we accept the year A.D. 885, would be one hundred and twenty years and this is not improbable. Therefore Kamban may safely be referred to the ninth century A.D. One characteristic feature of this period deserves to be noticed here. It is that the metre adopted by poets during this period is what is called Viruttam (Sans-Vritta). All the accepted Śaṅgam or earlier works are either in Ahaval or Veṅba metre. This would lead us to place the *Chintāmaṇi* at the commencement of this period, because it is a masterpiece in this line of composition and was, by tradition, the model for Kamban's *Rāmāyaṇam*. We have also reason to regard this as the period of great activity among the Jains. One reason chiefly insisted on by Pandit Vēdanāyagam for placing Māṇikkavāśagar in the third century is the transition we could notice in his works from the earlier metre to the later, as stated above.[1]

Before the seventh century A.D., then, we shall have to look for the early period of Tamil literature—to be called appropriately the Augustan Age—the age, that is, of great patrons. This is also the period of Śaṅgam activity. This is the period which has given us all the most important works extant in Tamil—*Śilappadhikāram*, *Maṇimēkhalai*, *Pattuppāṭṭu*, *Padiṟṟuppattu* and a number of others. The *Tolkāppiyam* is generally the grammar on which these works are based. I have set forth in full (in chapter xiv), the arguments in favour of regarding the early centuries of the Christian era—or more precisely the second and the first half of the third centuries—as the Augustan

[1] An Article in the *Christian College Magazine*, 1904.

Age. There is internal and external evidence in support of this conclusion in the works mentioned above and others of the time. Whether this actual conclusion, which I have arrived at (which is more or less in agreement with those of Mr. Kanakasabhai Pillai and the Hon'ble Mr. Kumaraswami of Ceylon), be the correct one or not, the day is long past when the works—the *Śilappadhikāram*, *Maṇimēkhalai* and the *Kuṛal*, can be ascribed to the period between the ninth and twelfth centuries A. D. *Śilappadhikāram* was composed by Iḷangō, the Chēra ascetic prince the younger brother of Śenguṭṭuvan, the reigning king; *Maṇimēkhalai* by his friend the corn-merchant Śāttan of Madura held in high esteem at the court of Śenguṭṭuvan at Vanji or Karūr (known at different times and circumstances, Koḍungalūr, Mahāudiyarpaṭṭaṇam, Vanjikuḷam, etc.); the *Kuṛaḷ* of Tiruvaḷḷuvar is quoted by the two authors, and as such, it must have been well known at the time. This king Śenguṭṭuvan had a contemporary ruler, by name Gajabāhu, of Ceylon, who was an honoured guest at his court. Which of the Gajabāhus of the Ceylonese Chronicle is this personage to be identified with? That the Chronicle is not a history in the modern sense of the term does not admit of doubt. Dr. Fleet[1] is of opinion that the very names in the Chronicle are not correct and much less, therefore, the dates. Professor Rhys Davids, on the contrary, finds the Chronicle borne out in important details by inscriptions in the Sanchi Tope.[2] For our present purpose, we find, in the whole list of kings in the *Mahāvamśa*, only two rulers of the name of Gajabāhu, one in the eleventh century A. D., and the earlier in the second century A. D. The reasons for identifying this Gajabāhu, the friend of

[1] Footnote, p. 16, *Journal of the Royal Asiatic Society*, 1904.
[2] *Buddhistic India*, pp. 299, 300 et seq.

Śeṅguṭṭuvan, with the first of the name, have been set forth in full in chapter xiv. It will be enough to state them briefly here: (1) The state of things as gathered from the works themselves shows that Tamil was the language of Chēra at the time. Mr. Logan has pointed out in the *Manual of Malabar* that in the latter half of the eighth and the earlier half of the ninth centuries Malayalam was in the making.[1] The work, therefore, must have been composed much anterior to the eleventh century A. D., the date of Gajabāhu II. (2) These works must have been much anterior to the *Kalingattuparaṇi* celebrating the conquest (rather the re-conquest) of Kalingam by the Pallava General Karuṇākara Toṇḍamān of Vaṇḍalūr for the Chola Kulōttunga. This event is placed by the late Professor Sundaram Pillai at about A. D. 1080.[2] In the genealogy of the Cholas given by the author, the Karikāla of the *Paṭṭinappalai* is placed much anterior to the ninth century A. D., and Dr. Hultzsch admits that he must have belonged to a dynasty anterior to that whose epigraphical records have come down to us.[3] (3) Sundaramūrti Nāyanār refers to Pāri of Parambunāḍu (one of the last seven patrons celebrated in the Śiṟupāṇāṟṟuppaḍai) whose name had, by the time the Nāyānar flourished, become proverbial for liberality. (4) The Śaṅgam is said by tradition to have passed out of existence in the reign of Kūn Pandya, *alias* Niṉṟa Śīr Nēḍumāran, the contemporary and convert of Gñāna Sambanda (in the seventh century) who was one of the Śaiva leaders of the Hindu revival. The works under consideration are Śaṅgam works—in the sense that they were either accepted by the Śaṅgam or were composed at the time as could be clearly made out. (5) Mahānāman, the

[1] By comparing the language of the three Syrian Christian Grants.

[2] *Christian College Magazine*, for 1891. Actual date about A. D. 1111.

[3] *South Indian Inscriptions*, vol. ii.

author of the *Mahāvamśa*, be he Sthāvira Mahānāman the first of the name (A. D. 538), or the second (A. D. 588),[1] mentions a Gajabāhu anterior to him. Whatever may be the actual date of Gajabāhu he must have flourished before the sixth century and perhaps much earlier. This is borne out by the fact that the Pallavas were gaining the ascendency in Southern India about this time and the Śaṅgam works do not show any trace of this ascendency. (6) The Chola capital was Kaveripūmbaṭṭinam, with the alternative Uraiyūr, and there is nothing of Tanjore or Gangaikoṇḍa Sōḷapuram, the capitals during the Chola Ascendency Period (A. D. 900–1300 nearly). (7) There are abundant allusions and references, which can be explained only on the assumption of the Śātavāhana rulers of the Dekhan and their wars with the Kshētrapas. The Śātavāhana power came to an end about the middle of the third century A. D.[2] These would warrant our regarding the Augustan Age—an age of great Buddhistic influence—to be coeval with the early centuries of the Christian Era, that is, A. D. 100–300 at the latest.

One word more about *Maṇimēkhalai*. Professor Vinson opines that this work must have been of a later period than *Vīraśōḻiyam*, because the latter work makes no mention of it. It would be equally sound to say that the *Śilappadhikāram* must have been composed after the days of Nachchinārkiniyar, as the great commentator has not commented on the work. This opinion of the learned Professor would have been received with respect had it not been that there is ample evidence of the two—*Śilappadhikāram* and *Maṇimēkhalai*—being companion works. The commentator of the former explains the connexion between the two and gives all the references in page ten of

[1] Footnote, p. 16, *Journal of the Royal Asiatic Society*, 1904

[2] Dr. Bhandarkar's *Early History of the Dekhan*.

Pundit Swaminatha Iyer's edition. Further, the introductory passage to the work states clearly that the corn merchant Śāttan it was, that induced the ascetic to take up the work, and the closing passage refers to its having been read out to him. All this apart, *Śilappadhikāram* alone would be a defective composition according to the rules of epic composition but for the supplementary *Maṇimēkhalai*. The first has reference only to the first three of the four objects of life, and the second deals with the fourth. If these were not enough, the same Chēra and the Chola rulers figure in both the works, and all traditional and other accounts agree in ascribing the latter to Śāttan, the corn-merchant of Madura, who, as the critic *par excellence* of the Śaṅgam used to plant his stile into his head every time he had 'the misfortune' to detect an error in works submitted to the Śaṅgam. The fact that one author of the eleventh or twelfth century does not mention a work of a number of centuries earlier is, at the best, very unreliable as evidence of relative chronology. There is a verse in praise of *Maṇimēkhalai*, ascribed to Ambikhāpathi the son of poet Kamban; and Śivaprakāsa Swami, a Śaiva of much later times, refers to the same work in glowing terms. Buddhamitra might not have known the work, or much rather, might not have seen occasion to mention it or refer to it.

It is high time that these time-honoured theories were given up and the question be approached with the disengagement demanded by historical research. The fact that we have not as yet come across inscriptions of a period earlier than the fifth century of the Christian era, leads to the inference in certain quarters, that the alphabets were not known in South India before the third century A. D. Most of the inscriptions we know of, are inscriptions found in temples, and the great majority of temples were built and old ones were endowed after the overthrow of the Buddhistic ascendency in the South. Literature till recently, was handed down mostly by word of mouth, though the stile and the palmyra leaf were often called into requisition as a valuable auxiliary. It will be some time before the literary history of the Tamil language attains definiteness but there is good reason to hope that the trend of it will be along the lines indicated above.

CHAPTER XVI

SELF-IMMOLATION WHICH IS NOT SATI

It is an undoubted fact in India, that self-immolation was practised from time immemorial, in one shape or another, the motive having been sometimes spiritual, but often entirely personal. The universally known practice called sati, where a woman burnt herself on the pyre of her husband, was only one form of it. Whether the practice was Dravidian or Aryan in origin, we have instances of it occurring pretty frequently in South India. The earliest known, of an historical character, is the death of the wife of Bhūta Pandya, an early celebrity in Tamil Literature. One poem ascribed to her is to be found in the collection known as the *Puranāṇūṛu.* That self-immolation was not confined to women who had become widowed, but was common even among men, sometimes great warriors or learned Brahmans, is amply borne out by the great epics of India and the lesser ones alike. Arjuna was about to slay himself more than once, but the supreme example is that of Bharata, the younger brother of Rāma, who was saved by the arrival of Hanumān with the happy message of Rāma, just at the moment of entering the sacrificial-fire. It is of self-immolation within historical times that I shall concern myself here.

There is a numerous class of archæological monuments in South India, known as Vīrakkal and Māstikkal. The latter term represents *Mahāsati-kal,* i. e. a stone erected in memory of one who performed a *mahāsati,* or act of self-immolation by a woman on the pyre of her husband. The former is a stone erected in memory of a man who displayed valour, either on the field of battle or by some other act of personal courage. The erection of memorial stones in honour of a fallen hero is as old as the days of the *Kuṛaḷ*, i. e. at least as early as the initial centuries of the Christian era, and there are innumerable examples scattered through the Mysore Province. There are, nevertheless, others recording cases of self-immolation, which were the result of a vow, and in the volumes of the *Epigraphia Carnāṭaka* brought out by Mr. Rice, a number of inscriptions on these memorial stones have been brought to light. Most of them record acts performed in pursuance of vows rather of a civil than of a religious nature.

That religion did indeed sanction self-immolation is borne out by the belief that such acts always forced open the gates of heaven to receive the performers, in spite of the cynical proverb that 'no one ought to pull out his tongue to die on an ekādaśī day,'[1] and of the popular notion that the suicide cannot go to heaven, except by spending the rest of his allotted earthly span as a wandering devil, hovering about his usual habitat. Notwithstanding these beliefs, we have numerous instances of Jains performing the act of sallēkhana, i. e. death brought on by starvation. The Chāḷukya emperor Āhavamalla Sōmēsvara, when attacked with a malignant fever, 'went to Svarga (heaven)' by plunging into the Tungabhadrā after a regular confession of faith in Śiva. In the sallēkhana ceremony, men and women alike took part and devoted themselves to contemplation of the divinity for days without food or water, and we have numbers of instances in the Śravaṇa Beḷagoḷa Records. I now give a number of

[1] The eleventh day after full or new moon, regarded as a particularly good day on which to die.

instances of men putting an end to themselves without any direct motive of religion, although faith, such as it was, did underlie most of the acts.

Two inscriptions found in the Arkalgūd Tāluq in the Hassan district record instances of friends having thrown themselves into the fire out of sorrow for their late masters, the Ganga kings Nītimārgga and Satya Vākya, respectively. A third case to the point is given in an inscription in Kadur, dated about A. D. 1180. The governor of Āsandināḍ died, or, as the inscription has it, 'laid siege to Indra's Amarāvatī'. On this Bammayya Nāyaka, the slave of Sankamalē, 'showed the way to Svarga'. The next instance, Maśaṇayya's younger brother Boppaṇṇa, 'making good his word for the occasion', went to heaven on the death of Tailappa, the ruler of Banavāse, etc., in A. D. 1030. What the occasion was and why he took this vow is not vouchsafed to us to know. Perhaps, it was a vow that the minister's brother took to show his attachment to his sovereign. Such vows, once made, were apparently not merely expected to be carried out; but sometimes the votary was asked to make good his word, as in the following instance. In the fifth year of Tribhuvanamalla Vīra Somēsvara, i. e. A. D. 1185 his senior queen Lachchaḷa Dēvī went to heaven. Bōka, an officer of the king, had previously taken a vow: 'I will die with the Dēvī.' 'On his master calling him, saying, "you are the brave man who with resolution have spoken of taking off your head," with no light courage, Bōka gave his head, while the world applauded, saying "He did so at the very instant". The word spoken with full resolve is not to be broken.'

The next instance I have to exhibit, records a vow taken even without a personal motive, as in the preceding cases. A certain Tuḷuva, Chanḍiya, took a vow 'not to let his finger-nails grow', if the Banavāse Fort should be disposed of in a manner he did not approve of. It so happened that Baḷḷavarasa and Satyāśraya Dēva jointly made a grant of the fort and a temple endowment in the twelve-thousand country. Upon this the Tuḷuva, Chanḍiya, 'cutting off the finger which he had given at the Permāḷu temple and climbing the Bhērunḍēsvara Pillar leaped upon the point of a spear and gained the world of gods.'

Here is another vow made from an entirely different motive. Votive offerings of the nature of that following are made nowadays also, but by the person who is the direct recipient of the favour sought. This case is, however, peculiar from the fact that the vow was taken, not by the party directly concerned, but by a friend. In A. D. 1123 while Vikramāditya VI was emperor, and his governor of Banavāse was Ramayya, the Mahāśāmanta (great lord) Bopparasa and his wife Śiriyā Dēvī, surrounded by all the subjects, were in the temple at the rice-fields, the cowherd, Mārana's son Dēki Nāyaka, made a vow, saying: 'If the king obtain a son, I will give my head to swing on the pole for the God of Konḍaśabhāvi. . . .' This is nothing more, so far as the details of the deed are concerned, than the hook-swinging of modern times, but, as has been pointed out above, the vow is taken by an attendant and not by the principal party.

All these instances show clearly that, when there was enough attachment to persons, or even to ideas, the people of India did not display much respect for life, but showed themselves ready to offer 'even the most precious thing on earth, as though it were a careless trifle.' The supreme instance of such throwing away of the most precious thing was the suicide, purely from personal affection, of the general of Vīra Beḷḷāḷa, Kuvara Lakshmaṇa (or Kumāra Lakshma) with his wife Suggalā Dēvī and the army which was attached to him (at least of a select part of it). Kuvara Lakshma was both minister and general of Vīra Beḷḷāḷa and cherished by him as his son. 'Between servant and king there was no difference; the glory and marks of royalty were equal in both.' 'His wealth and his life Kuvara Lakshma devoted for the gifts and victories of Vīra Beḷḷāḷa Dēva, and conquered the world for him as far as the southern ocean.' His wife was Suggalā Dēvī, who also wore a *toḍar* (a hollow anklet, with pebbles or precious stones inside) like the husband, as a mark of her unswerving devotion to her lord. He had a company of a thousand warriors, vowed to live and die with him. He set up a vīra śāsana (which is recorded on a pillar near the Hoysalēśvara temple at Haḷēbīd), on which are placed images of himself and Garuḍa, indicating the latter alone as his equal in devotion to his master. 'While all the world was praising him as the founder of the greatness and increase of king Beḷḷāḷa and the cause of his prosperity, the Danḍēsa Lakshma, together with his wife, mounted upon the splendid stone pillar, covered with the poetical vīra śāsana, proclaiming his devotion to his master: and on the pillar they became united with Lakshmi and with Garuḍa.' The inscription is left incomplete, but the sculptures on the pillar, being all figures of men with swords, cutting off their own arms and legs, and even their own heads, indicate unmistakably what had been done. This example was followed by others, and acts of such wholesale immolation are on record on the occasion of the death of each of the warlike successors of Vīra Beḷḷāḷa.

Useless waste of life as this appears to us, and entirely needless to demonstrate faithful attachment, it still shows a depth of devotion and a sacrifice of that most precious legacy, life in this world, which ought to evoke the admiration of all, however misguided was the zeal in a cause hardly calling for the sacrifice.

CHAPTER XVII

THE AGNIKULA: THE FIRE-RACE

In one of his interesting contributions entitled *Some Problems of Ancient Indian History*, published in the *Journal of the Royal Asiatic Society*, 1905, p. 1 ff., Dr. Hoernle regards the Paramāra Rājputs as the only family that laid claim to belong to the Agnikula or Fire-race before the time of the poet Chand (loc. cit., p. 20), and, so far, the evidence all seems to point to any such claim not being found earlier than the middle of the eleventh century. That, however, does not preclude an earlier existence of the legend. It would be interesting, therefore, if the legend could be traced to an earlier period than that of the Paramāras of Mālva. In the early classical literature of the Tamils, there is a reference to this same legend, and there appears to have been in that part of India a family of ancient chiefs who claimed descent from the sacrificial fire.

There have been in the Tamil land a certain number of chiefs, whose names have been handed down to posterity as the Last Seven Patrons of Letters, the patron *par excellence* among them having been Pāri of Paṛambunāḍu. This chief had a life-long friend in the person of a highly esteemed Brahman, Kapilar, who was a poet *sui generis* in a particular department of the poetical art. 'The three crowned kings of the south,'—the Chēra, the Chola, and the Pandya,—growing jealous of the power and prosperity of Pāri as a patron of poets, laid siege conjointly to his hill-fort, Muḷḷūr. Pāri having fallen a victim to this combination, it fell to the lot of his Brahman friend to get his daughters suitably married, to bring about acceptable marriages being one of the six special duties of Brahmans in the social system. He, therefore, took the girls over successively to two chiefs, Vichchikkōn and Puli Kaḍi Māl Iṛungōvēḷ of Aṛayam. This latter chief is addressed by the poet in these terms: 'Having come out of the sacrificial fire-pit of the Rishi—having ruled over the camp of Dvārapati, whose high walls looked as though they were built of copper—having come after forty-nine generations of patrons never disgusted with giving—thou art the patron among patrons.'[1] The allusion to the coming out of the sacrificial fire of the sage cannot but refer to the same incident as the other versions discussed by Dr. Hoernle. The chief thus addressed was a petty chief of a place called Aṛayam, composed of the smaller and the larger cities of that name, in the western hill-country, somewhere in the regions of the Western Ghāts in Mysore.

The more important question, exactly relevant to the discussion, is: What is the time of this author and his hero? This has, so far, reference to times anterior to epigraphical records, and has therefore to be considered on literary data alone. This poet, Kapilar, is connected with a number of chiefs and kings, and is one of a galaxy of poets of high fame in classical Tamil literature. According to the *Tiruviḷaiyāḍal Purāṇam*, Kapilar was born in Tiruvādavūr, and was a Brahman by birth. The tradition that he was one of the seven children of the Brahman Bhagavān, through the non-caste woman Àdi, is not well supported by reliable literary evidence. But if this tradition be true (there are some inconsistent elements in it), he must have been the brother of Tiruvaḷḷuvar, the author of the *Kuṛaḷ*, and of the poetess Avvaiyār. This

1 *Puṛanāṉūṛu*, 200, 201. Pandit Swaminatha Iyer's Edition.

relationship, however, is nowhere in evidence in contemporary literature.

So far as they are available at present, his works, all of them being a 'Paradise of Dainty Devices' in Tamil literature, are :—

1. The seventh of the *Padiṟṟuppattu*, the *Ten-Tens*, in praise of the Chēramān Śelvakkaḍuṅgōvāḻiyādan.

2. *Kuriñjippāṭṭu* of Pattuppāṭṭu, the *Ten-Idylls*, to teach Brahasta, the Aryan king, Tamil.

3. *Aiṅguṟunūṟu, Kuriñji Section*, the whole anthology having been collected and brought out by Kūḍalūr Kiḻār for the Chēra 'Prince of the Elephant-eye' (Yânaikkaṭchēy).

4. *Inna*, 'that which is evil and as such to be avoided,' 40.

5. Twenty stanzas in *Naṟṟiṇai*, 29 in *Kurunthogai*, 16 in *Ahanānūṟu*, and 31 in *Puṟanānūṟu*.

Kapilar appears, from his works, and from the high esteem in which he was held by his contemporaries, poets and potentates, and from the great approval with which he is quoted by grammarians and commentators alike, to have been a specialist in composing poems relating to *Kuriñji*, i.e. the hill-country, this being the scene of the inward feelings evoked, such as love, and the outward action induced by inward feelings. As to details of his life, we have but little information. Of course, he sang in praise of the Chēramān Śēlvakkaḍuṅgō, and received a large reward. Otherwise, he appears to have been the life-long guest and intimate friend of his patron, Pāri of Paṟambunāḍu. It was after the death of this chief that the poet went about with his daughters to obtain for them eligible husbands, and that the allusive reference to the Agnikula descent was made for Iṟungōvēḷ.

This Pāri of Paṟambunāḍu was one of the Seven Patrons, besides the Three Kings, who flourished about the same generation in South India.[1] All these are celebrated in the poem called Sirupāṇāṟṟuppaḍai of Nallūr Nattattanār, who sang in praise of Ērumānāṭṭu Nalliyakkōḍan, as a more liberal patron than the Three Kings and the Seven Patrons. These poems are rhapsodies of a Homeric character, sung on occasions by wandering minstrels, who received sumptuous rewards for their labour. The plan of the Sirupāṇ is that a wandering minstrel is at a loss to know where he could find a patron; and another, returning from the court of the patron, solves the puzzle by pointing to the particular personage who is the object of praise. As a rule, therefore, these poems are directly addressed to the patron by the poet. And this circumstance makes them of great importance for purposes of the history and social condition of those times. Unfortunately, however, the author does not mention the Three Kings by any specific names—a matter of indifference to them, as they could not have had any idea of the rise of laborious students of history among their posterity. But the Seven Patrons are referred to specifically enough. And certain of the details relating to the kings themselves give important clues. The Seven Patrons are, in the order given by the poet: Pēhan, round about the Paḷnis; Pāri, along the Western Ghāts further north; Kāri, round about Tirukkōvalūr in South Arcot; Āay, round about Padiyil Hill in the west of Tinnevelly; Adiyamān of Tagaḍūr, either the place of that name in the Mysore country or Dharmapuri preferably[2]; Naḷḷi, of Malanāḍu (there is nothing else by which to fix his exact locality); and Ōri, with his territory round about Kolli Malai in Salem. The Chola is associated with Uraiyūr, and the Chēra with Vanji, specifically, and not in the gencral terms in

[1] *Pattupāttu*, Pandit Swaminatha Iyer's Edition, 3rd Poem.

[2] See *Indian Antiquary*, vol. xxii, pp. 66 and 143, and *Epigraphia Indica*, vol. vi, p. 331.

which the Mahārājas of Travancore are nowadays styled.

Kapilar is generally associated with Paraṇar; and the two together are usually spoken of by the elder commentators Kapila-Paraṇar. That this is due to contemporaneousness, is proved by the fact that Kapilar was an elder contemporary of 'the Chēra of the Elephant-look' in whose reign the *Aiṅguṛunūṛu* collection, of which Kapilar composed the third part, was made by Kūḍalūr Kiḻar, a Śaṅgam celebrity. Further, both these poets, Kapilar and Paraṇar, interceded with Pēhan on behalf of his wife when he deserted her in favour of a sweetheart. Thus, then, Kapilar and Paraṇar were contemporaries, and the latter celebrated Śeṅguṭṭuvan Śēra in the third section of the *Ten-Tens.* This, therefore, takes the Agnikula tradition to the age of Śeṅguṭṭuvan, who was the grandson of Karikāla-Chola. This Karikāla is placed in the Leyden Grant and in the *Kalingattupparaṇi* far anterior to Parāntaka I; and the *Śilappadhikāram* itself makes Śeṅguṭṭuvan the contemporary of a Gajabāhu of Ceylon, whose date is held to be A. D. 113–135.

The name of Pāri had become proverbial for liberality in the days of Sundaramūrti-Nāyanār. This latter must have lived centuries before Rājarāja the Great, as some of his grants make donations to the image of the Nāyanār. It was Rājarāja's contemporary, Nambi Āṇḍār Nambi, who elaborated the *Tiruttoṇḍattogai* of Sundara. On these and other considerations, Sundaramūrti has been allotted to the eighth century of the Christian era, and therefore Kapilar and others have to be looked for at a respectable distance anterior to this. For, between the date of Sundara and the fifth century A. D., the Pallavas of Kānchī occupied the premier position in South India, and there is absolutely no reference to this in the body of the literature to which the works under consideration belong.

The Chēra capital, as given in all these works, is Vanji, on the west coast, at the mouth of the Periyār; while the Chola capital was Uraiyūr. In the later period, from the days of Kulaśēkharāḻvār, the Chēra capital certainly was Quilon. This change is said to have taken place, according to tradition, after the days of Chēramān-Perumāḷ, who was a contemporary of Sundara. Besides this, the language of the whole of the south was Tamil; Malayāḷam had not yet become differentiated from it. These considerations, again, would lead us to refer Kapilar and the galaxy to a period anterior to the seventh century, according to even the most unfavourable estimate. But, in point of fact, the time referred to is much earlier than this. The contemporaneousness of Gajabāhu refers the period of Kapilar to the second century A. D.; and this, so far, has not been shown to be incorrect. There was at any rate a king Gajabāhu previous to the days of Mahānāman, the author of the earlier part of the *Mahāvamśa*.

Thus, then, the tradition of a race of rulers whose eponymous ancestor was born from the sacrificial fire of a Rishi is far older than the period for which Dr. Hoernle has found authority. This does not necessitate the affiliation of the one dynasty to the other. It only shows that the legend is very much older, and might have been laid hold of by ruling families at great distances, and otherwise unconnected, for the embellishment of their genealogies, just as in the case of the heroic Greeks of yore.

CHAPTER XVIII

THE AGE OF NAMMĀḺVĀR

UNDER the unpretentious heading *Some Points in the Archæological Report for 1902-3*, Mr. Pichaimuttu, B.A., L.T., discusses in the pages of the *Christian College Magazine* for February, 1904, the date of Nammāḻvār, one of the twelve Vaishṇava saints of Southern India and arrives at the conclusion that 'it is likely he lived in the ninth century A.D.' Mr. Gopinatha Rao, M.A., arrives at the same conclusion by another line of argument. This conclusion, if correct, would be another mile-stone in Tamil literary history, and it will be excused if I venture in the same field and offer a few of my own observations on the same subject, having had occasion to study some parts at least of the literature bearing on this question. Before, however, proceeding to state my own views on the question, it will be well to pass in review the arguments adduced in favour of the conclusions already arrived at by those that have preceded me in this question.

Mr. Pichaimuttu arrives at his conclusion from the following considerations:—

'The works of Nammāḻvār are called *Drāviḍa Veda.* Madurakavi had them published and established their sacredness before a council of 300 men under the presidency of the royal poet, Kamba Nāṭṭāḻvār, during the Śaṅga days of the Pandya kings.' 'It is popularly supposed that Kambanāḍan visited the Pandya capital of Madura. It is likely that, in one of his visits, he approved of the works of Nammāḷvār, a descendant of the Pandya kings.' Mr. Pichaimuttu further observes that there was a Vaishṇava revival between the eighth and the eleventh centuries A. D. 'Before that the prevailing religion of South India was the Śaivitic religion. Before the days of Māṇikkavāśagar, the Pandya and Īḷa kings were Buddhists.'

Mr. Gopinatha Rao whose article appeared in a recent number of *Śeṅ Tamil*, the organ of the Madura Tamil Śaṅgam, argued that, as Nāthamuni learnt the *Tiruvōymoḷi* from Madurakavi, the disciple of Nammāḷvār, this last and Nāthamuni must have been contemporaneous, and inferred the ninth century A. D. from the recognized contemporaneity of Kamban and Nāthamuni.

Pending a fuller examination of the history of the Āḷvārs, which I hope to find time to make at an early date, I may here examine these considerations adduced as making for the ninth century A. D., as the epoch of this Āḷvār, one of the oldest and, in fact, the greatest among the Āḷvārs, and suggest what appears to me the more probable age of Nammāḷvār.

To take up Mr. Gopinatha Rao's case first, it is no doubt true according to the *Guruparamparai* (the traditional chronicle of successive gurus of the Vaishṇavas) that Nāthamuni the first of the Āchāryas (preceptors as opposed to the Āḷvārs or saints) went to Āḷvār Tirunagari to gain a knowledge of the *Tiruvōymoḷi* (the sacred word of Nammāḷvār) not from the Āḷvār or his disciple but to learn it from any one that knew it, having failed to obtain knowledge of it from every other probable source of the knowledge. This had been published and learnt up largely for a time; but had fallen into desuetude. Nāthamuni attempted a revival. No doubt the story has it that he got it at last from Nammāḷvār and Madurakavi both appearing to him for this special purpose. Long before the days of Nāthamuni, the latest of the Āḻvārs, Tirumangaimannan had built a shrine and arranged for the recital of the *Tiruvōymoḻi* in Srīrangam. This arrangement having been allowed to fall into desuetude, Nāthamuni had to revive it and for this very purpose he had to make the pilgrimage to Āḻvār Tirunagari. I shall show other reasons for regarding the view as being untenable and will take up the other case for consideration.

Nammāḻvār's works are not merely called, by the courtesy of posterity, the *Drāviḍa Veda,* but are professedly the rendering of the Vedas in Tamil. The *Tiruvōymoḻi* 1,000 being the substance of the Sāma Veda, the *Tiruviruttam* 100, the *Tiruvaśiriyam* 7 and *Periyatiruvandādi* 100 are respectively the rendering, in brief, of the Rig, Yajus and Atharva Veda.

According to tradition no doubt Madurakavi published the *Tiruvōymoḻi* and may have got its sacredness acknowledged in the Śaṅgam Assembly—but certainly not under the presidency of Kamban, for Kamban never did preside, nor ever could have, over the Śaṅgam, as will presently be shown.

Kamban, the author of the *Rāmāyaṇam,* often refers in the course of his work to a patron, not a royal sovereign, but a plain Mudaliar by name Saḍayappah of Veṇṇainallūr. It is highly improbable that, if ever he had a royal patron, he would not have mentioned his name, while he systematically refers to Saḍayappah at regular intervals. Again so far as I know the story, he is said to have betaken himself to the Chēra court and not to the Pandya, but the details of the story stamp it as untrue in the main. Even according to tradition the Śaṅgam is said to have gone out of existence with Kūn Pandya or Sundara Pandya or Neḍumāran the contemporary and disciple of Tirugñāna Sambanda (seventh century A.D.).

If Kamban was ever in a position to preside over the Śaṅgam, how was it that he had to wander from place to place seeking approval for his *Rāmāyaṇam*? He had to get the approval of the 3,000 Brahmans of Chidambaram and of the assembly of divines at Srīrangam. Over this assembly presided Nāthamuni, and it was to please him and his *confrères* that he had to compose and recite the *Shaḍagōparandādi* 100 in praise of Nammāḻvār. In the face of this work, it is passing strange that the two gentlemen should have so thoroughly ṃistaken the relation of Kamban to Nammāḻvār.

Further Mr. Pichaimuttu states that there was a Vaishṇava revival between the eighth and the eleventh centuries A. D. It may be so, but what is there to connect the Āḻvārs with this revival? It is, to say the least, misleading to state that the prevailing religion before that time was Śaiva. If it does nothing else, this begs the question. We have abundant reference to Vaishṇavas and their temples much anterior to this, not only in literature but also in inscriptions. Not to mention others Kōchengaṅ Chola built temples to Vishṇu and Śiva alike; and this could not have been merely for theoretical impartiality without a practical demand. Paramēsvara Varman Pallava and his grandfather built temples to Vishṇu at Kānchī and Mahābalipuram. That the Pandya and Īḻa kings were Buddhist before the days of Māṇikkavāśagar proves nothing in this connexion, as in fact Kūn Pandya was a Buddhist. The fact is that from very early times the votaries of these different religions lived together, and it did not make much difference generally what the particular persuasion of the ruler for the time being was.

To return to Nammāḻvār. I have already pointed out that Nammāḻvār's works had long been published and had acquired wide celebrity, but could not be obtained in the days of Nāthamuni except at the Āḻvār's birthplace. In those days this celebrity could not have been attained in a short period of time. Nāthamuni was, according to tradition, the contemporary of Kamban whose work *Shaḍagōparandādi* deifies the Āḻvār. This circumstance again suggests considerable lapse of time. Rāmānuja, the famous reformer of the Vaishṇavas, came in the fifth generation from Nāthamuni, not in official succession only but also in actual descent; and Rāmānuja's life, A. D. 1017–1137, is coeval with the Chola ascendency in Southern India. Therefore, we must assign Nāthamuni at least to a century earlier, and this brings us quite close to the traditional Saka 807 (A. D. 885) for Kamban's *Rāmāyaṇam*. No sound argument against this date for Kamban has, so far as I know, been brought forward except the statement that the Chola ruler at the time was a Rājēndra (identified with Kulōttunga I).[1] The name Rājēndra is so common among the rulers of the Chola dynasty that we cannot at all be positive as to which personage it actually refers to without extraneous support. Even for this mere statement there is no very good authority. If then Nāthamuni lived about A. D. 900 we must go back for Tirumangai Āḻvār a century or two, so as to allow time for his arrangements at Srīrangam for the worship of Nammāḻvār to fall into desuetude. We must go back again from this time for Nammāḻvār, if already he had become a saint worthy of being worshipped in a public place of worship of the dignity of 'The Temple' of the Vaishṇavas (Srīrangam).

Reserving a fuller examination of Tirumangai Āḻvār's history for a future occasion, it is quite in place to remark here that his and Kulaśēkharāḻvār's works were considered of sufficient sanctity to warrant provision

[1] *Vide* ante note on p. 378.

being made for their recital by Prince Chola Kērala, viceroy of Kongu about A. D. 1050. This apart, one of the most unfamiliar of the birudas or titles of Tirumangai Āḻvār had already become a name assumed by Vaishṇavas, as we have Araṭṭamukkidāsan among the inscriptions of Rājarāja II about A. D. 1150. To crown all, there are inscriptions in the temple at Ukkal near Māmaṇḍūr dated about A. D. 1000, which gives the name of the God as Tiruvōymoḻi Dēva. *Tiruvōymoḻi* is the work *sui generis* of Nammāḻvār, and that a god should be named after it speaks for considerable antiquity. Dr. Hultzsch is of opinion that 'Nammāḻvār must have lived centuries before A.D. 1000.'

Coupled with these considerations, there is the fact that Nammāḻvār deliberately worked at popularizing the 'hidden lore' the Vedas. This could have been only when the Dravidian Hindus were preparing for the supersession of Buddhism by Brahmanism, no more to be the recondite lore of the learned Brahmans only. This theory finds powerful support in the fact that the works of Nammāḻvār, in comparison with those of later Āḻvārs, are peculiarly free from any caustic reflections on the Śaivas. Under the circumstances, I am inclined to think that we shall have to look for the age of Nammāḻvār in the period of struggle between Buddhism and Brahmanism for mastery in South India, and that period is between A. D. 500 and 700.

CHAPTER XIX

TIRUMANGAI ĀḺVĀR AND HIS DATE

PARADOXICAL as it may seem, it is nevertheless the fact that, although a great deal has been written concerning the Vaishṇava saints and devotees, their history has yet to be written. There has, unfortunately, been too great a tendency in the writers, great and small, to refer them to periods, more as it suited their preconceived notions as to the recent origin of Vaishṇavaism in general, than on any dispassionate examination of such evidence, imperfect in its nature of course, as is available. It would not be going over quite a beaten track to bring together here such historical information as has been brought to light, setting aside the extreme Śaiva arguments of Tirumalaikkoḻundu Pillai and his school on the one side, and the ardent Vaishṇava view of A. Govinda Charlu and his school on the other. This is not because I do not appreciate their learning, but because the one school would deem nothing impossible of belief, while the other would see nothing that could not be made to lend itself to giving the most ancient of these saints a date somewhere about the end of the first millennium after Christ. Gopinatha Rao belongs to a different school, and in his recent ambitious attempt (in the *Madras Review* for 1905) at a history of Vaishṇavaism in South India, he has come to certain conclusions, which would certainly have commanded assent, but for a too transparent tendency to establish certain conclusions.

Without pretending to say the last word on the subject, I shall merely put forward certain facts and arguments I have been able to gather in my studies, and the notes that I have made from the writings of some of my friends, who have been pursuing similar research, and leave it to my readers to draw their own conclusions, while not depriving myself of the pleasure of making such inferences as appear to me warranted. I may at the outset acknowledge my obligations to my friend, Pandit Raghavaiyangar, Assistant Editor of the *Śeṅ Tamil*, who has with remarkable courtesy placed some of his notes at my disposal, and has been of great help to me in looking up references to literature.

The Vaishṇavas, like their *confrères* of other sects, trace their hierarchy of gurus (preceptors in religion) from God himself. Putting the translunary part on one side, and coming down to terra firma, their list consists of names divided into two broad classes, entitled, in Vaishṇava parlance, the Āḷvārs and Āchāryas. There are twelve among the former, and a large number among the latter, which is being added to by each separate sect or unit at the decease of the existing guru for the time being. Without going into the details of the hagiology of these saints and preceptors, we are enabled to collect the Āḷvārs, from the traditional accounts alone, into three groups—the ancient, the middle, and the last.

The list of the twelve Āḷvārs, with their traditional dates of birth, is as follows:—

Ancient.	Poygai Āḷvār	 4203	B.C.
	Bhūtattār	 4203	"
	Pēy Āḷvār	 4203	"
	Tirumaḷiśai Āḷvār...	... 4203	"

Middle.	Nammālvār	3102 B.C.
	Madhurakavi	3102 "
	Kulaśēkhara	3075 "
	Periy Ālvār	3056 "
	Āndāl	3005 "
Last.	Tondaradippodi	2814 "
	Tiruppān Ālvār ...	2760 "
	Tirumangai Ālvār ...	2706 "

Disregarding these apparently definite dates, in which, however, most Tamil works, particularly those of a religious character, are peculiarly weak, it is still possible to regard this traditional order as fairly in chronological sequence. Even the Vaishṇava hagiologists have very little to say about the first group. Their information about the second is meagre, while of the third they have something to say that may be historical. The name at the head of the paper is the very last, and there are certain facts concerning him, which cannot lightly be passed over by any one who tries to examine the chronology of the Āḻvārs.

Tirumangai Āḻvār is the author of the largest number (1,361 stanzas, of the 4,000 verses of the Vaishṇava *Prabhandam*), Nammāḻvār coming next with a number almost as great. He belonged to the Kaḷḷar caste and was born at Kurayalūr in Āli Nāḍu in the Shiyāḻi taluk of the Tanjore district. There he pursued, when he grew up to man's estate, the profession of his father, which was of a duplex character—the government of a small district under the reigning Chola and the playing the knight of the highway, in both of which capacities he appears to have achieved great distinction. The critical stage of his life was reached when he fell in love with the foundling daughter of a Vaishṇava physician, who would not marry him unless he reformed and became a Vaishṇava. He went to Tirunaraiyūr, near Kumbhakōnam, and there received the sacrament. He was not yet to gain the object of his desire, as the young lady insisted upon his feeding 1,008 Vaishṇavas a day for a whole year. This he could do only by plundering wayfarers, which he did, consoling himself with the idea that he was doing it in the name of God. A second transformation was yet in store for him. One night he waylaid a Brahman bridal party, and was probably stricken with remorse for the very enormity of this deed. He there received from the Brahman, who was no other than God himself come in human shape to fulfil his ends on earth, that mysterious 'mantra' the name Nārāyaṇa. On being thus blessed, he broke out into verse and his first decad of verse makes this confession. Thereafter he began visiting all the shrines sacred to Vishṇu, and at last settled in Srīrangam, to spend the rest of his days in the service of God, and to rebuild some parts and remodel others of the great shrine, the funds for which he had to find by demolishing the great Buddhist shrine at Negapatam. Having done this to his satisfaction and provided for the recital of Nammāḻvār's *Tiruvōymoḻi* annually at Srīrangam he passed away. This, without any of the embellishments of the hagiologists, is the life-story of the man but not of the saint, for which the curious may read A. Govinda Charlu's *Holy Lives of the Āḻvārs*.

Let us now proceed to examine what historical reliance can be placed upon this story. The materials for the history of these sainted personages are entirely traditional, and we can attach to the details only as much value as can safely be attached to mere traditions. The general tenor of the life may be correct, while we ought not to insist on details with too much certainty. Even in this modified sense the story does not enlighten us as to the age of the Āḻvār and his actual doings. But there are the monuments of the labours of Tirumangaimannan, namely, his works in the *Prabhanda* and the buildings he undertook in the temple at Srīrangam. It is certainly very unfortunate that tradition has not preserved the name of the Chola ruler whose vassal the Āḻvār was. This omission is significant of the fact that he was not contemporaneous with any great Chola ruler, although even these latter are never named specifically enough under similar circumstances. That he was the latest of the saints is amply borne out by the fact that he celebrates most, if not all, of the now well-known temples to Vishṇu in India, while others celebrate only a few. The destruction of the rich Buddhist sanctuary at Negapatam and the frequent references he makes to the Buddhists themselves in his works refer us to times anterior to the centuries of Chola ascendency, which is again indirectly borne out by the robber chieftain having been successful in his defiance of his Chola suzerain. That Negapatam was the head-quarters of a Buddhist sect is borne out by the references to the place in such Tamil classics as the *Permumbāṇāṟṟuppaḍai.* This fact is attested even to-day by a place not far off being known as Buddankōṭṭam, although it is now a Brahman village. These facts, in conjunction with references to the Pallavas in the *Periyatirumoḻi,* would refer the Āḻvār to the age of the Pallava ascendency previous to the rise of that Chola power which wielded imperial sway over South India from the tenth to the fourteenth century after Christ.

The Pallava ascendency was coeval with that of the early Western Chāḷukya period and vanished not long after the rise of the Rāshṭrakūṭas, who overthrew their enemies, the Western Chāḷukyas. Before adducing positive evidence that tends towards this conclusion, we have to examine critically the opinions offered by others as to the age of the Āḻvār. Bishop Caldwell and those that followed him could be excused, if they held that these were disciples of Rāmānuja, as nowadays Gopinatha Rao is willing to believe that Tirumangai Āḻvār and other later Āḻvārs were contemporaries, if not actually disciples, of Āḷavandār, Rāmānuja's great-grandfather. In support of this view he quotes a stanza from a work called *Koiloḻuhu*, which is a history of the Srīrangam temple. In the stanza a street, called after Tirumangai Āḻvār, comes next to a street called after a Rājamāhēndra. This latter is identified with the son and successor of the Rājēndra who fought the battle of Koppam in A. D. 1053. Hence he infers that Tirumangai Āḻvār must have lived in the latter half of the eleventh century.[1]

That Rāmānuja had read and had derived much wisdom from the works of this last of the Āḻvārs is in evidence, so as to satisfy the most fastidious student of history, in the centum known as the *Rāmānuja-nūṟṟandhādhi*, a work composed during the lifetime of Rāmānuja by a convert and pupil of his own disciple Kūrattāḻvār. This connexion between Amudan, the author of the centum, and Kūrattāḻvār is borne out by stanza seven of the centum and the old *Guruparamparai* of Pinbaḻagya Jīyar, stanzas 8–21. The former acknowledges Rāmānuja's indebtedness to all the twelve Āḻvārs and the two early Āchāryas, Nāthamuni and his grandson Āḷavandār. This inconvenient piece of evidence has been accorded no place in the array of evidence and authorities passed in review by Gopinatha Rao.

To pass on to the positive evidence available, the Vaishṇavas always regarded the Āḻvārs higher in spiritual estate than the Āchāryas, not merely as such, but also as being more ancient, and they must have had some reason for making this distinction. If Tirumangai Āḻvār and others of that class had been

1 *Madras Review*, February and May, 1905.—*History of the Srīvaishṇava movement.*

disciples of Āḷavandār, why call this latter only an Āchārya and his disciples Āḷvārs, the idols of the Āḷvārs being placed in temples and worshipped, while those of most of the Āchāryas are not. Leaving this aside as the outcome of a most unreasonable partiality on the part of the Vaishṇavas, we have other evidence to fall back upon. Inscriptions of Rājarāja II, about the middle of the twelfth century, contain the unusual name Araṭṭamukkidāsan—the first part of which is a special title of Tirumangai Āḷvār. Next, prince Chola Kērala, about the middle of the eleventh century, made provision for the recital of *Tiruneḍunḍānḍaham*,[1] one of the works of Tirumangai Āḷvār, which would be extraordinary if he had been living at the time and working to accumulate merit and earn his title to saintliness, especially as his life was, during the greater part of it, far from saintly.

That Tirumangai Āḷvār was not a disciple of Āḷavandār is also made probable by a stanza in praise of his work by Tirukkōṭṭiyūr Nambi, from whom Rāmānuja had to learn, which goes to show that this Āḷvār's works had been regularly studied and handed down from preceptor to disciple for some time at least. Again, the conquering Chola brothers, Rājādhirāja who fell at the battle of Koppam, and his younger brother Rājēndra who succeeded him, had an elder brother by name Āḷavandān. If this name was given to him because of the Āchārya, the latter must have been anterior to him by a considerable interval, as even now the name is specially Vaishṇava.

This would make Āḷavandār's grandfather Nāthamuni much prior to the age ascribed to him by Gopinatha Rao. He lays much stress upon the fact that Nāthamuni was accustomed to going to Gangaikoṇḍa Cholapuram, founded by Gangaikoṇḍa Chola,

[1] *Epigraphist's Report* for 1900, p. 10.

in A. D. 1024. This is a detail which cannot be looked upon as a crucial piece of evidence, as it is possible that the hagiologists alone are responsible for it. When the earliest among them wrote the lives of their saints, they were so accustomed to Gangaikonḍa Cholapuram as the Chola capital, that when they heard that Nāthamuni visited the Chola ruler, they naturally put down Gangaikonḍa Cholapuram as the Chola capital. It certainly would not be unreasonable to ascribe Nāthamuni to a period in the earlier half of the tenth century A. D. This is exactly the conclusion warranted by the proper understanding of the traditional account, which is that Nāthamuni was born in A. D. 582 and that he was in what is called *Yoga Samādhi* for 340 years. This would give the date A. D. 922 for the death of Nāthamuni, which is not at all improbable, taking all circumstances into consideration. But why did the hagiologists then ascribe this long life or long death in life to Nāthamuni? The explanation is not far to seek. They believed, and the Vaishṇavas do believe even now, that there was an unbroken succession of these saints, and unfortunately they found a gap between Nāthamuni and the last Āḷvār. This they bridged over in this clumsy fashion.[1]

If the above view of the connexion between the Āḷvārs and the Āchāryas is correct, then we shall have to look for Tirumangai Āḷvār two or three centuries earlier than Nāthamuni, and this takes us to the seventh or the eighth century of the Christian era. This is certainly warranted by the frequent references to the Pallavas[2] and by none at all to the modern Cholas, even to the Chola Rājamahēndra, who did so

[1] If Kalhaṇa, the professed historian of Kasmīr, did the same with respect to the early rulers of Kasmīr in the first centuries A. D., is it wonderful that these hagiologists fell into such a trap?

[2] See p. 486, vol. III, *Śen Tamil*, Pandit M. Raghavaiyangar's article.

much for the Srīrangam temple. Even according to Gopinatha Rao, the only Chola that is referred to elaborately by the Āḻvār is the ancient Chola Kōchchengaṉ in the decad regarding Tirunaraiyūr. This, in combination with references to the Śaṅgam in the body of the work, brings him later than the age of either. But another decad in praise of the Paramēśvara Viṉṉagar at Kānchī gives in great detail the achievements of a Pallava ruler, whom Dr. Hultzsch considers to be identical with Paramēśvaravarman II from the name of the shrine. This is not a necessary inference, as any other Pallava paramount sovereign might have had the title Pallava Paramēśvara, and the foundation, when contracted, might have become Paramēśvara Viṉṉagaram, e. g. Vidya Vinīta Pallava Paramēśvaram. And notwithstanding the details given in the decad, it does not find support from what is known of Paramēśvaravarman II. This Pallava sovereign, whatever his name, won victories over his enemies at Maṇṇai, Nenmeli, and Karūr. At Karūr he fought against the Pandya and at Nenmeli against the Villavan (Chēra), but the enemy at Maṇṇai is not specified. If these names could be identified with places where Udaya Chandra won victories for his master Nandivarman Pallavamalla or Nandipōttarāja, then the Āḻvār must have lived after Nandivarman, or, at the earliest, during his reign.

Among these victories we find mention of a defeat of the Pandyas at Maṇṇaikkuḍi and the taking of Kāḷidurgā.[1] Maṇṇaikkuḍi may be the Āḻvār's Maṇṇai, and Kāḷidurgā the Āḻvār's 'Kuṉrail'. Karūr as such does not find mention in the inscriptions. It may be that this name refers to an incident in which Udaya Chandra played no part. Then comes Nelvēli, where

[1] *Vide S. Ind. Ins.*, vol. ii, pt. iii, No. 74. Fleet, *Bombay Gazetteer*, vol. i, pt. ii, pp. 326-7.

Udaya Chandra won a victory; but the Āḻvār speaks of Nenmeli, and the war was between the Pallava and the Chēra (Villavan). It is probable that these separate incidents refer to different Pallava princes who worshipped Vishṇu at the Paramēśvara Viṇṇagaram shrine. Whatever be the real nature of these references, whether they refer to one Pallava Nandivarman or to several, such as Simha Vishṇu, Paramēśvaravarman and Nandivarman (in fact, all the Vaishṇava Pallavas), it is clear that we have to look for the date of the Āḻvār while the Pallavas were still in power and the Cholas had not come into prominence.

There is one reference, however, which should give us a narrow enough limit for his time. In the last stanza of the decad, immediately preceding that just considered in celebrating the shrine of Ashṭabhujkaram in Kānchī, he makes what, in his case, appears as a somewhat peculiar reference to a certain Vairamēghan, 'bowed down to by the ruler of the people of the Toṇḍa country whose army (or strength) surrounded Kānchī' In all references made to rulers, he has specified people who had made special donations to Vishṇu, whether with respect to Chidambaram, Triplicane or Tirunaraiyūr. In this case alone is the reference made in a secular fashion. Besides this, the language indicating the connexion warrants the inference that the reference is made to a living person. In the commentary of Periya Āchan Piḷḷai, Vairamēghan is explained by the term chakravarti (emperor). Thus it is clear that, at the time referred to, there was a Pallava ruler who was under the protection of an imperial personage, whose name (or rather title) was Vairamēghan. This again warrants the inference of the decline of the Pallava power.

Among the inscriptions so far brought out, we have not often come across the name, but to the Rāshṭrakūṭa Dantidurga II of the genealogical table of the family, in Fleet's *Kannaḍa Dynasties,* is ascribed this title in the Kaḍaba Plates published by Mr. Rice.[1] This was the personage who overthrew the natural enemies of the Pallavas, namely, the Western Chāḷukyas of Badāmī, and in their stead established the Rāshṭrakūṭa power. According to the Ellora inscription referred to by Dr. Fleet,[2] Dantidurga completed the acquisition of sovereignty by subjugating the ruler of Sandhubhūpa, the lord of Kānchī, the rulers of Kalinga and Kōsala, the lord of the Sriśaila country (Karnūl country), the Sēshas. This Dantidurga was deposed by his uncle Krishṇa I, about A. D. 755. The king of Kānchī (during the period including A.D. 754, the only known date for Dantidurga Vairamēgha) was Nandivarman who ruled for fifty years from about A. D. 710.[3] He is regarded as a usurper and is so far the last great Pallava ruler known in South Indian history. It is highly probable that when at last the Chaḷukya power was overthrown, the Pallavas advanced in the direction of Karnūl. The Rāshṭrakūṭa records, therefore, together with the statement of the Āḻvār, would lead us to believe that Dantidurga beat back the enemy and was in occupation of Kānchī. Nandivarman was a Vaishṇava, and Tirumangai Āḻvār's praise of him is admissible as that of a brother devotee, but any reference by him to an enemy would be far from complimentary. Hence, it can only have been made in the manner in which it is, and under circumstances when he could not get out of an unpleasant reminiscence such as the above. The inference, therefore, seems to be warranted that the Āḻvār flourished in this period exactly, and it would certainly be in keeping with the most cherished tradition of the Vaish-

[1] *Epigraphia Carnāṭaka*, Gb. 61, vol. xi, Tumkur.

[2] *Bombay Gazetteer*, vol. i, pt. ii, p. 389, and No. 4, vol. ix, *Epigraphia Indica*.

[3] *Śen Tamil*, vol. i, p. 80.

ṇavas that the arrangement made by the Āḷvār for the recital of the *Tiruvōymoḷi* of Nammāḷvār had fallen into desuetude in the days of Nāthamuni and that he had to revive it at Srīrangam after much ado. The date of Tirumangai Āḷvār then has to be allotted to the earlier half of the eighth century of the Christian era.

We have now to dispose of another Vaishṇava tradition, which has often led astray many a Śaiva scholar of repute, and has made him lose his balance of mind. It is the story that Tirumangai Āḷvār held a successful disputation with the Śaiva sage Tirugñāna Sambanda. It does not concern us here to examine whether the disputation was successful to the Vaishṇava or the Śaiva. Our only business is to examine whether the two could have been contemporaries. A late revered Śaiva scholar, in a letter to a friend of mine, who inquired if there was anything to warrant this, promptly wrote back to say that it was 'as false as any Vaishṇava tradition'. If Sambanda paid a visit to the man who destroyed Badāmī in A. D. 642, it may have taken place about the end of the seventh century, and so, if Tirumangai Āḷvār was at the height of his religious devotion about the middle of the eighth century, it is possible they were contemporary. Besides, they were both natives of the same place nearly. The Śaiva was born at Shiyāḷi, and the Vaishṇava at a village not far off. The dispute is said to have taken a curious form. It was not a religious question, but was only one of title to ability in composing poetry. The Āḷvār's disciples went about shouting 'here comes *Nālukavipperumaḷ* (he that excels in composing the four kinds of poetry).' The Āḍiyār's disciples objected and ushered the Āḷvār into their preceptor's presence. The Āḷvār was asked to compose a *kuṛal*, and burst out with a decad in praise of Śrī Rāma of Shiyāḷi, beginning with *Oṛukuṛaḷ* (unparalleled dwarf), a sense entirely different from that which the Āḍiyār would have given to the word. The story further goes on to state that Sambanda was satisfied and not only acquiesced in the titles of the Āḻvār, but even made him a present of the trident he used to carry. It is of no use to enter into the details of the story, as, so far, it has merely led to annoyance, but one particular, however, cannot be passed over here; and that is, that the Āḻvār, who generally gives himself one of the titles in the concluding stanza of each decad, breaks out at the end of this one into a rather provoking and assertive enumeration of all of them.

It would appear, therefore, after all has been said, that tradition combined with the results of historical research, so far as it bears upon the subject, would allot Tirumangai Āḻvār to the earlier half of the eighth century after Christ; and thus possibly he was a younger contemporary of Tirugñāna Sambanda, and perhaps an elder of Sundaramūrti Nāyanār.

NOTES

Page 18.—Kosambi: Mr. Vincent A. Smith writes in regard to the connexion between the Guptas and Kosambi. 'I do not know of any reason for connecting the Guptas with Kosambi. Chandragupta I, who established the Gupta Era, reigned from A. D. 319–20 to about 336 (not 326 as in the Early History of India), and his dominions do not extend beyond Allahabad. It was his grandson Chandragupta II (388 or 390) who annexed Surāshtra.'

Pages 49 *and* 131.—Chakrakoṭṭam and Ruler of Dhāra. Chakragoṭṭam or Chakrakoṭṭam was hitherto regarded as a fortress of strength in the territory of Dhāra: but Rai Bahadur Hira Lal holds that the former is in the Bastar State and its connexion with Dharavarāsa is accounted for as referring to Dharavarsha of the Nāgavamsi family (vide *Epigraphia Indica*, Vol. IX, pp. 178–9 and Vol. X, iii, pp. 25–7).

Page 245.—Vishnuvardhana's death is put down to the year A. D. 1141 on the authority of Mr. Rice, but there are inscriptions which imply that he lived about ten to fifteen years later. Pending a fuller examination of the question this date is given tentatively (vide *Quarterly Journal of the Mythic Society*, Vol. II, ii, p. 64).

Pages 153, 378 *and* 400.—Kamban had been regarded as a poet of the tenth century A. D. on the strength of certain stories connected with his life. It is more likely that he belonged to the thirteenth century for the following reasons among others:—(1) He refers to a Chola King Tyagamāvinōdhan (who seems to be Vikrama Chola). (2) His contemporaneity and hostility to Oṭṭakkūttan seems provable. (3) There is one story which connects him with Pratāpa Rudra of Warangal.

ERRATA

Page,	*line*
8	1.—*For* ' Bundlekhand ' *read* ' Bundalkhand '.
9	26.—*Omit* ' It was probably extended ' and *read* with the previous [sentence.
19	29.—*For* ' His father ' *read* ' his son '.
23	19.—*For* ' Hieun Thsang ' *read* ' Hiuen Thsang (Yuwan Chwang)'.
29	4.—*For* ' Mālva Dekhan ' *read* ' Mālva-Dekhan '.
32	23.—*For* ' idealized picture ' *read* ' an idealized picture '.
34	18.—*For* ' Sambahava ' *read* ' Sambhava '.
43	7.—*For* ' and probably under his father ' *read* ' and under his son '
44	34.—*Omit* ' a .
46	21.—*For* ' fathers A. D. 1044,' *read* ' fathers, A. D. 1044 '
	33.—*For* ' A. D. 1052 ' *read* ' A. D. 1053 '
54	19.—*Omit* ' the ' before Sophytes.
56	17 and 24.—*For* ' Yuet-chi ' *read* ' Yueh-chi '.
57	*head-line.*—*For* ' PoliticAl ' *read* ' Political '.
60	4.—*For* ' that ' *read* ' the '
69	3.—*For* ' war.craze ' *read* ' war-craze '
95	*head-line.*—*For* ' Iḷanirayan ' *read* ' Iḷandirayan '.
109	16.—*For* ' A. D. 1052 ' *read* ' A. D. 1053 '
114	26.—*For* ' Rajēndra Vīrārājēndra ' *read* ' Rājēndra and Vīrarājēndra '.
122	7.—*For* ' Kāśavadanda ' *read* ' Kēśavadanda '.
128	27.—*For* ' Vīrarājēndradēāva ' *read* ' Vīrarājēndradeva '.
130	26.—*For* ' நிலைமகள் ' *read* ' நிலமகள் '.
152	16.—*For* ' this father ' *read* ' his father '.
177	8.—*For* personalities ' *read* ' personalties '.
179	11.—*For* ' Kōnōrinmaikoṇḍān ' *read* ' Kōnērinmaikoṇḍān '.
182	16.—*For* ' kalanju ' *read* ' kalanju '.
211	36.—*Omit* the words ' those ' and ' in '.
216	32.—, 33.— *For* ' [illegible] ' *read* ' [illegible] '.
223	33.—*For* ' respective, emblemson ' *read* ' respective emblems on '.
226	16.—*For* ' A. D. 1052 ' *read* ' A. D. 1053 '.
234	26.—*For* ' Pramāras ' *read* ' Paramāras '
	36.—*For* ' regrant ' *read* ' re-grant '
239	4.—*For* ' Vigrahim ' *read* ' Vigrahin '.
	20.—*For* ' Belugoal ' *read* ' Beḷugoḷa '.
	26.—*For* Mārbala Irtha ' *read* ' Mārbala Tīrtha '.

Page, line

247 3.—*For* ‘ Banevase ’ *read* ‘ Banavasc ’.
248 6.—*For* ‘ who was to become ’ *read* ‘ who were to become ’.
36.—*For* ‘ Kākaiyas ’ *read* ‘ Kākatīyas ’.
253 25.—*For* ‘ Ywan Chwang ’ *read* ‘ Yuwan Chwang ’.
266 30.—*For* ‘ enemy’s ’ *read* ‘ enemy ’.
270 17.—*For* ‘ his late Highness ’ *read* ‘ His late Highness ’.
274 5.—*For* ‘ Remati Revati ’ *read* ‘ Remati, Revati ’.
285 24.—*Omit* ‘ Raja ’
287 25.—*For* ‘ Beṭad, Woḍeyar’s ’ *read* ‘ Beṭad Woḍeyar’s ’
302 28.—*For* ‘ method of the collection ’ *read* ‘ method of collection ’.
306 32.—*For* ‘ victory to Mysore ’ *read* ‘ victory for Mysore ’
308 5.—*For* ‘ herefore ’ *read* ‘ therefore ’
314 15.—*For* ‘ bandalism ’ *read* ‘ vandalism ’.
315 29.—*For* ‘ poetry ’ *read* ‘ poetics ’.
333 1.—*For* ‘ Saka A. D. 1021 or 1099 ’ *read* ‘ Saka 1021 or A. D. 1099 ’
334 23.—*For* ‘ Muduraikkānji ’ *read* ‘ Maduraikkānji ’.
354 *Note* 2, *line* 3.—*For* ‘ as the owner ’ *read* ‘ was the owner ’.
358 *Notes.—Before* Tuvarai *insert* ‘ (2) ’
364 25.—*For* ‘ Dhamilas ’ *read* ‘ Damilas ’
365 1.—*For* ‘ miselection ’ *read* ‘ mislection ’.

INDEX

(References to pages)

A

B

D

E

H

I

L

M

O

P

R

T

U

W

Y

FINIS

NOTE.—I am obliged to my friend Mr. V. Gopalasami Iyengar, B.A., of the Mysore Government General and Revenue Secretariat for this index in the preparation of which he bestowed considerable time and labour.

OPINIONS ON 'ANCIENT INDIA'

BASINGSTOKE,
November 26, 1911.

EARL CURZON.

Pray accept my thanks for sending me a copy of your interesting work. I am indeed glad that you have turned your attention to such topics.

OXFORD,
December 7, 1911.

DR. A. F. R. HOERNLE, M.A., PH.D., C.I.E. (OXFORD)
Author of 'History of India.'

It is a very creditable performance, and I promise to myself much pleasure and no less profit from the reading of it.

Let me express the hope that this may be the beginning of much more useful and successful work by you in the sphere of Indian Historical Research.

ROEHAMPTON,
December 3, 1911.

R. SEWELL, ESQ., I.C.S. (*retired*)
Author of a 'Forgotten Empire of Vijayanagar.'

I cannot express to you the pleasure I feel that a gentleman like yourself should take up so seriously and carefully and dispassionately the study of the History of South India. I have been hoping for many years that such a work should be attempted by a South Indian Brahman for many reasons; and I send you my warm congratulations on the happy climax of your labours.

OXFORD,
December 4, 1911.

VINCENT A. SMITH, ESQ., M.A., I.C.S., ETC., (*retired*)
Author of 'Early History of India.'

Your volume looks well and will be useful to me if I live to bring out a new edition of the Early History, as I hope to do.

CAMBERLY,
December 4, 1911.

DR. G. A. GRIERSON, PH.D., C.I.E., I.C.S. (*retired*)
of the Linguistic Survey of India.

I can see clearly that *Ancient India* is a most interesting book, and that I shall profit much from its perusal. I trust that it is only a preliminary to other works on a larger scale, such as the Early History of Southern India which as Mr. Vincent Smith says, is so much wanted by all students of the subject.

MADRAS,
October 27, 1911.

J. H. STONE, ESQ., M.A., F.R.HIST.S.,
Madras.

It was an excellent idea to collect your essays in the handsome volume which contains much of great interest.

MADRAS,
September 29, 1911.

SIR S. SUBRAMANYA IYER, K.C.I.E., LL.D., D.C.L.,
Madras.

It is scarcely necessary for me to add that your literary work will bring honour to your Alma Mater.

MYLAPORE,
November 10, 1911.

HON'BLE MR. V. KRISHNASWAMI IYER, C.S.I.

I congratulate you on the volume of historical essays you have issued.

MALLESVARAM,
November 1, 1911.

R. NARASIMHACHAR, ESQ., M.A., M.R.A.S.

'Stuffed with useful and suggestive information elucidating several important points in South Indian History.'

HALLE, GERMANY,
December 13, 1911.

FROM DR. E. HULTZSCH, PH.D.,
Late Epigraphist to Madras Government.

Many thanks for the copy of your interesting volume on *Ancient India* in which you have treated in a masterly manner several problems of South Indian History which have interested me for many years. Let me congratulate you on the vivid manner in which you have arranged and represented the *disjecta membra* of historical information. It is no small gratification to me to observe that you have so carefully examined and utilized every item which is brought to notice in my epigraphical publications. I shall often consult your volume, the value of which is enhanced by the full index.

INDIA OFFICE, WHITEHALL, S.W.
December 20, 1911.

FROM SIR W. LEE-WARNER, K.C.S.I.

I have to thank you for *Ancient India* into which I have dipped but which I hope to study more carefully. It is kind of you to remember me and I am always glad to see Mysore well represented in the field of letters as in other fields of knowledge and enterprise. Wishing you all the best compliments of the season etc.

THE TIMES OF INDIA ILLUSTRATED WEEKLY.

January 24, 1911.

* * * * *

This is a noteworthy book in many respects. It is a proof that the historical spirit is beginning to take hold of English-educated Indians, who can do invaluable work in throwing light on the obscure chapters of Ancient Indian History.